THE BEST OF AUGUSTINE
Selections from the Writings of St Augustine of Hippo

(Original Title: *Leaves from Saint Augustine*)

By

Mary H. Allies
Edited by T. W. Allies

Burns and Oates
New York, London
Catholic Publication Society Co.
1886

Etext corrected and further edited
by Darrell Wright, 2016

CONTENTS

PART 1. PERSONAL

1. ST. AUGUSTINE'S CONVERSION
   (*Confessions*, Bk. 8, ch. 5)
2. DEATH OF ST. MONICA …..16
   (*Confessions*, Bk. 9, ch. 10)
3. ST. AUGUSTINE'S EPISCOPAL LIFE AT HIPPO …. 24
   (*Sermon* 355)
4. HIS VIEW OF FUNERAL POMP
   (*On the City of God*, Bk. 1, ch. 12, 13)
5. DUTIES OF TESTATORS …..32
   (*Sermon* 355.3)
6. DUTIES OF KINGS ….37
   (*Letter* 185 to Boniface}
7. ANSWERS TO VARIOUS QUESTIONS ….43
   (*Letter* 54)
8. ST. AUGUSTINE AND THE COUNT OF AFRICA …. 47
   (*Letter* 220)
9. ST. AUGUSTINE AND THE HOLY SEE …..57
   (*Letter* 209)
10. ST. AUGUSTINE ON THE APPOINTMENT OF HIS SUCCESSOR IN THE SEE OF HIPPO….64
    (*Letter* 213)

PART 2. DOCTRINE IN DAILY LIFE

1. THE APPARITIONS OF GOD IN THE BIBLE ….71
   (*Sermon* 7)
2. ABRAHAM TEMPTED BY GOD ….76
   (*Sermon* 2)
3. THE LESSON OF THE NEW TESTAMENT ….81
   (*Sermon* 25)
4. THE ROYAL GIFTS OF SIGHT AND HEARING ….85
   (*Sermon* 28)
5. TRUE POVERTY ….89
   (*Sermon* 15)
6. TEARS OF THE JUST ….94
   (*Sermon* 31)
7. TEMPORAL PROSPERITY ….98
   (*Sermon* 19)
8. REST IN LABOR ….101
   (*Sermon* 69 and 70)
9. A HOUSE AND A TENT ….105
   (*On the Psalms*, 26. 6)

10. MYSTERY OF TEMPORAL PROSPERITY 108
    (On the Psalms, 91)
11. LAZARUS AND THE RICH MAN 119
    (Sermon 41)
12. YOU SHALL HIDE THEM IN THE SHADOW OF YOUR FACE 125
    (Sermon 362.3, On the Psalms, 30)
13. LANGUID FAITH 129
    (On the Psalms, 25.4)
14. REWARD OF NATURAL VIRTUE 131
    (On the City of God, Bk. 5, ch. 15 and 16)
15. DIFFERENT ACTION OF THE SAME FIRE 133
    (On the City of God, Bk. 1, ch. 8)
16. DEFICIENCY OF THE EVIL WILL 136
    (On the City of God, Bk. 12, ch. 7 and 8)
17. THE LAW FROM MOSES: GRACE AND TRUTH FROM OUR LORD 139
    (On the Gospel of John, 3)
18. GRACE ...143
    (On the Gospel of John, 26)
19. INTERIOR STRENGTH 146
    (On the Lord's Sermon on the Mount)
20. LIGHT AND DARKNESS 148
    (Sermon 49. 3)
21. FAITH AND WORKS 150
    (On the Psalms, 31)
22. HE IS OUR GOD 155
    (On the Psalms, 55)
23. THE OLD TESTAMENT THE FIGURE OF THE NEW 159
    (On the Psalms, 72)
24. THE JUST REJOICE IN GOD 163
    (On the Psalms, 32)
25. ONE IS TAKEN, ONE IS LEFT 167
    (On the Psalms, 36 and Questions on the Gospel, 1. 2. q. 44)
26. THE MOTHER AND THE BROTHERS OF OUR LORD 171
    (On the Gospel of John, 10.2)
27. THE VINEYARD AND THE LABORERS 174
    (Sermon 87.6, 7, 8, 9)
28. LEAVING OUR GIFT AT THE ALTAR 179
    (On the Lord's Sermon on the Mount, 1. 1. 26)
29. CURING OF THE TEN LEPERS 181
    (Questions on the Gospel, 1.2, q. 40)
30. CHARITY THE FULFILLMENT OF THE LAW 186
    (On the Letters of John, 5)
31. NO LIFE WITHOUT ITS BURDENS 188
    (Sermon 164. 4)
32. CHARITY IS THE MARK OF THE ELECT 191

(*Sermon* 350. 2)
33. FORBEARANCE WITH SCANDALS 194
(*On the Psalms*, 99)
34. INTERPRETATION OF THE SYCAMORE TREE 203
(*Sermon* 174.3)
35. OUR DAILY BREAD 207
(*On the Lord's Sermon on the Mount*, Bk. 2.25)
36. MARTHA AND MARY 210
(*Sermon* 103)
37. DIVINE LOVERS: WORLDLY LOVERS 215
(*Sermon* 126. 3.)
38. ST. PETER'S DENIAL OF OUR LORD 219
(*On the Gospel of John*, 66)
39. VISIBLE THINGS THE EVIDENCE FOR THINGS INVISIBLE 223
(*Sermon* 126.3)
40. HIDDEN MEANING OF OUR LORD'S MIRACLES 227
(*On the Gospel of John*, 17 and 24)
41. THE SEEING OF THE WORD 231
(*On the Gospel of John*, 18, 20-21)
42. THE DEAD RAISED TO LIFE BY OUR LORD 239
(*Sermon* 98)
43. THE CAUSE MAKES THE MARTYR 247
(*Sermon* 285.2)
44. JOY OF THE MARTYRS 250
(*Sermon* 273 and 286)
45. OUR LORD PASSING BY 254
(*Sermon* 349. 5)
46. ST. PETER AND ST. JOHN, TYPES OF TWO LIVES 256
(*On the Gospel of John*, 124)
47. THE WEARINESS OF JESUS 266
(*On the Gospel of John*, 15)
48. PASSING FROM DEATH TO LIFE 275
(*On the Gospel of John*, 22)
49. "THEY COULD NOT BELIEVE" 280
(*On the Gospel of John*, 53)
50. THE TWO GENERATIONS OF OUR LORD 285
(*On the Gospel of John*, 2 and 8)
51. THE MARRIAGE FEAST OF CANA 289
(*On the Gospel of John*, 8 and 9)
52. FROM THAT HOUR THE DISCIPLE TOOK HER UNTO HIS OWN 294
(*On the Gospel of John*, 119)
53. THE WEDDING GARMENT 297
(*Sermon* 90)
54. ADORATION OF THE HOLY EUCHARIST 304
(*On the Psalms*, 98.9)

55. MANNER OF RECEIVING THE HOLY EUCHARIST 307
    (*Sermon* 71.17)
56. JESUS DID NOT TRUST HIMSELF UNTO THEM 309
    (*On the Gospel of John*, 11.2, 3, etc.)
57. JESUS FLED 316
    (*On the Gospel of John*, 25.4)
58. LITTLE CHILDREN, IT IS THE LAST HOUR 321
    (*On the Letters of John*, 3.1, etc.)
59. TWO CITIES: BABYLON AND SION 326
    (*On the Psalms*, 136)

PART 3. THE KINGDOM OF OUR LORD ON EARTH

1. THE KINGDOM OF CHRIST FORETOLD FROM THE BEGINNING 341
   (*On the City of God*, Bk. 7, ch. 32; *Letter* 137, to Volusian)
2. THE STONE FROM THE MOUNTAIN WITHOUT HANDS 345
   (*On the Psalms*, 98)
3. "HE IT IS THAT BAPTIZES" 348
   (*On the Gospel of John*, 6)
4. THE VALIANT WOMAN 350
   (*Sermon* 37)
5. THE HEAD IN HEAVEN, THE BODY ON EARTH 356
   (*On the Letters of John*, 10, ch. 5)
6. THE SHIP AND THE PILOT 361
   (*Sermon* 75 and 76)
7. HERESIES AND HERETICS 368
   (*On the Psalms* 7, 21, 54)
8. THE CATHOLIC FAITH STRENGTHENED BY HERETICS 374
   (*On the City of God*, Bk. 18, ch. 51)
9. THE GIFT OF THE DOVE WITHOUT THE DOVE 377
   (*On the Gospel of John*, 6)
10. JACOB AND ESAU IN THE CHURCH 383
    (*Sermon* 4 and 5)
11. OUTWARD CATHOLICS AND BAD CATHOLICS 389
    (*On Matthew*, q.17.1)
12. HIDDEN CHILDREN OF THE CHURCH 392
    (*On the City of God*, Bk. 1, ch. 34, 35; Bk. 18, ch. 49)
13. PETER AND JUDAS IN THE CHURCH 395
    (*On the Gospel of John*, 1)
14. ON SACRIFICE 399
    (*On the City of God*, Bk. 10. ch. 4, 5, 6, 7)
15. SACRIFICES OF THE OLD LAW, TYPES 403
    (*Questions on the Gospel of Luke*, Bk. 2)
16. OUR LORD THE DAILY SACRIFICE OF THE CHURCH 404
    (*On the City of God*, Bk. 10, ch. 20; Bk. 17, ch. 20, *On the Psalms*, 33)

17. HOW CHRISTIANS HONOR THE MARTYRS 407
   (*On the City of God,* Bk. 8, ch. 27)
18. THE EUCHARIST A PERPETUAL MARRIAGE-FEAST 409
   (*On the Letters of John,* 2)
19. THE FOOD OF THE CHURCH 412
   (*On the Psalms,* 33, *On the Gospel of John,* 26 and 27)
20. SACRIFICE OF THE ALTAR APPLIED TO THE DEPARTED 419
   (Handbook to Laurentius, ch. 29)
21. SAVED YET SO AS BY FIRE 421
   (*On the Psalms,* 37)
22. ALMS, PRAYER, AND SUPPLICATION FOR THE DEAD 423
   (*Sermon* 172)
23. THE HOLY SPIRIT THE SOUL OF THE CHURCH 426
   (*Sermon* 267, 268)
24. THEY HAVE PARTED MY GARMENTS AMONG THEM 429
   (*On the Gospel of John,* 118)
25. THE TWO CAPTURES OF FISH 434
   (*On the Gospel of John,* 122)
26. CHURCH IN ST. AUGUSTINE'S DAY A CHURCH OF MIRACLES 443
   (*On the City of God,* Bk. 22, ch. 8)

PART 4. BEHIND THE VEIL

1. HAPPINESS OF THE SAINTS 455
   (*On the City of God,* Bk. 22, ch. 30)
2. VISION OF THE BLESSED IN ETERNAL LIFE 461
   (*On the City of God,* Bk. 22, ch. 29)
3. THOUGHT IS TRANSPARENT IN THE GLORIFIED BODY 469
   (*Sermon* 243)
4. ETERNAL LIFE: AMEN AND ALLELUIA 471
   (*Sermon* 362)

PREFACE

SOME years ago it was reported that an American sailor had fitted up for himself a small boat with a covered deck, in which he attempted to cross the Atlantic alone; and it was also said that he accomplished his task, and brought his boat safely to our shores.

Something like this sailor's "heart of oak, cased in triple brass," seems to me her courage who set her frail bark to traverse the ocean of St. Augustine, and to give in the compass of a small volume a notion of the beauty, the vastness, the proportion, and the grandeur of mind in one who is said to have acted upon a larger number of men than any one since the time of St. Paul. I would fain hope that she also has brought her bark safe to shore, and that such as think it worth their while to read the words herein selected of that great Saint and Genius no less great, will be able to form some notion of the personal character, the doctrine, the faith, the hope, and the charity of the man who ranks among the Fathers of the Church as St. Paul among the Apostles.

Works of St. Augustine, translated at Edinburgh, make [vi] fifteen octavo volumes; the Oxford translation of the Fathers makes several more. Both together are far from containing all that has been preserved to us. It is necessary to say that neither of these series has been used or even referred to by the Translator. Both the choice of passages and the translation itself are her own. My task has been only to review the whole when completed.

The [Latin] edition of St. Augustine used is that of the Benedictines, Paris, 1679.

T. W. ALLIES

PART 1. PERSONAL

1. ST. AUGUSTINE'S CONVERSION
(*Confessions*, Bk. 8, ch. 5.)

WHEN Your servant Simplician told me these things about Victor, I longed to imitate him, and this was Simplician's reason for telling me. Afterwards he indeed added that under the Emperor Julian a law had been passed forbidding Christians to teach literature and oratory, accepting which law, he had preferred rather to give up his teaching than Your Word. By this Your Word You make eloquent tongues of infants. I thought his happiness at least equaled his courage, inasmuch as he thus found an opportunity of spending time upon You. This was the happiness after which I was sighing, all bound as I was, not by external chains, but by the chain of my own will. The enemy had possession of my will, and in this way he had involved me in a chain by which he held me bound. An unlawful desire is indeed produced by a perverse will, and in obeying an unlawful desire a habit becomes established; and when a habit is not restrained it grows into a necessity. Thus, like links hanging together, which induced me to use the word " chain," a dire servitude held me fast. For the new will which began to be in me that I might offer You my heart's free worship, and enjoy You, O God, Who [4] alone are secure joy, was not yet strong enough to overcome the old will which habit had confirmed. So it was that these two wills, the old one and the new one, the former carnal and the latter spiritual, were at variance with each other, and dissipated my soul by their struggle.

In this way I understood by personal experience that which I had read, how the flesh may lust against the spirit and the spirit against the flesh. I indeed felt this double conflict, but I went rather with that in me which approved itself to me than with that in me of which I disapproved. With the latter indeed I did not go so much, because in a great measure I rather suffered it against my will than did it with a will. Still habit had acquired a greater power over me by my own fault, so that I had arrived by my will at a point which 1 did not will. . . . But I, who was weighed down by earthly necessities, refused to serve You, and I feared to be free from all impediments, as men ought to fear being held by them.

Thus the burden of this world held me in its easy yoke, after the fashion of sleep, and the thoughts which I had concerning You were like the efforts of men wishing to rouse themselves from sleep, who fall back again into it through excessive drowsiness. And as no man is to be found who would wish always to sleep, and in the sound judgment of all it is a good thing to be awake, still for all that, a man procrastinates much about throwing off sleep when he feels grievous weariness in his limbs, and he enjoys it the more even if distasteful in itself, although it be time for him to get up. So I knew for certain that it was better for me to give myself up to Your charity than to yield to my own desire. The one approved itself to me and conquered my judgment; the other flattered me and [5] won the day. For I had no answer to make to those words of Yours to me, *Awake, you who sleep, and arise from the dead, and Christ will enlighten you.* I, who was convinced of the truth, had nothing whatever to answer You, everywhere showing Yourself to speak true things, except slow words and sleepy words. "Later, later;" "Presently;" "Leave me alone for a little while." But "presently, presently," had no present, and my "little while" went on for a long while.

It was in vain that I delighted in Your law according to the inner man, while another law in my members was fighting against the law of my mind, and making me a captive unto the law of sin which was in my members. . . .

And I will now declare how You did deliver me from the chain of lustful desire which was holding me tight, and from the slavery of worldly business; and I will confess to Your name, O Lord, my Helper and my Redeemer. I carried out my usual occupations with increasing uneasiness, and I cried to You day by day. I frequented Your church as far as the burden of those cares which made me groan gave me time. Alypius was with me, free from his legal business after the third session, and looking for someone to whom he might again sell his advice, just as I sold my power of speaking, if indeed it is to be imparted by teaching. Nebridius had now, in consideration of our friendship, consented to teach under Verecundus, a citizen and a grammarian of Milan, and a very intimate friend of us all, who urgently desired, and by the right of friend ship challenged from our company, such faithful aid as he greatly needed.

On a certain day, therefore, I do not remember how it was that Nebridius was absent, a man called Ponti-
[6] tianus, a countryman of ours, inasmuch as he was an African, in high office in the Emperor's court, came to our house to see me and Alypius. I did not know what he wanted of us. We sat down to talk, and it happened that upon a table for some game before us he observed a book, took, opened it, and, contrary to his expectation, found it was the Apostle Paul, for he had thought it some of those books which I was wearing myself out in teaching. And so, smiling and looking at me, he expressed his joy and wonder that he had suddenly come upon this book, and that I alone saw it. For he was a Christian and one of the faithful, and often prostrated himself before You, our God, in the church in frequent and continued prayers. When then I had told him that I bestowed very great pains upon those Scriptures, a conversation arose (suggested by his account) about Anthony, the Egyptian monk, whose name was in high reputation among Your servants, though to that hour unknown to us. When he discovered this, he dwelt the more upon the subject, informing our ignorance, and expressing his wonder

that we should know nothing of one so eminent. But we stood amazed, hearing Your wonderful works most fully attested, in times so recent and so near to our own days, wrought in the true Faith and Catholic Church. We all wondered; we that they were so great, and he that they had not reached our ears.

Thence his discourse turned to the flocks in the monasteries and their holy ways, a sweet-smelling savour unto You, and the fruitful deserts of the wilderness, whereof we knew nothing. And there was a monastery at Milan, full of good brethren, without the city walls, under the fostering care of Ambrose, and we knew it not. He went on with his discourse, and we listened in intent silence. Then he told us how [7] one afternoon at Trier, when the Emperor was taken up with the Circus games, he and three others, his companions, went out to walk in gardens near the city walls, and there, as they happened to walk in pairs, one went apart with him, and the other two wandered by themselves; and these, in their wanderings, lighted upon a certain cottage inhabited by some of Your servants, poor in spirit, of whom is the kingdom of heaven, and there they found a little book containing the life of Anthony. One of them began to read it, and to admire and to be fired at it, and, as he read, to meditate embracing this manner of life, and giving up his secular state for Your service. These two were what they call agents for public affairs. Then, suddenly filled with holy love and quiet indignation, in anger with himself, he looked at his friend, saying, "Do tell me what we

are aiming at by all these labors of ours? what are we seeking? what are we contending for? Can our hopes at court rise higher than to be the Emperor's favorites? And is there anything in this which is not unstable and full of danger? By how many perils do we arrive at a greater peril? and when? But if I choose to be a friend of God, I can become one at once." Thus he spoke, and in pain with the travail of a new life, he turned his eyes again upon the book, and read on, and was changed inwardly before Your sight, and his mind was stripped of the world, as soon appeared. For as he read and his feelings were stirred up, he was vexed with himself for a bit, and then he discerned and determined on a better course. Being already Yours, he said to his friend, "Now I have broken with those worldly hopes of ours, and am resolved to serve God, and to begin from this very hour and place. If you do not care to imitate me, do not oppose me." The other answered that he would re-
[8] main with him as the sharer of so glorious a reward and so great a service. Both being now Yours, they were building the tower at the necessary cost of forsaking all they had and following You. Then Pontitianus, and the other with him, that had walked in other parts of the garden, came in search of them to the same place, and finding them, reminded them to return, for the day was now far spent. But they, relating their resolution and purpose, and how that will had arisen and become strengthened in them, begged their friends, if they would not join, not to molest them. But the others, though in no wise changed from what they

were before, were still grieved that they were the same (so he said), and piously congratulated their friends, recommending themselves to their prayers; and so, with hearts lingering on the earth, went away to the palace. The other two, however, fixing their heart on heaven, remained in the cottage. And both had affianced brides, who, when they heard of this resolution, also dedicated their virginity to God.

This was the story of Pontitianus; but You, O Lord, while he was speaking, did force me to look at myself, taking me from behind my back, where I had placed myself, unwilling to observe myself. You did set me before my face, that I might see how foul I was, how crooked and defiled, stained and ulcerous. And I looked and stood aghast, and there was no escape from myself. If I tried to turn my eyes away from myself, he went on telling his story, and You did again bring me before my eyes and make me look at myself, that I might find out my iniquity and hate it. I had known it, but tried not to see it, winked at it, and forgot it.

Then, indeed, the more I loved those of whose holy affections I was hearing, who had given themselves [9] wholly up to You to be cured, the more heartily I hated myself by comparison with them. For I had passed many years of my life, perhaps twelve, since, in my nineteenth year, after reading Cicero's Hortensius, I was moved to study wisdom; and instead of despising earthly happiness, so as to be able to give myself up to consider that of which not the possession, but the mere inquiry, was to be put before treasures even possessed, the kingdoms of the nations and the plenitude of all carnal delights, I procrastinated. Miserable, most miserable youth indeed that I was! At the beginning of that youth itself I had even asked You to give me chastity, and had said, "Give me chastity and continence, but not yet." For I feared lest You should quickly hear me, and cleanse me from the disease of concupiscence, which I wished to gratify, not to be delivered from. And I was walking by crooked ways in grievous depravity, not indeed secure in those ways, but as if preferring them to all others. I was in perverse opposition with regard to these latter, and did not honestly seek them.

I fancied it was because I had no certain light as to the direction of my life that I put off from day to day following You alone by despising all worldly hopes. The day came when my eyes were opened to myself, and the voice of my conscience asked me in a tone of reproach, "Where are you, O tongue? For you were saying that you would not give up the yoke of vanity for an uncertain truth. See, now, it is certain, and it is still knocking at your door, when those men, who have neither become broken by inquiry nor meditated on these things for ten years and more, put on wings, being less encumbered." Thus was I torn with anguish and buried in the depths of shame as Pontitianus went on telling his tale. Having said his say [10] and finished his visit, he went away, and I returned into myself. What thought did not come into my head? With what cogent reasons did I not scourge my soul, that it might be one with me, who was striving to go after You? It was refractory; it refused, and did not excuse itself. Every argument was answered and overcome: a mute fear alone remained, which dreaded, like death, being restrained from the force of a habit which led to death.

In that great travail of my inner man which I had stirred up against my soul in the secret sanctuary of my heart, agitated both in face and in mind, I made a vehement appeal to Alypius. "What are we doing?" I exclaimed to him; "what is this? what did you hear? The unlearned rise up and take heaven by force; and look at us! we with our lifeless learning are immersed in flesh and blood. Because they have gone before us, are we to be ashamed of following? Are we not rather to be ashamed of not even following?" I said something, I know not what, to this effect, and my warmth tore me away from him as he looked at me in silent astonishment. Nor had my words their natural sound; my face and look, eyes, color, and tone of voice spoke my mind better than the words which I uttered. Our establishment had a garden, which we used with the rest of the house hold, for the master of the house did not dwell in it. To there I was drawn by my mental agitation. There no man would impede that burning struggle in which I was fighting against myself, until it should end in the way You did know, though I did not know it. Only

I was out of myself for my good, and I was dying a living death, conscious of my wickedness, unconscious of the good I was to reach in a short time. I turned, therefore, into the garden, and Alypius followed closely [11] after me. Nor did his company make my secret not mine; for would he ever forsake me in this frame of mind? We sat down as far from the house as possible. I was groaning in spirit, and was burning with indignation at my not accepting Your pleasure, and making a compact with You, my God, for which acceptance all my bones were crying, and were sending to heaven the voice of praise. There was no getting there by ship or chariot or foot of man as quickly as I by one step had gone from the house into that place where we were sitting. For not only the going there, but also the getting there, was nothing else than the will to go. This will should be strong and genuine, not a half hearted will, which is irresolute and struggling, now with the wish to rise, now with the wish to fall.

Thus was I sick and in anguish, reproaching myself with more than usual severity, turning and re-turning in my chain, until its last snap should be broken; for, slight as it was, still it bound me; and You, O Lord, just Mercy, were speaking to my secret heart, putting before me motives of fear and shame, lest I should again turn away, and that small and frail link which remained should not be broken, and should grow strong to bind me afresh. For I said to myself, "Let it be now, let it be now." And so I went on, contenting myself with words. I was already doing and not doing;

neither did I fall back into my former ways, but I was standing still in near proximity to them, and taking my time. And again I tried, and was almost successful, and had almost reached the mark and held it in my grasp; and still I fell short of it, and neither reached nor held it, hesitating to die to death and to live to life. I inclined rather to follow the worse course, which was familiar, than the better, which was unfamiliar; and [12] as to that particular moment of time when I was to become different, the nearer it approached the more it struck me with horror. Only it did not vanish into the background, nor disappear, but was pending.

Small trifles, the vanity of vanities, the things which I had formerly loved, were holding me back. They were stirring up my covering of flesh, and murmuring, Will you send us away? And from this time forth shall we be with you no more? Will you be unable to do such and such a thing for evermore? And what were the suggestions they made in saying "such and such a thing"? What indeed, my God? Let Your mercy preserve the soul of Your servant from them. What pollution and what shame! And I heard them with much less than half an ear, not contradicting me openly before my face, but, as it were, murmuring behind my back, and disappearing like a runaway thief to induce me to look round. Still they delayed me in my desire to tear myself away from them, and to go where I was called, because the strong force of habit said to me, "Do you think to do without these things?"

But already the suggestion was faintly made. For, in the direction in which I had turned my face, and where I was fearing to pass, the pure glory of Chastity, with her serene and holy mirth, was disclosed to me. With honest words of encouragement she bade me come and not doubt, and held out her fair hands, full to overflowing with the examples of the good, to receive and embrace me. In them were crowds of boys and girls, and young people, and people of all ages; there were sober widows and aged virgins; and in no one of them was that same Chastity sterile, but she was the fruitful mother of sons of joy by You, O Lord, her spouse. And Chastity smiled at me in admonishment, [13] as if to say, "Can you not do what these have done? or indeed can they do it of themselves, and not rather in the Lord their God? The Lord their God gave me to them what are you doing and not doing? Cast yourself upon Him: fear not; He will not leave you to fall: cast yourself upon Him with confidence; He will receive and heal you." And I was filled with great confusion, because I still heard the murmurings of my vanities, and hesitated in suspense. And again it seemed to me that Chastity spoke: "Turn a deaf ear on earth to those unclean members of yours, that they may be mortified. They speak to you of delights, but they are not as the law of the Lord your God" This struggle in my heart concerned only myself against myself. Alypius, who clung to my side, awaited in silence the issue of my unusual emotion.

But when earnest contemplation abstracted from the secret depth of conscience and brought before the eyes of my heart all my wretchedness, then a tempest broke, bringing with it a great fountain of tears. In order that I might give them full play, I got up and left Alypius; solitude seemed to me more suited to the shedding of tears, and I went far enough from him, so as not to feel the restraint of even his presence. This is how I was, and he thought I know not what. I believe I had said something in which the tone of my voice, struggling with sobs, had betrayed itself, and thus I had got up. He therefore remained where we had been sitting in great astonishment. I threw myself down, I know not how, under a certain fig-tree, and put no check upon my tears. The floodgates of my soul poured forth a sacrifice acceptable to You. Not indeed in these words, but in the spirit of them, I spoke repeatedly to You: And You, Lord, how long? How long, Lord, will You be angry unto the end? [14] Be not mindful of our former iniquities. For I felt that they held me captive, and was crying out in my anguish. "How long? how long is it to be tomorrow and tomorrow? Why not now? Why may not this very hour put an end to my shame?"

I was saying these things and weeping in the bitterest sorrow of heart; and all at once I heard a voice, like the voice of a boy or a girl, I know not which, coming from the next house, repeating over and over again in a musical tone, "Take and read; take and read!" Composing myself instantly, I began most

earnestly to ponder whether there was any game what
ever in which children were accustomed to sing similar
words, nor could I remember ever to have heard them before. The violence of my tears being checked, I rose,
interpreting them in no other way than to mean that this
was a Divine intimation to me to open the Scriptures
and to read what first came in my way. For I had
heard that Anthony was admonished by a chance read
ing of the Gospel, as if the words, *Go, sell all that you
have and give to the poor, and you shall have treasure
in heaven: and come and follow me,* had been said to
him, and that by this sign he had been at once converted to You. Thus minded, I returned to the place
where Alypius was sitting, for I had put down the book
of Epistles in coming away. I took it up, opened it,
and read in silence the first chapter which met my eyes:
*Not in rioting and drunkenness, not in concupiscence and
impurity, not in contention and anger: but put you on
the Lord Jesus Christ, and provide not for the flesh in
impure lusts.* I would not read on, nor was there any
need that I should. For I had no sooner read to the
end of the sentence than a light as if of security being
infused into my heart, all the darkness of doubt was
dissipated.

[15] Then, having put my finger or some other mark in
the place, I closed the book and passed it to Alypius
with a countenance already composed. As to him,
this was how he showed me what was going on in
himself, which I did not know. He asked to see what
I had been reading. I pointed it out to him, and he

went on further than I, and I was not familiar with what followed, which was, but receive the weak man in faith. This he took for himself, and disclosed it to me. But he was strengthened by this advice, and without any painful hesitation he followed that which was in keeping with his life, by which he had far out distanced me for a long time past. Then we went in to my mother with our story, which rejoiced her. We told her how it had happened, and her joy was triumphant. She praised You, Who are powerful to do more than we ask or can understand, because she saw You had given her more in my regard than she had been accustomed to ask You for by her sighs and tears. For You had so converted me to You that I sought neither for a wife nor for anything else in this world, holding that rule of faith which You had revealed to her so many years before that I should hold. And You did turn her weeping into joy much more abundantly than she had desired, and concerning the relations due to my sin much more tenderly and chastely than she had demanded.

[16]
2. DEATH OF ST. MONICA
(*Confessions*, Bk. 9, ch. 10)

As the day approached on which she (Monica) was to bid farewell to this life, which day, O Lord, You did know, though we knew it not, it happened by the secret workings of Your providence (as I believe) that she and I were standing alone at a window which looked on to the garden of the house inhabited by us. Here, by the mouth of the Tiber, after a toilsome journey, we were resting apart from the crowd with a view to continuing it by sea. We were discoursing together alone very sweetly, and, forgetting the past in our desire to grasp the future, were asking each other in the presence of the unvarying Truth, which You are, what that eternal life of the saints would be which eye has not seen, ear has not heard, nor heart of man has imagined. But yet we gasped with the mouth of our heart after those heavenly streams of Your fountain, the fountain of life, of which You are the source, in order that, drawing from there what strength we were able, we might in some way or other form a picture of this ineffable mystery.

When, in our conversation, we had reached that point at which pleasure of the senses, however great, and corporeal light, however dazzling, seemed for the exceeding joy of eternal life to be unworthy not only of comparison, but even of mention, we raised our [17] hearts to God in still more burning love, and viewed successively all corporeal things, and heaven itself, from which sun, moon, and stars shine upon the earth. And still we rose higher by our secret contemplation, by our praise and admiration of Your works. Then we came to consider our own minds, and passed them by that we might attain the region of unfailing plenty, where You feed Israel for ever on the food of truth. There life is Wisdom, by whom all these things are made, and by whom all past and future things are.

Wisdom itself is not made, but is now what it was, and will be the same for ever; or rather, past and future time do not exist in it, but Being alone, because it is eternal. For past and future time have no place in that which is eternal. In the vehemence of our desires after wisdom, we grasped it for one moment with our whole heart; and then sighed as that foretaste of the Spirit left us, and we were forced to return to the distraction of human words, which have both beginning and end. What is like to Your Word, O Lord, which remains in itself without decay and renovates all things?

We were saying then: If to any the tumult of the flesh were hushed, hushed the images of earth and waters and air, hushed also the poles of heaven, yes, the very soul be hushed to herself, and by not thinking on self surmount self; hushed all dreams and imaginary revelations, every tongue and every sign, and whatsoever exists only in transition, since, if any could hear, all these say, "We made not ourselves, but He made us who abides forever." If, then, having uttered this, they too should be hushed, having roused only our ears to Him who made them, and He alone speak by Himself, not by them, that we may hear His word, not through any tongue of flesh, nor angel's [18] voice, nor sound of thunder, nor in the dark riddle of an allegory, but might hear Him whom in these things we love, might hear His very self without these (as we two now strained ourselves and in swift thought touched on that Eternal Wisdom which abides over all); could this be continued on, and other visions of kind far unlike be withdrawn, and this one ravish and absorb and wrap up its beholder amid these inward joys, so that life might be forever like that one moment of understanding which now we sighed after; were not this *Enter into the joy of your Lord*? And when is this to be? Will it be when we all rise again, but are not all transformed?

So we were talking, and if not exactly in this way and in these words, You, O Lord, know that on the day when we held this conversation, the world with all its pleasures seemed to us, as we spoke, a thing of no account. Then she said, "As for me, my son, nothing in this life delights me. I know not what more I can still do, or why I am left here, as I have no further hope from this world. There was one thing which made me desirous of dwelling here on earth a little longer, which was, that I might see you a Christian Catholic before I died. My God has abundantly granted my request in letting me see you even despise earthly happiness and become His servant. What am I doing here?" I cannot exactly remember what answer I made to these words of hers. In the meantime, within five days, or little more from that time, she was seized with fever. And one day, during her illness, she fainted away and lost her senses for a short time. We hastened to her, and she soon revived, and looking at my brother and me who were standing by, she said as if seeking to know something, "Where have I been?" Then seeing our

[19] pained surprise, she went on, "Will you bury your mother here?" I was silent, and was restraining my tears. My brother, however, said something to the effect that he would not have her die on a journey, but rather, as the happier lot, in her own country. When she heard this, she gave him an anxious look with her eyes, as if to depreciate his caring for such things, and then she turned to me with the words, "You hear what he says?" Soon she addressed us both again. "Lay this body anywhere: let it not be a care to you: this only I ask of you, that you would remember me at the Lord's altar wherever you be." When she had explained this her wish as best she could, she was silent again, and her illness came on with greater force, to try her.

But, O invisible Good, I, pondering on the gifts productive of admirable fruits which You put into the hearts of Your faithful, rejoiced and gave You thanks. For I recalled to mind how extremely anxious she had always been about her grave, which she had prepared for herself by the side of her husband's body. Inasmuch as they had lived together in great harmony, she had a further wish in addition to her former happiness for the human mind does not easily grasp divine things and she hoped its fulfillment might come to the knowledge of men. She desired that, after her wanderings beyond the sea, it might be given to her to be buried in the same earth as her husband. I know not at what moment this empty desire by the fullness of Your goodness began to decline in her heart, and I rejoiced in wonder at what she now told me, although at that conversation of ours at the window, when she said, "What have I to do here?" she seemed not to be desirous of dying in her own country. I also heard afterwards that, during our stay at Ostia, [20] she was talking one day with motherly kindness to some friends of mine about contempt of this life and the happiness of death. I myself was not present. In admiration at the strength of soul which You had given to her, they asked her whether she did not dread leaving her body so far from her native town. Her reply was, "Nothing is far to God; nor is it to be feared lest at the end of the world He should not recognize from where He has to raise me up." In the ninth day, therefore, of her illness, in the fifty-sixth year of her age, that devout and holy soul was released from her body.

I closed her eyes. Grief took possession of my very soul, and poured itself out in tears, so that my eyes with the violence of my sorrow wept themselves dry, and I suffered greatly from this anguish of sadness. When she breathed forth her last breath, my son, Adeodatus, began to weep, but he was silenced by us. In this way, too, force was put upon the childishness which was hidden in my own heart, and it was checked and repressed. Nor did we deem it fitting to celebrate that death with murmuring tears and groans, this being the ordinary way of showing grief for a certain destitution, or sort of total extinction, which men attribute to the dead. But she neither died unhappily nor was hers a death at all. This was firmly impressed on our minds both by the unerring example of her conduct and by her genuine faith.

When the body was removed we returned tearless to our home; for I did not weep even during the prayers we prayed to You, as the Sacrifice of our redemption was offered for her when the corpse was placed by the grave before it was lowered, according to the usual rite, but all day long I suffered great [21] anguish of heart, and in my agitation I asked You as best I could to calm my grief, yet You did not, impressing, I believe, upon my memory by this one instance how strong is the bond of all habit, even upon a soul which now feeds upon no deceiving word. . . . Then I slept, and, on awakening, found my grief not a little softened; and being as I was in the solitude of my bed, those true verses of Your servant Ambrose occurred to my mind; for You are the

"Maker of all, the Lord

And Ruler of the height,
Who, robing day in light, have poured

Soft slumbers o'er the night,
That to our limbs the power

Of toil may be renew'd,
And hearts be raised that sink and cower,
And sorrows be subdued."

But that wound, which seemed to prove an excess of human affection, being now healed, I offer up to You, our God, tears of a far other kind for this Your servant tears proceeding from a humble consideration of the dangers to which every soul dying in Adam is exposed. For although she was vivified in Christ, and while still in the flesh so lived as to glorify Your name by her faith and by her works, still I dare not say that from the time of her regeneration through You by baptism no single word against Your commands ever escaped her lips. The Truth, Your Son, spoke the words, *If any man shall say to his brother, You fool, he shall be guilty of hell fire.* And it is woe even to the virtuous life of good men if You judge them without mercy. But because You do not search eagerly after sins, we confidently hope to find some place of indulgence with You. For what does [22] any man do who enumerates his good deeds to You except tell You of so many gifts of Yours? Oh, if men did but know themselves, and if he who glories in himself would only glory in the Lord!

Therefore, O God of my heart, my glory and my life, putting aside just now her good actions, for which I give You joyful thanks, I beg Your mercy for the sins of my mother; hear me through the redemption which was shown on the cross for the healing of our wounds, and may He Who sits on Your right hand be our Mediator. I know that her life was merciful, and that she forgave her enemies from her heart; do

You forgive her now her debts, if she contracted any during the course of so many years after the salutary waters of baptism. Forgive her, O Lord, forgive her, I beseech You, and enter not into judgment with her. Let Your judgment praise Your mercy, because Your words are true, and You have promised mercy to the merciful. You gave them power to be this. You will have mercy on the man who inspires Your compassion, and will show mercy when You are merciful.

I believe You have already done what I am now asking, but do You commend, O Lord, the voluntary offering of my lips. For as the day of her death was at hand, she did not give a thought to having her body magnificently laid out or embalmed; nor did she crave for a choice monument, nor wish to be buried in her family tomb. These were not the recommendations which she gave to us. She desired only to be commemorated at Your altar, which she had served without a single day's intermission. From the altar she knew that the Holy Victim is dispensed, by whom the handwriting which was against us has been blotted out. By that Victim the enemy was conquered who [23] keeps an account of our transgressions, and who, seeking something with which to reproach us, finds nothing against Him whose victory is ours. Who will give Him back His innocent blood? Who will restore to Him the price which He paid for us, that His enemy shall thus have power to take us away from Him? Your handmaid enchained her soul to His sacrament of our redemption by the bond of faith. Let no one withdraw her from Your protecting arm. May the lion and the dragon not interpose main force or artifice in her path. Neither will she answer and say that she has no debt, lest she be convicted by the wily accuser, and fall a prey to him; but she will answer that her debts were forgiven her by Him to whom none may restore that which He, all innocent of debt, gave for us.

May she rest, then, in peace, with the husband before and after whom she never had any, whom she obeyed with patience, bringing forth fruit unto You, that she might win him also unto You. And inspire, O Lord my God, inspire Your servants, my brethren, Your sons, my masters, whom with voice, and heart, and pen I serve, that so many as read these Confessions may at Your altar remember Monica, Your handmaid, with Patricius, her deceased husband, by whose bodies You brought me into this life, how I know not. May they with devout affection remember my parents in this transitory light, my brethren under You our Father in our Catholic mother, and my fellow citizens in that Eternal Jerusalem which Your pilgrim people sighs after from their exodus unto their return. So that my mother's last request of me, through my Confessions more than through my prayers, be, through the prayers of many, more abundantly fulfilled to her.

3. ST. AUGUSTINE'S EPISCOPAL LIFE AT HIPPO
   (*Sermon* 355)

I ASKED you yesterday to come in greater numbers today, because of what I am now going to say. We live here with you and for you; and it is our intention and our desire that we may live with you for ever with Christ. You see, also, what our conversation is, so that possibly we, too, may dare to say what the Apostle said, though we are so far beneath him, *Be my imitators, as I am an imitator of Christ.* This is why I would not have any one of you find in us a pretext for himself leading a bad life. For we provide good things, as the same Apostle says, not only in the sight of God, but also in the sight of men. The testimony of our conscience is sufficient for our own sakes; for yours our good name should not be sullied, but should be strengthened in you. Listen to what I have said, and make this distinction. Conscience and reputation are two things. Conscience is for your own sake, and reputation for your neighbor's. The man who relies on his conscience and neglects his reputation is cruel to himself, especially when he is placed in the position of which the Apostle speaks in writing to his disciple, showing yourself a good example with regard to all men.
[25] Not to detain you too long, especially as I am sitting and you are standing, you, all of you, or almost all of you, know that we live in the house which is called the bishop's house, so as to imitate as far as we can

those holy men whom the Book of the Acts mentions: *No man called anything his own, but all things were common unto them.* It may be that some of you do not inquire diligently enough into our lives to know this as I would have you know it: I say what it is, and I have said it in a few words. I, whom by God's grace you see before you as your bishop, was young when I came to this city, as many of you know. I looked for a place where I might found a monastery and live with my brethren. I had indeed given up all my worldly hopes, and would not be that which I might have been; nor did I seek to be what I now am. I chose to be rather an abject in the house of my God than to inhabit the tents of sinners. I broke off from those who loved the world, but I did not put myself on a footing with those who govern the people. Nor did I seek an exalted place at my Lord's banquet, but a low one, and it pleased Him to say to me, Go up higher. I so much feared the episcopate, that, as I had begun to be of some reputation among the servants of God, I did not go to the place where I knew there was no bishop. I avoided it, and did all I could to be saved in a low place, lest I should be endangered by an exalted one. But, as I have said, the servant may not oppose his lord. I came to this city to see a friend whom I thought I might gain to God and have with us in the monastery, and I fancied myself safe because there was already a bishop in the place. They laid hands upon me and made me a priest, and in this way I reached the episcopate. I brought nothing with me, and came to this see having only the clothes which I

[26] wore at the time. And as I purposed living in a conventual house with my brethren, Valerius, of blessed memory, having become acquainted with my institute and my wish, gave me the garden in which the convent now stands. I began to collect together men of good will, who were of my own standing, possessing nothing, as I had possessed nothing, and imitating my example, that as I had sold my slender inheritance and distributed it to the poor, so they who wished to be with me should also do, that we might live a community life, in which God Himself should be our great and all-sufficing prize. I came to be a bishop, and I found it necessary that a bishop should show unwearying kindness to all who called upon him or were passing his way, and if a bishop did not so act he would be called inhuman. But if this custom had been tolerated in a monastery it would have been out of place. And this was why I wished to have with rne in this my episcopal house a community of priests. This then is how we live. In our community nobody is allowed to have private property; but perhaps some have it notwithstanding. It is against our rule, and if any have property, they are breaking it. I have, however, a good opinion of my brethren, and having this good opinion, have refrained from asking them questions, because it seemed to me that in questioning them I might appear almost to suspect some evil. I knew, and I know, that all those who have lived with me are familiar with our scheme and our rule of life. . . .

You remember, my brethren, that I recommended

those who remain with me, that if any among them have private property, they either sell and distribute it, or make it over to the common fund. They have the Church by which God feeds us. And I gave them a delay up to the Epiphany, on account of those who either [27] had not estimated their property and given it up to their brothers, or of those who had as yet done nothing with their property, because they were waiting to be of age. Let them do as they like, provided that they keep me company in poverty and in confidence in God's mercy. But should they object to this, and perhaps some do, I who laid down the law, as you know, had resolved to ordain no man a priest who would not remain with me, so that if he wished to change his mind, I could lawfully remove him from the office of a priest, because he would have been unfaithful to the promise of our holy society and to the common purpose of our life. Mark my words: before God and before you I retract what I then laid down. I do not take the functions of a priest from those who wish to have private property, who are not satisfied with God and with His Church; let them live where they like and where they can. I will have no hypocrites. For does any man doubt that hypocrisy is an evil? It is wrong to fall away from a purpose, but it is worse to make pretence of one. Listen attentively to what I am saying: he who falls away from that community life which is praised in the Acts of the Apostles is unfaithful to his vow and falls from his holy calling. Let him be mindful of his Judge, who is God, not Augustine. I do not deprive him of the priestly functions. I have

put before him the greatness of the danger; let him do
as he pleases. For I know that if it pleases me to
degrade a priest for so acting, men will be found to
patronize and support him, and who say, both in this
place and to other bishops, "What evil has he done?
He cannot endure this life with you; he does not wish
to live in the episcopal house, he wishes to have his
own means. Shall he therefore be deprived of his
priestly functions?" I know how great an evil it is
[28] to promise something holy and not to accomplish
it. Vow and pray to the Lord your God; and again, It
is better not to promise than to promise and not fulfill.
A virgin who has never lived in a convent is still a
virgin, and she may not marry though she is not obliged
to be in a convent. But if she was in a convent, and
has left it, being still a virgin, she is half ruined. So
a priest has promised two things holiness and the
priesthood. The holiness is to be interior; the priesthood God has imposed upon him for the sake of His
people, and it is rather a burden than an honor; but
who is wise and will understand these things? He has
therefore taken upon him the calling of holiness, and
also of the common life; he has seen how good and how
pleasant it is for brethren to dwell together in unity.
If he fall away from this purpose, and in his desertion
is still a priest, then he, too, is half ruined. What is
this to me? I am not his judge. If after his withdrawal
he keep up the appearance of holiness, he is half lost,
but if he remain within as a hypocrite, he is wholly
lost. I will not give him an opportunity for making
pretenses. I am aware how men prize the priesthood,

and I degrade no one from it simply because he refuses to live with me in community life. He who chooses to remain has God with him. If he be ready to be fed by God through His Church, to have no private means, but either to distribute his money to the poor or to put it into the common fund, then let him stay with me. As for him who does not agree to this, let him be free, but let him consider what chance he has of happiness hereafter. . . .

4. ST. AUGUSTINE'S VIEW OF FUNERAL POMP
(*On the City of God*, Bk. 1, ch. 12, 13)

IT is written in the psalm, *They have given the dead bodies of Your servants to be meat for the fowls of the air, the flesh of Your saints for the beasts of the earth*; but the words bear witness rather to the cruelty of those who inflicted this treatment than to the unhappiness of those who suffered it. Although this treatment seems a hard and cruel one in the sight of men, still precious in the sight of God is the death of His saints. Hence all these things, that is, the care of funeral, burial-place, and pomp of interment, are rather a solace to the living than a consolation to the dead. If the possession of a magnificent tomb is to profit the wicked man anything, then having a poor one or none will prove detrimental to the good man. A crowd of his servants gave that wicked man in the Gospel, who was clothed in purple and fine linen, a splendid funeral in the sight of men; but how much more beautiful in the eyes of God was the ministry of the angels in the case of the poor man covered with sores, whom they bore not into a marble tomb, but into Abraham's bosom!

Nor are dead bodies, especially those of the just and righteous, either to be thrown aside or to be treated with contempt. The Holy Spirit has made use of [30] them like organs or vessels for all manner of good works. If a father's garment or ring, or anything else of the kind, is dear to his family in proportion as their love for him was great, the body itself, which is far more a part of ourselves than clothes of whatever description, is by no means to be looked down upon; for it is not an outside ornament or attire which is put on, but it belongs to the very nature of man. Hence the funerals of the just in ancient times were the objects of tender piety; they were celebrated with due pomp, and their burial place was a matter of fore thought. During their lifetime they gave directions to their sons about the burying, or even transferring of their remains; and Tobias is commended by the angel for having pleased God in burying the dead. Our Lord Himself, who was to rise on the third day, speaks of the good work of Mary Magdalen, saying, that in pouring precious ointment over His Body she was to become known, and that she had done it for His burial; and the Gospel records with praise the deed of those who received His Body from the cross, and were diligent in covering It and giving It honorable burial. These instances do not indeed prove that there is any sense in dead bodies, but they signify that the bodies of the dead belong to God's providence, and that these works of mercy are pleasing to Him as a token of faith in the resurrection. From this we may gather the worth of almsgiving to the living, if even that which is done for the inanimate limbs of departed men is not lost in God's sight. In speaking of the burial or removal of their bodies, there are other things, too, which the holy patriarchs said, and which they wished to be understood in a prophetical spirit. But this is not the place for going into them, in as much as what I have said may suffice. If things so [31] necessary for the support of the living as food and clothing fail, grievous though the want of them may be, it does not break either the endurance or the fortitude of just men, nor does it destroy piety in their hearts, but, by proving their religion, renders it more fruitful. How, then, does the absence of such things as are accustomed to be used for the service and burial of dead bodies make those souls miserable who are already at rest in the hidden abode of the just?

5. DUTIES OF TESTATORS
(*Sermon* 355.3)

THE priest Januarius also joined our community. He seemed to have almost given away his whole property in genuine alms; but this was not the case. He had some money left that is, some property which, he said, was his daughter's. This daughter of his, by the

grace of God, is in a convent, and gives good promise.
May God guide her, that she may fulfill our hopes in
the strength of His mercy, not in her own merits.
And because she was under age and could not dispose
of her money (for, although we saw what a beautiful
calling hers was, we feared the snares to which her
youth was subjected), it was put by as if for the girl
till she should be of full age, to do with it as it behooves
a virgin of Christ, at which time she could best lay
it out. In the meantime her father drew near death.
Some time back, swearing that the property was his,
and not his daughter s, he had made a will as if the
money had been his own to leave. I say, a priest and
member of our society, one of us, who lived on the
Church and professed the common life, made a will
and appointed heirs. What a grief for that society!
a fruit not produced by the tree which the Lord has
planted! But he made the Church his heir! I refuse
to take the gift, for I love not the fruit of bitterness.
I sought him out in order to give him to God. He
[33] was a member of our community. Would that he
had kept to it, and carried out its rule, and possessed
nothing, and not made a will. If he did possess any
thing, he should not have pretended to be our companion, as if he too were one of God's poor. This is
a great grief to me, brethren, and because of it I have
settled that the Church shall not receive the inheritance
itself. Let his children have what he has left, and let
them do with it as they please. For it seems to me
that if I take it, I become a partaker in an action
which displeases and grieves me. I wished you to

know this. His daughter is in a convent, his son in a monastery. Praising the daughter and speaking soft words to the son, that is, treating him with indignity, he has disinherited both. It was my advice that the Church should not receive those small portions which belong to these disinherited children until they are of age. The Church is keeping their property for them. Januarius has bequeathed strife to his children, and I have now to contend with it. The girl says, "It is mine; you know that my father always said it was." The son says, "Let my father be believed, because he would not die with a lie in his mouth!" What an affliction this quarrel is! But if these children be really servants of God we shall soon put an end to the dispute. I hear all they have got to say as a father would, and perhaps better than their father. I shall see what justice requires, according to God's good pleasure, with some few faithful brethren of unblemished reputation. These I shall choose by His grace from your number, that is, from this people. I shall confer with them on the subject, and bring the matter to a termination in the light of God.

Still I ask of you let no man reproach me because I am unwilling that the Church should accept this in-
[34] heritance. In the first place, I am unwilling because I detest that man's action; and in the second, it concerns my own society. Many will applaud what I am going to say, but some may blame me. You have just heard the Gospel words, *We have piped to you, and you have not danced; we have lamented, and you*

have not mourned. John came neither eating nor drinking, and they say he has a devil. The Son of Man came eating and drinking, and they say, Behold a man that is a glutton and a wine-drinker, a friend of publicans and sinners. What am I to do with those who are ready to reproach me, and to grind their teeth at me if I accept the inheritance of those who have dis inherited their children in a fit of anger? On the other hand, what shall I do with those who will not dance when I sing to them? who say, "The reason why nobody gives the Church at Hippo anything, and why no wills are made in its favor, is that Bishop Augustine is too kind (even their praise is biting; their words are soft, but not without sting); he gives every thing away, and refuses to take gifts! "I do indeed take gifts; I promise to take good and holy ones. But if a dying man in anger at his son disinherit him, should I not, if he recovered, try to appease his wrath? Would it not be my duty to reconcile the son to his father? How then is my wish that he should be on good terms with his son sincere if I covet that son's inheritance? A man may indeed follow the course which I have often advised. If he had only one child, he might make Christ the second; or if he had two, he might make Christ the third; or if he had ten, he might make Christ the eleventh, and then I would accept his inheritance. And because I have acted in this way in several instances, they want to put a bad construction on my good nature, or to injure my good name, so that they may have a ground for blaming me, and for saying that I will not receive the offerings of good men. Let them think how many gifts I have accepted. What need is there of enumerating them? I can mention one. I accepted the inheritance of Julian's son; and why? Because he died without children.

I would not have Boniface's inheritance, not out of kindness, but out of fear. I would not have the Church of Christ made into a shipowner. There are many certainly who make money even by their ships. But one day a tempting offer would come, and the ship might take it and be wrecked; then we should have men put to the torture in order that the usual judicial inquiry might be instituted as to the wreck, and those who had escaped drowning would be subjected to the judge's torture. But we would not give them the men, for under no circumstances would this conduct befit the Church. Would it then pay the fine? But with what funds? We are not allowed to place money at interest. [1] For laying by gold is not a bishop's province, any more than his turning a deaf ear to the poor man is. ... We may not hoard, for laying by money is not a bishop's province, nor should he reject the poor man. Every day how many beg of us in tears and poverty, and we leave the greater number in their sorrow, because we have not something to give to all. ... When indeed I gave to the son what his father in his anger had taken away at his death, I did well. Let those who like praise me, and let those who will not praise me spare me. What more shall I say, brethren? Let the man who wishes to make the Church his heir by disinheriting his son find some other person than Augustine to receive the inheritance,

1 This shows the different discipline of the time. The Church forbade usury, but she was the first to obey her own law.

[36] or rather, by God's grace, may he not find any one. What a praiseworthy act was that of the holy and venerable Aurelius, Bishop of Carthage, and how it made all those who knew of it loud in their praises of God! A certain man, having no children nor the prospect of any, gave all his property to the Church, keeping the interest only for himself. He had children in course of time, and the bishop returned him his gift without his even giving the matter a thought The bishop had it in his power to keep the property but by the law of earth, not of heaven.

[37]
6. DUTIES OF KINGS
(*Letter* 185 to Boniface, 8)

As the Apostle says, *While we have time, let us work good to all men.* Let those who can, do this good by the words of Catholic preachers; let those who can, do it by the laws of Catholic princes. Let all be called to salvation and be recalled from bad ways by the joint action of those who obey the divine behests and by those who obey the imperial commands. Because when emperors enact bad laws in favor of falsehood against truth, true believers are proved, and, persevering, they are crowned. But when emperors enact good laws in favor of truth against falsehood, fierce opposers are awed, and are corrected by coming to a right understanding. Whoever, therefore, will not obey those laws of emperors which are enacted against God's truth acquires a great reward; but whoever will not obey those laws of emperors which are enacted in favor of God's truth merits a great punishment. For in the times of the prophets all kings who did not prohibit or put an end to anything instituted against God's precepts are blamed; and those who did prohibit and did put an end to them are praised more than the rest. And King Nebuchadnezzar, being, as he was, the slave of idols, enacted a sacrilegious law that a statue should be adored; but those who would [38] not obey his impious commands acted with piety and faithfulness. Still the same king, corrected by a divine miracle, enacted the holy and praiseworthy law for truth, that whomsoever should speak blasphemy of the God of Shadrach, Misach, and Abdenego should immediately be put to death, together with his household. If any were found to contemn this law and to suffer its just penalty, they no doubt said what the others said, i.e., that they were just, because they were suffering persecution from a law of the king's. And this most certainly they would have said if they were as bereft of sense as these men who divide the members of Christ, and insult the sacraments of Christ, and glory in persecution, because they are prohibited from doing these things by the laws which emperors have enacted for the unity of Christ. And they boast falsely of their innocence, and seek from men that glory of martyrs which they cannot receive from God. But those are true martyrs of whom the Lord says, Blessed are they who suffer persecution for justice. Therefore, not those who suffer persecution for iniquity, and for the impious division of Christian unity, but for justice sake, are true martyrs. For Hagar suffered persecution from Sara, and in this case the persecutor was holy and the persecuted was wicked. Is the persecution of holy David, whom the iniquitous Saul persecuted, to be compared to this persecution which was suffered by Hagar? Indeed, his differed widely from hers, not because he suffered, but because he suffered for justice. And our Lord Himself was crucified with thieves; but those whom suffering united the cause separated. Therefore those words of the psalm are to be understood as the cry of true martyrs, who wish to be distinguished from false martyrs: *Judge me, God, and distinguish my cause from that of the* [39] *unrighteous people.* He did not say, Distinguish my suffering; he says, *Distinguish my cause.* For the pain of the impious may be the same, while the cause of their pain is not the same; and these two are mentioned in the psalm in the words, *They persecuted me unjustly; do help me.* He deemed himself deserving of just help because they were persecuting unjustly; for if they had been persecuting him justly, he should not have expected help, but correction.

....If the true Church be that Church which suffers persecution and does not persecute, let men ask the

Apostle which Church it was that Sara typified when she persecuted her handmaid. He says, indeed, that our mother, the Heavenly Jerusalem, that is, the true Church of God, was typified in that woman who persecuted her handmaid. But if we penetrate further, it was rather Hagar who pursued Sara by her pride than Sara who repressed Hagar; for Hagar was offensive to her mistress, while Sara put a curb on Hagar's pride. Next I ask, if good and holy men never persecute any one, but only suffer persecution, who it is they suppose to be speaking in the psalm where we read, *I will pursue after my enemies and overtake them; and I will not turn again till they are consumed*? If, therefore, we would say and acknowledge what is true, that persecution which impious men wage against the Church of Christ is unjust, and that is just which the Churches of Christ wage against impious men. This Church, therefore, which suffers persecution for justice is blessed, and those men who suffer it for injustice are truly miserable. Hence the Church persecutes with love, and they persecute with cruelty; the Church that she may correct, they that they may destroy. The Church persecutes that she may convert men from their errors, and they that they may draw men into error. The [40] Church, in short, persecutes her enemies and embraces them, until, vanity being consumed in them, they are able to make progress in the truth; but they, returning evil for good, strive to take away even our temporal things because we are anxious for their eternal salvation, and they are so addicted to murder that they perpetrate it on themselves (1) when they cannot perpetrate it on others. For just as the charity of the Church is in labor to save them from that perdition, so that no one of them should die, so does the fury of these men labor either to kill us that they may give an aliment to their own cruelty, or to kill even themselves lest they should seem to have lost the power of putting men to death. . . .

As to those men who object to just laws being enacted against their own impiety, saying that the Apostles asked for no such laws from the kings of the earth, they do not consider the different nature of the times, and that all things have their own time. For what emperor then believed in Christ so as to serve Him out of piety against impiety, while those words of the prophet were still being carried out, *Why have the Gentiles raged, and the people devised vain things? The kings of the earth stood up, and the princes met together against the Lord, and against His anointed one.* That which is spoken of a little farther on in the same psalm had not yet come about, *And now, you kings, understand: receive instruction, you that judge the earth. Serve the Lord with fear; and rejoice unto Him with trembling.* How, then, do kings serve the Lord in fear unless by prohibiting and censuring with reverent severity those things which are done contrary to the commandments of God? For the king serves in one way

1 This is a reference to the Donatists, who frequently committed suicide.

because he is a man, and in another way because he

is also a king. Because he is a king, he serves God by enforcing with due vigor laws which enact just things and repress unjust ones. This was what Ezekiel did when he destroyed the woods and temples of the idols, and those high places which had been raised against the command of God; and Josias also, who did similar things, and the king of the Ninevites by ordering the whole city to appease the Lord. Thus, too, Darius served God by giving the idol into Daniel's hands to be broken, and by throwing his enemies to the lions. So also did Nebuchadnezzar, of whom we have already spoken, by prohibiting severely all his subjects from blaspheming God. This, then, is how kings, as kings, serve the Lord, that is, by doing those things for His service which only kings can do.

Whereas, therefore, kings did not already serve God in the days of the Apostles, but were still devising vain things against the Lord and against His Christ, in order that all the sayings of the prophets should be fulfilled, it was not then that impiety could be forbidden by the laws; it was rather enforced by the laws. Thus time ran its course, so that the Jews put to death those who preached Christ, thinking they were thereby doing service to God, as Christ had foretold, and peoples raged against Christians, and the patience of the martyrs conquered them all. After that which is written, *And all the kings of the earth shall adore Him, all peoples shall serve Him,* had begun to be accomplished, what reasonable man would say to kings, "Do not pay any attention to the fact of a man holding or oppressing the Church of your Lord in your kingdom? It is no matter to you whether a man in your kingdom chooses to be religious or sacrilegious!" For to these same kings it cannot be said, "Does it not matter to you [42] whether a man in your kingdom chooses to be moral or immoral?" Why, therefore, as free will has been divinely given to man, is adultery to be punished by the laws, (1) and sacrileges to be tolerated? Is it easier for a soul not to keep faith with God than it is for a woman to keep her marriage vow? Or if those things which are committed, not out of contempt, but out of ignorance of religion, are to be more mildly treated, are they to be altogether overlooked?

1 It is here to be remembered that adultery was punished as a crime by the Roman law.

[43]
7. ANSWERS TO VARIOUS QUESTIONS
(*Letter* 54, to Questions of Januarius)

WITH regard to your questions, I should like first to know how you yourself would answer them, for in this way, by my approval or disapproval of them, I could answer you in a much shorter way, and easily either confirm you in your mode of thinking, or point out your errors. This is what I should prefer, as I say. But in order to send you an answer now, I have chosen rather a lengthy letter than a lengthy delay. In the first place, I would have you hold what comes first in our disquisition, i.e., that our Lord Jesus Christ, as He says Himself in the Gospel, has laid on us His own sweet yoke and light burden. Hence He has put together a society of the people of the New Law by sacraments, few in number, easy of observance, most ineffable in their signification, such as baptism, which is consecrated by the name of the Trinity, the communion of His Body and Blood, and whatever else is commended in the canonical books of Scripture, except those things which burdened the people of old, being in keeping with their disposition of heart and the needs of that age of prophecy. These are contained in the five books of Moses. But those things which we keep as handed down and not written, which indeed the whole world holds, are explained to us either by the Apostles themselves, or by the commendations and [44] decisions of plenary councils, which the Church possesses the happy authority of calling together. Thus, for instance, the Passion and Resurrection and Ascension of our Lord into heaven, and the descent from heaven of the Holy Spirit, are kept by a yearly solemnity, and in the same way other festivals of a like kind are kept by the universal Church wherever she may have penetrated.

But there are other practices which vary according to the region; for instance, some fast on Saturday, and some do not; some partake every day of the Body and Blood of the Lord, some only on certain days; in one place It is offered up every day without fail, at another on Saturday and Sunday, elsewhere on Sunday only;

and so on with other practices of the kind, which may be observed with perfect freedom. On this point a wise and prudent Christian can do nothing better than conform himself to the custom of the Church as he may happen to find it; for that which is contrary neither to faith nor morals imposes no obligation, and is to be kept or not for the sake of those with whom a man has to live.

I think you must at some time or other have heard what I am going to say, but I will repeat it here. My mother followed me to Milan, and when she found that it was not the custom of the Church there to fast on Saturday, she began to be disquieted and to hesitate about what she should do. Though I took no interest in such matters at the time, for her sake I consulted Bishop Ambrose, of blessed memory, on the subject. His answer was, that he knew of no better way than his own, for that if he did he would rather follow it. On my observing that, in quoting his own example alone, he had given no sufficient reason for his wish that we should not fast on Saturday, he went [45] on to say, "When I go to Rome I fast on Saturday, but here I do not fast. And this is what you should do: wherever you go, follow the custom of the Church as you find it, if you wish to avoid giving or taking scandal." When I reported this to my mother, she willingly adopted the advice. And as to myself, I have pondered it over and over again, and always viewed it in the light of an oracle from Heaven. For I have often seen with sorrow and affliction much disquietude produced amongst weak people by the quarrelsome obstinacy or the superstitious fear of certain brethren, who, in questions of this kind, which cannot be determined by the authority of Holy Scripture, nor by the tradition of the universal Church, nor by any bearing which they have on the correction of life (merely for a particular reason a man may have, or because he was accustomed to do so and so in his own country, or may have seen a thing during the course of his wanderings, and the farther from home the better he deems it), stir up so many contentions, that they think nothing right unless they do it themselves. Someone will say that the Holy Eucharist should not be received every day. You ask, "Why not?" Because, the objector says, those days on which a man lives with greater purity and chastity are to be chosen, so that he may approach worthily to so great a sacrament; For he who eats unworthily, eats and drinks judgment to himself. Another man, on the contrary, says, " Indeed, if sin be so grievous, and the force of the disorder so great that remedies so ineffable are to be delayed, then the sinner should be deprived of the altar by the bishop's authority in order to do penance, and he should be reconciled by the same authority." This is receiving unworthily, if he receive at a time when he ought to be doing penance; for a man should not take it upon himself to stay away from the altar [46] or to approach it again as he feels inclined. For the rest, if sin be not so heinous as to make a man incur excommunication, he should not deprive himself of the daily medicine of our Lord's Body. Perhaps the man who advises both parties to aim principally at being in the peace of Christ goes the furthest towards settling the question between them; but let each one act according to the pious suggestions of his own faith. Neither of them dishonors the Body and Blood of the Lord, but they vie with each other in honoring so ineffable a sacrament. Nor did Zachceus and the Centurion dispute together, nor either prefer himself to the other, and still one of them received Our Lord with joy into his house, and the other said, "I am not worthy that You should enter under my roof" They both honored Our Lord in a different, and, as it would seem, an opposite way; they were both sinners, and they both found mercy. With regard to this comparison, it may be urged that the flavor of the manna varied amongst the people of old according to the will of the individual, and thus it is in each Christian heart with that sacrament by which the world has been overthrown. For one man honors it by not daring to receive it every day, and another man honors it by not daring to let one day pass without receiving it. It is contempt alone which must not be shown for this food any more than disgust for the manna. Hence the Apostle says that it is unworthily received by those who did not discern this food, to which so singular a reverence is due, from other foods. Immediately after the words, He eats and drinks judgment to himself, he added, by way of explanation, not discerning the Body of the Lord; and this is sufficiently evident from the whole passage in the first Epistle to the Corinthians, if it be carefully read.

8. ST. AUGUSTINE AND THE COUNT OF AFRICA
(*Letter* 220)

AUGUSTINE to his lord and son, Boniface, whom he commends to the protection and providence of God's mercy for present and eternal salvation.

I have not been able to find a more trustworthy man, with at the same time a freer access to your ear, to carry my letters than that minister and servant of Christ whom the Lord now offers me in the person of the Deacon Paul, most dear to us both, in order that I may say something to you, not on account of your power and the honor which belongs to you in this wicked world, nor for the health of your corruptible and mortal body, because it too is transitory, and the length of its life is always uncertain. What I say concerns that salvation which Christ promised to us, Who was despised and crucified here on earth for the purpose of teaching us rather to look down upon the good things of this world than to set our hearts on them, and to rest our hearts and hopes on that which He showed forth in His resurrection. For He rose from the dead, and dies not now, nor shall death have any further power over Him.

I know that men are not lacking who care for you according to the life of this world, and who counsel you, sometimes well, sometimes ill, according to it. This they do because they are mortal men, and consult as they best can the interests of the moment, not knowing what the morrow may bring forth. It is not easy, however, for any man to offer you advice according to God, lest your soul perish; not that counselors are lacking, but that it is difficult for them to find a time when they can say these things to you. For I myself have always desired this, and have never found either place or time to bring before you those subjects which it was my duty to bring before a man who is dear to me in Christ. You know, too, in what a state you found me at Hippo when you honored me with a visit. I could scarcely speak for bodily weakness. Now, then, listen to me, my son, exhorting you at least by letter, which I was never able to send you in your troubles, fearing, as I did, for the safety of the bearer, and that it might fall into unacceptable hands. I ask your pardon, therefore, if you think that I was too timorous. I say only why I was timorous.

Listen to me, then, or rather listen to our Lord God speaking to you through the medium of my infirmity. Call to mind what your feelings were when your first wife of pious memory was still alive; and at her recent death how the vanity of this world inspired you with disgust, and how you longed for the service of God. We heard and can bear witness to what you told us at Tubunae about what was in your mind and will. My brother Alypius and I were alone with you. For I think the worldly cares, of which your course is full, will hardly have been so overpowering as to obliterate this entirely from your memory. You were desiring, indeed, to give up all public business in which you were engaged, and to withdraw into a holy leisure, and even to embrace that life which those servants of [49] God, the monks, live. What else prevented you from carrying out this intention than the consideration, on our showing, of how much that which you were doing benefited the churches of Christ, provided you were doing it solely to enable them, safe from the incursions of barbarians, to lead a quiet and tranquil life, as the Apostle says, in all piety and chastity; and that you yourself, girded with a most chaste continence, and amidst the clash of arms, more surely and powerfully protected by arms of the Spirit, sought nothing from the world except those things necessary for the support of you and yours?

While, then, we rejoiced at your being in this mind, you set out on your course and married a wife. The setting out belonged to that obedience which, according to the Apostle, you owed to the higher powers, but you would not have married a wife unless, giving up that chastity which you had vowed, you had been conquered by concupiscence. When I found out that you had done this, I own that I was struck dumb with amazement, but I was partly consoled by hearing that you had refused to marry her unless she first became a Catholic. Still the heresy of those who deny the true Son of God so far prevailed in your house that your daughter was baptized by one of them. If, indeed, things have been truly reported to us I wish heartily that they may be false i.e., that even virgins consecrated to God have been rebaptized by those same heretics, with what fountains of tears ought we not to weep over so grievous an evil? Men say, too, per chance without truth, that you have not been contented with your wife, but have contaminated yourself by unlawful intercourse with I know not what other women.

How shall I characterize the numerous and grievous [50] evils, patent to all, which have been brought about through you since your marriage? You are a Christian, you have a heart, and you fear God. Consider, then, you yourself that which I will not commit my self to say, and you w r ill see how urgently evils so flagrant solicit you to penance. I believe the Lord spares you on account of it, and delivers you from all dangers that you may carry it out as it should be carried out, provided you listen to those words, *Be not slothful in being converted to the Lord, and put not off your conversion from day to day.* You say, indeed, that your cause is just, and of this I am not a judge, because I cannot hear both sides; but, however this may be there is no need of discussing it, or disputing about it at the present moment before God, can you deny that you would not have fallen into this state if you had not loved the things of this world, which, as the servant of God we knew you formerly to be, you ought to have altogether despised and accounted as nothing. You were bound indeed to take what came in your way in order to use it for good purposes, but not so to seek out forbidden things or to undertake matters for others as to bring yourself to this pass on account of them. When the goods of this world are loved, then sin is committed; though you personally may commit it only a little, yet you are the cause of others sinning much, and while those things which are prejudicial for a time if indeed they are so are feared, that which is to be prejudicial for all eternity is committed.

To take one instance of this, who does not see that many men cleave to you for your defence and protection, that although they may be all faithful to you and judged incapable of any treachery by you, they are still desirous of reaching through you those goods which [51] they love not according to God, but according to the world? For this reason, you, who should have controlled and restrained your own desires, are forced to satisfy those of others. And to do this, many things which are displeasing to God are bound to be done, and yet not even so are these desires satisfied. For they are more easily put down entirely in those men who love God than they are even partially satisfied in those who love the world. Consequently Holy Scripture says, *Love not the world nor the things of the world. If any man love the world, the love of the Father is not in him: because all that is in the world is concupiscence of the flesh, and concupiscence of the eyes, and the pride of life, which is not from the Father, but from the world. And the world and its concupiscence pass away. But he who does the will of God abides for ever, as God also abides for ever.* How, then, will you be able, I say, not to satisfy the concupiscence of those who love the world, of so many men of arms, whose cupidity has to be quenched, whose cruelty is a matter of dread for this is an utter impossibility but to feed this concupiscence only a little, so that the whole people be not lost, unless you yourself do what God forbids, who threatens the doers of such things? This is why you see so much havoc worked, that there is hardly the most paltry thing left to take.

But what shall I say about the laying waste of Africa, the work of African barbarians, who meet with no resistance? You, in the meantime, are taken up with the matters I have specified, and do nothing to avert this danger. Who would believe, rather, who would fear, that while Boniface, Count of the Domestics, and also of Africa, is himself in Africa with so huge an army and so great a power, who, as a Tribune, with only a few confederates, beat down those very [52] barbarians by valorous deeds of arms and of terror, these same should become so daring, push their incursions so far, commit so many acts of devastation and rapine, make desolate so many places which were full of people? Was it not the talk of all when you assumed the power of a count, that you would not only subdue the barbarians of Africa, but even make them vassals of the Roman Republic? And now you see how these hopes are reversed; nor need I enlarge further upon the subject with you, because you can better think it than I can speak it.

But, perhaps, in answer to these things, you will say, that they are rather to be imputed to those who did not acknowledge the virtues you had shown in office, but made you a bad return for them. I can neither hear nor judge these points. Do you rather look at and consider your own cause, for this you know to be between you and God, not between any men whatsoever. You are living as a faithful member of Christ, therefore it is Christ Whom you should fear to offend. I look rather to higher causes in this matter of Africa having to suffer so grievously, and think that men should impute it to their own sins. Still I would not have you belong to the number of those wicked and iniquitous men through whom God chastises whom He pleases with temporal afflictions.

For, if they be not corrected, He reserves eternal punishment for them, Who makes a just use of their wickedness to inflict temporal evils on others. Do you look to God, do you consider Christ, Who has given us goods so great, and Who bore evils so grievous. Who soever desire to belong to His kingdom, to live for ever happily with Him and under Him, love even their enemies, do good to those who hate them, and pray for those who persecute them, and if they are ever obliged [53] to show a hard severity for the sake of discipline, they do not on that account lose charity. If, then, good things, although earthly and transitory, be given to you by the Roman Empire, for the reason that it too is earthly, not heavenly, and can only give what it has got, if, then, I say, good things are yours, do not re turn evil for good. But if evil be inflicted on you, do not return evil for evil. Which of these two suppositions is the real case I will not discuss, nor am I able to judge in the matter. I am speaking to a Christian, and I say, Do not return either evil for good, or evil for evil.

Perhaps you will say to me, What would you have me do in so dire a necessity? If you are seeking of me advice after the fashion of this world, how this transitory life of the body may be secure, how the power and riches which you now have may be continued to you, or may be even increased, I know not what to say. These uncertain things can command no certain counsel. But if you seek counsel of me according to God lest your soul perish, and are fearing the words of the Truth who says, *What does it profit a man if he gain the whole world and lose his own soul?* then, indeed, I have something to say I have advice which I may give. Why should I say anything more than what I have already said? *Love not the world nor the things of the world. For if any man love the world, the charity of the Father is not in him; because all things which are in the world are lust of the flesh and lust of the eyes and pride of life, which are not from the Father, but from the world: and the world and its concupiscence passes away. But he who does the will of God abides for ever, as God also abides for ever.* Here, then, is my advice: take it and act upon it. Show now that you are a man; overcome those desires

[54] by which this world is loved; do penance for past wrongs, when, conquered by those lusts, you were led away by unrighteous desires. If you accept this advice of mine, and hold to it and act upon it, you will attain to those certain good things, and work out your soul's salvation in the midst of these uncertain ones.

But, once more, you may ask me how you are to do this, involved as you are in so many cares of this world. Pray earnestly, and say to God those familiar words of the psalm, *Deliver me from my necessities*. For when those desires are overcome, then are these necessities at an end. He who heard your prayers, and mine for you, when we asked Him to spare you from so many dangers of visible and corporeal war, in which only this mortal life is at stake, but the soul does not perish, unless it be held captive by bad passions, He will help you to conquer, invisibly and spiritually, the invisible and interior enemies, that is, those desires. Thus you will use this world as not using it; you will resist becoming evil in order that you may do good with its good things; for they are good things, and are given to man by Him alone Who has power over the heavens and the earth. Yet, lest they should be deemed evil things, they are given also to the good; and lest they should be looked upon as great goods or the highest goods, they are given also to the wicked. And again, they are taken away from good men for their trial, and from bad men for their chastisement.

For who is so ignorant and foolish as not to see that

the health of this mortal body, the strength of corruptible members, victory over enemies, temporal honor and power, and all other temporal goods, are given both to good and bad men, and taken away from them? But the salvation of the soul with immortality of the body, and the virtue of justice, and victory over pre-[55] vailing passions, and eternal glory and honor and peace, are given only to the good. Love these, then, and desire them and seek them in all possible ways. To gain and acquire them, give alms, offer up prayers, practice fasting as far as you can without injuring your health. But as to those temporal goods, do not put your heart in them, however abundantly they may be yours. So use them as to do much good with them, and no evil on their account. They will perish for a certainty; but good works done even with perishable goods perish not.

If you were not married, I would repeat what we said at Tubunae, and tell you to live in holy chastity. I would add, what we then forbade your doing, that, as far as human affairs and your peace of mind would allow it, you should withdraw yourself from these wars and rumors of wars, and, in the society of holy people, should give yourself up to that life which you were then desiring. In it the soldiers of Christ fight in silence, not that they may kill men, but that they may utterly defeat the principalities and powers and spiritual wickedness, that is, the devil and his angels. For the saints conquer the enemies whom they cannot see, and still, not seeing them, they conquer by conquering those things which they feel. But your wife is a difficulty in the way of my advising you to lead a similar life, because without her consent you may not lead a life of continence. Although you should not have married her after those words of yours at Tubunae, she married you in all innocence and simplicity, knowing nothing about them. Would indeed that you could induce her to adopt a state of continence, that you might thus give to God without any obstacle that which you know you owe Him. But if you cannot obtain this of her, at least keep chastity according to [56] the married state, and ask God, Who is to deliver you from your necessities, that you may be able to do at some future time what you cannot do now. Nevertheless, your wife does not prevent you, or should not prevent you, from loving God, not loving the world, keeping faith in your wars, if you must still be engaged in them, and seeking peace; she does not or she should not prevent you from doing good with the good things of this world, nor from not doing evil on account of them. That charity in which I love you according to God, not according to this world, has urged me to write you this letter, beloved son, because in thinking of the words, *Correct the wise man, and he will love you; correct the fool, and he will hate you*, I was bound to look upon you not as a fool, but as a wise man.

9. ST. AUGUSTINE AND THE HOLY SEE
(*Letter* to Pope Celestine, 209)

To my most blessed Lord, to be venerated with due charity, the holy Pope Celestine, Augustine sends greeting in the Lord.

In the first place, I acknowledge the worth of your own merits, inasmuch as the Lord our God has placed you in the eminent See which you occupy without, as I hear, any dissension among His people. In the next place, I should wish to say something to your Holiness of our own business, that you may help us not only by praying for us, but also by counseling and by intercession. Being indeed in great tribulation, I am writing this letter to your Holiness. Wishing then to do good to certain members of Christ in our neighborhood, I, improvident and incautious that I am, have brought a great destruction upon them.

Fussala is the name of a township on the confines of the territory of Hippo. Formerly it had no bishop, but, together with the region adjacent to it, belonged to the jurisdiction of the Church of Hippo. This part of the country numbered few Catholics. The Donatist errors had unhappily obtained with the rest of the population, who were very numerous, so that at Fussala itself there was not a single Catholic. It happened by God's mercy that all those places returned to the unity of the Church. It would be long to relate what labors and dangers this has cost us, seeing that the priests whom we had put there in the first instance to draw them together were robbed, beaten, deprived of their bodily strength, blinded, put to death, whose sufferings nevertheless were neither vain nor barren, because of the security thus given to unity. Seeing, however, that the said township is forty miles distant from Hippo, and that in administering to these people and in collecting together the number, small as it was, who in both sexes had fallen away, no longer violent, but out of reach, I found myself extending my pastoral care farther than was due; nor could I suffice for all that I most clearly saw ought to be done, and I set about getting a bishop consecrated and having him established there.

In order to do this, I looked for a man suited and suitable for that place, one who should also know the Punic tongue. I had in my mind one who was already ready for the priesthood, and I wrote and begged the holy bishop who was then Primate of Numidia that he would undertake the long journey and come and ordain him. When he had come, and the minds of all were in anxious suspense over the grave business, he, whom I had looked upon as ready, defeated us by resisting us in every way. But I, who, as the result proved, ought to have chosen delay rather than a precipitate action, not wishing that the aged and holy bishop, after the trouble of coming so far to us for nothing, should go home, offered him, without being asked, a certain young man, Anthony by name, who was with me at the time. He had been kept by us in a monastery from his early childhood, but beyond the office of lector he was not known by his labors or [59] priestly orders. The poor people, ignorant of the future, most fully trusted me in my recommendation of him. What more shall I say? The thing was done, and he began to be their bishop.

What shall I do? I will not trouble your Paternity about the man whom I had educated, neither will I forsake those whom I had just drawn into the fold and then begotten with fear and anguish; yet I see not how I can carry out both these wishes of mine. The thing had become so scandalous that those who had yielded to us in receiving his episcopal ministrations, as if thus consulting their own interests, brought accusations against him to us. Inasmuch as these accusations of flagrant immorality, made against him, not by his own flock, but by others, could not be in the least proved, and that he seemed to be free of the reproaches which were so slanderously rumored concerning him, he inspired both us and others with so great a compassion, that whatever complaints were raised by the people of Fussala and the inhabitants of that region as to his overbearing government and diverse acts of robbery, oppression, and tyranny, we still did not think him bad enough to be deprived of his bishopric, either for this or for all these things put together. We judged rather that he should make restitution of those things which he could be proved to have taken away. In short, we so softened our sentence as to let him remain bishop without leaving unpunished that which he had no right either to do himself or to propose to the imitation of others. By our correction, therefore, we kept the youth's honor intact; but in correcting we diminished his power, preventing him, that is, from governing any longer those whom he had so treated, that with just sorrow they could by no possible means bear to see him over them; for, at their risk and his [60] own, they might possibly have shown their impatient grief by some new crime.

But what need is there of further words? I beseech you, venerable and most blessed Lord, holy Pope, who are so dear to our charity, do you labor with us, and have the whole case, as it has been sent to you, brought before you. Consider how he used his power as a bishop; how he accepted our judgment, and was deprived of communion unless he should make entire restitution to the Fussalians; how, after sentence had been passed upon him, he kept back money from the restitution that he might be restored to communion. Consider what undue persuasion he used with so grave and holy a man as our Primate to make him believe all his assertions, so as to commend him to the venerable Pope Boniface as a man entirely blameless, and the rest, which I have no need of entering upon, since the same venerable Primate has told the whole case to your Holiness.

But in all these dealings which our judgment of him has called forth, I should rather fear that we seem to you to have judged him less severely than we ought, did I not know how inclined you yourself are to mercy, so that you would not only be for sparing us because we spared him, but also for sparing him. He, however, is striving to turn that which we did, whether kindly or remissly, into a sophism. He is calling out, " Either I ought to sit in my own episcopal chair, or not to have been a bishop at all," as if he were not sitting now in his own. On this account the same places are allowed and conceded to him which he formerly occupied as bishop, lest he should be said to be illicitly enthroned in another man's seat against the canons of the Fathers. Either the man who is an exactor, whether of severity or of mercy, should by no manner of means [61] make any accusation against those who have not been openly degraded from the episcopal dignity, or those who have been judged worthy of some reproach should be deprived of the episcopal dignity.

Examples are extant when this Apostolic See was itself the judge or the confirmer of the decisions of others, in which some men, for certain faults, were neither deprived of the episcopal dignity nor left without any punishment. Not to go back to times very remote from our own, I will recall recent instances of this. Let Priscus, bishop of the province of Caesarea, be heard. He says, "Either the road to the primacy should be open to me as well as others, or the episcopacy should be removed from me." Let Victor, another bishop of the same province, be heard, who finding himself in the same sad plight as Priscus, is nowhere in communication with any bishop except in his diocese. Let him speak, I say: "I ought to be everywhere in communion, or else not in communion at home." Let Laurence, a third bishop of the same province, speak, and let him speak in these words: "Either it was my right to sit in my own episcopal seat, to which I was consecrated, or not to be a bishop at all." But who will blame these sentiments except the heedless man? Neither is everything to be left unanswered, nor are all things to be answered in the same way.

As, therefore, the most blessed Pope Boniface wrote in his epistle with pastoral and vigilant caution, in speaking of Bishop Anthony, "If he has faithfully laid before us the facts in their order," so do you now hear the facts in their order which he withheld in his statement, and then listen to what has taken place in Africa since those words of that man of holy memory were read. Give your help to men who in the mercy of Christ are imploring it of you far more earnestly than he from [62] whose disturbance they desire to be delivered. For either he or common report threatens them with judgments and processes, and a martial law which is to carry out the sentence of the Apostolic See, so that wretched Christian Catholics have graver evils to fear from a Catholic bishop than they had as heretics to fear from the laws of Catholic emperors. I beseech you, through the Blood of Christ, through the memory of the Apostle Peter, who admonished the rulers of the Christian people against the violent oppression of their brethren, not to suffer these things. I commend both the Catholics of Fussala, my children in Christ, and Bishop Anthony, my son in Christ, to the benign charity of your Holiness: I commend both, because I love both. Nor am I angry with the Fussalians, be cause the complaint which they pour into your ears is just of my having inflicted upon them a man whom I had not proved, not sufficiently old, who was thus to torment them. Neither do I will to harm Anthony, because the sincerer my charity is in his regard, the more do I deplore his wicked cupidity. May each deserve your mercy; they, that they may not suffer evils, he, that he may not do them; they, that they may not hate the Catholic faith, if Catholic bishops, and most particularly the Apostolic See itself, does not take their part against a Catholic bishop, but he, that he may not involve himself in sin so grievous as to wean from Christ those whom he strives to make his against their will.

As to me and this I must confess to your Holiness in this danger besetting them both, I am so torn by fear and anguish, that I would contemplate giving up my office of a bishop and devoting myself to bewail my mistake in a fitting way, if through him whose episcopal consecration I imprudently supported I should [63] see the Church of God devastated, and see her perish even with the perdition of the devastator; which may God Himself avert. For, calling to mind what the Apostle says, If we would judge ourselves, we should not be judged by God, I will judge myself, in order that He Who is to judge the living and the dead may spare me. But if you release both the members of Christ who are in that region from a fatal sadness and fear, and console my old age in merciful justice, He will return you in this life and in the life to come good for good, Who consoles us through your person in this affliction, and Who placed you in the eminent See which you occupy.

[64]
10. ST. AUGUSTINE ON THE APPOINTMENT OF HIS SUCCESSOR IN THE SEE OF HIPPO
(*Letter* 213)

(ST. AUGUSTINE'S speech to the clergy and people on the sixth day of the Kalends of October 426, in the Church of Peace in the Diocese of Hippo, when he was almost seventy-two years old.)

"That which I promised you yesterday, dear brethren, on account of which I asked you to come in greater numbers and I see that you have done this must now be accomplished without the slightest delay. For if I say anything else, your attention might be diverted, so that you would not hear this. We are all of us mortal in this life, and every single man is ignorant concerning his last day. Still childhood is looked for after infancy, and in childhood we look forward to youth, and in youth we look for its further ripening; in our youth's maturity we hope to see graver years,

and when we are old we hope to see real old age. It
is all uncertain. Still we may hope. But old age has
nothing further to hope; it is even uncertain how
long it will be in man's possession. One thing, however, is certain, and that is, that no age can follow old
age. Because God so willed it, I came to this city in
the vigor of my age, when still young, however, and
I have grown old. I know that after the death of bishops
churches are accustomed to be disturbed by ambitious and contentious men. I am bound as far as
I can to keep from this city that which I have often
seen with sorrow. As you, my brethren, know, I was
then in the church of Milevis. Some brethren there,
especially some servants of God, begged me to go
there, because after the death of my brother of blessed
memory, and my co-bishop, Severus, a great disturbance was feared. I went, and God in His mercy so
helped us that they peaceably received for their bishop
him whom their bishop had appointed during his life
time. For when this had become known to them,
they willingly embraced the will of their late and
deceased bishop. Still there was a small cause of
grievance to not a few, because my brother Severus
had thought it might be sufficient to name his successor to the clergy, and hence he did not speak to
the people. Some were very aggrieved in consequence.
Why need I enlarge upon this? By God's good plea
sure the sadness vanished and joy took its place. He
whom the former bishop had designated was consecrated. Therefore, that no one of you may complain
of me, I make known to you all my will, which I

believe to be the will of God: I wish the priest Heraclius to be my successor."

Here the people responded three times, *Thanks be to God, Christ be praised*; six times, *Hear, Christ, long live Augustine*; and eight times, *Hail our father and bishop*.

When they were silent Bishop Augustine went on: " I have no need to speak anything in his praise; I value his wisdom and spare his humility. It is sufficient that you know him; and this I say is my will, which I know to be yours, and if I was not aware of it before, I should prove it today. This, then, is my will this I ask of our Lord God in most fervent petition, [66] although I am even now in the deadness of age; in this I exhort, admonish, and supplicate you to join your prayers to mine, that all minds being at one in the peace of Christ, God may confirm what He has worked in us. May He who sends Heraclius to me keep him keep him without spot or stain, that, as he is my joy now that I am alive, so he may supply my place when I am dead. As you see, the scribes of the Church are taking down what is said, what you say and what I say, and your acclamations do not fall upon a dead soil. To put it less ambiguously, we are now writing the annals of the Church, and I would have them confirmed, as far as may be, by the approval of men."

The people answered by responding thirty-six times,

Thanks be to God, praise be to Christ; thirteen times, *Hear, Christ, long live Augustine*; eight times, *Hail our father and bishop*; twenty times, *He is worthy and just*; fifteen times, *He is indeed deserving and just*; six times, *He is worthy and just.*

When they were silent Bishop Augustine said: " Therefore, as I was saying, I wished my will and your will, as far as it pertains to men, to be confirmed in the annals of the Church; but as far as the hidden will of the Almighty is concerned, let us all pray, as I said, that God may confirm what He has worked in us."

The people exclaimed sixteen times, We give thanks for your judgment; twelve times, Amen, amen; six times, Hail, father and bishop Heraclius.

When they ceased speaking, Bishop Augustine said: " I know that you know what I am going to say, but I would not have the same thing happen to him which happened to me. Many of you know what this was; those only are in ignorance who either were not born [67] at the time, or were too young to understand. While my father and bishop, the old man Valerius, of blessed memory, was still in the body, I was consecrated bishop, and administered the diocese with him. I did not know that this was forbidden by the Council of Nicaea, nor did he. Therefore I wish that my reproach may not be found in my son."

The people responded thirteen times, *Thanks be to God, praised be Christ.*

When they had ceased Bishop Augustine went on: "He will be what he is now, a priest, when God shall be pleased to require the new bishop. But, indeed, I am going to do now, by the mercy of Christ, what I have never hitherto done. You know what I wished to do some years ago, which you were against. According to my desire and yours, I was to have five clear days to myself, without a single interruption from any one, in order to see to the Scripture documents which my brethren and fathers, the co-bishops in the two Councils of Numidia and Carthage, deigned to entrust to me. The annals were written; you gave your consent by acclamation; your pleasure and responses are chronicled. This rule was kept only for a brief time, and then my solitude was violently disturbed, and I am not allowed leisure for what I want to do. Before twelve o'clock in the day, and after twelve, I am involved in the business of other men. I pray and beseech of you, for Christ's sake, that you would suffer me to order afresh the burden of my occupations for this youth, that is, the priest Heraclius, whom I propose today in the name of Christ as my successor." The people responded six times, *We give thanks for your judgment.*

When they were silent Bishop Augustine said: "I give thanks for your charity and goodness, with our Lord God, or rather, I thank God for it. Therefore, [68] brethren, let whatsoever was brought to me be taken to him; whensoever he have need of counsel, I do not refuse my help - God forbid that I should withdraw it. Still, let anything which used to be brought to me be now taken to him. Let him either consult me, if perchance he finds himself in a perplexity, or let him appeal to me, whom he knows to be his father, that nothing may be lacking to you, and that I may at least sometimes be able, if God should allow me to live for a little while longer, to devote whatever remains to me of life, not to idleness, nor to inertness, but to the Holy Scriptures, as far as He gives and allows. This will benefit Heraclius too, and you also through him. Consequently, let no man envy me my leisure, because my leisure is full of a great undertaking. I see that I have brought before you all that I had to say in asking you to come today. I now make you a last request, which is, that all of you who can would be good enough to put your signature to what has taken place today. I require to have your answer in this matter. Give it to me; let me have some outward token of your assent." The people responded five times, *Amen, amen*; eight times, *It is right and just*; fourteen times, *Amen, amen*; five times, *He has ever been worthy and deserving*; thirteen times, *We give thanks for your judgment*; eighteen times, *Hear, Christ, health to Heraclius*.

When they were silent Bishop Augustine continued: " It is a good thing for us to settle things concerning God's service at the time of His sacrifice, in which hour of our supplication I specially recommend you, dear brethren, to leave alone all your business and occupations, and to offer up prayers to God for this Church, for me, and for the priest Heraclius."

PART II: DOCTRINE IN DAILY LIFE

1. THE APPARITIONS OF GOD IN THE BIBLE
(*Sermon* 8)

IN reading the Divine account of the great miracle which so greatly struck God's servant Moses, we too were in anxious expectation, because we too were much struck by the fact of the fire appearing in the bush and not consuming it. Next we notice that Holy Scripture says, in the first place, that it was an angel of the Lord who appeared to Moses in the bush. Secondly, Moses seems to have conversed, not with an angel, but with God. Thirdly, when Moses asked God how he should answer the inquiries of the children of Israel respecting the Divine name and his own mission, the reply was, "*I am Who am.*" . . .

It is a very important matter that the same person who spoke to Moses should be called at once the angel of the Lord and the Lord; nor is it one which should he decided in unseemly haste, but with earnest inquiry. There are two views which this passage may call forth; whichever be the true one, they are both in accordance with faith. . . . Some say that the Scripture speaks of an angel and of the Lord because it was really Christ,

whom the prophet literally designates as the Angel of Great Counsel. The name *angel* describes office, not nature, and is the Greek term for the Latin *messenger*. ... And who shall deny that Christ did announce the kingdom of heaven? Hence, an angel, that is, a mes-
[72] senger, is sent from Him to tell us something in His name. Who will say that Christ was not sent when He Himself so often used the words, I have come not to do My will, but the will of Him who sent Me? He was indeed sent. ...

Here, however, we must be careful not to fall into error. Heretics are not lacking who say that the natures of the Father and of the Son are different and distinct, and who deny the identity of one and the same substance in both. But the Catholic faith believes the Father, Son, and Holy Spirit to be one God, a Trinity of one substance, equal, inseparable, not confused by commixture, not separated by distinction. They, therefore, who seek to prove that the Son is not of the same substance as the Father allege that the Son showed Himself to the patriarchs; for the Father, they say, was not seen. The invisible and the visible make two natures; hence, according to them, the words Whom no man has ever seen or can see, refer to the Father. This would be to believe that He who appeared, not only to Moses, but also to Abraham, to Adam himself and the other patriarchs, was not God the Father, but the Son; that thus the Son may be viewed as a creature. The Catholic faith does not say this. What does it say? That the Father is God and the Son is

God; that the Father is incommutable and the Son is incommutable; that the Father is eternal and the Son is eternal; that the Father is invisible and the Son is invisible. For if you say that the Father is invisible and the Son visible, you distinguish, or rather separate, the substance of both. . . . Therefore, the question is solved in this way: the Father, Son, and Holy Spirit God, is by nature invisible; but He has appeared when He willed to appear, and to whom He willed to appear, not as He is, but in the manner He willed, Whom all [73] things obey. If the soul, which is invisible in the human body, speaks in order to show itself, and if the voice in which it manifests itself is not part of its substance, the soul is one thing and the voice is another, yet the soul shows itself in that which it is not. In like manner, if God appear in fire, He is not fire; if in smoke, He is not smoke; if in sound, He is not sound. These things are not God, but they show forth His presence. Bearing this in mind, we may believe without fear that the vision which appeared to Moses could be called at once the Son, God, and the Angel of God.

As to those who think that it was truly an angel of the Lord, not Christ, but an angel who was sent, they must tell us why he is spoken of as the Lord. . . . I have shown how those who think that it was Christ escape from the difficulty of His being called an angel, because the prophet spoke without ambiguity of Christ the Lord as the Angel of Great Counsel. . . . These men say: As in the Scriptures, when a prophet speaks,

God is said to speak, not because God is a prophet, but because He is in the prophet; so when God deigns to speak through an angel, as He does through an apostle or a patriarch, the angel is still truly called an angel on his own account, and the Lord on account of the indwelling God within him. It is certain that St. Paul was a man and that Christ was God; yet St. Paul says, *Will you have a sign of Christ who speaks in me?* and the prophet, *I will hear what the Lord God shall speak in me.* The same who speaks in man speaks in the angel; therefore it was an angel of the Lord who appeared to Moses and said, *I am Who am.* It was the voice of the inmate of the house, not of the house. . . .

An angel, then, and in the angel, God, said to Moses, who asked Him His name, *I am Who am*: you shall say to the children of Israel, He Who is sends me to you. *To be* is the name of the unchangeable. All changeable things cease to be what they were and begin to be what they were not. He alone who is immutable has true and perfect being being in its essence. He has true being of whom the psalm says, *You shall change them, and they shall be changed; but You are the same.* What is the meaning of *I am Who am*, if not "I am the Eternal"? What does it mean if not, "I cannot be changed"? No creature is this, nor heaven, nor earth, nor angel, nor virtue, nor thrones, nor dominations, nor powers. Whereas, then, this name is the name of Eternity, His condescension in giving Himself the name of Mercy was the greater. *I am the God of Abraham, and of Isaac, and of Jacob.* The one He is by essence, the other He is with regard to us. For if He had willed to be only that which He is in Himself, what should we be? If Moses understood, or rather because he understood, the words which were said to him, *I am Who am, He Who is, has sent me*, he believed that this being was full of purport to man, and he saw that it was far removed from man. For he who really understands that which is and is truly, by whatever light of truest essence he may thus understand, or in a brief moment of revelation, sees himself far below, far beneath, in immeasurable unlikeness; as he who said, I spoke in my rapture of mind. In his rapture of mind he saw I know not what which more concerned him. This was true being. I spoke, he says, in my rapture of mind. What? I am cast away from the face of Your eyes. When, therefore, Moses saw himself to be far removed rather from what was said than from what was seen, and felt, as it were, his incapacity, he was thus inflamed with very desire to see that which is, and he said to God, with whom he [75] was speaking, Show me Yourself. As if, when finding himself so far removed from that excellence of being, he might despair, God encouraged the humbled man, because God saw that he feared. It was as if God had said, "Because I have said *I am Who am*, and *He Who is has sent me*, you have understood what Being is, and you have despaired of reaching it. Lift up your hope. *I am the God of Abraham, and of Isaac, and of Jacob.* I am what I am; I am Being itself; I am identical with being; all this in such a way that it is my will not to be foreign to man." If in any way we can seek the

Lord and search out Him who is, who truly is not far removed from each one of us, for in Him we live and move and have our being, let us, therefore, ineffably praise His being and love His mercy. Amen.

2. ABRAHAM TEMPTED BY GOD
(*Sermon* 2.2)

THE Scripture says that God "tempted" Abraham. Is God, then, so ignorant of what passes and of the human heart that He should require to tempt a man in order to know him? Far be it from us to think so. He tempts in order that a man may know himself. Let us briefly consider this question for the sake of those who are opposed to the Holy Scriptures of the Old Law; for not a few men, when they do not understand, are more apt to criticize than to search that they may understand. They become not humble inquirers, but overbearing calumniators, imagining that they may be in the true way, and able to walk properly with only one foot, because they are not scribes instructed in the kingdom of heaven, who bring forth out of their treasures new things and old. . . . We say to men of this kind, "You accept the Gospel; the Law you do not accept. But we hold that the terrible Giver of the Law and the most merciful God of the Gospel is one and the same." . . .

What reason does the perverse man allege for accepting the Gospel and not admitting the law?

Because it is written that *God tempted Abraham.* . . . Where, then, do we read of Christ tempting? The Gospel records that He said to Philip, *From where shall we [77] buy bread that these may eat?* And the Evangelist continues, *This He said to try him; for He Himself knew what He would do.* Go back now to God trying Abraham. This God also said to try him; for He Himself knew what He would do. ... A heretic does not tempt as God tempts. God tempts a man that He may enlighten him; a heretic tempts himself in order that he may shut his eyes to God. God, then, does not try a man that He may learn something which He knew not before, but that by the fact of His tempting, which amounts to an interrogation, that which is hidden in a man may be revealed. For a man does not know himself as his Creator knows him, nor does a sick man know himself as his doctor knows him. When a man is sick, it is he who suffers, not the doctor; and it is the patient who expects in formation from the physician. Therefore man says in the psalm, *Deliver me, Lord, from my secret sins,* because there are things in a man which are hidden from himself, and which are not called forth nor revealed except by temptations. If God leave off tempting, our Master leaves off teaching. God tempts that He may give us a lesson; the Devil tempts in order to deceive. . . . What, then, brethren, do we say? Supposing even that Abraham did know him self, we did not know him. He was to be revealed either to himself, or, beyond a doubt, to us: to himself, that he might know his own cause for thankfulness; to

us, that we might know either what we should ask of
God or what we should imitate in man. What, then,
does Abraham teach us? To put it briefly, he teaches
us not to prefer the gifts of God to God. . . . There
fore, put not even a real gift of God before the Giver of
that gift; and if He should choose to take it away, let
Him not lose His worth in your eyes, because God is
to be loved for His own sake. For what sweeter
reward is there from God than God Himself?

When Abraham had accomplished his devoted act
of obedience, he heard the words, Now I know that
you fear God, which means that God had revealed
Abraham to himself. . . .

Before all things, brethren, we both admonish and
exhort you in God's name, to the best of our power,
that, in hearing the narrative of the events recorded in
Holy Scripture, you first believe that those events took
place in the way in which the Scripture tells them,
lest, taking away the foundation of the thing described,
you seek to build without basis. Abraham our father
was an upright man in those days, believing in God
and justified by faith. Sarah bore him a son when
they were both old, and the thing was, humanly speaking, impossible. But what may not be hoped for from
God, to Whom nothing is difficult? He does great
things as He does small things; He raises the dead
just as He creates the living. . . . What is difficult
to Him who produces by a word? It was as easy to
Him to create the angels above the firmament as to

create the heavenly bodies, the fishes in the sea, and trees and living things on earth. Great things He has created with the same facility as small things. Whereas, then, it was most easy to Him to create all things out of nothing, is it wonderful that He should have given a son to an aged father and mother? This, then, was the type of man; these were the men whom God used, and whom in those days He made the prophets of His Son to come, that, not only in the words which they spoke, but in their actions, or in those things which befell them, Christ may be sought for and found. Whatsoever the Scripture records of Abraham is at once a fact and a prophecy, as the [79] Apostle somewhere says, *It is written that Abraham had two sons, one by a bond woman, and one by a free woman. Which things are said by an allegory, for these are the two Testaments.* . . .

Abraham believed God, and it was reputed to him to justice, and he was called the friend of God. That he believed God in his heart was a matter of pure faith, but in taking his son to the slaughter, in fearlessly preparing his right hand to strike, which he would have done had not the voice prevented him, he showed forth both a great faith and a great action; and God praised this action in saying, *You have heard My voice.* How then does St. Paul say, *We account a man to be justified by faith without the works of the law*? and again, *And faith that works by charity*? How does faith work by charity, and how is a man justified by faith without the works of the law? Observe how, brethren. A man becomes a believer, receives the sacraments of the faith on his deathbed, and dies: he has not had time to work. Shall we say that he is not justified?

Of course we consider him justified, as believing in Him who sanctifies the unrighteous. This man then is justified without works, and the Apostle's words are fulfilled: *We account a man to be justified by faith without the works of the law. The thief who was crucified with the Lord believed with the heart unto justice, and made confession with the mouth unto salvation.* For faith that works by charity, even if it find no external outlet, keeps its inner warmth in the heart. There were certain men of the law who glorified themselves because of the works of the law, which possibly they did rather out of fear than charity, wishing to appear just, and to be preferred to the Gentiles, who did not accomplish the work of the law. When [80] the Apostle was preaching the faith to the Gentiles, and saw those among them justified by faith who approached the Lord; so that believing they were able to do good works who did not believe because they were first righteous, but who were justified by believing, he exclaimed with confidence, *That a man may be justified by faith without the works of the law*, so that they were not just who acted through fear, for faith by charity works in the heart, even if it does not exercise itself by outward deeds.

3. THE LESSON OF THE NEW TESTAMENT
(*Sermon* 25.1)

TAKE up that Testament which is called the Old Testament, and learn its lesson. The law of God was promulgated then also. Read it, or listen to it when it is read to you, and consider what its promises were. In it an earth was promised to the earth, an earthly country flowing with milk and honey, but still an earth. If, however, we understand it in a spiritual sense, then that earth did not run with milk and honey; the land which will flow with milk and honey is something quite different; it is that land of which the Psalmist says, *You are my hope, my portion in the land of the living.* Do you seek for milk and honey? *Taste and see how sweet the Lord is.* His grace is signified by the milk and honey; it is sweet and nourishing. But this grace, which is typified in the Old Testament, is revealed in the New.

In short, on account of those who are worldly-wise and seek material rewards from God, and choose to serve Him for the sake of those things which were then promised, that law deserved to be characterized by the Apostle St. Paul as Engendering unto bondage. And why? Because the Jews interpreted it in a material sense, for in its spiritual meaning it is the Gospel. It engenders then unto bondage. What men? Those who serve God for temporal goods, who return thanks when they have them, and blaspheme when they have them not. Such worship of God is not that of a true heart. For they look at those who do not serve our God, and see that they have those things for which they themselves are serving Him, and they say in their heart, "How does the service of God profit me? Have I as much as that man, who blasphemes every day of his life?" One man says his prayers and starves, another blasphemes and feasts. He who takes account of these things is human indeed, a man of the Old Testament. But he who serves God in the New has to look for a new inheritance, not for the old. If you hope for the new inheritance, go farther than the earth, soar higher than the mountain tops, that is, despise the heights of the proud. But in doing this be humble, lest you fall from your high place. Listen to the words *Sursum cor* [Lift up your heart]; lift it up to God, not against God. All proud men have lifted up their hearts, but against God. If you would in truth have your heart lifted up, let it be lifted to the Lord. . . .

Blessed is the man whom You shall instruct, Lord, and shall teach him out of Your law; that You may give him rest from the evil days.

The evil days. Are these not evil days which are determined by the course of the sun? Evil men make evil days, and nearly the whole world is evil. The few good groan in the vast crowd of the wicked. . . .

Therefore these days are evil; but let us soften them. And how can this be done? Let us not be angry with God's ordering of events. ... In the evil days a man learns to seek for the good ones. What are these good days? Do not look for them on earth. Believe me, or rather believe as I believe, you will not find them. The evil days will pass and the good ones will come, [83] but they will be for the good. Worse days will come for the wicked.

I ask you in my turn, who is the man who wishes for life? and I know that you will all answer with one voice, Who is there that does not wish for life? I add, and who is there who does not wish to see good days? . . . *Keep your tongue from sin and your lips from evil speaking.* The past is no more: your tongue may have been wicked; you may have misused your tongue; you may have been a criminal, a calumniator, a male factor; you may have been all these things. May they pass away with the evil days, but do not you pass away. . . .

Keep, then, *your tongue from sin and your lips from evil speaking.* You who wished for life, or who now wish for life and good days, turn from evil and do good. Seek peace, which we all desire in this flesh of our mortality, in this weakness of our mortality, and in this most deceitful vanity. Seek peace and go after it. Where is it? Where am I to go? What is peace? Listen to St. Paul, who said of Christ, *He is our peace, Who has made both one.* Christ, therefore, is Himself peace. Which way did He pass? He was crucified and buried; He rose from the dead and ascended into heaven. This was the way of Peace. How am I to follow after it? *Sursum cor.* This is how you are to follow. You hear it indeed said to you briefly every day when you listen to the words *Sursum cor.* (1) Ponder them well, and you will reach peace. Listen to them in a wider sense that you may follow true peace.

Your Peace, Who bore strife for you, Who prayed for the enemies of peace, and said, as He hung on the Cross, "*Father, forgive them, for they know not what*

---

1 An evident allusion to the words of the Mass, *Sursum corda* [Lift up (your) hearts].

---

[84] *they do.*" Strife had reigned, but peace came from the tree. . . . *You are dead, and your life is hidden with Christ in God. When Christ shall appear, Who is your life, then you, also shall appear with Him in glory.* Then will come the good days. Let them be the object of our desires. Let our life and prayer and almsgiving be directed unto this end.

4. THE ROYAL GIFTS OF SIGHT AND HEARING
   (*Sermon* 27.1, 2)

LET the heart of them rejoice that seek the Lord. It is certain that each of our senses has its particular gratification. Sound does not delight our eyes, nor does color please our ears. God is at once the light and fragrance and food of our heart; and therefore He is all things, because He is no one of these things; and because He is no one of these things, He is the Creator of them all. He is the light of our heart; for we say to Him, *To my hearing You shall give joy and gladness.* He is its fragrance, of whom it is said, *We are the pleasant fragrance of Christ.* If you seek food because you are fasting, blessed are they who hunger and thirst after justice. . . . He says of Himself, *I am the living Bread that comes down from heaven.* This is the Food which gives life and is never lacking, which is taken and not consumed, which feeds the hungry and remains whole. . . .

And do not wonder either that our hearts are so fed as to be themselves refreshed, while the source of their refreshment remains undiminished. God has given food of a similar kind to our mortal eyes. For this material light is the food upon which they feed; and if a man remain for some space of time in darkness, his eyes fail him as if for want of nourishment. Men [86] have lost their sight through sitting in the dark; and this has not been brought about by external irritation, or by receiving a blow from any one, not by bad humors from without, nor smoke, nor dust. A man is brought out into daylight from the darkness, and he sees not what he saw before. His eyes have died of hunger, and have failed through not partaking of their food, that is, the light. Observe, therefore, what I proposed to you as to the food of our eyes. This material light is seen by all and feeds the eyes of all; while it refreshes the sight, it remains whole and entire itself. If two see, its power is undiminished; if many see, it remains the same; whether it be for the rich or for the poor, it is alike for all. No man limits the light; the need of the poor man is satisfied, the rich man's avarice has no play. For does he who is richer see the more, or can he for a sum of money take the poor man's place and buy sight for himself, so as to deprive the other of it? If, then, this be the food of our eyes, what is God Himself to our mind?

Sound is a kind of food for our ears, and of what sort is it? From these, our bodily senses, we may form a conjecture about the capacity of our mind's understanding. ... I have named our ears and our mind, which contain two things, sound and understanding. They are simultaneous, and strike the ear at the same time. Sound remains in the ear, understanding penetrates into the heart. But from sound itself let us first see the superior excellence of understanding. Sound is, as it were, the body, understanding the soul. Sound, as soon as it has struck the ear, passes away and is beyond recall. Thus it is that words succeed and follow one another, so that the second cannot be spoken until after the first. Nevertheless, in this way, and in a sense, a certain transitory [87] thing is a very wonderful thing. If, for instance, I were to put bread before you when you were hungry, it would not do for all. You would divide it amongst yourselves, and have so much the less; but now, when I speak, you do not divide the syllables amongst yourselves, neither do you break my discourse into pieces, so that each may take a part, and thus minutely partake of what I am saying; the whole is heard by one, or two, or many, and, in fact, by all who come to listen. It is sufficient for all and entire for all. Your ear is listening, nor does your neighbor's ear in any way defraud it. If this be the case with the word which passes away, what must it be with the Omnipotent Word? For as this human voice of ours reaches wholly and entirely the ear of every single listener nor have I as many voices as there are ears among you, but one voice fills many ears with the whole, not a part of what it says so think of the Word of God, whole and entire in heaven, on earth, in the angels whole and entire with the Father, in eternity, in the flesh, in limbo, which that Word in His integrity visited whole and entire in Paradise, which He gave to the thief. These things I have said with regard to sound.

What if I say something about the understanding? How far inferior it is to the Word of God! For I do not recall sound, but if I want to be heard I follow the first sound up by another and another, or there will be silence; but with regard to the sense of my words, I both give it to you and keep it myself. You are in possession of what you have heard, and I do not lose what I have said. See how true the Psalmist's words are, *Let the heart of them rejoice who seek the Lord*. For God is the principle of truth itself. The understanding, therefore, which is in my heart passes into yours without leaving mine. Whereas, indeed, a certain understanding is in my heart, and I want to convey it to yours, I seek a mode of transfer which is supplied by the vehicle of sound. Having taken sound, as it were, I convey understanding through it; I speak and produce it, and teach it without losing it. This is what understanding, if it indeed was able, has done with my voice. Consider how the Word of God, God with God, the Wisdom of God, remaining substantially with the Father, sought our flesh as a sort of vehicle of sound, in order that He might come to us. He took it upon Himself, and came to us without leaving the Father. Understand and ponder well that which you have heard; think how great it is, and what it is, and conceive greater things of God. He is to be desired and to be longed for by charity that the heart of those who seek the Lord may rejoice.

5. TRUE POVERTY
(*Sermon* 14.1, etc.)

WE have sung to the Lord, and have said, *To You is the poor man left; You will be a helper to the orphan.* Let us seek to find out the orphan and the poor man; and do not be astonished at my exhorting you thus to seek out those whom we see and feel to be so plentiful. Is there any place where the poor are not, or where orphans are not to be found? Still I have to seek out both in the crowd. In the first place, brethren, we have to show you that apparent poverty is not what we are trying to find. The race of men, indeed, abounds who are looked upon as poor, and who are poor; who are by God's commandment the objects of almsgiving; of whom we acknowledge the words to be written, *Shut up alms in the heart of the poor, and it shall obtain help for you from the Lord*; but the poor man I have in view is to be understood in a higher sense. He belongs to the class of those of whom it is written, *Blessed are the poor in spirit, for theirs is the kingdom of heaven*. There are the poor who have no money, and can scarcely manage to get their daily bread, and who are so much in need of their neighbor's substance and pity that they are not ashamed to beg. If the words, *To You is the poor man left*, apply to such as these, what will become of us who do not fall under this category? We who are [90] Christians, are we therefore not committed to God's care? . . .

For no vice is more to be feared than pride in these visible riches which are commonly called riches, and to which poverty, as it is ordinarily understood, is opposed. The man who has neither money nor much substance has not anything to be proud of. If, there fore, he who has nothing to make him proud be not praised because he is not proud, let praise be given to that man who, having what might make him proud, is not proud. Why should I praise a poor man in his lowliness who has not something to be proud of? But who shall bear a man who is both needy and proud? Praise the rich man who is humble and who is poor in spirit. This is the sort of rich man to please the Apostle St. Paul, who says, writing to Timothy, *Charge the rich of this world not to be high-minded.* . . . Give me wealthy Zaccheus, the prince of tax collectors, the penitent, who was short of stature, and shorter in his own opinion; he climbed up a tree in order to see Christ passing by, Who was to hang for him on a tree. Give me a man who will say, "The half of my goods I give to the poor." Still, O Zaccheus, you are rich indeed! . . .

But perhaps a beggar, who is weak with neediness, covered with rags, languid with hunger, will come and say to me, "The kingdom of heaven is due to me; for I am like Lazarus, who lay at the rich man's door covered with sores, which dogs licked, and who sought to stay his hunger with the crumbs which fell from the rich man's table. The kingdom of heaven is for the like of us, not for those who are clothed in purple and fine linen, and who feed sumptuously every day.... Let us distinguish, then, between the rich and the poor. Why do you try to put other meanings upon me? It is manifest enough who the poor are."

I answer, "Listen, my fine beggar, to what I have to say on the point which you have raised. In calling yourself that holy beggar, covered with ulcers, I fear that pride prevents you from being what you pretend. Do not despise the rich, who are also charitable, humble, and poor in spirit. Be poor in reality, that is, humble. If you glory in your rags and ulcers because you are thus like Lazarus who lay before the rich man's door, you are thinking of his poverty, but you are not thinking of anything else. You ask, of what else should I think? Read the Scriptures and you will see what I mean. Lazarus was poor, but the man into whose bosom he was taken up was rich. . . . Read, or, if you cannot read, listen, and you will know that Abraham was most wealthy in land, in gold, and silver, and children, and flocks of sheep, and possessions; and still he was poor, for he was humble." . . .

You see that, though the poor are plentiful, we do well to seek the poor man. We look for him in the crowd and can scarcely find him. A poor man comes to me, and still I go on looking. In the meantime, put out your hand to the poor man whom you come across. . . . You say, "I am a beggar, like Lazarus;" my rich man, who is humble, does not say, " I am like Abraham, who was rich." You, therefore, are exalting yourself, while he is humbling himself. . . . You say, "I, being a poor man, am taken up to Abraham's bosom." Do you not see that a rich man receives the beggar? If you look down upon those who have money, and say that they do not belong to the kingdom of heaven, whereas they may be humble and you are not, do you not fear that Abraham may say [92] to you at your death, "Depart from me, for you have blasphemed me"? . . .

Consider another sort of poor man. They who wish to become rich fall into temptation, and into many and foolish desires, which lead men to death

and perdition. Who are these who have fallen away from the faith and entangled themselves in much sorrow? They who wish to become rich. Let me see now what the beggar has to say; let us put it to him if he does not wish to become rich; let him answer the truth. ... If he does wish it, he falls at once into temptation and many and foolish desires. For I speak not of possessions, but of desires. ... Why convince me that such a man has no substance, when I convince him of so much lusting after it? I put two men together. The one is rich, the other poor; but the rich man no longer desires what he has got. His riches come to him from his fathers, or from gifts and succession. Let us suppose even that he has gained his riches by sin. He has left off desiring further increase to his wealth; he has put a limit to his wishes, and is sincerely seeking after piety. "He is rich," you say. "Yes," I answer. But again you become an accuser? and you say, "He is rich through sinful gains." What if he should make friends of the mammon of iniquity? ... You are without substance, but you wish to become rich, and you fall thereby into temptation. Possibly you have fallen into miserable poverty and need through the calumny of a rival, depriving you of whatever you may have received as your portion for your sustenance. I hear you groaning and accusing the bad times; you would remove if you could the cause of your groans. Do we not see these things with our eyes? are they not of daily occurrence? ...
[93] Look at Him who, being rich, made Himself poor for us. All things were made by Him, and without

Him nothing was made. It is a greater thing to make gold than to have it. Who is able to form a notion of His riches? How does He make Who is not made, or create Who is not created, or form Who is not formed? How does the Immutable One create mutable things, or the Eternal One that which passes away? Who can form a true conception of His riches? . . . He is conceived in the virginal womb of a woman, and is enclosed in His mother's womb. What poverty is this! He is born in a narrow stable, and, wrapped in swaddling clothes, is laid in a manger. . . . Then the Lord of heaven and earth, the Creator of the angels, the Maker and Creator of all things, visible and invisible, sucks at His mother's breast, cries, is nourished, grows up, bears His years, and hides His majesty. Later on He is taken. He is despised, scourged, mocked, scorned, struck, crowned with thorns, hung upon a tree, pierced by a lance. Oh, what poverty! See here the Head of those poor whom I am seeking. Of Him we find the true poor to be members.

[94]
6. TEARS OF THE JUST
(*Sermon* 31.1, etc.)

THEY who sow in tears shall reap in joy. Going they went and wept, casting their seeds; but coming they shall come with joy fullness, carrying their sheaves.

Where are they going, and from where do they come? Why are they sowing in tears, and what is the seed? What are the sheaves? They are going to death, and they come from death. They are going in their birth, and coming in their rising again; sowing good works, and reaping an eternal reward. Our good seeds, therefore, are whatever good we do, and that which we are to receive at the end constitutes our sheaves. If, then, our seeds be good and our works good, why does the Psalmist speak of tears, seeing that *God loves a cheerful giver*?

In the first place, dear brethren, consider that these words apply principally to the blessed martyrs. For no men have staked so much as those who have staked themselves, according to St. Paul's words, *I will myself be spent for your souls*. By confessing Christ they spent themselves, and by His help fulfilled that which is written, Are you set at a great table? know that these are the things which you are to prepare. What is the great table if not that from which we take the Body and Blood of Christ?

[95] But have they perished who have heard from the Lord that even their hair is in His keeping? Does the hand perish when the hairs of the hand do not perish? Does the head perish when its hairs do not perish? Can the eye fail and not the eyelid? . . .

Why then in tears, when all our good works should

be done in joy? It may indeed be said of the martyrs, because they sowed in tears. For they fought a strong fight, and were in great tribulations. And in order to comfort them in their tears Christ bore them up, and transformed them into Himself, and said the words, *My soul is sorrowful even unto death*....He transformed then into Himself the infirm members of His Body. And perhaps it is of those weak ones that it is said, *They who sow in tears shall reap in joy*. For not in tears did that great champion of this same Christ sow who said, *I am even now ready to be sacrificed, and the time of my dissolution is at hand. I have fought a good fight, I have finished my course, I have kept the faith. As to the rest, there is laid up for me a crown of justice,* a crown made from the sheaves. *There is laid up for me,* he says, *a crown of justice, which the Lord, the just Judge, will render to me in that day.* As if he would say, He for whom I spend myself sowing will give me the harvest fruit. As far as we understand these words, brethren, they are the words of a man exulting, not of a man who weeps. When he spoke them, was he not in tears? Was he not like the joyful giver whom God loves? Let us, therefore, apply these words to the weak, that even they who have sown in tears may not despair; for supposing that they have thus sown, sorrow and weeping will pass away; sadness has an end; joy will come that has no end.

Still, dear brethren, see how it seems to me that these words apply to us all, *They who sow in tears shall*

[96] *reap in joy. Going they went and wept, casting their seeds; but coming they shall come with joyfulness, carrying their sheaves.* Listen to me, and judge, if by God's help I am able to show how the words *Going they went and wept* concern us all. We are going from the moment of our birth. For what man is stationary? Who is not forced to be in progress from the time of his entering on the path of life? A child is born; he walks by his growth: death is the term. We must attain that end, but in gladness. Who is there who does not weep here in this evil way when the very infant begins by tears. The infant, indeed, when it is born, is cast into this immense world from the small prison-house of its mother's womb, and proceeds from darkness unto light, and for all that it comes out of the darkness into light it can weep, but it cannot laugh. Men both laugh and weep, and their laughter is a matter of weeping. One man grieves over a loss, another at his difficult circumstances, another because he is imprisoned, another weeps because death has deprived him of one of his best beloved ones, and so it is with each. But why does the just man weep? In the first place, all these things are subjects of grief to him, for he weeps with genuine grief over those whose weeping is vain. He weeps for those who weep, and he weeps for those who rejoice; for those who weep foolish tears weep for nothing, and those who rejoice in vanity rejoice at their peril. The just man weeps under all circumstances, therefore he weeps more than any others. . . . There are the tears of the good, the tears of the

saints, which their prayers show forth. . . . The tears of
the just are plentiful, but only in this world. Will they
be found in the heavenly city? Why will they not be
found there? Because coming they shall come with
[97] joyfulness, carrying their sheaves. Happiness will
come, and will tears come with it? Those, indeed,
who weep useless tears here and rejoice in emptiness,
given over to their inordinate desires, groan when they
are cheated, and exult when they cheat others; these,
too, then, weep here, but not in joy. *Coming!* they
shall come with joyfulness, carrying their sheaves.
What can they reap when they have not sown? Or
rather, they *do* reap, but they reap what they have
sown. Because they have sown thorns they reap fire;
and they go not from tears to joy, like the saints.
Going, they went and wept, casting their seeds, but
coming, they shall come with joyfulness. They go from
weeping to weeping, from weeping with joy to weeping
without joy. . . . Where are they to go after the resurrection? Where, if not to that place of which Our
Lord spoke when He said, *Bind him hand and foot,
I and cast him out into external darkness*? What then?
Will there be darkness, and will there be no pain?
No, indeed. Not only will there be darkness; not only
will sight, in which they were used to rejoice, be taken
away, but in addition to this they will groan for all
eternity. . . . Eternal will the tormentor be, eternal
the torment. Neither will the tormentor grow weary,
nor the tortured die. Eternal weeping, therefore, will
be the portion of those who have so lived; eternal will
be the joys of the saints, when *coming they shall come*

in joyfulness, carrying their sheaves. For in the time of the harvest they shall say to their Lord, "Lord, by Your help we have done according to Your command; do give to us that which You have promised."

7. TEMPORAL PROSPERITY
   (*Sermon* 19.4)

My feet were almost moved, says the Psalmist; *my steps had almost slipped,* that is, I nearly fell. Why was this? Because I had a zeal on occasion of the wicked, seeing the prosperity of sinners. He was not silent as to the cause of his feet being moved and of his steps nearly slipping; therefore it is an admonishment to us. He had expectations from God according to the sense of the Old Testament, not knowing that in it the signs of future things are shown forth. He expected, then, to receive temporal happiness from God, and sought to have on this earth that which God reserves for His own in heaven. He wished to be happy here, whereas happiness is not here. For happiness is a real good and a great good, but it has its own region. Christ came from the land of happiness, and not even He found it on earth. He was scorned and mocked, taken prisoner, scourged, loaded with chains, struck by the hand of man, defiled by spittle, crowned with thorns, hung to a cross: and at last, of the Lord are the issues of death. . . . Why, then, do you, a servant, seek happiness in a place where the issues of death are of the Lord? That man of whom I had begun to speak was looking for happiness out of its proper place, and cleaving to the service of God in the hopes of obtaining it in this present life. He saw [99] that this great good, or great in his estimation, which he besought of God, and for which he served God, was enjoyed, not by those who worshiped God, but by those who worshiped the devil and blasphemed the true God. He saw this, and he was troubled, as if he had lost the fruit of his toil, which is expressed by his wrath against the wicked at witnessing their peace. ... I worship God; they blaspheme God. They are prosperous; I am wretched. Where is justice? Hence his feet were almost moved, his steps had almost slipped, and his ruin was at hand.

Consider to what a dangerous pass he had come by seeking temporal prosperity of God as if it were a great reward. Learn, then, dearly beloved, to look down upon it if you possess it, and not to say in your hearts, "Things go well with me because I serve God." For you will see men who do not serve God doing well according to your notion of prosperity, and your steps will be moved. Either, serving God, you are prosperous, and you will find others equally so who do not serve God, and you will therefore conclude that it is needless to be His friend because another man is prosperous without God; or you are not prosperous, and then you will lay the blame all the more upon God, Who gives happiness to His blasphemers and denies it to His servants. Learn, therefore, to despise temporal things, if you will serve God with a faithful heart. . . .

Indeed, on reflection, this ardent sinner, witnessing the peace of sinners, corrects himself for beginning to I think evil of God; he corrects himself, saying, *What have I in heaven, and besides You what do I desire upon earth?* Already coming to himself with a converted heart, he acknowledges the worth of the service of God, on which service of God he had put a low price indeed when he had sought to exchange it for [100] temporal prosperity. He acknowledges the reward which is awaiting God's servants in that place towards which we are admonished to lift up our hearts, and towards which we declare that we have lifted them up. (1) May we not lie, at least at the hour and in the moment of time during which we make the response. . . . *What have I in heaven?* What have I there? Eternal life, incorruption, a kingdom with Christ, the society of the angels, neither insecurity, nor ignorance, nor danger, nor temptation, but true and certain and lasting security. This is what I have in heaven. *And besides You what do I desire upon earth?* Have I desired riches, which are temporary and perishable? What have I desired? Gold, the mustiness of the earth; silver, the strife of the earth; honor, the smoke of time? These are the things which I desired from You upon the earth; and because I saw them in the hands of sinners my feet were almost moved, and my steps had almost slipped.

For what have I in heaven? What? He who made heaven; your God is the reward of your faith; you will have Him; He reserves Himself as the reward for His servants. Consider, dear brethren, the whole universe, the heavens, the earth, the sea, consider those things which are in heaven, on the earth, and in the sea, their wonderful and perfect and faultless ordering. Do they move you? Yes, indeed they do. Why? Because of their beauty. What is He who made them? I imagine you would be transfixed if you were to see the beauty of the angels. What, then, is the Creator of the angels? He is the reward of your faith. Oh, avaricious man, what is to satisfy you if God Himself is not enough for you?

1 An evident allusion to the words of the Mass, "Sursum corda" and "Habemus ad Dominum."

8. REST IN LABOR
(*Sermon* 69.1, and 70.1)

COME to Me all you who labor. Why do we all labor if it is not because we are mortal men, weak and infirm, carrying earthen vessels, with which our fellow men come into painful collision? . . . What then do the words signify, *Come to Me all you who labor*, if not, "Come to Me that you may not labor?" . . .

Take up My yoke upon you and learn of Me, not to make the universe, or to create all visible and invisible things, not to work miracles in this our world, or to raise the dead to life; but, that *I am meek and humble of heart*. Would you be great? Then begin from the very beginning. If you contemplate raising a high and noble edifice, be first intent upon the basis of humility. When a man wishes and prepares to raise a solid structure, the greater the building is to be the deeper he goes for the foundation. When the structure is finished, it is raised aloft in the air, but he who digs the foundation goes deep into the heart of the earth. Thus, before reaching its height, the building has a lowly beginning, from which it is raised high into the air. . . .

Listen to Him saying, *Come to Me all you who labor*. You do not cease your labor by flight. [102] Would you fly from Him and not to Him? Find a place where He is not, and go there. ... If, there fore, He fill heaven and earth, and there be no place of escape from Him, labor not: fly to Him now that He is nigh, lest you should feel His wrath at His coming.... By leading a good life you may be hopeful about seeing Him by whom you are seen when leading a bad one. For in doing this you are seen, and cannot see; but in leading a good life, you are both seen and you see. . . . Nathaniel said to God, whom he did not yet know, "How did You know me?" And Our Lord replied, "While you were under the fig-tree, I saw you." Christ sees you in these shadows; shall He not see you in His eternal light? . . . Prepare yourself to see Him in glory by whom you were seen in mercy. But as the building is lofty, give special attention to the foundation. You ask, what sort of foundation this is? Learn of Him, because He is meek and humble of heart. . . .

It seems a strange thing to some men, my brethren, when they hear Our Lord's words, *Come to Me all you who labor and are burdened, and I will refresh you. Take up My yoke upon you and learn of Me, for I am meek and humble of heart, and you shall find rest for your souls. For my yoke is sweet, and my burden light.* They think of those who have fearlessly taken up this yoke, and most meekly laid this burden on their shoulders, and who have been so tried and exercised by the strife of this world that they seemed to be called, not from labor to peace, but from peace to labor, as the Apostle also says, *All they who wish to live holy in Christ shall suffer persecution.* Some one, then, will say, "How is this yoke sweet and this burden light, when bearing both one and the other is equivalent to living holy in Christ?" And instead of *Come to Me all you that labor and are burdened, and I will refresh you,* why is it not rather "Come to Me all you who are idle that you may labor?" He found idlers, and took them into the vineyard that they might bear the burden of the day and of the heat. And under that sweet yoke and that light burden we hear the Apostle saying, In all things let us exhibit ourselves as the ministers of God, in much patience, in tribulation, in necessities, in distresses. And again, in another part of the same Epistle, *From the Jews five times did I receive forty lashes save one. Three times was I beaten with rods, once I was stoned, three times I suffered shipwreck; a night and a day was I in the depth of the sea*; and many more perils which may be counted indeed, but not tolerated except by the help of the Holy Spirit.

He was bearing therefore constantly those hard and grievous trials which he mentions; but the Holy Spirit was indeed with him, Who in the corruption of the outward man renewed the interior man day by day; and having tasted spiritual rest in the abundance of God's delights, the Apostle found all trials softened and all afflictions lightened by the hope of future blessedness. What a sweet yoke of Christ this was, and what a light burden for him to call all those hard and severe afflictions which he has just enumerated, and which fill every listener with dread a slight tribulation! He saw with the enlightened eyes of his soul at what a price of temporal things that eternal life is to be bought which consists in not suffering the eternal labors of the wicked, and in enjoying with perfect security the eternal happiness of the saints. Men suffer themselves to be cut and burnt in order to be free, at the price of excruciating suffering, from the pains of an abscess, which is not everlasting, but some-[104] what tedious. In the weak and uncertain repose of his old age the soldier is disturbed by bloody wars; instead of rest, years perhaps of anxious toil lie before him. What storms and tempests, what winds and ocean do not merchants brave that they may acquire their perishable riches, which are beset by dangers and storms at ever greater risk! What cold and heat, and dangers from horses and ditches and rivers and wild beasts do not sportsmen encounter! What hunger and thirst and privations of the first necessaries of life that they may catch their prey! and all the time they have no need of the flesh of the animal for which they endure so much. Even when the wild boar or the deer are caught, the sportsman's soul rather rejoices at their capture than his palate in eating them. In schools, too, how youths are tried by sitting up at night, and going without food, not for the sake of learning wisdom, but for vain honor and gain, that they may acquire mathematics, and letters, and skillful arts.

In all these things, however, men who do not care about them suffer the same hardships in their pursuit; but they who do care about them go through the same hardships, it is true, without seeming to feel them. For love makes all hard and bitter things easy, or as nothing. How much more surely and easily does charity, then, lead to true happiness, when cupidity exerts all its influence to lead men to misery. . . . Not in vain did St. Paul, that vessel of election, say in deep joy, *The sufferings of this time are not worthy to be compared to the glory to come, which shall be revealed in us.* This is how His yoke is sweet and His burden light. . . . *For the sake of the words of Your lips*, says the Psalmist, *I have avoided evil ways.* But things that are hard to toilers become easy to lovers.

9. A HOUSE AND A TENT
(*On the Psalms*, 26.6)

IF war shall arise in me, David says, *in this will I hope.* In what? *One thing,* he says, *I have asked of the Lord.* He expresses a certain benefit by the feminine gender (*unam petii a Domino*), as if his meaning were one petition. . . . Let us see what he who fears nothing has to ask. A great peace of heart. Do you wish to fear nothing? Ask for this one thing, which one thing he who fears nothing asks for, or which he asks for in order that he may fear nothing. *One thing,* he says, *I have asked of the Lord: this will I seek.* This is the one thing which they who walk righteously do in this world. What is it? what is the one thing? *That I may dwell in the house of the Lord all the days of my life.* This is the one thing; for that house is here signified which will be our eternal dwelling place. In this exile we speak of a house, but it is properly called a tent. A tent is the abode of pilgrims, and in a certain sense, of soldiers, of those who are fighting against an enemy. As, therefore, we have a tent in this life, it follows that there is an enemy; for you know that in military language inhabiting the same tent belongs to fellow comrades. Hence we have a tent in this world and a house in the next. But this very tent is sometimes erroneously called a house, and [106] in the same way a house is called a tent. Strictly speaking, however, the house belongs to heaven, and the tent to this world.

Another psalm expressly says what it is we are to do in that dwelling place: *Blessed are they who dwell in Your house: they shall praise You for ever and ever.* The Psalmist, burning, if we may so speak, with this desire and this love, desires to dwell in the house of the Lord all the days of his life; and these days in the house of the Lord are not to be as days which pass, but they are to last for ever. Days here are used in the same sense as those years of which it is said, *Your years shall not fail.* For the day of eternal life is one long day without an end. This, then, is what he had in view in saying to the Lord, I have desired this, one thing I have asked for, this will I seek. And as if we were to say to him, "And what will you do there? what enjoyment will you have? what food for your heart? what delights? from where the joy? You indeed will not endure it unless you are happy. And how will that happiness come about?" Here below the human race has diverse kinds of enjoyment, and any man is called miserable when that which he cares for is taken away from him. Men, therefore, love various things, and when a man seems to have that which he likes he is called happy; but the truly happy man is he who loves what is worthy of love, not he who possesses the object of his desires. For many men are to be pitied rather for having what they love than for being deprived of it. They are wretched from loving harmful things, but when they possess them they are still more wretched. And God is merciful when He holds back from us that which we love in a wrongful way; but He is angry when He satisfies the

desires of an unrighteous lover. You have the clear
[107] evidence of the Apostle, God delivered them up
to the evil desires of their hearts. He gave them, therefore, what they wished for, but unto damnation. Again,
you find Him turning a deaf ear to St. Paul's petition,
*For this I besought the Lord three times that He would
take it away from me* (the lust of the flesh), *and
He said to me, My grace is sufficient for you, for
strength is perfected in weakness.* See how He gave
them up to the desires of their hearts, and refused to
listen to the Apostle Paul. He granted their request
for their condemnation, and refused St. Paul for his
good. But when we love that which God would have
us love, He will most surely give it to us. This is that
one thing which ought to be loved, that we may dwell
in the house of the Lord all the days of our life.

10. MYSTERY OF TEMPORAL PROSPERITY
   (*On the Psalms*, 91.7) (1)

WHAT are we to think of those who lead bad lives
and flourish? This disquiets the man who loses the
sabbath. He is conscious of doing good works day
by day, and of being pressed down by narrow means,
or of not having enough for his family, or of being
in hunger, thirst, and nakedness. Or perhaps he,
being virtuous, finds himself in prison, whereas the
man who sent him there is a sinner, rejoicing in his
wickedness; and an evil thought against God enters

into his heart, and he says, "O God, why am I serving You and obeying Your words? I have not taken my neighbor's goods, nor stolen; I have not committed murder, nor desired anybody's property; I have not borne false witness against any man; I have not dishonored my father or my mother; I have not turned myself towards idols; I have not taken the name of the Lord God in vain; I have kept myself from sin." He touches upon the ten chords, that is, the ten commandments of the Law, and questions himself concerning each, and finding that he has not offended even against one, he is grieved at the misfortunes which have fallen upon him. And they who give no thought, I say not to

---

1 The title of this psalm is, *A Psalm of a Canticle on the Sabbath Day*.

[109] the commandments, but even to the Psalter itself, doing no sort of good, are serving idols; and maybe they seem to be Christians as long as no adversity befalls them or theirs. As soon as some misfortune appears they run to the pagan priest, or to a sorcerer, or an astrologer. When Christ is mentioned to them they smile scornfully, or when they are asked, "Do you, a Christian, consult an astrologer?" they will answer,
"Get out of my presence; he has been of use to me, otherwise I should have been ruined and miserable!"
"My good man, do not you sign yourself with the cross of Christ? and the Law forbids all these things. You rejoice at your success in money matters; and are you not sad at the loss of yourself? How much better it would be for you to suffer the loss of your clothes than

that of your soul!" He laughs these objections to
scorn, ill treats his parents, hates his enemy and pursues
him unto death, thieves when he gets an opportunity,
ceases not from false testimony, destroys the peace of
other marriages, covets his neighbor's goods; he does
all these things, and flourishes in the riches, honors,
and reputation of this world. That poor man in his
virtue, who is suffering wrongs, sees him, and is disquieted. "O God," he says," I believe the wicked
find favor before You, and that You hate the good
and love those who do evil." If he be so unhinged
as to consent to this thought, he loses his peace
of heart, and begins not to heed the teaching of the
psalm. He departs from its meaning, and the words,
*It is good to give praise to the Lord; and to sing to
Your name, Most High*, lose their significance on his
lips. When the sabbath of the inner man and peace
of heart are destroyed, and good thoughts are put
away, he begins to imitate the prosperous sinner before
his eyes, and he too turns himself to evil. But God is
patient because He is eternal, and He knows the
day of His reckoning in which He examines all things.

This being the drift of the Psalmist's teaching, what
does he say? *Lord, how great are Your works! Your
thoughts are exceedingly deep.* In truth, my brethren,
there is no ocean more unfathomable than this thought
of God's, that the wicked should be prosperous and the
good should labor: there is nothing so deep, nothing
so far above us. This impenetrable mystery is infallible shipwreck to the infidel. Would you grasp this

depth? Depart not from the cross of Christ; hold to Christ, and you are safe from drowning. What am I saying, hold to Christ? This is why He chose toil on earth. You heard when the Prophet was read to you that He did not withdraw His shoulders from lashes, or His face from the spittle of men, or His countenance from their blows. Why did He choose to suffer these things if not to console the suffering? He too might have reserved His resurrection for the end of time; but you who had not seen it would have been without hope. He did not delay His resurrection lest you should still doubt. Bear, therefore, and suffer tribulations here below with that same end in view which you see that Christ had, and let not evil doers, who are prosperous according to this world, disturb you. The thoughts of God are exceedingly deep. Where is God's thought? For the present He loosens the reins, but hereafter He will draw them in. Do not share the pleasure of the fish who is relishing his food. It is true the fisherman has not drawn his line, but already the fish is biting at the hook. That which seems long to you is short: all these things pass rapidly away. What is a man's long life compared to God's eternity? Would you be long-suffering? Consider God's eternity. You are thinking of your own short days upon earth, and would have all things fulfilled during their brief course. What are these things? That all the wicked should be condemned, and all the good should he crowned. Would you see these things in this life of yours? God will carry them out in His own time. What if you suffer and cause weariness? He is eternal,

He is slow, He is long-suffering. But you say, "I am not long-suffering, because I am finite!" You have it in your power so to be. Unite your heart to God's eternity, and with Him you will be eternal. For what is written of transitory things? *All flesh is grass, and all the glory thereof as the flower of the field: the grass is withered and the flower is fallen.* All things, therefore, wither and die, only not His word. *For the word of the Lord endures for ever.* Grass passes away, and its glory passes away; but you have an abiding thing for your support, The word of the Lord endures for ever. Say to Him then, Your thoughts are exceeding deep. You have held to the plank, and are passing through this abyss. Do you see or understand any thing? You say you do. If you are already a Christian, and are well instructed, you say, God reserves all things for His own judgment. The good are in toil, because they are punished as sons; the wicked rejoice, because they suffer the penalty of aliens. A man has two sons: he chastises the one and leaves the other free. One does evil, and he is not corrected by his father; while no sooner does the other move than he is beaten and bruised with blows. Why is the one left alone and the other beaten, unless it be that the inheritance is reserved for the bruised one and the other is already disinherited? The father views his state as hopeless, and leaves him to do as he pleases. But if the boy who is whipped has neither sense nor prudence nor understanding, he envies his brother for getting no [112] blows, and groans over himself, saying in his heart, " To think of all my brother's evil deeds, how he disobeys my father's orders as much as he pleases, and no one has a word to say to him, whereas if I only move my little finger I am beaten!" He is a senseless and foolish boy, thinking only of his present suffering, not of his future inheritance.

Therefore after saying *Your thoughts are exceedingly deep,* he went on immediately to add, *The senseless man shall not know; nor will the fool understand these things.* What are the things which the fool shall not understand and the senseless man shall not know? When the wicked shall spring up as grass. What does *as grass* mean? They are green during the winter, but are burnt up in summer time. Look at the flower of the field. What passes away so quickly? What is brighter or fresher to behold? Delight not in its freshness, but fear its withering. You have heard that the wicked are like grass; hear now the voice of the just: *for behold.* In the meantime consider how sinners flourish like grass; but who is it that does not understand? Fools and senseless men. When the wicked shall spring up as grass, and all the workers of iniquity shall look on. All those who have not right thoughts concerning God in their hearts have gazed at sinners springing up like grass, that is, prospering for a time. Why do they look at them? *That they may perish for ever and ever.* For they consider their temporary prosperity, make them objects of imitation, and wishing to prosper with them for a time perish for ever. This is the meaning of that they may perish for ever and ever. *But You, Lord, are most high for evermore.*

From out of Your eternity on high You are waiting [113] for the sinner's day to pass, that the time of the just may come. *For behold.* Listen, brethren, with all your ears. Already he who speaks these words (for he speaks for us by the mouth of the body of Christ, and Christ speaks in His body, that is, in His Church) has been received into the eternity of God: as I told you in a former part of this psalm, God is patient and long-suffering, and He bears with all these evil deeds which He sees the wicked doing. Why? Because He is eternal, and He knows what He is reserving for them. Would you too be patient and long-suffering? Unite yourself to God's eternity, and with Him expect those things which are beneath you; for when your heart cleaves to the Almighty One, all mortal things will be beneath your estimation: *For behold Your enemies shall perish.* They who flourish now shall perish hereafter. Who are God's enemies? Brethren, maybe you look upon blasphemers alone as God's enemies? It is true that they are His enemies, and most disgraceful enemies, who spare not their reproaches of God either by word or evil thoughts.

And what do they do to the most high and eternal God? If you strike a blow with your fist at a lofty column, you hurt yourself; and do you imagine that you can strike God by blasphemy with impunity to yourself? You cannot touch God. But blasphemers of God are openly His enemies, and every day secret enemies are discovered. Beware of all such; for Holy Scripture makes manifest certain hidden enemies of

God, that, not being able to discern them with your own heart, you may recognize them in the inspired page, and avoid being one of their number. St. James says plainly in his Epistle *Do you not know that the friend of this world is constituted the enemy of God?* You hear the words. Do you wish not to be God's [114] enemy? Be not the friend of this world; for if you are the friend of this world, you are God's enemy. Just as a wife cannot break her marriage vow without being hostile to her husband, so a soul cannot become an adulteress through love of worldly things without being God's enemy. This soul fears, but does not love; it fears punishment, and does not delight in justice. Therefore, all lovers of this world, all seekers after trifles, all those who consult sorcerers, astrologers, and pagan oracles, are God's enemies. Whether they frequent churches, or whether they do not, they are God's enemies. They may flourish for a time like grass, but they will perish when He begins to examine them and to pass His judgment upon all flesh. Be on the side of God's Scripture, and repeat with it the words of this psalm, *For behold Your enemies shall perish.* May you not be found in that place of their damnation. *And all the workers of iniquity shall be scattered.*

What is it to you who are now in toil, if the enemies of God are to perish, and all the workers of iniquity to be scattered? What if you who, in the midst of these scandals, are groaning with the sins of men all around you, and are suffering according to the flesh but re-

joicing in spirit? What is your hope, O body of
Christ? O Christ, Who sit at the right hand of
the Father, but are laboring on earth by Your feet
and Your members, You say, Saul, Saul, why persecutest you Me? What hope is yours if the enemies
of God are to perish, and all the workers of iniquity
to be scattered, how will you fare? *My horn shall be
exalted like that of the unicorn.* Why did the Psalmist
say like the unicorn? Sometimes the unicorn signifies
pride and sometimes the exaltation of unity; because
unity is praised all heresies shall perish with God's
[115] enemies. *And my horn shall be exalted like that
of the unicorn.* And when will this be? *And my old age
in plentiful mercy.* What does he mean by *my old age*?
My last end. As old age is the last period in our
human lives, so all that which the body of Christ is
now suffering in labors, and trials, and vigils, in
hunger and thirst, in scandals and sins and oppression,
constitutes its youth: its old age, that is, its last end,
shall be gladness. And think not, my brethren, that
in speaking of old age the Psalmist meant to imply
death. Man, as he is in the flesh, grows old in order
to die. The old age of the Church will be bright with
just deeds, but it will not suffer the corruption of
death. That which his head is to the old man, that
our good works will be to the body of Christ. You
see how the hair grows gray and white as old age
approaches. Sometimes you vainly seek a dark hair
on the head of a man whose growing old is perfectly
healthy and natural; and so when our life is such that
the blackness of sin may be looked for in it and not

found, this green old age is like a second youth, and will always be vigorous. You have heard sinners likened to grass; now listen to what the old age of the just is to be. *My old age in plentiful mercy.*

The grass passes away and the flowering of sinners. What of the just? *The just shall flourish like the palm tree. The wicked spring up like grass,* but *the just shall flourish like the palm tree.* He has taken the palm-tree in order to signify loftiness. Perhaps he wishes also to signify that its beauty is in the top, that you may trace its beginning from the earth, and see how its top is high in air, with all its proud beauty; the root which is in the earth is rugged to the eye, the beautiful foliage is exposed to the light of heaven. So [116] your comeliness is to be hereafter. Let us take firm root, but let us turn our minds heavenwards; for Christ, Who ascended into heaven, is our foundation. He shall be exalted in His humility. *He shall grow up like the cedar of Lebanon.*

Consider the kind of tree he specifies: *The just shall flourish like the palm tree; he shall grow up like the cedar of Lebanon.* Does the palm wither when the sun shines, or does the cedar dry up? But when the sun is somewhat powerful, grass is burnt up. Judgment, therefore, will come in order that sinners maybe withered, and that the just may flourish. *He shall grow up like the cedar of Lebanon.*

They that are planted in the house of the Lord shall

flourish in the courts of the house of our God. They shall still increase in a fruitful old age; and shall be tranquil that they may proclaim. This is the Sabbath which I have already commended to you, from which this psalm takes its title: *They shall be tranquil that they may proclaim.* Why do peaceable ones proclaim this message? They are not affected by the grass of sinners. The cedar and the palm are not bent even by tempests. Therefore let them be at peace that they may deliver their message. Their peace must be real, because it is even now they have to speak in the teeth of deriding men. O wretched lovers of this world, they who are planted in the house of the Lord, give you a message; they who confess the Lord by hymn and instrument, by word and deed, speak to you and say, "Be not seduced by the happiness of sinners; give not a thought to the flower of the field; envy not those whose happiness is transitory, and whose misery is to be eternal." Nor is this visible happiness, as it appears to us now, true happiness; nor are they happy in their hearts who are tormented by a bad conscience. But do you have peace, hoping in the promises of the Lord your God. What message will you preach from out of your peace? *That the Lord God is righteous, and there is no iniquity in Him.* Examine yourselves, brethren, and see if you are planted in the house of the Lord, if you wish to flourish like the palm tree, to be multiplied like the cedar of Lebanon, and not to be burnt up like grass by a scorching sun, as those who seem to flourish without the sun. If, therefore, you wish not to be as grass, but as the palm and the cedar, what will you proclaim by your life? That the Lord our God is righteous, and there is no iniquity in Him. How is there no iniquity? Take the case of a bad man who has committed all kinds of sin. He has perfect health; he has children, and plenty of means, and an abundance of show. He is courted to the skies; he has satisfaction from his enemies; and his life is full of transgressions. Another man, whose life is blameless, not taking his neighbor's goods, doing no harm to anybody, is toiling in chains and imprisonment, or is struggling with hunger and want. *How is there no iniquity in Him?* Have peace and you shall understand this mystery. You are disturbed, and are hiding the light from your own chamber. The eternal God would enlighten you; make not a cloud for yourself of your uneasiness. Have peace in your heart, and receive the words which I have to say. Because God is eternal, because He spares the wicked in this life, bringing them to repentance, and chastises the good, making them wise for the kingdom of heaven, therefore there is no iniquity in Him. Fear not. "I call not myself just," says one man. "See how I have been chastised; it is my sins that have done it, arid I acknowledge it." This is the language of many men. If it happens that any one be in trouble or pain, and another strive to console him, he will reply, "I have sinned; my sins have done it, and I acknowledge it; but have I sinned as much as such a man? I know what a grievous sinner he has been; I recognize my own sins, and confess them to God, but they are not so great as his, and he has nothing to suffer." Be not disquieted; be calm, that you may know *that the Lord is righteous, and that there is no iniquity in Him.* What if He chastises you now for the reason that He does not reserve you for eternal fire? What if He be leaving that other man alone now because he is one day to hear the words, Depart into everlasting fire? But when shall this be? When you are standing at His right hand, He will say to those on His left, Depart into everlasting fire, which is prepared for the devil and his angels. Be not therefore moved by these things; have peace and calm, and proclaim the message that the Lord our God is righteous, and there is no iniquity in Him.

11. LAZARUS AND THE RICH MAN
(*Sermon* 41.4)

KEEP fidelity with a friend in his poverty, that in his prosperity also you may rejoice. Consider poor Lazarus lying at the rich man's door. He was miserably ill, not having as much as that bodily health which is the patrimony of the poor. He even had ulcers, which the dogs licked. There lived a rich man in that house, who was clothed in purple and fine linen, and feasted sumptuously every day, and who would not "keep fidelity" with the beggar. Truly Our Lord Jesus, the lover and giver of faith, thought more of that very faith in the beggar than He did of the rich man's gold and pleasures, more of the beggar's possession than of the rich man's pride. For this reason He named the beggar, whereas He deemed it expedient not to name the rich man. There was, He says, a certain rich man, who was clothed in purple and fine linen, and who feasted sumptuously every day, and a certain beggar called Lazarus. Does it not seem to you that He was quoting from that book in which He found the beggar's name entered, but not the rich man's? the book of the living and of the righteous, not of the proud and of sinners? The name of that rich man was in the mouths of men, but no one spoke of Lazarus. God, on the contrary, gave the [120] beggar his name, and passed over the rich man's in silence. *It happened that the poor man died and was carried by angels into Abraham's bosom. The rich man also died and was buried* (for perhaps Lazarus was not even buried); *and when he was suffering torments in hell,* as we read, *lifting up his eyes he saw Lazarus,* whom he had despised at his house door, *in Abraham's bosom.* He could not share the rest of a man with whom he had refused to share a common faith. *"Father Abraham,"* he said, *"send Lazarus that he may dip the tip of his finger in water to cool my tongue, for I am tormented in this flame."* He was answered, *"Son, you did receive good things in your lifetime, and likewise Lazarus evil things; but now he is comforted, and you are tormented. And besides all this, between us and you there is fixed a great chasm; so that they who would pass from here to you cannot, nor from there come here."* He saw that mercy was denied to him, because he had denied it to others. He recognized the truth of the words, *Judgment without mercy to him that has not shown mercy.* And he, who in his day had closed his heart against the poor, was tardily touched with compassion for his brothers. *"Send Lazarus,"* he said to Abraham, *"for I have five brothers. Let him testify unto them, lest they also come into this place of torture."* And the answer was, *"They have Moses and the prophets: let them hear them."* That man who derided the prophets found kindred spirits in his brothers. For I believe indeed I am certain that when they spoke together of the prophets who preach goodness and condemn evil, and speak with a warning voice concerning future punishments while promising future rewards, he would laugh all these things to scorn. "What life will there be after death?" they would say. "What [121] memory in corruption, or what sense in ashes? All men die and are buried. Who has ever been known to come back? " Remembering these his words, he wished Lazarus to return to his brothers that they might no longer say, " Who has ever come back from the dead?" A suitable and appropriate answer was made to this demand. The rich man seems to have been a Jew, and therefore to have addressed Abraham as father. The answer, then, *"If they hear not Moses and the prophets, neither will they believe if one rise again from the dead,"* was perfectly pertinent. It was carried out in the Jews, who neither heard Moses and the prophets, nor believed in Christ rising from the dead. Had He not foretold it to them in the words, *If you believed Moses, you would believe Me also?*

That rich man, therefore, now that his temporal

pleasures were over, remained without consolation in eternal torments. He had not done just deeds, and had been answered accordingly. Remember that you have received your good things during your life. Therefore this life which you see is not your life. That which you see and desire from afar is not for you. Where are now the words of the rich and of flatterers of the rich, when they see someone brimming over with worldly goods, abounding on the face of the earth, drawing the world after himself with exaggerated homage, and pulling towards him the weight which may sink him? For it was that great weight which took the rich man to hell, and that heavy burden which pressed him down to the lowest depths. He had not heard the words, *Come to Me all you who labor and are burdened. My yoke is sweet, and My burden light.* The burdens of Christ are wings, and Lazarus had been borne on them to Abraham's bosom. The rich man would not listen, but he [122] had lent his ear to the voice of flatterers, who had made him deaf to the prophets. These evil men had said, "You have no one but yourself to consult." Therefore, *You have received your good things during your life.* You looked upon them as yours, neither believing nor hoping in any others: you have had your good things during your life. For you looked upon this mortal life as your all when you hoped for nothing after death and feared no terrors. You have received your good things in your life, but Lazarus evil ones. Abraham does not say his evil things, but only evil things, as men understand them, and fear and shun them. Lazarus received evil things in this world, not your good things, which neither did he lose. For as the evil things are not specified as his, so neither does the text add here during his life. He looked for another life in Abraham's bosom. In this world he was as one dead; he did not live. He was amongst the number of whom the Apostle speaks, *You are dead, and your life is hidden with Christ in God.* The beggar suffered temporal crosses; but God only delayed his good things, and did not take them away. What, then, O Dives, do you desire in hell? When you were enjoying your riches you were without hope. Are you not that man who, in despising the poor man, laughed to scorn the Prophet Moses? You would not keep faith with your neighbor in his poverty, and would you now enjoy his good things? When you heard the words, Keep faith with your friend in his poverty that you may rejoice in his prosperity, you scorned their teaching. Now you see his good things from afar, and do not share them with him. They were goods to come invisible goods. While they were invisible they were to be believed in, lest when visible you should be able to feel regret, but vain regret.

[123] It seems to me, brethren, that we have said enough on these words. The text in its Christian meaning to Christians means that we are not to keep faith with a poor friend in the mere hope of his coming into temporal riches, and of our sharing them with him. This is not at all the sense of these words. How, then, shall we do it if not by fulfilling Our Lord's precept? *Make to yourselves friends of the mammon*

of iniquity, that they may receive you into everlasting dwellings. There are poor men here who have no dwellings in which to receive us. *Make friends of the mammon of iniquity*, that is, of the gains which iniquity calls gains; for there are gains which justice calls gains, and these are in the treasures of God. Do not look down upon the poor who have not where to go. In eternity they have dwelling places, and dwelling places in which you will vainly long to be received, like the rich man, if you receive them not now in your houses. Because *he who receives a just man in the name of a just man will have the reward of the just man, and he who receives a prophet in the name of a prophet will have the reward of a prophet; and he who shall give to the least of My little ones a glass of cold watery even in the name of a disciple, Amen, I say unto you, he shall not lose his reward.* He keeps faith with his friend in his poverty, therefore he shall enjoy his prosperity.

Your Lord, who made Himself poor whereas He was rich, puts a further and fuller meaning on these words. Perhaps you are hesitating in your mind as to whether the beggar whom you have taken into your house is genuine, or rather a hypocrite; you are thus troubled in your charity because you cannot see into hearts. Be kind even to the sinner, that you may thus reach the just. He who fears to see his [124] seeds fall upon the wayside, amongst thorns, or on stones, and is idle during the winter, has to suffer hunger in summer time. . . . *Keep fidelity with a friend in his poverty*.... See Christ in the friend, and accept Him in humility.

Where the inspired Word speaks of a friend, read Christ; for Christ was signified in the prophetical meaning, and you see the nourishment contained in the text, which is poured forth from the fountain of truth in order to allay your thirst. Keep fidelity with Christ in His poverty, that in His prosperity you may rejoice. What does this mean, *Keep fidelity with Christ*? Because He became man for you, was born of a virgin, endured insult, was scourged, hung upon a tree, was wounded by a lance, and buried. Do not despise these things, nor look upon them as incredible, and in this way keep faith with your friend; for this is His poverty. But what is *That in His prosperity you may rejoice*? Because He willed it, and, willing it, therefore came to you in poverty. Listen to the voice of Him Who is poor for your sake, the Lord your God, Who makes you rich. See how you may rejoice in His prosperity if you keep faith with Him in His poverty. *Father*, He says, *I will that where I am they whom You have given Me may be with Me.*

12. "YOU SHALL HIDE THEM IN THE SHADOW OF YOUR FACE."
(*Sermon* 362.3; *On the Psalms* 30.8)

THE kingdom of heaven is like to a net that was

cast into the sea, and gathered of every kind, which, when it was filled, they drew out, and sitting by the shore, they chose out the good into vessels, but the bad they cast forth. Our Lord wished to show that the Word of God is sent to nations and peoples in the same way as a net is cast into the sea. It gathers together now by the Christian sacraments both the good and the bad; but not all whom the net takes are put away into vessels. For these vessels signify the thrones of the saints and the great mysteries of the beatific life, which not all who are called Christians shall be able to attain, but those whose life answers to their name. The good and the bad, indeed, are together in the one net, and the good bear with the bad till their final separation at the end. It is also written in another place, *You shall hide them in the shadow of Your face.* This was spoken of the saints. *You shall hide them*, the Psalmist says, *in the shadow of Your face*, that is, where neither the eye nor the thought of man can penetrate. Wishing to signify a most hidden and mysterious place, he expressed it by the shadow of the face of God. Are we to understand this in a material [126] sense, and to suppose that God has a spacious countenance, and in it a place where the saints are to be hidden? You see, brethren, that this is a gross interpretation, and it is to be rejected by the faithful. What, then, is to be understood by the shadow of God's face, if not that which is known to the face of God alone? When granaries are spoken of as secret places - vessels, as they are elsewhere called - neither such grainaries nor such vessels as we are familiar with are signified. For if one of these things were really meant, it would not be called by two names. But as things to us unknown are expressed by analogies familiar to men, take both things, the granary and the vessel, as implying a mystery. But if you seek to know what manner of secret thing this is, listen to the Prophet's words, *You shall hide them in the shadow of Your face.*

This being so, brethren, we are still as wandering pilgrims in this life, and we are still sighing by faith after an unknown country. And how is it that we are citizens of an unknown country, unless it is that we have forgotten it in our remote wanderings, and in this way it is that we have to call our true country an unknown land? Christ, Our Lord, the King of that country, put forth this forgetfulness from our hearts when He came down to pilgrims; and by His incarnation His Godhead is made our path, that we may walk by the Man Christ, and may abide in Christ, Who is God. In what language, then, brethren, are we to explain to you that secret which *neither eye has seen, nor ear has heard, nor heart of man has conceived,* or how are we to contemplate it? At times we may experience some thing, which we cannot however put into words; but if we have never experienced a thing, we are unable to speak about it at all. As, then, it might happen that, if I knew these things, I could not describe them to you, how much more difficult is it for me to speak about them when I too, brethren, am walking with you by faith, and have not yet their vision. But am I different in this from the Apostle? He comforts our ignorance and strengthens our faith in saying, *Brethren, I do not count myself to have apprehended. But one thing I do: forgetting the things that are behind, and stretching myself forth to those that are before, I press towards the mark, to the prize of the heavenly call;* by which words he shows himself to be still a pilgrim in this world. And in another place he says, As long as we are in the body we are absent from the Lord. For we walk by faith, and not by sight. And again he says, *For we are saved by hope. But hope that is seen is not hope. For what a man sees, what is there to hope for? . . . . You shall hide them in the shadow of Your face.* What may this place be? He did not say, "You shall hide them in Your heaven" nor, "You shall hide them in Your Paradise" nor, "You shall hide them in Abraham's bosom." For the future dwelling-places of the saints are spoken of in Holy Scripture as reserved for many of the faithful. Let everything which is not God become worthless. He Who protects us during this life will be Himself our dwelling place after this life, for so the 30th psalm makes petition to Him, *Be You unto me a God, a protector, and a house of refuge.* Therefore we shall be hidden in the shadow of God's face. Do you expect to hear from me what the shadow of God's face is? Purify your hearts, that He Whom you invoke may enter in and enlighten you. Be His dwelling place, and He will be yours; let Him dwell in you, and you will dwell in Him. If you receive Him into your heart during this life, He will receive you after this life into the shadow of His countenance. *You shall hide them,* He says. Where? *In the shadow*

[128] *of Your face, from the disturbance of men.* Hidden there, they are not disquieted. In the shadow of Your face they are not disquieted. Do you think there is any man in this world so happy that, when he is insulted by men for serving Christ, he turns his heart to God and begins to experience His sweetness, and enters into the face of God by his conscience from the disturbance of the men who are insulting him? . . .

You shall hide them in the shadow of Your face from the disturbance of men. You shall protect them in Your tabernacle from the contradiction of tongues. Some times You so hide them in the shadow of Your face from the disturbance of men that no human anxiety any longer exists for them; but because they who serve You suffer much persecution from bitter tongues, what do You do for *them*? *You shall protect them in Your tabernacle.* What is this tabernacle? The Church militant is called a tent because it is still in a land of exile, for a tent is the dwelling place of soldiers who are engaged in war. A house is not a tent. As an exile, take your part in the war, that, safe in the tent, you may be received with all honor into the house. Your eternal dwelling place will be in heaven if you now pass your life completely in the tent. Therefore in this tabernacle You shall protect them from the contradiction of tongues. Many are the tongues of contradiction; respective heresies represent so many schisms; numerous are the lips which deny true doctrine. As for you, hasten to the tabernacle of God, hold to the Catholic Church, go not away from the rule of truth, and you shall be protected in the tabernacle from the contradiction of tongues.

13. LANGUID FAITH
(*On the Psalms*, 25.4)

... THE ship was in danger on the lake, and Jesus slept. We are, as it were, sailing on a lake; neither winds nor tempests are lacking; our ship is nearly filled by the daily temptations of this world. How does this come about, unless it is because Jesus sleeps? If Jesus were not sleeping in you, you would not have these storms to suffer, but you would have inward peace in the companionship of Jesus. What does this mean Jesus is asleep? Your faith, which comes from Jesus, has fallen asleep. Storms arise on the lake; you see the wicked nourishing, the good being tried: this is a temptation; it is an angry wave. You say to yourself, "O God, is this Your justice, that the unjust are prosperous and the righteous in sorrow?" You say to God, "Is this Your justice?" And God answers, "Is this your faith? Did I promise you these things? Were you made a Christian that you might be prosperous in this world?" You are vexed because the wicked nourish here, when they are to be tormented hereafter by the devil. Why is this? Why are you disquieted by the storms and tempests of the lake? Because Jesus is asleep, that is, your faith, which comes from Him, is slumbering in your breast. What can you do to be saved? Arouse Jesus, and say,

"Lord, we perish. The lake is stirred up; we are [130] perishing." He will awake, that is, your faith will return to you, and with His help you will see, by meditating, that those things which are given now to the wicked will not remain always with them. Either they will forsake them during their lifetime, or be forsaken when the hour of death comes. But that which is promised to you will last for all eternity. Their good is temporal, and it is soon taken away, for it has blossomed like the flower of the field. *All flesh is grass; the grass has dried up, and the flower has withered, but the word of the Lord endures for ever.* Turn, then, your back to that which perishes and your face to that which perishes not. The tempest will not frighten you if Christ is watching, nor will the waves fill your ship, because your faith has power over the winds and the waves, and the danger will pass away.

14. THE REWARD OF NATURAL VIRTUE
(*On the City of God,* Bk. 5, ch. 15 and 16)

IF God had not bestowed that earthly glory of a magnificent empire on those to whom He was not to give eternal life with His holy angels in His heavenly city, for true religion, which exhibits the worship called *Latria* by the Greeks to the one true God alone, leads to the enjoyment of His society, their skillful arts, that is, their natural powers, would have been left unrewarded. For the Lord Himself says of those men who are seen to do some good action that they may be glorified by men, *Amen, I say unto you they have received their reward.* Thus the Romans despised their possessions for the common good, for the commonwealth, in other words, and for its treasury; they resisted the promptings of avarice, and thought of their country's good with disinterested minds; nor were they guilty of crime or voluptuousness according to that country's laws. They used all these means as the true way to honors, to empire, and glory: their name was glorious amongst the majority of peoples; they imposed their laws upon many nations; and in these times they are renowned in most lands for their letters and their history. They have no cause to complain of the justice of God, the almighty and true God. *They have received their reward.* But far other is the reward of the saints, even though they may suffer insult on [132] earth for the city of God, which is odious to the lovers of this world. That heavenly city is eternal: in it there is no birth because there is no death. There is true and perfect happiness, not personified by a goddess, but the gift of God. From that heavenly city we have received the token of faith as long as we sigh after its beauty in the days of our exile. There the sun does not rise upon the just and unjust, but the sun of justice protects the good alone; nor will it be necessary to expend great labor on enriching the public treasury from small private means, because the truth will be the treasure common to all. Therefore the Roman *imperium* was open to human glory, not only that the earthly reward should be granted to men so minded, but also that the citizens of that eternal commonwealth, as long as they are pilgrims in this world, might carefully take to heart their examples, and judge what love is due to the heavenly country on account of eternal life, if the earthly one is so cherished by its citizens for human glory.

[133]
15. DIFFERENT ACTION OF THE SAME FIRE
(*On the City of God,* Bk. 1, ch. 8)

SOMEONE will say, "Why, then, does this divine mercy of God reach even impious and ungrateful men?" What reason shall we allege if not that this mercy has been shown by Him *Who makes His sun to rise over the good and the wicked, and His rain to fall over the just and the unjust*? Although some of their number, pondering these things, are converted from their impiety, some others (as the Apostle says), despising the riches of His goodness, and patience, and longsuffering, treasure up to themselves wrath, according to their hardness and impenitent heart, against the day of wrath and revelation of the judgment of God. Still the patience of God invites the wicked to repentance, just as the chastisement of God makes the good wise unto patience. Again, the mercy of God surrounds the good for their protection, as His severity strikes the wicked for their punishment. It pleased Divine Providence to prepare good things for the just, which the wicked will not enjoy, and evil things for the unjust, by which evil things the good will not be tormented. But He willed that these temporal goods and evils should be common to both, in order that neither those good things which the wicked also are seen to possess may be too eagerly desired, nor those [134] evil things may be sinfully avoided which often fall to the share of the good. But it matters much what use be made both of that which is called prosperity and that which is called adversity. For the just man is neither elated by temporal goods nor oppressed by trials, but the unjust man is chastised by this mode of adversity for the very reason that he deteriorates in prosperity. God often shows His hand in the distribution of these things; for if every sin were to meet with a manifest punishment here, there would seem to be nothing left for the last judgment. Again, if God were to punish openly no single sin, men would deny the existence of Divine Providence. In like manner, as to the good things of this world, if God were not to grant them generously to certain men who ask for them, we should say that these were not His to give; and also, if He were always to give them to those who ask, we should conclude that He was to be served merely for these rewards; nor would a worship in this manner make us good, but rather grasping and avaricious. This being so, when it happens that the good and the wicked are both afflicted together, it does not follow that there is no distinction between them because they have been struck with a common misfortune. Dissimilarity in men who suffer is apparent even in the same suffering, and whereas the torture is identical, there are varieties in strength and weakness. For as under the action of the same fire gold glows and straw burns, and under the same threshing machine chaff is reduced to dust while the grains of wheat come out full and pure, and the weight of the same press separates the oil from the refuse, so one and the same propelling power tries the good, purifies and perfects them, while it condemns the wicked, confounds and exterminates them. Hence [135] under the same sorrow the unrighteous curse God and blaspheme Him, but the righteous invoke and praise Him. The nature of the man, not what he suffers, is the all-important point. For one and the same pressure produces a foul stench from mud and a sweet fragrance from ointment.

[136]
16. DEFICIENCY OF THE EVIL WILL
(*On the City of God*, Bk. 12, ch. 7 and 8)

LET no one seek for the efficient cause of evil will, for it is not efficient, but deficient, because that evil will itself is not an efficiency, but a defect. For to be deficient from that which is highest to that which is lower is to begin to have an evil will. Moreover, to wish to find the causes of these defects, when, as I have said, they are deficient, not efficient, may be compared to a man who would like to see darkness or to hear silence. And yet we are familiar with both, the one through our eyes only, the other through our ears only, not indeed by a representative image, but by the privation of that image. Let no one, therefore, seek to know from me that which I know that I do not know, unless, perhaps, that he may learn to be ignorant of that which we ought to know to be beyond the limit of our knowledge. I mean those things which are known, not by their representative image, but by its privation, if such a thing can be expressed or understood, are in a certain sense known by being unknown, with the condition that this knowledge is ignorance. For when the glance of even the bodily eye ranges over [137] corporeal representative images, it sees darkness nowhere until it begins not to see. In the same way, hearing silence pertains to the ears alone, not to any other sense; this silence, however, is only felt by not hearing. Thus our mind beholds representative images of intellectual things by the act of intelligence, but where these are defective, it gains knowledge as it becomes sensible of ignorance. For *what man understands sins?* This one thing I know; never and nowhere and in no degree can the nature of God be deficient: and things made out of nothing can be deficient. These things, however, in proportion as they possess being and do good things (for then they do something), have efficient causes; but in proportion as they are deficient, and from this do evil things, (for what is their doing then but vanity?), they have deficient causes. I also know that in one with an evil will, that takes place in him which would not take place if he were unwilling; and therefore not necessary but voluntary defects are followed by merited punishment. The defect consists not in following evils, but in doing after an evil manner; it is a defect not to evil natures, but after an evil manner, because it is contrary to the order of nature to decline from that which is in the highest to that which is lower. For neither does the sin of avarice lie in the gold, but in the fact of a man's perverse love of it, by forsaking justice, which ought to be put immeasurably before it. Nor is the sin of luxury to be charged to beautiful and fascinating bodies, but to the soul which perversely loves sensual pleasures by neglecting that temperance which makes us cleave to things possessing the higher beauty of the spirit and the incorruption of immortality. Nor is human praise accountable for the sin of vainglory, but the soul which inanely desires [138] the praise of man against the testimony of conscience. Nor is the sin of pride to be charged to the giver of power, nor to that power itself, but to the soul which has an excessive love of its own power by despising one who has a juster power. So it is that the man who has an inordinate love for whatever sort of natural good it may be, even if he gain it, he himself becomes evil in the possession of a good thing, and wretched by the privation of a greater good.

17. THE LAW FROM MOSES: GRACE AND TRUTH FROM OUR LORD
(*Tractates on the Gospel of John*, 3.19)

PUT forth carnal thoughts from your hearts, that you may truly be under the law of grace and belong to the New Testament. This is why eternal life is promised in the New Testament. Read the Old Testament, and you find that the same commandments were given to the people of Israel, who were still carnal, as to us. We also are commanded to serve one God and not to take the name of the Lord God in vain. The commandment Keep, holy the Sabbath day is even more stringent for us, because we are to keep it holy in a spiritual sense. For the Jews observed the Sabbath day in a servile way by enjoying themselves with wine and luxury. How much better it would have been for Jewish women to spin wool on the Sabbath-day than to indulge in dissolute dances! Far be it from us, brethren, to admit that these people kept the Sabbath. The Christian keeps it in a spiritual way by abstaining from servile work. What is abstaining from servile work? Abstaining from sin. And how do we prove this? Consider our Lord's words, *Every man who commits sin is the servant of sin*. We are admonished then unto the spiritual observance of the Sabbath. All the other precepts of the law are specially impressed upon our observance, i.e., You shall not kill; you shall not commit adultery; you shall not steal; you shall not bear false witness against your

neighbor; honor your father and your mother; you shall not covet your neighbor's wife; and you shall not covet your neighbor's goods. Are not all these commandments, for us also? But look for the reward, and you will find these words in the same Old Testament, *That Ike enemy may be expelled from before your face, and that you may possess the land which God promised to your fathers.* They could not understand invisible things, therefore they were held by visible ones, and why? Lest they should perish entirely and turn to idols. For this they did, my brethren, as we read, oblivious of the great wonders which God had wrought before their eyes. The sea opened; a path was made in the midst of the waves, and the enemies who pursued them were buried in those very waters through which they had passed. When Moses the servant of God had departed from them, they asked for an idol, and said, *Make us gods who may go before us, for that man has left us.* All their hope was in man, not in God. Behold the man died, but was God dead, who had delivered them from the land of Egypt? And when they had made themselves the image of a calf, they adored it, saying, *These are your gods, Israel, who delivered you out of the land of Egypt.* How soon they forgot a grace so manifest! How then was this people to be attracted except by carnal promises? Those same commandments of the law are made also to us, but the promises of the law are not our promises. What is promised to us? Eternal life.
This is eternal life, that they may know You, the one true God, and Him Whom You have sent, Jesus Christ.

The knowledge of God is promised, a grace itself for a
[141] grace. Brethren, we believe now without seeing;
the reward of our faith will be to see what we believe.
The prophets knew this, but before His coming it was
hidden. For a burning lover speaks in the Psalms
when he says, *I have asked one thing of the Lord; this
will I seek for.* Do you ask what he sought for?
Maybe for a land overflowing with milk and honey -
though this land is to be sought and asked for in the
spiritual sense or for the subjection or the death of
his enemies, or for riches and high places in this world:
He is on fire with love, and is sighing, and thirsting,
and groaning much. *One thing I have asked of the
Lord; this will I seek after: that I may dwell in the
house of the Lord all the days of my life. . . .*

My brethren, why do you cry out, and exult, and
love in your hearts, except it be that you have here a
spark of the self-same charity? I ask you what do
you desire? Can it be seen with the eyes or touched
with the hands? Is it a beauty which can delight the
sight? Were not the martyrs an object of intense
love, and when we commemorate them do we not
burn? What do we love in them, brethren? Is it
their limbs torn by wild beasts? What is more
horrible if we consult only human vision? what is
more beautiful to the eyes of the heart? . . . These
are the rewards which are promised to us, my brethren;
set your heart upon one of this kind; sigh after that
kingdom and that home, if you would arrive at that
which Our Lord brings to us at grace and truth. But

if you desire temporal rewards of God, you are still under the law, and for that very reason you will not observe the law; for when you see those who offend God abounding in worldly goods, you stumble, and say to yourself, "Here am I, who am serving God and running every day to church, with knees worn with [142]kneeling, and I am always ill; whereas men who commit robberies and murders rejoice, and abound, and are sound." Were these the things which you asked of God? If so, you certainly did not belong to the dispensation of grace.

If grace be a gift because it was gratuitous on the part of God, love Him for Himself. Do not love Him for a reward; let the reward be Himself. Say in your heart, *One thing have I asked of the Lord; this will I seek after: that I may dwell in the house of the Lord all the days of my life, that I may see the delight of the Lord*. Have no fear of growing weary; that delight will be so great that you will have it always and never be satisfied, or rather you will always be satisfied and never satiated. If I said that you would not be satisfied, I should imply hunger; and if I said that you will be satisfied, I fear the imputation of weariness. I know not how to express that place where there will be neither hunger nor weariness.; but God has a means of speaking to those whom human language fails, who are believers in their reward.

18. GRACE
(Tractates on the Gospel of John, 26.2)

MURMUR not among yourselves. No man can come to Me, except the Father, Who has sent Me, draw him. This is a great commendation of grace. No man comes unless he is drawn. Do not set yourself to criticize whom He draws and whom He does not draw, or why He draws one man and not another, if you would not err. Accept the fact once for all. Have you not yet been drawn? Pray that you may be drawn. What are we saying, brethren? If we are drawn to Christ, then do we believe against our will? Violence, then, is done to us, and our will is not appealed to. A man may enter a church against his will, and he may go to the altar and receive the sacrament in the same way. He cannot believe against his will. If faith were a bodily act, it might be found in men against their will; but it is not a bodily act. Listen to the Apostle: *With the heart we believe and are justified.* And what follows? *With the mouth confession is made unto salvation.* This confession is made from the depths of the heart. Sometimes you hear a man make professions without recognizing him as a believer. Nor should you even call him a professor if you judge that he is no believer. To confess is to give voice to that which is in the heart; but if you think one thing and say another, you are speaking with your lips, not confessing. Since, then, it is the heart which believes in Christ, this being an act which no man accomplishes against his will, one who is drawn seems to be compelled in spite of himself. How are we to solve this difficulty, *No man can come to Me, unless the Father, Who has sent Me, draw him*?

If a man be drawn, someone will say he comes unwillingly. If he comes unwillingly, he does not believe; if he does not believe, he does not come. We do not go to Christ by walking with our legs, but by believing; nor by a bodily movement, but by the will of our hearts. Therefore, the woman who reached for the hem of His garment touched Him more than the crowd who pressed upon Him. Hence Our Lord's words, *Who has touched Me?* The disciples, wondering, said, *The crowd is pressing upon You, and You say, Who has touched Me?* And He repeated, *Someone has touched Me.* The woman touches Him, the crowd presses upon Him. What is touching if not believing? Thus He said to the woman who wished to fall at His feet after the resurrection, *Touch Me not, for I have not yet ascended to the Father.* "You believe Me to be only what you see; touch Me not." What does this mean? "You think that I am no more than I now appear to you; believe not thus." This is implied in the words, *Touch Me not, for I have not yet ascended to the Father.* "I have not ascended for you, but I have never left My Father." Mary Magdalen did not touch the Man on earth; how should she touch Him ascending to the Father? Yet in this sense He did wish to be touched. Thus He is touched by those who relish Him truly, that is, who recognize

Him as ascending to the Father, remaining with the Father, equal to the Father.

Consequently, when you read the words. *No man [145] can come to Me except the Father draw him*, do not think that you are drawn against your will; the soul is drawn by love also. Nor in this passage of Holy Scripture should we fear the possible objection of men who measure words, and are far remote from the comprehension of divine things in particular, when they may urge, "How do I believe with my will if I am drawn?" I answer: It is a small thing to be drawn by your will; you are also drawn by delight. What is being drawn by delight? *Rejoice in the Lord, and He will give you the desires of your heart.* There is a certain joy of heart which gives flavor to that bread from heaven. Indeed, if a poet could say, Each man is drawn by his passion, by his pleasure, not by his necessity; by delight, not by obligation; how much more have we reason to say that the man is drawn to Christ who takes pleasure in truth, in happiness, in justice, in life eternal, all which things Christ is? Or have the bodily senses their particular pleasures and the soul none? If the soul have not its own delights, how are the Psalmist's words to be explained, *The children of men shall put their trust under the cover of Your wings; they shall be inebriated with the plenty of Your house, and You shall make them drink of the torrent of Your pleasure; for with You is the fountain of life, and In Your light we shall see light*? Give me a lover, and he will understand what I say. Give me a man of desires, one who hungers; give me in this desert a pilgrim who is athirst; give me one who is sighing after the eternal fountains he will understand what I say. But if my words fall on cold ears, they will have no sense. Such were they who murmured one to each other. *He whom the Father draws comes to Me,* says the Lord.

[146]
19. INTERIOR STRENGTH
(*On the Lord's Sermon on the Mount,* 13)

WHOEVER seeks the delights of this world and the abundance of temporal goods in the strength of the Christian name should note that our happiness is an interior thing, just as the soul of the Church is thus described by prophetical lips, *All the glory of the King's daughter is from within*; for from without, curses and persecutions and calumnies are promised, of which, however, the reward will be great in heaven; and this reward is felt in the heart of those who thus suffer, of those who can say, *We glory in our tribulations, knowing that tribulation works patience, and patience trial, and trial hope, and hope confounds not: because the charity of God is poured forth in our hearts by the Holy Spirit who is given to us.* To bear these things is not fruitful in itself, but what is fruitful is to bear them for the name of Christ with even more than an equable mind with joy. For many heretics, deceiving souls with the Christian name, constantly suffer similar things, and are cut off from the promised reward; because not only is it said, *Blessed are they who suffer persecution*, but also unto justice. Where the right faith does not exist there can be no justice, because *the just man lives by faith*. Nor may schismatics promise themselves any part of this reward, because, in like manner, justice cannot exist where there is no charity, for love of our neighbor does not work evil. If they had this love, they would not tear asunder the body of Christ, which is the Church.

20. LIGHT AND DARKNESS
   (*Sermon* 49.3)

WE shall see each other's hearts one day, but hereafter: now we are still bearing about us the darkness of this mortality, and we are walking by the light of Scripture, as the Apostle Peter says, *We have the more firm prophetic word, to which you do well to attend, as to a light that shines in a dark place, until the day dawn, and the day star arise in your hearts*. Hence, through this same faith by which we believe in God we are as day compared to unbelievers. While in infidelity, we were, as they are, night, and now we are light according to the Apostle's testimony, *You were once darkness, but are now light in the Lord. Darkness in yourselves, light in the Lord*. Again he says in another place, *You are all children of light and of the day: we are not of the night nor of the darkness. Let us walk honestly as in the day*. We are therefore day as compared with unbelievers. But compared with that day when *the dead shall rise, and this corruption shall put on incorruption, and this mortality shall be clothed with immortality,* we are still the night. The Apostle St. John speaks to us as if we were already in the daylight. *Dearly beloved, we are now the sons of God.* And yet, because it is still night, what follows? *It has not yet appeared what we shall be. We know* [149] *that when He shall appear, we shall be like Him, because we shall see Him as He is.* But this is the reward, not the task. *We shall see Him as He is,* our true reward; then will come a day of unsurpassable brightness. Now therefore in our present day let us walk honestly: in the night which is still upon us let us not judge one another. For consider that the words of the Apostle St. Paul, *Let us walk honestly as in the day,* do not differ from those of his co-Apostle St. Peter, *To which you do well to attend, that is, to the divine Word, as to a light that shines in a dark place, until the day dawn, and the day star arise in your hearts.*

21. FAITH AND WORKS
   (*On the Psalms*, 31. 2)

THE Apostle Paul has testified that this, the 31st Psalm, pertains to that grace by which we are Christians: this is why I wished to propound it to you. In commending the justice which comes of faith against those who glory in the justice which is from works, the

Apostle said this: *What then shall we say that Abraham our father found according to the flesh? For if Abraham is justified by works, he has glory, but not glory unto God* (Rom. 4.1, 2). May God preserve us from this glory, and let us rather hear those other words, *Let him who glories glory in the Lord* (1 Cor. 1.31). Many indeed glory in their works, and you find many pagans who will not become Christians because they seem to rest satisfied with their good life. So a man says, "We must live good lives. What will Christ advise me to do? To live purely? That is what I am doing already. What do I want with Christ? I commit neither murder, nor theft, nor robbery; I do not covet my neighbor's goods; I am not stained with adultery. Now, let anything worthy of reproach be found in my life, and let him who blames me make me a Christian." This man has glory, but not unto God. It was not thus with our father Abraham. These words of Scripture would turn our attention in this direction. Be-
[151] cause we acknowledge - and this is the teaching of our faith concerning the holy Patriarch who pleased God - that we know him to have glory unto God, the Apostle says, *It is certainly known and manifest to us that Abraham has glory unto God: for if Abraham is justified by works, he has glory, but not unto God: he has then glory unto God, and therefore he is not justified by works. If, then, Abraham is not justified by works, by what is he justified?* He goes on to say how. *For what does the Scripture say?* that is, by what does it say that Abraham was justified? *Abraham believed in God, and it was reputed to him unto justice. Abraham*

then was justified by faith.

Now let the man who hears this by faith, not by works, beware of the abyss of which I have spoken. You see that Abraham was justified by faith, not by works, and you say, "Then I will do whatever I please, because even if I have not good works, and merely believe in God, it is reputed to me unto justice." If a man has so spoken, and has acted upon his words, he is lost: if he still hesitate, he is in danger. But the Scripture of God in its true reading not only delivers a perishing man from danger, it also raises up a fallen man from the depths. I answer, then, as if against the Apostle, and say of Abraham that which we find in the Epistle of another Apostle who wished to correct the misinterpreters of St. Paul. For in answer to those who, presuming on faith alone, would not work good works, St. James in his Epistle commended the works of that Abraham whose faith St. Paul had exalted; and there is no diversity in the two Apostles. St. James speaks of the action, familiar to all, of Abraham's offering up his son as a sacrifice to God. This was indeed a great action, but it was prompted by faith. I praise the building up of the work, seeing all the [152] time its foundation - faith. I praise the fruit of a good deed, but I acknowledge faith to have been its root. For if Abraham had done this without genuine faith, his action, whatever it had been, would not have profited him anything. Again, if Abraham's faith had been such that when God commanded him to offer up his son, he had said to himself, "I shall not do this thing, and still I believe that God is my salvation, even though I spurn His commands, a similar faith without works would be a dead faith, a root which, bearing no fruit, would be barren and sterile.

What then? Must we put no works before faith, that is, shall we say no man has done well before arriving at faith? For these very works, as they are called, without faith, although they may appear to men praiseworthy, are of no avail. They seem to me to be like great strength and rapid speed out of bounds. Let no one, therefore, take account of his good works before having faith; where faith was not, neither was there any good work. For the intention makes a good action, and faith directs the intention. Do not make a great matter of what a man does, but of his aim in acting; notice the direction in which he is steering. For supposing that a man who pilots his ship well has lost his course, does it avail him anything to manage her admirably, to govern her movements wisely, to shelter her prow from the waves, and to steer her clear of rocks? His strength may be so great that he can urge his ship forward as he pleases, and yet, supposing he be asked, "Where are you going? and he answer, "I know not, or "I am going to such a port," while in reality he is hastening to destruction.... So it is with the man who is an excellent runner out of the straight path. Would it not then be preferable that our pilot should be less robust, so that he should have some trouble and difficulty in steering, provided that he kept to a straight course; and again, that the man who runs should be slower and less agile, keeping to the right path, than swift outside it? He is, therefore, best who keeps to his course with a good pace; and he comes next who, though he may occasionally stumble, does not quite lose his way, nor remain behind, but walks on by slow degrees; for perchance we may hope that, even late, he may reach his destination.

Therefore, brethren, *Abraham was justified by faith*; for if works did not precede this faith, they certainly followed it. Is your faith to be sterile? If you are not sterile, neither is your faith sterile. If you have believed anything evil, you have burnt up the root of your faith in the flame of your perversity. Hold, then, to the faith with the intention of doing good works. But you object, "This is not what St. Paul says." Indeed he does. He speaks of *faith which works by love*; and in another place, *Love is the fulfillment of the law*; and again, *The whole of the law is fulfilled in one word*, in that which says, *You shall love your neighlour as yourself.* Judge if he does not require you to work when he says, *You shall not commit adultery, you shall not kill, you shall not steal; and if there be any other commandment it is involved in this, You shall love your neighbor as yourself. Love of our neighbor works no evil; for charity is the fulfillment of the law.* Does charity ever allow you to do evil to him whom you love? But perhaps you merely do no evil, but do no good. Then does charity allow you not to do your best for him whom you love? Is not charity that virtue which prays even for its enemies? Does a man forsake his friend, who wishes well to an enemy? Therefore if faith be without charity it will be with-[154] out works. So that, therefore, you should be troubled concerning the works of faith, add to it hope and charity, and be not in difficulty as to what you are to do. Love knows not how to be idle. What is it but love which exerts even a bad influence in any man you please? Give me an idle love which is accomplishing nothing. Does not love bring about crimes, adultery, and murder and every kind of luxuriousness? Purge, therefore, your affections; turn the water, which is running waste, into your garden; let those torrents which were formerly given to the world be devoted to the world's Creator. Are you told to love nothing? God forbid! If you love nothing, you will be idle, dead, miserable, and detestable men. Love, then, but be careful what you love. Love of God and of our neighbor is called charity; love of the world and of these passing things is called lust. Lust is to be restrained and charity is to be enkindled; for the very charity of a good man gives him the hope of a good conscience. A good conscience gives hope: as a bad conscience is full of despair, so a good one is full of hope. There are three of which the Apostle speaks, faith, hope, charity. And in another place he mentions the same three again, but he makes a good conscience stand for hope: The end of the commandment are his words. What is the end? It signifies not the consummation of the commandments, but their perfection. In saying, "I have finished my meal," and "I have finished my garment" (which was being woven), we mean different things. The food is taken so that it is consumed, the garment is finished so that it may be completed, and the end of both is called by the same name. St. Paul, therefore, had here in view the end of the commandment; not an end by which they perish, but an end by which they are perfected, and, without being consummated, are brought to their completion....

22. HE IS OUR GOD
(*On the Psalms*, 55.16)

IN whatever day I shall call upon You, behold I know You are my God. Herein lies great wisdom. He does not say, "I know You are God, but that "*You are my God.*" For He is yours when He comes to your assistance; He is yours when you put no obstacles in His way. Hence the psalm says, *Happy is that people whose God is the Lord.* Whose, then, is He not? He is indeed the Lord of all, but specially the God of those who love Him, and cling to Him, and worship Him. His household is, as it were, composed of a great family, the men redeemed by the most precious blood of His only Son. What has God not given us that we might be His and He ours? But the aliens are far removed from the saints; they are strange sons. Listen to what another psalm says of them. *Lord, rescue me,* David says, from *the hand of my enemies, whose mouth has spoken vanity, and their right hand is the right hand of iniquity.* Consider their prosperity, although it was a temporary prosperity, that is, the pride of life. *Whose sons*, he continues, *are as new plants in their youth; their daughters decked out, adorned round about after the likeness of a temple.* He is describing the happiness of this world, by which men are deceived; for, making [156] great account of it, they neglect to seek for true and eternal happiness. Here is the reason why, instead of being sons of God, they are strange children: *Whose sons are as new plants in their youth; their daughters decked out, adorned round about after the likeness of a temple; their storehouses full, flowing out of this into that; their sheep fruitful in young, abounding in their going forth; their oxen fat: there is no breach of wall, nor passage, nor crying out in their streets.* And what follows? They have called the people happy that has these things. Who is meant by they? *Strange children, whose mouth has spoken vanity.* What do you say? *Happy is that people whose God is the Lord.* He has taken from their midst all those other things which are His gifts, and He has given them Himself. For God gives all those things which the aliens have chronicled; but He gives them to aliens, and to the wicked, and to blasphemers, as *He makes His sun to rise over the good and the bad, and the rain to fall on the just and the unjust.* Sometimes He gives these things to the good, and sometimes not; and so with the wicked also. Still He reserves Himself for the good, but eternal fire for the wicked. There is, then, an evil which He does not give to the good, and there is a good which He does not bestow on unjust men, and there are certain middle things, both good and evil, which He gives to one and the other.

Let us love God, brethren, with purity and innocence. A heart which serves Him for a reward is not pure. What then? Shall we have no reward for serving Him? We shall indeed, but it will be that very God Whom we are serving. He will be our reward, *because we shall see Him as He is.* Consider what this will be. What does Our Lord Jesus Christ say to those who love Him? *He who loves Me keeps [157] My commandments; and My Father loves him who loves Me, and I will love him.* What, then, will You give him, Lord? *I will manifest Myself to him.* This is a small thing if you are not a lover. If you love and desire Him, and are serving Him generously Who redeemed you out of love - for you had not merited it for yourself - if you long for Him when you consider His benefits, and are impatient to possess Him, do not ask Him for anything beyond Himself; He is sufficient for you. However avaricious you may be, He suffices. For if ambition would seek to possess the whole earth, and even heaven, He who made both is greater than these. Take the instance of marriage, and let it illustrate the meaning of serving God with a pure heart. In human marriages, a man who loves his wife for her money does not love her, neither does a wife truly love her husband if she loves him either because he has given her something or been very generous. In riches and in poverty a husband is equally a husband. How many men who have been imprisoned have been all the more loved by their devoted wives. The misfortunes of husbands have tested the virtue of many marriages, in which the wives, lest they should seem to love anything besides their husbands, not only did not forsake them, but clung to them the closer. If, then, an earthly husband is thus loved, and an earthly wife, how is God to be loved, the true and faithful Spouse of our souls, Who is making us fruitful for eternal life, and Who will not have us sterile? Let us therefore so love Him that we may love nothing else; and let us realize in ourselves those words of the psalm which were spoken for us, *In whatever day I shall call upon You, behold I know You are my God*. We call upon Him truly when we do it without self-seeking. Hence what is said of some, that *they did not call* [158] *upon God*. They seemed to themselves to be calling to Him, and they asked Him for earthly inheritances, and for more money, and for long life, and for other temporal things. What does the Scripture say of them? *They did not call upon God*, and what was the result? There have they trembled for fear where there was no fear. Where was there no fear? They were afraid of losing their money or of having something taken out of their house, and, again, of not living for so many years as they had hoped. Indeed, they trembled for fear where there was no fear. Of this kind were the Jews who said, *If we allow Him to live, the Romans will come and take away from us our place and people*. They trembled for fear where there was no fear. *Behold, I know that You are my God.* In these words are great riches of heart, sure light in the eye of the soul, and unfailing hope. *Behold, I know that You are my God!*

[159]
23. THE OLD TESTAMENT THE FIGURE OF THE NEW
(*On the Psalms*, 72.3)

UNDER the Old Testament, brethren, the promises of Our God to the carnal Jewish people concerned earthly and temporal things. An earthly kingdom was promised, that promised land into which the people who had been delivered from Egypt were indeed led. They were introduced by Joshua into the land of promise, where the earthly Jerusalem was built and where David reigned. The people delivered out of Egypt took possession of it, passing through the Red Sea. After the fears and anguish of the desert were over, they received a promised land and a kingdom; and later on, because these their gifts belonged to the earth, they began by reason of their sins to meet with opposition, to be driven out and taken captive, and at last the city itself was overthrown. Such were the promises which were not to prove stable, but were yet to foreshadow those other promises of the times to come which should remain, that the whole course of those temporal promises should be a figure, and as it were a prophecy of the future....

And consider now briefly that which was a figure of ourselves. The people of Israel were under the dominion of Pharaoh and the Egyptians; the Christian people, [160] before the faith, were already predestined to God's service, and still were given up to devils and to Lucifer, their prince. Here was a people enslaved to the Egyptians and to their sins, for it is only through our sins that the devil can have dominion. The people of Israel is delivered by Moses from the Egyptians; the other is delivered from their past life of sins by Our Lord Jesus Christ. The one passes through the Red Sea, the other passes by baptism. All the enemies of the former perish in the Red Sea; all our sins are destroyed in baptism. Mark this, brethren, the land of promise is not given immediately after the Red Sea, nor is the triumph at once complete, as if enemies were no more; the solitude of the desert still remains, and the wayside enemies: so after baptism the Christian life is carried on in temptation. In that desert of old they sighed after the promised land; what else do Christians long for when they are cleansed by baptism? Do they already reign with Christ? We have not yet come to our promised land; but it is not a transitory promised land, for there the praises of David shall not fail. So may all the faithful hear these things and realize where they are: they are in the desert, sighing after the promised land. . . . Whatever that people suffered there in the desert, brethren, and whatever God bestowed upon them, both their punishments and their gifts are signs of the things which we, who are walking with

Christ, and seeking our true land in the solitude of this life, receive for our consolation and suffer for our good. It is not, therefore, wonderful if that which was a figure of the future passed away. For the people were taken into the promised land. Was it to last forever? If this had been so, it would not have been a figure, but a reality. Because it *was* a figure that [161] people were led to a temporal thing. And if this was a temporal thing, then it was bound to fail, so that in its passing away they might be forced to seek that which does not pass away.

The Synagogue, then, that is, those who sincerely worshiped God in it, but for temporal and present things - there are impious men who seek temporal goods of the demons - was therefore better than the Gentiles, inasmuch as though, seeking temporal and passing goods, it sought them of the one God, Who is the Creator of all, both in the spiritual and the physical order. Consequently those pious men, that is, that Synagogue which was based on men who were naturally good, not spiritual men, as were the prophets and the small number of those who apprehended the eternal kingdom of heaven, had expectations according to the flesh. That Synagogue recognized what it had received from God, and what God had promised to the Jewish people - an abundance of worldly goods, country, peace, an earthly happiness. But all these things were figures. Not understanding what was hidden in them, the Synagogue imagined that God gave those goods as great gifts, and that He could not give better things to those who love and serve Him. They looked and saw certain sinners, impious men, blasphemers, sons and slaves of the evil one, living in great sin and pride, and abounding in these earthly and temporal goods, for which goods the Jews themselves served God. A wicked thought arose in their hearts which made their feet totter and nearly slip away from God. This was the mind of the people of the Old Testament. Would that it may not be that of our carnal brethren, now that the delights of the New Testament are openly preached. For what did the Synagogue say of old? What said that people? "We serve God, and we are [162] chastised and scourged; those things which we love, and which we have received as great gifts from God, are taken away from us; whereas the most wicked of men, who are proud, intolerant, and blasphemers, abound in all those things for which we are serving God. We see no use in serving Him." This is the sense of the psalm and the mind of a failing and irresolute people. In considering the wealth of temporal blessings enjoyed by those who did not serve God, and for which they themselves did serve Him, they were shaken almost to falling and failed with their song of praise; for such hearts as these ceased to give thanks. What does this signify? That they were full of worldly things, and did not praise God. For how should they praise Him when He seemed to them as it were perverse, bestowing so much happiness on the wicked and taking it away from His servants? God did not appear to them to be good. He was not praised by those who looked upon Him in this light, and hymns ceased in those by whom God was not praised. Later on, indeed, this people understood what it was God admonished them to seek in taking away these temporal things from His servants and bestowing them upon His enemies, blasphemers and impious men. Being enlightened, they understood that above all things which God gives both to the good and the wicked alike, or withdraws, there is one thing which He reserves for the good. What do we mean by reserving something for the good? What is it which He reserves? It is Himself.

24. THE JUST REJOICE IN GOD
(On the Psalms 32, 1)*

THE unjust rejoice in this world, and their exultation will finish with it. But let the just rejoice in the Lord, because, as He endures for ever, so will their joy. Rejoicing in the Lord, we must praise Him, Who alone cannot displease us; and no one is in so many ways displeasing to unrighteous men. This counsel is short. He pleases God whom God pleases. Do not look upon this as a slight thing, for you see how many fight against God, and to how many His works are distasteful. When He wills to cross the will of man, because He is the Lord and He knows what He does, seeking rather our good than our inclination, men who prefer the accomplishment of their own will to that of God desire to bend His will to theirs, not theirs to His.

Such men, unfaithful, impious, unrighteous (which it is grievous to say, but I will say it, for you know how true it is), naturally take more delight in foolish amusement than in God!

But because we cannot exult in Him unless we praise Him, and we praise Him Whom we please in proportion as He is pleasing to us, after the words, *Rejoice, you just, in the Lord*, the Psalmist says, *Praise is fitting for the righteous*. Who are the righteous? They who conform their heart to the will of God. If human [164] frailty disquiets them, divine justice strengthens them. Should they even have their human desires, according to the nature of any present business or necessity, when they have once understood and realized that God wills something else, they put the will of the One Who is greater than they before their own, the will of the Almighty before a weak will, the will of God before the will of man. For the will of God is as far above the will of man as God Himself is removed from man. Thus, when Christ became man, and proposed Himself to us as an example, teaching us how to live, and being Himself our help, He gave proof of a certain human will in which He showed forth both His own will and ours; for He is our Head, and we belong to Him, as you know, like members. *Father*, He said, *if possible, let this chalice pass away from Me*. This was a human will, wishing for something in particular which was, as it were, personal to Himself. But because He willed man to be simple of heart, He added the words, *Not as I will, but as You will, Father*, that He might turn man in any possible perversity which might be in him to that One who is ever righteous. But could Christ have an evil desire? What, in short, could He desire which the Father did not desire? Where there is unity of Godhead there cannot be dissimilarity in evil. But in the person of man, transforming His own into Himself, whom He had transformed, as His words show, *I was hungry and you gave me to eat*; and again, whom He had transformed, as shown when He cried out from on high to Saul as he was persecuting the saints, *Saul, Saul, why do you persecute Me?* when no man had laid hands upon Him, He showed a certain human will. He showed you yourself and corrected you. "Behold yourself in Me," He says. Human frailty is allowed [165] sometimes to have some personal wish in which God wills otherwise. It would be difficult for you never to have any personal wish; but lift up your eyes at once to Him Who is over you. You are subject to Him and He is above you; He is the Creator and you are a creature; He is the Lord and you are the servant; He is the Almighty and you are a weak man. He corrects you and unites you to His will by the words, *Not what I will, but what You will, Father.* How are you separated from God when you will what He wills? Therefore you will be righteous, and praise will become you, because praise becomes the righteous.

But if you are unrighteous, you praise God when things go well with you, and you blaspheme Him when things go ill (which ill, indeed, if just, is not an evil, and it is just because it comes from Him who can do nothing unjust); and you will be a foolish son in the paternal house, loving your Father when He flatters you and hating Him when He chastises, as if both by prosperity and adversity He were not preparing you an inheritance. But see how praise becomes the righteous. Listen to the words of a true praiser in another psalm: *I will praise the Lord at all times; His praise is always in my mouth.* At all times and always mean the same, and so I will bless and His praise is in my mouth. At all times and always, in prosperity or adversity; for if it be only in prosperity and not in adversity, how can it signify *always*? We have heard an abundant voice of praise from many men at some happy bit of good fortune befalling them, when they rejoice and bless and magnify God. They are not, therefore, to be blamed; but we should share their joy, for multitudes do not even thank Him for their good things. They who have already praised God in their prosperity are to be taught to recognize their Father when He chastises, and not to murmur against that rebuking Hand, lest, remaining in their evil mind, they should lose their inheritance. Having been made righteous (what does righteous mean? that no one of God's works should displease them), let them praise God in adversity and say, *The Lord has given, the Lord has taken away; as it pleased the Lord, so it has been done: may His name be praised.* Praise becomes those who are thus righteous, not those who praise first and curse afterwards.

25. ONE IS TAKEN, ONE IS LEFT
(*On the Psalms*, 36.2 and *On the Gospel of Luke*, 2.44)

ONE shall be taken and one shall be left. The good man shall be taken, the bad man shall be left. *Two are seen in the field*; the occupation is identical, but not the heart. Men see the state, God knows the heart. Whatever then the field may signify, *one shall be taken, and one shall be left.* It is not as if one half were to be taken, the other half left; but in these words He tells us of two classes of men. Although one class may be rare and the other may be common, still one will be taken and one will be left; that is, one class will be taken and one will be left. And it is the same with regard to the bed and to the mill. Perhaps you are wondering what these things may mean. You see that they are obscure, and that they are clothed in allegory. It may strike me in one way, and another man in some other; but I neither force my interpretation as mine upon him, nor he upon me for our mutual acceptance, if each be in accordance with the faith. They who govern churches seem to me to be laboring in the field, as the Apostle says, *You are God's garden; you are God's building.* For he calls himself both architect and farmer, saying, *As a wise architect I have laid the foundation*, and again, *I have planted, Apollos watered, but God gave the increase.* Two women, not two mills, are spoken of. This figure I view as applying to the people, because rulers govern and people are governed. I think the mill signifies the world, which turns on the wheel of time, so to speak, and grinds those who love it. Thus, there are those who take part in the duties of this world, but here again some are good and some are evil: some make to themselves friends of the mammon of iniquity, by whom they may be received into the eternal dwelling-places and to these are addressed the words, *I was hungry, and you gave Me to eat*; others neglect similar duties, and to them the same Gospel says, *I was hungry, and you gave Me nothing to eat.* Therefore, as some who are engaged in the business and cares of this world love to do good to the needy, while others neglect them altogether, it is with them as with the two women at the mill one will be taken and one will be left. But I think the bed signifies repose, for there are those who neither take their part in the duties of the world, which are marriage and the care of a house and wife and children, nor work anything in the Church as do rulers who labor after the fashion of farmers; as if incapable of these things, they sit idle and love their quiet, mindful, as it were, of their weakness, not venturing upon great actions, and praying to God from a sort of bed of infirmity. This class too has its good men and its false men; for here again one shall be taken and one shall be left. Whatsoever may be the state which you embrace, be prepared to suffer false brethren; for if you are not prepared, you will find what you did not look for, and you will either break down, or be perturbed in mind. He prepares you for every emergency Who speaks to you now when it is the hour both for Him

[169] to speak and for you to hear, and not yet that of judgment or of fruitless penance; for penance is not now in vain, but it will be then. It is not that men will not be sorry in that day for having led evil lives, but the justice of God will refuse to give them back that which they have lost through their own injustice.
... Who are in that night *the two in one bed*, and *the two women grinding together*, and *the two men in the field*? In the case of all these couples, one is to be taken and one is to be left. Three classes of men seem to be here signified. In the first, it is they who choose leisure and quiet, and have to do neither with worldly nor with ecclesiastical affairs, which rest of theirs is implied by the figure of the bed. The next points to those who, forming part of the people, are governed by the more learned, and do the works of this world; these our Lord expressed by the female sex, because, as I say, it is good for them to be led by counsel, and He speaks of them as grinding on account of the wide domain involved in temporal affairs, and grinding together, in so far as they allow their private affairs and business to serve the needs of the Church. The third signifies those who are engaged in the ministry of the Church, as if in the field of the Lord, of which husbandry the Apostle speaks. Each of these three classes, therefore, contains two kinds of men, who are discerned by their fortitude.

For whereas all appear outwardly to be members of the Church, some endure and some fall, both of those who are enjoying leisure and of those who are engaged in worldly affairs, as also of those who are ministering to God in the Church, when affliction comes to try them: those who remain are taken, those who fall are left. Therefore *one shall be taken and one shall be left* is said not as of two men, but of two classes of [170] minds in each of the three avocations. He spoke of that night, meaning that tribulation.

I think the names of those three holy men, Noah, Daniel, and Job, the only three of whom the Prophet Ezechiel says that they are to be delivered, belong also to those same three classes. For Noah seems to be one of those by whom the Church is governed, as he it was who directed the ark on the waters, which was a figure of the Church. Daniel, however, who chose an angelic life, in despising earthly nuptials, that, as the Apostle says, he might live without solicitude, in the constant thought of the things of God, signifies the class of those who are at leisure, but who are still most strong in temptation, so that they may be taken. Job, who had a wife and children and a great abundance of worldly goods, belongs to that class whose work it is to grind, and still to prove themselves most valiant under temptation, as Job was; because otherwise they could not be taken. Nor do I think, among the men who make up the Church, that there are other classes than these, each with its two kinds of men who fall under the taking or the leaving. Although there is an immense diversity of aim and will in individuals, they may be found equally tending to peace and unity.

26. THE MOTHER AND THE BROTHERS OF OUR LORD
(*Tractates on the Gospel of John*, 10.2)

AFTER this He went down to Capharnaum, the Gospel says, He, and His mother, and His brethren, and His disciples; *and they remained there not many days.* Behold, He has a mother, and brethren, and also disciples. He has brethren as He has a mother. For our Scripture is accustomed to call brethren not only those who are born of the same husband and wife, or of the same mother, or of the same father, even by several wives, but likewise cousins on the side of the father or of the mother who stand in the same grade of relationship. The Scripture does not restrict the title of brother to the first of these.

We must understand its manner of speaking. It has its own language; and if a man is ignorant of this, he is disquieted, and says, "How could Our Lord have brothers?" Had Mary more than one child? Most certainly not. In her the dignity of virginity began. She might be a mother, but she could not cease to be a virgin, for she is called a woman because of her sex, not because her virginity was ever sullied, and this is the language of the Scripture itself. For you know that Eve, as soon as she was drawn from her husband's side, before she became his wife, was called a [172] woman; *and He made her into a woman.* Who, then, are the brethren? Mary's kinsmen, of whatever degree, were Our Lord's brethren. How do we prove this? From the Scripture itself. Lot was called Abraham's brother, as the son of his brother. Read and you will see that Abraham was Lot's uncle, and they were called brothers. Why, unless it was that they were kinsmen? Again, Laban the Syrian was maternal uncle to Jacob, for Laban was brother to Jacob's mother, that is, to Rebecca, Isaac's wife. Read the Scripture and you will find that a maternal uncle and a sister's son are called brethren. Having taken cognisance of this usage, you will see that all Mary's kinsmen are brethren of Our Lord.

But the disciples were more particularly brethren, for those kinsmen of Our Lord's would not have been brethren if they had not been disciples; there would have been no meaning in their being brethren if they had not recognized their Master as a brother. For at a certain place, when it was told Him that His mother and brethren were waiting outside, and He was talking with His disciples, He said, *Who is My mother, and who are My brethren? And raising His hand over His disciples, He said, These are My brethren.* And *whoever shall do the will of My Father is My mother and brother and sister.* Hence Mary was His mother, for she had done the will of the Father. This was what the Lord praised in her; not that, being flesh, she had brought forth flesh, but that she had accomplished the will of the Father. . . . Therefore when Our Lord showed His power in the crowd, doing signs and wonders, certain persons said in their astonishment, *Blessed is the womb which bore You.* And His answer was, *Yes, rather blessed are they who hear the word of God and keep it*, which was to say, My [173] mother, whom you call blessed, was blessed because she kept the word of God; not because the Word was made flesh in her and dwelt amongst us, but because she kept that Word of God by whom she was made, and which was made flesh in her. Let not men rejoice over human births; let them be glad if they are united in spirit to God. . . .

[174]
27. THE VINEYARD AND THE LABORERS
   (*Sermon* 87.6-9)

IN that reward of eternal life we shall therefore all be equal, when, as it were, *the first will be last and the last will be first*; for that penny of the Lord of the vineyard is eternal life, and in eternal life all will be equal. Although some will shine more and some less, according to their degree of merit, still, as far as eternal life is concerned, it will be the same for all. That which is to last for ever will not be longer for one and shorter for another; that which has no end will not end for either you or me. Conjugal chastity will have one reward in eternity, virginal purity another; and so will the fruits of good works be distinct from the martyr's crown. One thing will be rewarded in one way, and another in another; still, with regard to eternal life itself, one man will not live longer in it than another. They all live equally for ever, each one living with a personal glorification, and the great reward is eternal life. Let him who comes to it after a long time not murmur against him who receives it after a short time. It is given to each, but the same thing is given to both.

Except for the solution of this parable, by which we understand Abel and the just of his age to be called in the first hour, Abraham and the just of his day in the [175] second, Moses and Aaron and the just of their times in the sixth, the prophets and just of their age in the ninth, and all Christians in the eleventh, which marks, as it were, the end of time; except, I say, for this interpretation of the parable, our life on earth offers something similar to it. They who, as soon as they are born, begin to be Christians, are, as it were, called in the first hour; and, carrying on the similarity, children may be likened to those hired at the third hour, young people to the sixth, elderly persons to the ninth, while they who are quite worn out by years belong to the eleventh hour. Still all are to receive the same reward of eternal life.

But listen, my brethren, and understand the meaning of this, lest anyone should put off coming to the vineyard because he is confident that whenever he comes he is quite certain to receive the reward. He has indeed the certainty that the reward is promised to him, but he is not exhorted to delay. For when the lord of the vineyard went out in order to bring in those whom he found at the third hour, did they say to him, for instance, "Wait a little, we are not going there till the sixth hour"? Or did those whom he found at the sixth hour say, "We are not going till the ninth hour"? Or did those whom he found at the ninth answer him by saying, "We are not going till the eleventh? He means to give the same thing to all; why then should we have needless fatigue"? What He means to give and to do is His own secret. As to you, come when you are called. The same reward is promised to all, but the particular hour of labor is a great mystery. If they, for instance, who are called at the sixth hour, being in that phase of the body when youthful veins are full of life and fire, were to say, " Wait a little; for we have heard in the Gospel that [176] one reward awaits us all, and when we are grown old we will come at the eleventh hour. If we are to be rewarded at last, why should we labor more than is necessary"? they would be answered in this way, "Do you refuse to labor when you know not whether you will live to grow old? If you are called at the sixth hour, obey the call. The householder did certainly promise the laborer who came even at the eleventh hour a reward, but no one promised that you should live up to the seventh." I say not, till the eleventh; I say, till the seventh. Why then do you put off listening to Him who is calling you? for certain as you may be of the reward, you are uncertain of the day. See that by your delay you do not deprive yourself of that which He promises to give you. If it be true to say this of infants, who belong, as it were, to the first hour, of children, as typifying the third hour, and of young people who are in the fire and heat of the sixth hour, how much truer it is to say of those who are broken down by years, "See, now it is the eleventh hour, and still you tarry, and are slothful to come to the vineyard." Possibly the Householder did not go out to call you. If He did not, what are we saying? For we are servants belonging to His family, and we are sent to bring laborers to the vineyard. Why, then, do you delay? You have run through your course of years; hasten to possess yourself of the penny. The going forth of the Householder is His becoming known, be cause he who is in His house is hidden, and is not seen by those outside. When he goes out of His house, he is seen by those outside. Christ is hidden when He is not understood or recognized; when He goes out to seek for laborers He is recognized. From being hidden He has come forth before the eyes of men. Christ is known; Christ is everywhere preached; all things [177] under heaven proclaim His glory. He was in some sort an object of contempt and reproach to the Jews. He appeared in His lowliness and was despised; for He was hiding His majesty and bearing the appearance of infirmity. This appearance in Him was despised, nor was that which was hidden in Him recognized. For if they had known it, they would never have crucified the Lord of Glory. Is He to be still despised Who sits in heaven, because He was despised as He hung on the tree? They who crucified Him shook their heads, and standing before His cross as if they were now in possession of the fruits of their cruelty, they said in a mocking tone, *If He be the Son of God, let Him get down from the cross. He saved others, can He not save Himself?* "Let Him get down from the cross and we will believe in Him." He did not get down because His Godhead was hidden. For He could easily have descended from the cross Who rose from the grave. He showed forth His patience for our instruction, and delayed the manifestation of His power, and He was not recognized. It was not then that He went forth to look for laborers, because He did not manifest Himself. *On the third day He rose again and showed Himself to His disciples.* Then He ascended into heaven, and sent down the Holy Spirit on the fiftieth day after His resurrection and the tenth after His ascension. The Holy Spirit thus sent filled all those who formed part of that one assembly, one hundred and twenty men. They, being filled with the Holy Spirit, began to speak the languages of all peoples; the vocation was expressed in words - the Lord of the vineyard had gone forth; for the power of the truth began to be manifested to all. Then even one man who had received the Holy Spirit spoke the languages of all nations. But now in the Church unity itself, like one man, speaks the tongues of every people. Where is the nationality which the Christian religion has not reached? To what extremity of the earth has it not been carried? There is no one that can hide himself from its heat; and still he who has reached the eleventh hour delays to answer the call.

28. LEAVING OUR GIFT AT THE ALTAR
(*On the Lord's Sermon on the Mount*, Bk. 1.26)

IF therefore you offer your gift at the altar, and there you remember that your brother has anything against you, leave there your offering before the altar, and go first to be reconciled to your brother; and then coming, you shall offer your gift. . . . We are told, then, that when we are about to offer a gift at the altar, if we remember anything which our brother may have against us, we should leave our gift before the altar and go and be reconciled to our brother, and then coming back, offer our gift. If this be taken in a literal sense, a man may consider himself so bound if his brother is on the spot; for as you are commanded to leave your gift before the altar, a longer delay would be impossible. But if the case be supposed as applying to a brother who is absent, or even beyond the seas, it is absurd to imagine that the gift is to be left before the altar and offered to God after you have traveled over land and sea. Therefore we are constrained to penetrate into the spiritual meaning of this passage, that a rational construction may be put upon it.

We may therefore accept the altar in a spiritual sense in the hidden sanctuary of God to signify our faith itself, of which the visible altar is the sign. For whatever gift we offer to God, be it prophecy, or theological learning, or prayer, or hymns, or psalms, [180] or any other spiritual gift which is in the soul, it can not be acceptable to God unless it be based on a sincere faith, and placed securely on this foundation, as on an altar, that the gift may correspond to our words in purity and integrity. Many heretics, not having an altar, that is, the true faith, have spoken blasphemies for the voice of praise, by which I mean that, swayed by human opinion, they have, as it were, poured their gift upon the ground. But the man who offers a gift should have purity even of intention. And therefore when we are about to make an offering of this kind in our hearts, that is, in God's secret sanctuary, as the Apostle says, *For the temple of God is holy, which you are, and Christ dwells by faith in your hearts*, if we should remember that our brother have anything against us, if, that is, we have offended him in anything, in which case we are in his debt, as he is in ours if he should have offended us, and if so, there is no need of proceeding to a reconciliation, for you do not ask pardon of the man who has done you an injury. You merely forgive him as you hope God will forgive you your offenses against Him. We must seek to be reconciled if we should chance to remember that we have in any way wounded our brother; but this reconciliation is effected by a movement of soul, not of body, by a humble disposition of mind towards your brother whom you seek out in spirit by a kind thought in the sight of Him to whom you are to offer your gift. In this way, should he be on the spot, you can do your best to soften him, and to make him relent by asking his pardon, if you first pray to God about it, going out to him, not by a slow movement of body, but by the swift wings of the heart, and coming back, that is, recalling your mind to what you were about, you can offer your gift. . . .

29. CURING OF THE TEN LEPERS
(Questions on the Gospel, Bk. 2.40)

IN the matter of the ten lepers whom the Lord cleansed when He said, *Go, show yourselves to the priests*, many questions may be asked which are of real interest to the inquirers. Not only do we ask ourselves what their being ten signified, and why only one of the number returned thanks - this is a detail which, even if it be not examined, does not materially affect the reader's mind, or slightly; but why rather did Our Lord send them to the priests, that in going they might be cleansed?

We find that, out of all those whom He cured, He sent none to the priests except only the lepers; for He had cleansed also the man to whom He said, *Go, show yourself to the priests, and offer for yourself the sacrifice commanded by Moses as a testimony unto them.* Then, again, how are we to understand the spiritual cleansing of men whom He reproached for their in gratitude? It is easy indeed to see that a man may be without bodily leprosy and yet that he may not be good, but, according to the sense of this miracle, it is puzzling to understand how an ungrateful man can be called clean.

We must try, then, to find out what the leprosy itself signifies. They who were without it are called clean, not sound. Leprosy is a defect in color, not [182] an organic ailment or a failure in the power of senses or members. It is not, therefore, beside the mark to understand by lepers those who, not having the knowledge of the true faith, hold various doctrines of error. They do not hide their ignorance, but bring it forth to the light as the greatest cleverness, and boast about it in their speech. There is not one single false doctrine which has not in it something of truth. True doctrine, therefore, which is confused with an undue amount of false doctrines in the mouth of one man, like that which becomes apparent on the human body by color, signifies leprosy, a leprosy composed, as it were, of healthy and unhealthy dyes, spots, and stains; mortal bodies with various hues of color. These men are to be so shunned by the Church that, if possible, they should cry out at a great distance with a loud voice to Christ, as did these ten in the Gospel, who stood afar off, and lifted up their voice saying, *Jesus, Master, have mercy on us.* Their calling Him Master, a name which, as far as I know, no man in search of physical health ever addressed Him by, is, I think, a sufficient proof that leprosy signified false doctrine, which our Divine Master destroyed.

As to the priesthood of the Jews, scarcely one of the faithful doubts that it was a figure of the future regal priesthood which is in the Church. By it all who belong to the body of Christ, who is the true and supreme Prince of priests, are consecrated; for all are now anointed, which only kings and priests then were; and when Peter, in writing to the Christian people, uses the words kingly priesthood, he declared that both names were suitable for the people to whom that anointing belonged. God then checks and cures those vices which may be likened to diseases of the body, and to organic failure in sense or member, by speaking [183] in the secret depths of the heart and conscience. But that doctrine which is either infused through the sacraments or taught by sermon or book, which doctrine has the semblance of a perfect harmony of color, as it strikes the eye and is evident to all (for its effects are not in hidden thoughts, but in manifest works), is entrusted to the Church as her peculiar province. Thus when St. Paul heard the Lord's voice saying, *Why are you persecuting Me?* and again, *I am Jesus, Whom you are persecuting*, he was still sent to Ananias, that by that priesthood which is set up in the Church he might grasp the mystery of faith's teaching, and receive himself the true color which should make him acceptable. It is not that the Lord is unable to do all things by Himself? For who else, if not He, does these things even in the Church, except in order that the society itself of all the faithful gathered together, by approving each other and exchanging the doctrine of the true faith, in everything spoken by word or shown forth by mysteries, may bear, as it were, one appearance of healthy color?

To this also pertains to what the same Apostle says: *Then after fourteen years I went up again to Jerusalem with Barnabas, taking Titus also with me. And I went up according to revelation, and communicated to them the gospel which I preach among the Gentiles, but alone with them who seemed to be something: lest perhaps I should run or had run in vain.* And a little farther on: *And when they had known the grace that was given to me, James, and Cephas, and John, who seemed to be pillars, gave to me and Barnabas the right hand of fellowship.* This very union pointed out doctrine to be of one kind, without any variance whatsoever; and he admonishes the Corinthians also in the same sense, saying, *I beseech you, brethren, by the name of Our Lord Jesus Christ, that you all agree in what you say.* Again, when Cornelius is told by an angel that his alms are accepted and his prayers heard, he is ordered to send for Peter for the sake of unity in doctrine and sacraments, as if the words, *Go, show yourselves to the priests* had been said for him and for those like himself; for *as they went they were cleansed.* Peter had already come to them; but as they had not then received the sacrament of baptism, they had not reached the priests in a spiritual sense, yet still by the infusion of the Holy Spirit and their wonder at the Apostle's gift of tongues, their cleansing was manifested. This being the case, it is easy also to conceive it possible that a man in the communion of the Church, holding pure and true doctrine, confessing by his lips the whole scheme of the Catholic faith, and discerning the creature from the Creator, may thus prove himself free from the errors of disunity, from leprosy, as it were, and still he may be ungrateful to the Lord God his cleanser. He may be puffed up with pride, and not condescend to give thanks in prostrate humility, and he becomes like those of whom the Apostle speaks, *Because even though they knew God they have not glorified Him as God, or given thanks.* In saying that they knew God, he shows indeed that they had been cleansed of their leprosy, but at once accuses them of ingratitude. Thus such men will belong to the [other] nine, being, as it were, imperfect. By the addition of one to nine a sort of type of unity is attained; so great is the completeness of ten, that numbers only progress from it by again returning to one, and this rule is carried out through every complication of numbers. Therefore the number nine requires one more to give it a certain form of unity which ten has; but one by itself is a unity which does not require the [185] nine. Just as the nine who did not return thanks becoming wicked, were excluded from the bosom of unity, so the one who did give thanks was praised as signifying the one and only Church. And because those men were Jews, they are declared to have lost through pride the kingdom of heaven, where unity is most kept. He who returned thanks was a Samaritan, which is interpreted *a keeper*. Rendering to the Giver that which he had received, he seemed to repeat the Psalmist's words, *I will keep my strength to You*; subjecting himself to the King through thanksgiving, he preserved the unity of the kingdom by his humble devotedness.

30. CHARITY THE FULFILLMENT OF THE LAW
(*On the Epistles of John, 7*)

THIS, if you remember, is what I begged you to observe when we began to read this first Epistle of St. John, that he exhorts us before all things to charity. And if he seems to speak of other things, he goes back to charity, and he would refer everything he says to this same charity. Let us see if he does this in the passage before us, *Whoever is born of God does not commit sin.* We ask what sin, because if every kind of sin be meant, this passage will contradict those other words of St. John, *If we say that we have no sin, we deceive ourselves and the truth is not in us.* Let us ask, then, what sin he has here in view; let him instruct us, for fear I should say without sufficient grounds that sin signifies a violation of charity, because of his words a little before, *He that hates his brother is in darkness, and walks in darkness, and knows not where he goes because the darkness has blinded his eyes.* But perhaps he made some allusion to charity in his later words. Consider how what he then said leads up to charity and ends with it, *Whoever is born of God does not commit sin, for His seed abides in him.* The seed of God is the Word of God, hence the Apostle says, *For by the Gospel I have begotten you.* And he cannot sin because he is born of God. Well, let us see in what he cannot sin. *In this the children of God are manifest and the children of the devil. Whosoever is not just is not of God, nor he that loves not his* brother. . . . Therefore charity alone distinguishes the children of God from the children of the devil. All men may sign themselves with the sign of the cross, they may answer Amen to our prayers, and may echo our Alleluia; they may all be baptized, and frequent the church, and go the round of the basilicas; the distinctive mark of the children of God as opposed to the children of the devil is charity alone. *They who have charity are born of God*; they who have it not are not born of God. This is a great and infallible sign. You may have whatsoever you please, and if you have this not it profits you nothing; other things you may not have, but if you have charity you have fulfilled the law. *For he who loves his neighbor has fulfilled the law*, the Apostle says, and again, *Love is the fulfillment of the law*. I take this to be that pearl of great price which the merchant in the Gospel is spoken of as having sought, and, finding it, he sold all that he possessed and bought it. Love is the costly pearl, without which all that you may have besides is of no avail; with it alone you have sufficient. Now you see by faith, one day you will see in reality. For if we love while we do not see, what will be our transport when we do see? But how are we to practice charity? By brotherly love. You may tell me that you cannot see God, but you will never be able to tell me that you do not see man. Love your neighbor, for if you love your brother whom you see, in loving him you will see God, because you will thus see charity itself, and God dwells in the inner man.

31. NO LIFE WITHOUT ITS BURDENS
   (*Sermon* 164.4)

THE burdens which each man has to bear are his sins. It is to them who are weighed down by this grievous load that the Lord says, *Come unto Me, all you who labor and are burdened, and I will refresh you.* How does He refresh men who are laden with sin if not by His mercy? He who framed the world, looking down, as it were, from His loftiness, exclaims, "Listen, O human race, O sons of Adam, laborious and unfruitful people; I see your labors, and do you look at My gift. I know that you labor and are burdened, and, what is more distressing, that you load yourselves with evil burdens; that you petition to have further burdens of the same kind, not to be relieved of them, which is worse."

Which of us is able in a short time to go into the multiplicity and variety of these burdens? Still, let us give a few instances of them, and from these draw our conclusions as to the rest. Look at the man who is weighed down with the burden of avarice, how he sweats and pants and toils and thirsts in adding to his burden. What are you looking for, O miser, as you grasp your burden, and fasten its evil weight to your shoulders with the chains of lustful desires? What do you expect? Why do you labor and gasp and lust? You want to satisfy your avarice. Oh, vain desires [189] and most evil result. Do you expect, then, to satisfy your avarice? It may weigh you down, but you cannot satisfy it. ... And perhaps you are bearing together with this the burden of sloth, and the opposite claims of the two are tearing you to pieces. Sloth says, "Sleep on;" Avarice says, "Get up." Sloth says, "Keep out of the cold;" Avarice says, "Go through even storms at sea." The one says "rest"; the other will leave a man no rest. . . .

How many are bearing burdens of this kind! How many are even now exclaiming at me for speaking against those burdens which are weighing them down! They came in here with their burdens, and they go out with them; they came in misers and they go out misers. I have labored against these burdens. . . . I do not ask you to hear my words; listen to your King saying, *Come to Me, all you who labor and are burdened.* You do not come to Me unless you cease from your labor. You wish to come to Me, but your grievous burdens hold you fast. *Come unto Me, all you who labor and are burdened, and I will refresh you.* I offer pardon for past sins; I will take the dust from your eyes and the heavy burden from your shoulders. I will indeed remove your burdens, but I do not promise to free you from all burdens. I will take the evil ones and put good ones in their places. For after the words, *And I will refresh you*, He added, *Take My yoke upon you*. Lust had conquered you for evil, let love conquer you for good.

Take My yoke upon you and learn of Me. If human teaching of whatever kind has disgusted you, learn of

Me. These are the words of Christ our Master, the only Son of God, the only truth. He says, *Learn of Me*. What? That *the Word was in the beginning, and the Word was with God, and the Word was God, and all things were made by Him*. Can we learn of Him [190] to make the world, to fill the heavens with light, to regulate the course of day and night, to direct the progress of time and century, to make seeds to fructify, or to multiply animals on the earth? Our heavenly Lord does not command us to learn these things, which are the works of His Godhead. But because He is God, and has deigned also to be man, hear Him as God for your renovation, and as man for your imitation. *Learn of Me*, He says, not to make the world and to create natures, nor to do those other things which the hidden God in His manifest manhood worked upon earth. He does not say even, *Learn of Me* to drive away fevers from the sick, to put devils to flight, to raise the dead, to command the winds and waves, or to walk upon the waters; learn of Me implies none of these things which He gave to some of His disciples and not to others. *Learn of Me*, He said for all, and let no man hold himself excused from the precept *Learn of Me, because I am meek and humble of heart*. Why are you in doubt about bearing this burden? Are humility and piety heavy to carry? or faith, hope, and charity? They make a man humble and meek. And consider that if you listen to Him you will not be burdened. *For My yoke is sweet and My burden is light*. . . . What if it should weigh less heavily than other burdens? Is avarice

heavier to bear, justice less heavy? I would not have
you understand it in this way. This burden does not
add weight, but wings, and birds have to bear the burden
of theirs. . . . They carry their wings and are carried
by them. On the earth they bear the burden of their
wings, in the heavens they are borne by them. . . .
Carry, therefore, the wings of peace, put on the wings
of love. This is the burden of Christ, and thus
will His law be fulfilled.

32. CHARITY IS THE MARK OF THE ELECT
(Sermon 350.2)

CHARITY, by which we love God and our neighbor,
is in secure possession of the divine promises in all
their breadth and magnitude. The teaching of our one
Heavenly Master is contained in these words, *You
shall love the Lord your God with your whole heart, and
with all your strength, and all your soul; and you shall
love your neighbor as yourself. In these two commandments are contained all the law and the prophets*. If,
therefore, you have no time to study through every
sacred page, nor to draw out the hidden meaning of
the words, nor to penetrate every secret of Scripture,
have at least charity, on which all things depend. In
this way you will carry out what you have learned from
these pages, and even what you have not yet learned.
For if you have learned charity, you have learned that
upon which depends what possibly you have not learned.
Love is manifest in that Scripture page which is in-

telligible to you, and it is hidden in the obscure page. Hence the man who practices charity in his life understands both the plain and the obscure page of the divine words.

Wherefore, brethren, cultivate charity, that sweet and efficacious bond of minds. Without it the rich man is poor, and with it the poor man is rich. Love [192] softens adversity and tempers prosperity; it is strong in torture, cheerful in good works, most secure in temptation, most magnificent in hospitality, most joyful amongst true brothers, most patient with the false ones. Love made Abel's sacrifice acceptable, gave hope to Noah through the deluge, was Abraham's trust in his wanderings, caused Moses to bear injuries most meekly, and consoled David in his tribulations. The same charity which in the innocence of the three children led them to expect that the flames would be harmless endured with fortitude in the Maccabees - flames which tortured. In Susanna it produced chastity towards a husband; in Anna, chastity after a husband's death; in Mary, an absolute chastity.
Love was fearless in Paul to correct and humble, in Peter to obey. It is human in Christians to confess, and divine in Christ to pardon. But what words of mine can exceed that praise of charity which God speaks through the mouth of the Apostle, who points it out to be the most excellent way of salvation: *If I speak,* he says, *with the tongues of men and of angels, and have not love, I have become as sounding brass or a tinkling cymbal. And if I should have prophecy, and should*

know all mysteries, and all knowledge, and if I should have all faith, so that I could remove mountains, and have not love, I am nothing. And if I should distribute all my goods to feed the poor, and if I should deliver my body to be burnt, and have not love, it profits me nothing. Love is patient, is kind. Love envies not, deals not perversely, is not puffed up, is not ambitious, seeks not her own, is not provoked to anger, thinks no evil, rejoices not in iniquity, but rejoices with the truth; bears all things, believes all things, hopes all things, endures all things. Love never falls away. How great is this love? In literature it is the soul, in prophecy it is its virtue, in sacraments the salvation they confer, in knowledge its foundation, in faith its fruit, to the poor their wealth, to the dying their life. What is so generous as to die for the wicked, or so kind as to love our enemies? It is charity alone which is not jealous of another's happiness, because it has no envy. It is charity alone which takes no pride in its own happiness, because it is not puffed up. It is charity alone which suffers no torment from an evil conscience, because it deals not perversely. In verbal abuse it is firm, in hatred it is kind; it is equable in the fire of angry passions, and simple-hearted in the midst of snares; it groans amongst sinners and revives in the atmosphere of truth. What is stronger than charity, not at repaying injuries, but at making no account of them? What is more enduring, not for vanity, but for eternity? For because it has an unshaken faith in the promises of the future life, it tolerates all things in this present one, and suffers whatever may be sent here below because it hopes in the promises of that world hereafter. Truly charity falls not away. Cultivate it then, and, with it in your hearts, bring forth the fruits of justice. And whatever else, which I have not been able to express, you may find out for yourselves in praise of charity, let it be apparent in your lives...

[194]
33. FORBEARANCE WITH SCANDALS
(*On the Psalms*, 99.7)

Serve the Lord with joy. Every servitude is full of bitterness, and all those who bear a yoke upon them serve with groanings. Fear not the servitude of our God; in it there is neither murmuring, nor groaning, nor anger. No man considers that it makes him a hireling, because it is sweet to feel that we are all redeemed. It is an ineffable happiness, brethren, to be in this great house amongst servants, even if we wear chains. Be not afraid, fettered servant; confess to the Lord; attribute your chains to your own fault; and if you would have your fetters transformed into ornaments, praise God in them. It is not said in vain, *Let the sighing of the prisoners come in before You*; nor was the prayer left unanswered. *Serve the Lord with joy.* With God servitude is free, where charity, not necessity, prompts the server. *For you, brethren*, St. Paul says, *have been called into liberty; only make not liberty an occasion to the flesh, but by love of the Spirit serve one another.* Let love inspire your servitude, because the truth has freed you. *If you remain in My word you are truly My disciples, and you shall know the truth, and the truth shall set you free.* You are at once a servant and a free man - a servant, because you were made; a free man, because you are loved by God [195] Who made you; or rather, you are free because you love Him Who made you. Serve not in murmuring, for your murmuring will not make you less a servant, but a bad servant. You are God's servant and God's free man; seek not your emancipation by deserting the house of your Emancipator.

Serve the Lord with joy. That joy will be full and perfect when this corruption shall put on incorruption and this mortal life immortality. Then joy and delight will be made perfect; praise will be without ceasing, love without scandal, fruition without fear, and life without death. And is there no joy here? If there be no joy and no exaltation, how does the Psalmist say, *Sing joyfully to God, all the earth*? There is joy even here, for we taste now the hope of that future life by which we shall then be replenished. But it is inevitable that corn has to struggle up with tares: seeds are intermingled with chaff, and the lily is amongst thorns. What are the words addressed to the Church? *As the lily among thorns, so is my love among the daughters.* It does not say "among strange women," but among the daughters. O Lord, how do You console, and comfort, and terrify us? What do You say? *As the lily among thorns.* What thorns are these? *So is my love among the daughters.* What daughters? Whom do You call thorns and whom daughters? He answers, "Their works make them thorns, though My sacraments make them daughters." Would, then, that we might groan amongst strangers; it would be a less bitter groaning. This is a worse one, because *if my enemy had reproached me I would have borne it, and if he that hated me had spoken great things against me, I would have hidden myself away from him.* These are the Psalmist's words, and he who knows our Scriptures follows them. Let him who does [196] not know study them in order to follow. *If he that hated me had spoken great things against me, I would have hidden myself away from him*; but you, a man of one mind, my guide and my familiar companion, who did take sweetmeats together with me. What sweetmeats do they take together with us who are not always to be with us? What are these sweetmeats if not *Taste and see how sweet the Lord is*? We must of necessity groan in the midst of these men.

But how is the Christian to avoid groaning amongst false brethren? Where can he go? What is he to do? Is he to retire into solitude? Scandals follow him there. Is he who is making good progress to put up with no man whatsoever? What if, before he began himself to be fervent, he had not been borne with by any one? If, therefore, he be totally lacking in forbearance because of his own progress, he is fully convicted by this very fact of not progressing. Understand my meaning, brethren. The Apostle says, *Supporting one another in charity, careful to keep the unity of the Spirit in the bond of peace.* Supporting one another; do you give no man any cause for forbearance? I should be surprised if you do not. But we will suppose that you do not. Then you are so much the more able to practice forbearance with others, inasmuch as others have nothing to suffer from you. Men do not practice forbearance with you; then practice it with them. "I cannot," you say. Therefore they have to forbear even with you. *Supporting one another in charity....*

I exhort all - the voice of God exhorts you all in these words, *Supporting one another in charity.* What will he who presides, or rather who serves the brethren, in those places which are called monasteries, have to say to me? What will he say? He will say, "I will be cautious, and not admit any bad subject.... I will not open the door to any evil man; I will not admit the false brother seeking admission, and with a select few I shall prosper. How will you know whom to exclude? A bad man has to stand the burden of proof in order to be known; how then will you prevent a man from entering who is only proved later on, and cannot be proved without entering? Will you exclude all evil men? For you say you will, and you know how to examine them. Do they bare their hearts when they come to you? They who are to enter do not know themselves; how much less do you?

For many have had the intention of carrying out that holy life which has all things in common, wherein no man calls anything his own, each having one heart and one soul in God. They were put into the furnace, and they gave way. How then are you to know a man who is still unknown even to himself? Will you separate evil brethren from the community of the good? You, whoever you may be, put out of your own heart evil thoughts if you can; let not even a suspicion of evil enter into it. "I do not consent," you say, "but still the suggestion entered in." We all indeed wish to keep our hearts fortified against the suspicion of evil. Who knows how this evil enters in? Daily we fight in this single heart of ours; one man struggles with a crowd in his heart. Avarice, lust, gluttony, worldly delight, each whispers its own temptation; they are all tempting. He keeps himself clear of all, answers each, is opposed to each; but if he do not receive some wound or other, it is a wonder. Where, then, is security? There is no other security here in this life than in the hope of God's promises. But when we reach eternity, and the portals are closed, and the bolts of the gates of Jerusalem are strengthened, [198] it will be perfect; there we shall know the fullness of delight and joy. Now, however, lest you should be too confident in your praises of any life whatsoever, praise no man before his death. For this is how men are deceived. Either they do not take upon themselves a better life, or they undertake it rashly; because when they wish to praise, they so praise as not to speak of the evils which are to be found in [life]; and those desirous of condemning utter reproaches with so much bitterness, that they close their eyes to the good, only exaggerate the evils which either are there or which they believe to be there. Hence it follows that any manner of life which receives indiscreet, that is, incautious, praise, while this very praise invites men, those who adopt it find in it some whom they did not think to find, and, rebuffed by the wicked, they withdraw from the good. Brethren, compare this method of proceeding with your own life, and so hear me that what I say may profit you unto life. The Church of God, taking it altogether, is an object of praise. Christians, and Christians alone, are great; the Catholic Church is great. Each loves his neighbor, and each does all he can for each; throughout the whole earth prayers and fasting and hymns are offered up, and God is praised in one bond of peace. Perhaps some one hears all this, and does not know that silence is kept as to the evil men who coexist with it. He comes on the strength of the praise, and finds those evil men whom he was not warned about beforehand; he is scandalized at false Christians, and he shuns the true ones. On the other hand, bitter tongues break out in reproaches: What are Christians like? Who are Christians? Avaricious and money-loving men. Are not those very men who fill the churches on feast-days to be seen filling theatres and amphitheatres with [199] games and other spectacles, inebriated, voracious, envious, haters of each other, as they are? There are some such, but there are others. This harsh critic shuts his eyes to the good, and the other man is equally indiscreet in shutting his to the wicked. If this be the praise which the Church of God meets with on earth, how does the Scripture praise her? I have said how. *As the lily in the midst of thorns, so is my love amongst the daughters.* A man hears this and ponders it in his mind. The lily finds grace in his eyes; he enters in, and, cleaving to the lily, he bears with the thorns. He who says, *As the lily in the midst of thorns, so is my love amongst the daughters,* will deserve to be in the praise and in the embrace of the Spouse. So it is with priests. The praisers of the clergy see in them virtuous ministers, faithful dispensers, who are patient with all, spending themselves on those they wish to profit; *not seeking their own advantage, but the things of Jesus Christ.* They praise these qualities, and forget that there are evil men too among the number. Again, they who inveigh against the avariciousness and immorality of the clergy, against their lawsuits and lusting after the goods of others, denounce them as drunkards and gluttons. Both of you are indiscreet - the one in praising, the other in blaming. You who praise disclose the fact that there are bad men together with the good: you who blame recognize the good. So is it with that common life of the brethren which is passed in monasteries. Great and holy are the men who spend their lives day after day in hymns and prayers and the praises of God, and make devout exercises their care. They labor with their hands, passing from prayer to labor; no man takes for himself what another has not got; they all love and support each other. This is unmitigated praise. He who is ignorant concerning what passes inside, who knows not of that tempestuous wind which destroys even the vessels in harbor, enters in, hoping, as it were, for peace, and thinking not to find disagreeable men to bear with. He finds there are evil brethren within, who could not have been proved to be so unless they had been admitted (it is necessary, first, that they should be borne with, for they might be corrected; nor can they easily be dismissed, unless they have first been tolerated), and he himself altogether loses patience. "Who tried to send me here," he asks, "where I thought to find charity?" And, irritated by the unseemliness of a few men, while he does not persevere in carrying out his promises, he gives up his holy purpose, and is guilty of not fulfilling his word to God. On coming out, he too becomes a fault-finder and a harsh critic, and speaks of those things alone which he represents as having been found insufferable, and sometimes they are true things. But real grievances caused by bad men are to be borne with for the sake of the society of the good. The Scripture's warning to such is, *Woe to them who have lost endurance.* And what is more, this man's indignation calls up a picture so untempting as to dissuade those who would wish to enter from entering, and this because, after he had taken up this life, he was lacking in endurance. What does he call his former brethren? *Envious, quarrelsome, uncharitable, avaricious*; one did this thing, and another did that. *Evil men, why do you keep silence about the good?* You boast of those you could not endure, but you say nothing of others who bore with *your* own sinfulness.

Truly, dear brethren, that is a wonderful saying of Our Lord's in the Gospel, *There are two in the field; one shall be taken and one shall be left: there are two* [201] *women grinding at the mill; one shall be taken and one shall be left: two are in bed; one shall be taken and one shall be left*. Who are the two in the field? The Apostle tells us. *I have planted, Apollo watered, but God gave the increase.* You are God's farmers. We are laboring in the field. The two in the field are priests. *One shall be taken, the other shall be left*; the good shall be taken, the bad shall be left. The two women grinding at the mill He applied to the people. Why are they grinding? Because, vanquished by the world, they are held as by a weight in the circle of temporal things. Here, too, *one shall be taken and one shall be left*. Which of the two shall be taken? That one who does good works, sees to the need of the servants of God and of the poor, who is true in faith, and has the true joyfullness of hope, who is mindful of God, wishing no man evil, loving as far as he can, not only his friends, but his enemies. It is the one who knows no woman other than his wife, or, in the case of a woman, no man other than her husband; so shall one be taken from the grinding, but the one whose life is not in this manner shall be left. Other men say, "We seek for quiet, and want no man's society. Let us get away from the crowd, and when we have some peace we shall do well." If you wish for quiet, you seem to seek a bed where you may rest without any anxiety. And here, too, *one shall be taken and one shall be left*. Let no man deceive you, brethren. If you would not be deceived, and if you would love the brethren, know that every calling in the Church has some false professors. I do not say that every man is false; I say that every calling has some false professors; there are bad Christians, but there are also good Christians. You seem to see more bad because they form the chaff and hide the wheat from your [202] sight. Nevertheless, the wheat is there, and you have only to approach it, to see, touch, examine, and use the testimony of your palate. You find some people whose profession is holy, undisciplined; are you therefore to condemn the calling? Many religious women do not keep within their own houses; they go about with idle curiosity, talking more than they ought, and are proud, talkative, and given to wine. If they be virgins, what does chastity of the flesh profit when the mind is corrupt? Lowliness in the married state is better than virginity with pride; for if a virgin so minded had married, she would not have been able to glory in the name of the thing, and she would have had a curb to restrain her. But because of evil virgins, are we to condemn those women who are holy in body and in soul? or, for the sake of the good ones, are we to be forced to praise the reprobate? Everywhere one shall be taken and one shall be left.

34. THE SYCAMORE TREE
(*Sermon* 174.3)

AND behold, there was a man named Zacchaeus, who was chief of the tax collectors, and he was rich. And he sought to see who Jesus was, and he could not for the crowd, because he was low of stature. Be not sad on account of the crowd; climb the tree on which Jesus hung for you, and you will see Him. And what kind of tree was it that Zacchaeus climbed up? It was a sycamore. In our countries it either does not exist at all, or is of exceedingly rare growth; but in those regions both the tree and the fruit are very common. The sycamore fruit is said to be a kind of apple like a fig, but somewhat different, as those may know who have seen and tasted it. As to the etymology of the word, the sycamore means tasteless figs in its Latin interpretation. Look at Zacchaeus, look at him, I ask you, wishing to see Jesus in the crowd, and not being able. He was humble and the crowd was proud; and in pressing on to get a good sight of Our Lord, the crowd, as is the custom of crowds, impeded itself. Zacchaeus rose above it, and saw Jesus unmolested by it. The crowd is insulting in its language to the humble, to those who walk in the path of humility, offering to God their being wronged, and not seeking revenge on their enemies. It calls them "helpless people, who cannot take care of themselves." The crowd stands in the way of Jesus; the crowd, boasting and glorying in revenge when able to take it, prevents us from seeing Him Who said as He hung on the cross, *Father, for-*

give them, for they know not what they do. Wishing to see Him, Zacchaeus, who was the type of the humble, paid no attention to the crowd which sought to impede him, but he climbed the sycamore, the tree, as it were, of insipid fruit. *For we,* says the Apostle, *preach Christ crucified, a scandal indeed to the Jews.* Look at the sycamore: *a folly to the Gentiles.* The wise men of this world reproach us with the cross of Christ, and say, "What sort of mind have you to adore a crucified God?" What sort of mind have we? Certainly not the same mind as you have. The wisdom of this world is folly with God. We do not think as you do. But you call us foolish. Call us what you like. Let us climb the sycamore and see Jesus; for you have not been able to see Jesus because you are ashamed of mounting the sycamore. Let Zacchaeus, the humble man, climb the cross of the sycamore. Getting up is a small matter. Lest he be ashamed of the cross of Christ, let him engrave it upon his forehead, which is the seat of modesty.... I imagine that you laugh to scorn the sycamore, which has been the cause of my seeing Jesus. But you jeer because you are a mortal man. The folly of God is wiser than men.

And Our Lord saw Zacchaeus. Zacchaeus was seen and he saw; but unless he had been seen he would not have seen. *For those whom He has predestined He has also called.* He Himself said to Nathaniel, who was already, so to speak, giving his testimony to the Gospel, and saying, *Can anything good come from Nazareth? Before Philip called you, when you were under the fig tree, I saw you. . . .* What is signified in these [205] words if not, "You would not have come to be purified of your sin unless I had first seen you under the cloud of sin?" We were seen that we might see; we were loved that we might love. The mercy of my God will go before me.

Then Our Lord, Who had taken Zacchaeus into His heart, deigned to be received in his house, and said, *Zacchaeus, make haste and come down: for this day I must abide in your house.* He held it as a great privilege to see Christ; and he, who esteemed it a great and wonderful privilege to look upon Our Lord as He passed by, deserved at once to have Him in his house. Grace is poured out, and faith works by charity. Christ is received in the house of the man who already possessed Him in his heart. Zacchaeus says to Christ, *Lord, the half of my goods I give to the poor; and if I have wronged any man of anything, I restore him fourfold*; as if he meant, I keep the half, not for itself, but that I may have something to make restitution with. This is receiving Jesus in truth, receiving Him in the heart; for Christ was already there in Zacchaeus's heart, and He knew the words which He heard from Zacchaeus's lips. Thus the Apostle says that *Christ dwells by faith in your hearts.*

But because, in the first place, it was Zacchaeus; in the second, because he was chief of the tax collectors; and, in the third, because he was a great sinner, that crowd, which had impeded the sight of Jesus, was full of astonishment, and, as if confident of its own righteousness, reproached Jesus for having entered the house of a sinner. This was upbraiding the doctor for visiting a sick man. Because, therefore, Zacchaeus was laughed to scorn, but laughed to scorn by the unrighteous, whereas he himself was made whole, Our Lord answered the scoffers by saying, *This day salvation has* [206] *come to this house*. This is why I entered it; this day salvation has come to it. If indeed the Savior had not entered in, salvation would not have been shown to that house. Why, then, being sick, are you astonished? Then you, too, call upon Jesus, and think not that you are whole. The patient who receives the doctor is hopeful, but the man who is violent enough to strike the doctor is in a desperate state. What, then, is the madness of the man who kills the doctor? What must be the goodness and power of the Physician who has made His own blood a remedy for the insane man, his slaughterer? Nor did He who came to seek and to save that which was lost say without cause as He hung on the cross, "*Father, forgive them, for they know not what they do*. They are mad: I am their healer. Let them rave as they may, I will bear with them; and when they kill Me, I will make them whole." Let us be among those whom He heals. *A faithful saying, and worthy of all acceptance, that Christ Jesus came into this world to save sinners*; whether great or small, to save sinners. The Son of Man comes to seek and to save that which was lost.

35. OUR DAILY BREAD
(On the Lord's Sermon on the Mount, Bk. 2.25)

THE fourth petition of the Lord's Prayer is, *Give us this day our daily bread.* Our daily bread stands either for all those things which go to support our physical life, and in teaching us concerning them Our Lord said, *Be not solicitous for tomorrow*, so that daily bread was added with a purpose; or for the sacrament of Christ's Body which we receive every day; or for spiritual food, of which the same Lord says, *Labor not for the food that perishes*, and again, *I am the living bread which came down from heaven.* We may examine which of these three is the more probable meaning. Someone, indeed, may be troubled at our praying for those things which are necessary for the support of this life, such as food and clothing, when the Lord Himself says, *Be not solicitous what you shall eat, or what you shall put on.* Or can a man not be solicitous about a thing which he is praying to obtain, when his prayer has to be made with so great a fervor that the whole of the passage relating to closing our chamber may be applied to it? And so may those other words, *Seek first the kingdom of God and His justice, and all these things shall be added unto you.* He does not say, "Seek first the kingdom of God, and then seek these things;" but, [208] *all these things shall be added unto you*, that is, even unto those who do not seek them. I know not if anyone can explain how a man may be said not to seek a thing which he is imploring God to grant him.

With regard to the sacrament of the Lord's Body, there are many in the East who do not partake of It every day. Whereas, in the Lord's Prayer our *daily bread* is spoken of. Let them not raise a question here; let them keep silence, and not uphold the opinion which they act upon without scandal, perhaps by ecclesiastical authority itself. They are neither prohibited from so doing by those who govern the Church, nor condemned as disobedient when they do otherwise. Hence it is proved that in those parts this is not considered our daily bread, for those who do not receive it every day would thus be convicted of great sin. But, as I have said, not to make either custom a matter of discussion, this one thing must necessarily occur to our minds as we reflect, i.e., that we have received from Our Lord a rule of prayer to which we must faithfully adhere, neither adding nor subtracting anything. This being so, who will dare to say that we may recite the Lord's Prayer only once a day, or that even if we may repeat it twice or three times up to the hour of receiving the Lord's Body, we are not to use it at all during the rest of the day? We could not say, *Give us this day,* if we had already received it, nor could anyone force us to celebrate this sacrament in the latest part of the day.

It remains, therefore, for us to understand this daily bread in a spiritual sense, as signifying the divine counsels which we have each day to ponder and to act upon. It is of these that Our Lord says, *Labor for the bread which does not perish.* This food is called our daily bread during our mortal life, which is made up [209] of successive days. And in truth, as long as the mind is attracted now to higher, now to lower things, that is, now to spiritual, now to material things, after the fashion of one who is sometimes fed with food and sometimes suffering hunger, daily bread is necessary in order to refresh the hungry, and to fortify the man prone to fall. As in this life our body, before its transformation, is refreshed with food, because it is sensible of expenditure in the vital organs, so the soul, because suffering, as it were, the expenditure caused by temporal affections which draw it off from God, may be refreshed with the food of divine precepts. But give us this day is said as long as this day lasts, that is, during this mortal life. Thus, after this life we shall be so filled with spiritual food for all eternity, that it will not then be called daily bread, because the speediness of time which makes day succeed day, from which comes the expression today, will no more exist. As the words, *This day, if you shall hear His voice,* which the Apostle in the Epistle to the Hebrews interprets to mean "as long as today exists, so are we here to understand the expression give us this day. If any one wish also to interpret the words as applying to the necessary food of the body or to the sacrament of the Lord's Body, we must join the three together, asking, that is, at once for that daily bread which is necessary for our bodies, for that sacred and visible Bread of the altar, and for the invisible bread of the Word of God.

36. MARTHA AND MARY
(*Sermon* 103.2)

MARTHA and Mary were two sisters, not only according to the flesh, but also according to the spirit; both of them adhered together to the Lord, both of them were at one in serving Our Lord in the flesh. Martha received Him in the way travelers are accustomed to be received, but it was a servant receiving her Lord, a sick woman her Savior, a creature her Creator. She was to feed Him with material food, and to be herself fed according to the spirit; for Our Lord chose to take upon Himself the form of a servant, and in that form to be fed by His servants, not as one of them, but out of condescension. This condescension it was which made Him offer Himself as a guest at table. According to His human flesh, indeed, He could feel hunger and thirst, but do you not know that in the desert angels ministered to Him when He was hungry? His allowing Himself to be fed, then, was in itself a gift. What wonder was it that He granted to the widow the care of the holy Prophet Elijah, whom He had previously fed by the ministry of a raven? Did He fail the Prophet when He sent him to the widow? By no means, but He held a blessing in reserve for the widow on account of her service to His servant. In like manner, therefore, Our Lord was received as a [211] guest, *Who came unto His own, and His own received Him not; but to those who did receive Him He gave power to become the sons of God*, adopting His servants and making them brothers, liberating captives and making them heirs. Let no one among you be tempted to say, "Oh, happy people, who deserved to receive Christ into their own house!" Do not be vexed and troubled because you live in times when you do not see Our Lord in the flesh. He has not withdrawn this privilege from you, for He says, "When you did this for the least of My creatures, you did it for Me." . . .

As Martha was preparing to feed Our Lord, she was occupied about many things. Her sister Mary chose rather to be fed by Our Lord. She left her sister, in a way, to her numerous material cares, and sat down herself at Our Lord's feet, with nothing else to do but to listen to His words. Her faithful ears had heard the Psalmist's call, *Be still and see that I am God*. The one was troubled, the other was feasting; Martha was tending to many things, Mary had eyes only for one. Both occupations were good, but which shall we say was the better? We know whom to ask about it; let us hear Him. . . . Martha questions her guest, referring her cause to Him as to a judge, that her sister left her alone and would not help her in her material cares. Mary does not answer, but she is there when Our Lord gives judgment. She preferred to leave her cause, as it were, to the judge, troubling not to answer for herself. For if she had attempted an answer, she would have defeated her purpose in listening. Our Lord, then, answers for her. He was at no loss for words, because He was the Word. What did He say? *Martha! Martha!* The repetition of the name is a sign of love or of a desire to move her. He called her twice [212] in order the better to gain her attention, "Martha, Martha, listen to Me. You are troubled about many things; there is only one thing to be done, that is, one thing is necessary." He does not commend any one extraordinary action, but He says one thing is necessary, and that Mary has chosen.

Bring unity before your minds, my brethren, and see if it be not the point of unity which gives savor to the multitude. By God's grace you are many; who would bear with you if you did not relish unity? How does this peace come amongst so many? Give unity and we have a people; take away unity and it is a crowd. For what is a crowd but a multitude in disorder? But listen to the Apostle: *I beseech you, brethren, that you all speak the same thing, and that there be no schisms among you, but that you be perfect in the same mind and in the same judgment.* And in another place, *That you be of one mind, being of one accord. Let nothing be done through contention, neither by vainglory.* And Our Lord prayed to His Father concerning His followers. *That they may be one as We are one.* In the Acts of the Apostles we read that the multitude of believers had one heart and one soul. Therefore *magnify the Lord with me, and let us together extol His name.* For one thing is necessary, that one thing from above, one thing in which the Father, Son and Holy Spirit are one....

It is good to have a care for the poor, and especially

to render becoming services and religious respect to God's saints. They are a return, not a gift, as the Apostle says, *If we have sown spiritual seed in you, is it a great thing if we reap your material gifts? . . . Some men, being not aware of it, have entertained angels.* The gifts of hospitality are good, but Mary chose a better part. Necessity makes the occupation [213] of the one, charity constitutes the sweetness of the other. ... If Martha had sufficed to her task, she would not have asked her sister's aid. These things are many and various, because they are material and temporal; although they are good things, they are transitory. But what does Our Lord say to Martha? *Mary has chosen the best part.* Not that yours is bad, only hers is better. Listen further why it is better: *Which shall not be taken away from her.* Sometimes the burden of want is removed from you; the sweetness of truth is lasting. That which she has chosen shall not be taken away from her. It shall not be taken away, but it shall be increased. It will be increased in this life and perfected in the next, but never taken away.

For the rest, O Martha, if you will allow me to say it, you are happy in your worthy service, and as a reward for this your labor you seek rest. Now you are busy about your heavy service, and you wish to feed mortal bodies, holy bodies though they are. Do you think to find a traveler in need of hospitality when you come to your eternal home? Will you find a hungry man with whom to break bread, or a thirsty man to refresh with water, or a sick man to visit, or a quarrelsome man to appease, or a dead man to bury? None of these things will be there; but what will be there? That which Mary has chosen. We shall be ourselves fed; we shall not feed others. Therefore that which Mary has chosen here will be carried on and perfected hereafter. She picked up crumbs from the rich table of the Word of God. Would you know what we shall find in heaven? We have Our Lord's own words to His disciples: *Amen, I say unto you that He will make them sit down, and, passing, will minister unto them.* What is the meaning of sitting down if it [214] be not to imply leisure and rest? What is *passing, He will minister unto them*? He passes first, and afterwards ministers. But where? In that feast above of which He speaks: *Amen, I say to you that many shall come from the east and the west, and shall sit down with Abraham, and Isaac, and Jacob in the kingdom of heaven.* There Our Lord will feed us, but first He passed through this world. The Passover is interpreted to mean passing, as you know. Our Lord came; He did divine things and suffered human things. Is He still spit upon, and given a reed for a scepter, and crowned with thorns? or scourged, or crucified, or wounded by a lance? He has passed. This, then, is the Gospel expression in speaking of the Passover which He made with His disciples. What does the Evangelist say? *The hour had come when Jesus was to pass out of this world to the Father.* He therefore passed out that He might feed us; let us follow that we may be fed by Him.

37. DIVINE LOVERS: WORLDLY LOVERS
(*Sermon* 344)

IN this life two loves are striving in every trial for mastery - love of the world and love of God. The conquering love, whichever it be, puts force upon the lover and draws him after itself. For we do not walk to God with the feet of our body, nor would wings, if we had them, carry us to Him, but we go to Him by the affections of our soul. On the other hand, we cleave to the earth not by physical chains, but by earthly affections. Christ came to transform our love, and to change earthly man into a lover of the heavenly life. He Who made us men became man for us, and God assumed the nature of man that He might make men divine. This is the combat of our earthly course, a battle with the flesh, a battle with the devil, and a battle with the world. But let us have confidence, because He Who has imposed this warfare does not look on it without offering us His assistance, nor does He require us to trust to our own strength. For he who presumes upon his own strength, because he is a mortal man, rests upon his human powers, and *Cursed be the man that trusts in man.* The martyrs, who were on fire with this holy love, consumed by the strength of their mind [in] this house of flesh, and they themselves in the fullness of the spirit, reached Him for Whom they had burned. Due honor will be shown in the great resurrection of the dead to the man who despised his flesh; and therefore it was sown in corruption that it may one day rise in glory.

Our Lord speaks these words to those who are kindled with this love, or rather that they may be so inflamed: *He who loves father or mother more than Me is not worthy of Me; and he who does not take up his cross and does not follow Me is not worthy of Me.* He did not take away the love of parents and wife and children, but regulated it. He did not say, "He who loves," but *He who loves more than Me*. This is what the Church says in the Canticle of Canticles, *He set in order charity in me*. Love your father, but do not put him before God; love your mother, but not before your Creator. The father was the begetter of this progeny, but not the one who formed it; for in the act of being a father he knew not what or what kind of man his child would be. The human father gives food to his child, but he has not fed the hungry with bread from his own substance. In short, whatever your father may have to give you on earth, he gives it to you at his death. By his death he makes way for your life. But that which God your Father bestows upon you He bestows with Himself, so that in order to possess your inheritance with the same God the Father, you have not to wait for His death, but to cleave to Him Who will endure for ever, and to remain in Him forever. Love your father, therefore, but do not put him before God. Love your mother, but not before the Church, who brought you forth unto eternal life. In short, judge from the love of these human parents how much you should love God and the Church. For if those who brought forth a mortal man are to be so loved, how are those to be loved who have generated one for the abiding dwelling place of eternity? Love [217] your wife and your children according to God, so that you may induce them to serve God with you. When you are united to God you will have no separation to fear. You should not then put before God those whom you do not really love if you neglect to lead them to Him. Possibly the hour of martyrdom may strike for you, and you may have the will to confess Christ. Your confession of Him may draw down upon you the temporal penalty, that is, the punishment of death. Father, wife, or children are all entreating you not to die, and they succeed in producing your spiritual death. If not, Our Lord's words will occur to your mind in that hour, *He who loves father or mother or wife or children more than Me is not worthy of Me.*

But human affection is moved by the entreaties of relations, and a man's resolution is shaken. Draw in the excess of your material expansiveness, and gird yourself with strength. Are you tormented by earthly love? Take up your cross and follow the Lord. Your Savior Himself, though God incarnate, showed you human affection when He said, *Father, if it be possible, let this chalice pass from Me.* He knew that that chalice could not pass, and that He had come to drink it with His free will, not being bound by necessity. He was omnipotent; at His will it would have passed from Him, because He is God with the Father, and He and God the Father are one God. But in the form of a servant, in that being which He had

taken from us for our sakes, He cried out with
the human affection of man. He deigned to transfigure you into Himself that you might be able to
speak of infirmities in Him, and in Him might learn
strength. He showed in Himself that will which is
the source of our own temptation, and He went on to
teach us which will it is in us that we have to obey.
[218] *Father,* He says, *if it be possible, let this chalice
pass from Me.* "This is the human will; I am speaking
as a man, in the form of a servant." *Father, if it be
possible, let this chalice pass from Me.* It is the voice
of the flesh, not of the spirit; the voice of infirmity,
not of the Godhead. *If it be possible, let this chalice
pass from Me.* This is the will which is signified to
Peter in the words, *But when you shall be old you
shall stretch forth your hands, and another shall gird
you and lead you where you do not want to go.* How,
then, did the martyrs triumph? By preferring the
will of the spirit to the will of the flesh. They loved
this life, and were weighed down. From this they
went on to consider how much eternal life should be
loved if this perishable life be so highly prized. The
man who has to die does not wish to die, and still he
must of necessity die, although he may have the perpetual wish to live.

It is in vain that you would avoid death; you can
gain nothing by the most strenuous efforts; you have
no power of removing the necessity of death. That
which you fear will come upon you against your will,
and that thought which you put away from your mind

will have its fulfillment in spite of your resistance. You strive indeed to delay death, but can you do away with it? If, therefore, lovers of this life labor so much to defer death, how much should we not toil to remove it altogether? You most certainly wish not to die. Change the object of your love; death is shown to you not as coming upon you against your will, but as ceasing to exist by your will.

[219]
38. ST. PETER'S DENIAL OF OUR LORD
(Tractates on the Gospel of John, 66)

WHEN Our Lord Jesus commended to His disciples that holy charity by which they should love one another (St. John 13. 34, 35), Simon Peter says to Him, *Lord, where are You going?* Thus indeed the disciple spoke to his Master and the servant to his Lord as if ready to follow Him. Our Lord, Who read his soul and saw why he asked this question, answered him thus: *Where I go, you can not follow Me now, but you shall follow hereafter*; as if He would have said, "Because you ask, you can not follow now." He does not say, "You can not." You can not now puts a delay upon him without removing hope; and this same hope which He did not remove but rather gave, He confirmed by the words which He added, *But you shall follow hereafter*. Why so eager, O Peter? Christ, the rock, has not yet strengthened you with His own spirit. Be

cautious against presumption; You can not now.
Be not cast down with despair; You shall follow
hereafter. But still what does he say? *Why cannot I
follow You now? I will lay down my life for You.* He
saw the desire which was in his soul but he did not
see what strength was there. The sick man boasted
of his desire; the physician measured his weakness.
Peter made promises; Our Lord foresaw the future.
[220] The ignorant man was presumptuous, and He
Who could foretell what was to come to pass rebuked
his eagerness. How much did Peter not take upon himself in considering what he wished to do without knowing how much he could do. How much he had taken
upon himself; for whereas Our Lord had come to lay
down His life for His friends, and consequently for
Peter himself, he, Peter, went so far as to offer this
very thing to the Lord, and at a time when Christ's
life had not yet been offered for him he promised to
lay down his own life for Christ. Jesus, therefore,
answered him, *Will you lay down your life for Me?*
Will you do for Me what I have not done for you?
Will you lay down your life for Me? Would you
go before when you can not even follow? What
do you think yourself? Listen to what you are: *Amen,
amen, I say to you, the cock shall not crow till you
deny Me three times.* See, this is how you will shortly
be revealed to yourself, who speak great words and
do not know your own weakness. You, who promise
to die for me will three times deny your life. You,
who already deem yourself able to die for me, first
live for yourself, for in fearing the death of that body,

you will inflict death on your soul. For great as is the life which confesses Christ, so is the death which denies Him.

Did not the Apostle St. Peter, whom some try perversely to excuse, deny Christ, because, being questioned by a maidservant, he said he knew not the man, as the other Evangelists state more explicitly? As if denying the Man Christ were not equivalent to denying Christ. He who thus denies Him, denies in Him that which He was made for our sakes in order to save that which He had made us from perishing. Therefore Christ did not die for the man who so confesses Christ the Lord as to deny His humanity, because Christ died according to His human nature. He who denies Christ the Man is not reconciled by the Mediator to God. *For there is one God, and one Mediator of God and men, the Man Christ Jesus.* He who denies Christ the Man is not justified, because, *as through the disobedience of one man many are constituted sinners, so through the obedience of one Man many are constituted just.* He who denies Christ the Man will not rise again in the resurrection unto life, because *death came through man, and the resurrection of the dead came through man; for as all died according to Adam, so all are to be vivified in Christ.* But how is He the Head of the Church if not by Man, as in the words, *The Word was made flesh*? That is to say, God, the only-begotten Son of God the Father, was made man. Therefore, how does he who denies Christ the Man belong to the body of Christ? How

is he a member who denies the head? But what need
have I of further words, when Our Lord Himself removes all the subtleties of our human arguments?
He does not say, "The cock shall not crow before
you deny the Man, nor does He use the more familiar expression which, in His condescension, He was
accustomed to use, "The cock shall not crow before you
three times deny the Son of Man," but He says, *Before
you deny Me three times*. What does *Me* signify unless
that Person which He bore, and who else but Christ
was that Person? Therefore, whatsoever of His Peter
denied, it was Christ Himself Whom He denied, his
Lord and his God. For when his fellow-disciple,
Thomas, cried out, *My Lord and my God*, it was not
the Word, but the Flesh which he touched. He laid
his curious hands, not on the incorporate nature of
God, but on the Body of the Man. He touched the Man,
[222] and still knew his God. If, then, Peter denied
that which Thomas felt with his hands, Peter offended
against the faith contained in Thomas's words. "The
cock shall not crow before you deny Me three times.
Say, if you will, *I know not the man*; or say, *I know
not what you say*; or again, I am not one of His disciples; you shall deny Me." If Christ said this and
it is grievous to doubt in the matter if He foretold
the truth, then most surely Peter denied Him. In defending Peter let us not accuse Christ. Weakness
should confess its sin, for the truth knows no falsehood.
Peter freely acknowledged the sin of his weakness, and
by his tears he showed the extent of his guilt in denying Christ. He reproves his own champions, and shows

them his tears as witnesses against himself. Nor do we, in saying these things, take a delight in impugning the first of the Apostles; but in looking at him, we should be warned not to presume on our human powers. For what else had our Master and Redeemer in His mind than to show us that no one of us should have an excessive confidence in his own powers by the example of the very first of the Apostles himself? The offering which Peter made in his body took place in his soul. He did not indeed die first for Our Lord, as he presumptuously offered to do, but he still preceded Him in a different way to what he had thought. For before the death and resurrection of Our Lord he both died by denying Him, and lived again by his tears. He died because of his own presumption, but he lived again because Our Lord looked at him in mercy.

39. VISIBLE THINGS THE EVIDENCE FOR THINGS UNSEEN
(*Sermon* 126.3)

FAITH, then, as it has been elsewhere defined, *is the hope of things to come, the firm belief in that which is unseen.* How are we to be convinced that unseen things do exist? But from where do these visible things come if not from Him Who is invisible? You do indeed see something in order to- believe at all, and from that which you see you believe in that which you do not see. Be not ungrateful to Him who has given you sufficient light to believe what you cannot yet see. God has given you the eyes of your body, and put reason into your mind; stir up this reason, this inhabitant of your inward consciousness; give it light, that it may look at the creature of God, for there is an inward force in yourself which sees through your eyes. When your mind refuses to lend itself to a thought, you do not see that which is before your eyes. Windows are in vain when there is nobody to use them. It is not therefore the eyes which see, but somebody who sees through them; rouse this inner consciousness, for it is capable of being roused. God has made you a reasonable creature, has raised you above the animal creation, and has fashioned you after His own likeness. Should you use your powers like the beasts, only to consider what you may put into your mouth, not into your mind? Rouse then the sight of your reason; use your eyes as it becomes a man; look at the heavens and the earth, the heavenly bodies, the fruitfulness of the earth, the flight of birds, the swimming of fish, the bearing of seeds, and the order of the seasons; contemplate these facts and seek their Maker; look at what you see, and seek Him whom you do not see. Believe in Him whom you do not see on account of these things which you do see. And lest you should think I am alone in thus advising you, hear the Apostle, *The invisible things of Him from the creation of the world are clearly seen, being understood by the things that are made.*

You were setting aside these things, and not considering them with the mind of a man, but like an irrational animal. The voice of the Prophet called upon you in vain, *Be not as the horse and the mule, who have no understanding.* You had these things before your eyes and took no notice of them. God's daily miracles were lightly viewed, not because they were any the less miracles, but because they happened so often. For what is more difficult of comprehension than that a man should be born; that in dying he who was retires into mystery; that in being born he who was not is before the public gaze? What is more wonderful or so mysterious? But this is easy of accomplishment to God. Wonder at these things; have you been astonished at unusual phenomena, and are they more extraordinary than that which so frequently passes before your eyes? Men wondered at our Lord Jesus Christ feeding so many thousands with five loaves, and they do not wonder at the earth being filled with wheat from a few ears of corn. Men saw that water which was turned into wine, and were astonished; what else [225] is done with rain water through the root of the vine? He is the Author of both one and the other: of the natural wonder that you may be fed; of the second, that you may be filled with astonishment.

But both are wonderful because both are the work of God. Man sees extraordinary things and is astonished. What does this wondering man himself come from? Where was he before? How did he get here? How does he come by his body or his different members? How has he this fair apparel of human flesh?

What was his origin? How lowly was not it? And he who is himself the great miracle looks and wonders at other miracles. From where then come these things which you see if not from Him Whom you do not see? But as I was beginning to say, because you had grown used to these things, He came Himself to work extraordinary wonders, that you in the ordinary ones might recognize your Maker. He to whom it is said, *Renew Your signs,* and again, *Show forth Your wonderful mercies,* came. He was pouring those mercies forth broadcast and no man wondered. . . . He came to raise up the dead, and in the sight of wondering man He Who was in the light came to restore man to the light, for every day He gives light to those who were not.

He did these things, and was despised by many who, instead of considering His great works, looked down upon Him in His lowliness, as if saying to themselves, "These things are divine, but He is only a man." You see then two things here, divine wonders and a man. If divine wonders can be done by God alone, do you not think that God is hidden in the man? Look, I say, at visible things, and believe in the invisible ones. He Who has called you to faith has not deserted you; although He has commanded you to believe what you do not see, still He has not sent you away with no out-[226] ward sign of the invisible things which you are to believe. Is man himself a small sign or a small indiction of the Creator? But He also came and worked miracles. You could not see God, but you could see man. God became man to unite in one Person the object of your sight and of your faith. *In the beginning was the Word, and the Word was with God, and the Word was God.* So far you heard and had not seen. Then He comes and is born, and is born of a woman, Who had made man and woman. He Who made man and woman was not Himself made by man and woman. Possibly man might have despised Him Who was to be born, but he cannot despise the manner of His birth, because before it He always was. Then, I say, He took to Himself a body, and was clothed in flesh, and came forth from the womb. . . .

In the very birth itself there are two things, one which you see and one which you do not see, but this is in order that through that which you see you may believe what you do not see. Seeing Him Who is born, you were inclined to look down upon Him: believe what you do not see, because He is born of a virgin. Man says, "Who is He since He is born?" But how great is He Who is born of a virgin? And He Who was thus born has worked a miracle in time for you. He was not born of a father, that is, of a human father, and yet He was born of flesh. But let it not seem impossible to you that He was born only of a mother Who made man before father and mother.

40. HIDDEN MEANING OF OUR LORD'S MIRACLES
(Tractates on the Gospel of John, 24 and 17.1)

THE miracles wrought by our Lord Jesus Christ are truly divine works, and they are a lesson to the human mind to see God in visible things. But because God is not visible to mortal eyes, and His miracles, by which He governs the whole world and all creatures, have ceased to cause wonder by reason of their frequency, so that hardly any one will deign to consider the great and stupendous works of God in each separate seed; according to that mercy of His, He reserved to Himself certain things which He would do in their appointed time above the usual and ordinary course of nature, that men, who made light of the everyday miracles, seeing not greater, but unusual ones, might wonder and be amazed. For the government of the whole universe is a greater miracle than feeding five thousand men on five loaves. Still no man wonders at the first, whereas men wonder at the second, not because it is greater, but because it is rarer. Who is even now feeding the entire universe if not He Who makes corn grow out of small seeds? Our Lord, then, worked as God. Just as He multiplies corn from insignificant seeds, so He multiplied the five loaves in His hands. For power was in the hand of Christ. Those five loaves were like seeds, which were not indeed put into the earth, but multiplied by Him Who made the earth. This was addressed to the senses that the mind might be raised on high, and it struck the eye for the exercise of the intellect, that we might wonder at an invisible God through visible works, and that, keen to believe and purified by faith, we might desire to see Him Himself with the eye of faith, Whom, through visible things, we should know to be invisible.

Nor is it sufficient to view the miracles of Christ only in this way. Let us question the miracles themselves to see what they tell us of Christ, as, if rightly understood, they have their language; for, because Christ Himself is the Word of God, what He does is likewise a word for us. As we have heard what a great miracle this multiplication of the loaves was, let us see also what a deep meaning it has: let us delight not only in the surface part of it, but let us penetrate into its deep significance. That which we admire outwardly has an inward meaning. We have seen and gazed at a great and wonderful action, at a divine action which God alone could do, and we have praised the Doer for His deed. But just as if we were to see somewhere some fine writing, it would not be sufficient to praise the writer's hand for producing even and neat and pretty characters, without also reading what he had to say to us by their medium; so it is with this miracle. The man who merely looks at it makes his delight at the magnificence of the action a reason for being filled with wonder at the Doer of it; but he who understands is as one who reads the writing. A picture and writing have a different appearance.

When you look at a picture and have praised it, you have seen the whole thing; but with writing, look-[229] ing is not all, because you are also admonished to read. . . .

A miracle worked by God should not be a matter of wonder; it would be if a man had worked one. We should rather rejoice than wonder at Our Lord and Savior Jesus Christ becoming man, than that God did divine things amongst men. For His being made man for men was of greater consequence to our salvation than that which He did amongst men; and when He healed the wounds of souls, He did more than when He cured the ills of mortal bodies. But because that soul of man had not known Him Who was to cure it, and because man had eyes of flesh with which to see corporeal things, and had not yet a perfected interior sight by which to recognize a hidden God, He worked a visible thing that He might cure man's incapability of seeing the invisible ones. He went to a place where a great multitude of sick, blind, lame, and palsied men were lying, and being, as He was, the Physician of both souls and bodies, Who had come to save the souls of all future believers, He chose one out of those sick men to cure in order to signify unity. If we consider Him in this His action with slow hearts, and with a sort of human comprehension and measure, He did no great thing as regards His power, and He did a small thing as far as kindness goes. So many men were lying prostrate, and He cured only one, when by one word He might have cured them all.

What are we to understand by it if not that, as He was incited chiefly by His power and goodness, He considered rather what souls would learn from His actions for their eternal salvation than what bodies would gain for their physical health? For the real health of the body which we expect from the Lord will be at the end, at the resurrection of the dead: [230] then that which lives will die no more; that which is cured will no longer be subject to illness; that which is replenished will never again hunger or thirst; and that which is renewed will know no decay. But now in those deeds of Our Lord and Savior Jesus Christ, both the eyes of the blind which were opened were afterwards closed in death, and the paralyzed limbs which He restored to vigor again became stiff in death, and whatever else He cured of bodily ills in mortal members remained sound only till the hour of death, but the soul which believed passed to eternal life. Therefore, in the curing of this sick man, He showed forth a great figure of the soul who was to believe. He had come to forgive the sins of that soul, and He had humbled Himself in order to make it sound.

41. THE SEEING OF THE WORD
(On the Gospel of John, 18.7, 20.8, 21.3)

AMEN, amen, I say unto you, the Son cannot do anything of Himself, but what He sees the Father doing.

How, dear brethren, are we to explain the point which we have raised how the Word sees, how the Father is seen by the Word, and what is meant by that seeing of the Word? I am not so bold and rash as to promise to explain this clearly both to you and to myself. I may make a guess at your capacity for understanding, but I know what my own is. If you like, then, without further delay, we will go over this Gospel passage, and we shall find worldly men disquieted by Our Lord's words. They are troubled in order that they may not cleave to what they now hold. It is as if they were boys who have to divest themselves of some foolish habit or other which may lead them astray, that they may acquire more useful ones as they grow older, and, instead of groveling on earth, may make progress. As for you, arise, seek, sigh, be on fire with longing, and strive to penetrate into hidden things; for if we are not as yet sighing and thirsting in our desires, upon whom shall we cast our pearls, or shall we find any pearls at all? I would therefore stir up your heart's desire, dear brethren. Moral conduct is the road to understanding; the life of the heart leads to the life of the mind (*genus vitae perducit ad* [232] *genus vitae*). An earthly life is one thing, a heavenly life is another thing. The life of the brute beasts, the life of man, and the life of angels are all different. The life of the beasts is cast in gross pleasures, embraces only things of earth, cares for that to which it is prone. The angel's life is only heavenly. The life of man holds a middle place between the angels and the brute creation. If man live according to the flesh, he places himself on a level with the beasts; if he live according to the spirit, he is the companion of angels. ... But when men are still craving for gross delights, think deceitfully, do not avoid lies, and add perjury to their falsehoods, how can they whose hearts are thus unclean venture to say, "Tell me what is the seeing of the Word?" even if I could answer their question, and had already arrived at vision? For if I, who am perhaps not living this sort of life, am still far removed from this vision, how much more he who is not carried away by this desire from on high, and is weighed down by earthly ones? There is a wide difference between a man of opposition and a man of desires, and, again, between a man of desires and a man who is enjoying their fulfillment. If you live the life of the beasts, you are leading a life of opposition. The angels are in perfect happiness. If you are not living like a beast, there is no radical obstacle in you against that higher life. You are in unsatisfied desires, and by this very fact you have begun to live the angel's life. May it grow and be perfected in you, and may you attain your desires, not through me, but through Him Who made both you and me.

Our Lord did not leave us with half and half knowledge in this matter, because by the words, *The Son cannot do anything of Himself, but what He sees the Father doing,* He meant us to understand that the [233] Father does not do particular works for the Son to see, nor the Son some others when He sees the Father working, but that the Father and the Son do the same works. He goes on to say, *For what things soever He does, these the Son also does in like manner.* It is not that the action of the Father implies a simultaneous though different action in the Son, but what things soever He does, these the Son also does in like manner. If the Son does the same works as the Father, the Father works through the Son; and if the Father works that which He works through the Son, the Father does not do one thing and the Son another, but their works are one and the same. And how does the Son do the same works? He does both the same and in like manner. Lest we might think He meant the same but in a different manner, He says the same and in like manner. How could He do the same not in like manner? Take an instance which, I imagine, will be sufficiently familiar to you. In writing, our mind first thinks of the words, and then our pen writes them.

Why do I see assent on all your faces if not that this has been a matter of personal experience to you? What I say is clear and evident to every one of us. Words are first formed by our minds, and then, by the bodily instrument, the hand obeys the mind's behest, and the mind and hand produce the same letters, for does the mind compose one thing and the hand write another? The hand indeed writes the same words as the mind has invented, but in a different way; for our mind is their intellectual agent, while our hand is their visible medium. Well, this is how the same things are done in a different way. Hence it would have been too little for Our Lord to say, *Whatsoever the Father does, these the Son also does*, unless He had added, *in like manner*. What if my example should [234] have made you understand that whatever the mind does the hand does, but not in the same way? Here He adds, moreover, *These the Son also does in like manner*. If He both does the same things and in the same way, there is something to cause your wonder, to silence the Jew, to give faith to the Christian, to convince the heretic; for the Son is equal to the Father. *For the Father loves the Son, and shows Him all works which He Himself does*. Here, again, we have the word *shows*, and to whom would it seem? Beyond a doubt to one who would appear to be looking on. Let us go back to that which we cannot explain, how the Word is spoken of as seeing. Man indeed was made by the Word, but man has eyes and ears and hands and various members in his body. He can see with his eyes, and hear with his ears, and work with his hands; his different members have their special functions. One member cannot do what another can; but through the unity of the body the eye sees for itself and for the ear, and the ear hears for itself and for the eye. Are we to suppose something of this sort in the Word by Whom all things are? And the Scripture says in the psalm, *Understand, you senseless among the people; and you fools, be wise at last. He that planted the ear, shall He not hear? or He that formed the eye, does He not see?* If, therefore, the Word formed the eye, and if the Word planted the ear, because all things are by Him, we may not say the Word does not hear, or the Word does not see, lest the psalm should upbraid us with the words, *You fools, be wise at last.* Therefore, if the Word hears and sees, the Son hears and sees; but are we to search for His eyes and ears in separate places, as in our own bodies? Do His hearing and His seeing come from different sources? and are His ears unable to do what His eyes [235] do, and His eyes what His ears do? Or is He all seeing and all hearing? It may be so, or rather, there is no *may be* in the matter; but He truly indeed is so. Still His seeing and His hearing are far removed from our seeing and our hearing. The seeing and the hearing of the Word are one and the same thing; nor are they separate operations in Him, but His hearing is sight and His sight is hearing.

How do we know this, who hear and see in a different way? We return possibly into ourselves if we are not amongst the number of those deceivers to whom it is said, *Return, you deceivers, to the heart.* Return to your own heart; why do you go out of yourselves to perish? why do you walk the ways of solitude? You are wandering in the dark; return. Where? To God. He is easily found. First come back into yourself, for you are wandering out of yourself; you do not know yourself, and would you ask who made you? Return, return to your heart; forget your body; it is your earthly habitation; and your heart, though it feels through your body, does not feel as your body feels. Leave your body and return to your heart. In our human body we find eyes in one place and ears in another, but do we find this in our heart? Have we not ears in our heart, of which ears Our Lord spoke when He said, *He who has ears let him hear.* Have we not eyes in our heart, which prompts the Apostle to say, *The enlightened eyes of your heart?* Return to your heart, and see in it what you are to think of God, because His image is there. Christ dwells in the inward man, and in the inward man you are renovated unto the likeness of God, by which likeness recognize its Author. See how all the bodily senses make the heart sensible of their outward impressions; how many ministers this one interior ruler possesses, and what its personal work is even apart from these ministers. Through the eyes the heart sees black and white objects; through the ears it hears harmonious and discordant sounds; through the nostrils it smells pleasant or unpleasant odors; through the taste it is sensible of bitter or palatable things; through the touch it feels soft or rough things; through itself the heart recognizes that which is just or unjust. Our heart sees, and hears, and appreciates all other objects of sense; and where the bodily senses fail, it discerns what is just and unjust, and what is good and evil. Show me the heart's eyes, and ears, and nostrils. Many are the impressions conveyed to it, yet the impressions themselves are not found there. In our human body we hear by one organ and see by another; in our heart the seat of seeing and hearing is the same. If this be done in the image, how much more powerfully will He do it Who is Lord of the image? Therefore the Son both hears and sees, and the Son is vision itself and hearing itself. Hearing with Him is one and the same thing as being, and sight with Him is one and the same thing as being. With us seeing and being are not the same things, because we may lose our sight and go on living, and we may lose our hearing and go on living.

The works of the Father and the Son are therefore inseparable. But the words, *The Son can do nothing of Himself*, mean the same as if He had said, "The Son is not of Himself." For if He be the Son, He was born; and if He was born, He is of Him from Whom He was born. God the Father begot One equal to Himself. Nothing was lacking to Him Who begot, nor did He Who begot One co-eternal to Himself seek a time in which to beget; neither did He seek [237] a mother in order to beget Him Who brought forth the Word out of Himself; nor was the Father Who generated older than the Son, so as to generate a Son less than Himself. As the Father knew not age, so the Son knew not increase; the one grew no older, neither did the other increase, but the Father generated One co-equal to Himself, and the Eternal One generated an Eternal One. How does an Eternal Person generate an Eternal Person? someone will ask. In the same way as a physical flame generates physical light. For the flame which generates the light dates from the same time as the light; nor does the generating flame precede the light which it generated, but both flame and light spring into being at the same moment. Show me a flame without light, and I will show you God the Father without the Son. This, then, is the meaning of the words, *The Son can do nothing of Himself, but what He sees the Father doing,* because the seeing of the Son is one and the same thing as His being born of the Father. His vision and His substance are not different things, nor are His power and His substance different things. All that He is is of the Father; all that He can do is of the Father, because His power and His being are one and the same, and all is from the Father. . . .

What does the Father see, or rather, what does the Son see in the Father, that He should do likewise? Possibly I might be able to explain this, but who shall understand it? Or I might be able to picture it to myself, and unable to express it; or I might even be unable to imagine it. For that ineffable Godhead is beyond us, as God is beyond man, and the Immortal One beyond mortals, and the Eternal One beyond creatures of time. By His gift and inspiration may He deign to grant us now some dew from that fountain of life for the quenching of our thirst, lest we become parched up in this desert land! Let us call Him "Lord," as we have been taught to call Him Father. We will venture thus far, because it was His own will that we should, if, that is, our lives do not cause Him to say to us, "If I am your Father, where is your honor of Me? If I am your Lord, where is your fear of Me?" Let us therefore call Him Our Father. To whom do we say "Our Father"? To the Father of Christ. He, then, who calls Christ's Father "Our Father," should he not call Christ "Our Brother"?

But He is not our Father as He is Christ's Father, for never did Christ draw us into so close an union as to make no distinction between Himself and us. That Son is equal to the Father, eternal with the Father, and co-eternal with the Father; but we are made through the Son, and adopted by the Only-begotten One. Again, in speaking to His disciples, never was Our Lord Jesus Christ heard to speak of His Father, God Almighty, as Our Father. His expression was either "My Father" said so and so, or "your Father." He did not talk of "our Father;" and this is so marked that in a certain passage He speaks of Him twice, saying, I go to My God and to your God. Why did he not say "Our God"? He also spoke of "My Father" and "your Father," not of "Our Father." Thus He joins us with Himself while He distinguishes us from Himself; and distinguishes us while He does not disjoin us from Himself. He wishes us to be one in Himself, while the Father and He are One.

[239]
42. THE DEAD RAISED TO LIFE BY OUR LORD
(*Sermon* 98)

IT is most true that the miracles of Our Lord and Savior Jesus Christ have power to move those who hear about them and believe in them; but some are affected in one way and some in another. Some men, for instance, contemplating the miracles which He wrought on diseased bodies, think that none could be greater. Others wonder more when they hear of those same miracles worked on souls. Our Lord Himself says, As the Father raises up the dead and gives them life, so the Son gives life to whomsoever He wills. Not indeed that the Father gives life to some and the Son to others, but the Father and the Son to the same, because the Father does all things through the Son. Let, therefore, no man who is a Christian doubt that the dead are still raised to life. Every man has eyes with which he is able to see the dead rise again, as the son of the widow rose again; . . . but all men have not eyes with which to see those who are spiritually dead arise. Only they who have spiritually arisen them selves are able to see it. It is a greater thing to raise one from the dead who is to live always than to raise one who has again to die.

The widowed mother rejoiced over her son raised from the dead; the Church, our mother, rejoices over those who are every day raised from spiritual death. [240] That young man was dead indeed according to the body, but the others are dead according to the soul. His death, evident to all, was wept over by physical tears; their invisible death is neither evident nor a matter of inquiry. He has sought after the dead Who knew the dead; He alone knew the dead Who could raise them to life. For unless the Lord had come to raise the dead, the Apostle would not have said, *Rise, you that sleep, and arise from the dead, and Christ shall enlighten you.* In saying, *Rise, you that sleep,* you must understand that he alluded to a sleeper, but in the words, *Arise from the dead*, to a dead man. They who are dead according to the body are often spoken of as those who sleep; and indeed nearly all men are asleep with regard to Him Who has power to rouse them. A dead man is really dead to you; however much you may pull, and shake, and pinch him, he remains insensible. He to whom the word Arise was said was asleep with regard to Christ. No man can rouse another out of his bed as easily as Christ can raise one in his grave.

We find that Our Lord three times raised the visible dead to life, but those whom He raised from invisible death are numbered by thousands. What man, however, can know how many He raised from physical death? for not all the things which He did are written. St. John tells us this: *There are also many other things*, he says, *which Jesus did, which, if they were written every one, the world itself, I think, would not be able to contain the looks that should be written*. Beyond a doubt, therefore, many others were raised by Him; but it is not for nothing that three are recorded. Our Lord Jesus Christ wished those things which He worked in bodies to be understood also in a spiritual sense. Nor did He work His miracles for the sake of working miracles, [241] but that those things which He did might strike wonder into the hearts of eyewitnesses and carry truth to understanding minds. Just as the man who sees words written in a beautiful handwriting and cannot read, praises the handwriting indeed, admiring the regularity of the letters, but knows not what it is all about nor what the letters mean, and is a praiser with his eye, not with his mind. Another man both praises the writing and can understand the writer's meaning. This the man does who not only can see, which is common to all, but who can read, which a man can not do unless he has been educated. So those who witnessed Christ's miracles and did not understand their meaning nor what they were intended to signify, merely looked on in wonder, while others were both astonished at the deeds and understood their language. This is what we should do with regard to the teaching of Christ; for the man who asserts that Christ worked His miracles only for the sake of working them, may say also that He did not know figs were out of season when He looked for them on the tree. It was not the season for that fruit, as the Gospel says, and still He, being hungry, looked for it on the tree. Was Christ ignorant on a matter which is familiar to every peasant? Did not the Creator of the tree know as much as its nurturer? When, therefore, He sought fruit from the tree in His hunger, He signified that He was hungry, and that He was looking for something besides figs. He found that tree full of foliage without fruit, and He cursed it, and it withered. . . . What harm was there in the tree bearing no fruit? But there are those who have no will to bear fruit. Sterility is the sin of those whose fruitfulness is in their will. Thus the Jews had the letter of the law without its deeds, and were full of leaves which bore no fruit. [242] This I have said to convince you that Our Lord Jesus Christ worked His miracles in order to signify some thing very special by them, that, apart from their being wonderful, and great, and divine, we might also learn a lesson from them.

Let us see then what He wished to teach us in the three dead whom He raised to life. He raised to life the daughter of the chief of the Synagogue, whom He was asked to visit in her sickness that He might restore her to health. And as He was on His way, her death was announced, and, as if His labor were in vain, they said to her father, "*The girl is dead, why do you still weary the Master?*" But He went on, and said to the girl's father, *Do not: fear, only have faith.* When He reached the house, He found them making the necessary preparations for the funeral, and He said to them, *Weep not, for the girl is not dead but sleeping.* He spoke truth: she was sleeping, but only for Him Who had power to raise her up. *Taking her by the hand, He restored her living to her parents.* He took also by the hand the young son of the widow. . . . *The Lord was approaching the city, and a dead man was being carried out of its gate.* He was touched with pity at the tears of the widowed mother who was deprived of her only son, and He did what you know, saying, *Young man, I say to you, arise. That dead man arose and began to speak, and He restored him to his mother.* He raised Lazarus too from the tomb. *And when the disciples with whom He was speaking heard that Lazarus was ill (for Jesus loved him), He said, Lazarus, our friend, is sleeping.* They, looking upon the sleep of a sick man as a good sign, answered, *If he be asleep, Lord, he is safe.* And Our Lord, speaking more plainly, made answer, *I tell you that Lazarus, our friend, is dead.* Both were true, for this was His meaning: a To you he is dead, to Me he is sleeping."

These three types of dead people represent the three sorts of sinners whom Christ is raising at this present time from the dead. The daughter of the ruler of the Synagogue lay dead in her home; they had not yet borne her away amongst the people. It was within the paternal walls that she was raised to life and restored to her parents. The youth of Nain was no longer in his house, neither was he as yet in his grave; he had been taken from his home, and was not committed to the earth. He Who raised to life the dead girl still under her father's roof, raised also the dead youth who had been taken out, but not yet buried. A third degree remained, and this was that He should raise up a dead man from his grave; this He did in the case of Lazarus. There are some people, therefore, who sin in the secret of their heart, though not as yet by act. Supposing that a man gives way to a sinful desire, the words of Our Lord Himself are, *Whosoever shall look on a woman to lust after her has already committed adultery with her in his heart.* He has not sinned by action, but in his heart: he has his dead man within, and has not yet carried him out. And thus it comes about, as we know, for every day men are experiencing it, that hearing on some occasion the word of God, as if the Lord were saying, Arise, consent to sin is withheld, and they live anew unto salvation and justice. The man who lies dead in his own house arises, and his heart is converted in the secret of his breast. This resurrection of a soul spiritually dead takes place in the sanctuary of conscience, within the paternal walls, as it were. Other men, after consenting to sin, go on to sinful actions, as if bearing out their dead, so that what was hidden [244] in their own heart may be manifested. Are not these men, sinners of commission as they are, in a hopeless state? Were not the words, I say to you, arise, spoken also to the widow's son? Was not he too restored to his mother? So also is it with the man who has done evil, if, troubled and moved at the word of truth, he arises at the voice of Christ, and is given new life. He could go on committing sins for a time; he could not perish for ever. But those who, in doing evil, contract also the habit of sin, which prevents them from seeing that it is sin, excuse their own evil deeds and are angry when they are upbraided. This was so much the case with the inhabitants of Sodom, that some of them answered the just man who reproached them with their most corrupt will by saying, "You earnest here to dwell, not to legislate." Foul sin was so common there, that iniquity was viewed as justice, and the man who lifted the voice of warning was blamed rather than the sinner. They who are thus weighed down by depraved habits are, as it were, buried. But what shall I say, brethren? They are buried as Lazarus was buried, of whom the Gospel says, *By this time he stinks*.

The stone which was laid over the tomb is the power of depraved habits, which weigh down the soul, and keep it from breathing or rising.

It is written also, *He has been dead four days.* In truth the soul has reached the sin of habit, of which I am now speaking, by a sort of fourth stage of progress in evil. For the first is, as it were, a throb of secret pleasure, the second is consent, the third is deed, the fourth is habit. There are some who meet evil desires by turning their thoughts away so as not even to take delight in them. Some feel pleasure without consenting. In this case death is not complete, but it has begun in a certain sense. Consent follows pleasure, and this is damnation. After consent comes deed; and deed is turned into a constant practice, which makes the case a desperate one, and induces the words, He has been dead four days; *by this time he stinks.* Our Lord, therefore, to whom all things were indeed easy, appears, and in this case He manifests a certain difficulty. He groaned within Himself, to show that it needs a loud voice of supplication to turn those who are hardened by habit. Still, at the voice of the Lord calling, the compulsory chains fell off. The power of hell was shaken, and Lazarus came forth a living man. The Lord, then, delivers those who, by the force of evil habit, have been dead four days. Lazarus himself, who had been dead four days, was asleep, that is, insensible to Christ, who wished to raise him to life. What does He say? Consider the mode of this raising to life. He came forth from his grave alive, and he could not walk. Our Lord said to the disciples, *Loose him, and let him go.* He had raised the dead, and *they unbound him.* You see here something which belongs to the majesty of God Who raises the dead man. Someone who is held down by an evil habit is admonished by the word of Scripture. How many are admonished and give no heed to the warning! Who, then, operates interiorly in the listener's heart? Who breathes life into his inner powers? Who puts forth that death which is in secret, and gives life which is in secret? After entreaties and reproaches, are not men left to their own thoughts, and do they not begin to turn over in their hearts what a bad life they are leading, and what evil habits weigh them down? Hence becoming distasteful to themselves, they determine to amend their lives. These men have risen from the dead: those have lived again who have been dissatisfied with what they were, but in their new life they are unable to walk. These chains are the chains of their guilt. Hence someone must unbind the man who has risen again, and must give him the use of his limbs. This was the office He entrusted to His disciples when He said to them, *Whatsoever you shall loose upon earth shall be loosed also in heaven.*

Dear brethren, let us then hear these things so that the living may live and the dead may live again. Be it that the sin is in the heart and has not extended itself to deed; let there be repentance of mind and thought, let the dead man in the house of conscience arise; or be it that he has given consent to his thought, even so let him not despair. . . . Let him be sorry for what he has done and hasten to live again; let him not descend into the darkness of the tomb, nor suffer the weight of evil habits to be laid upon him. But perhaps I am addressing him who is already suffocating under the hard stone of his own ways, and is pressed down by the load of habit, who already stinks and has been four days dead. Neither must this man despair. He is in the depths of death, but Christ is the height of life. . . . May, then, the living truly live. But as to those who are dead, in whichever of these three classes of death they may find themselves, let them endeavor without delay to rise again.

[247]
43. THE CAUSE MAKES THE MARTYR
(*Sermon* 285.2)

You are especially to remember and always to bear in mind that it is not the penalty but the cause which makes the martyr of God; for God delights in our justice, not in our torments. Nor does His almighty and all truthful judgment seek to know what a man suffers, but why he suffers. It was the cause of Our Lord, not His suffering, which has enabled us to sign ourselves with the cross of Our Lord. For if it were the penalty, then the cross of the thief would have been equally efficacious. The three crosses occupied one spot. Our Lord was in the middle, *Who was reputed with the wicked*. They put a thief on each side of Him; but they had not the same cause as He. They were placed beside Him as He hung on the cross, but they were far removed from Him. It was their own crimes which crucified *them*, and ours which crucified *Him*. Still in one of their number the great worth, not of the crucifixion in itself, but of loving confession, was clearly shown forth. The thief in his sorrow gained what Peter lost by his fear; he confessed his guilt and ascended the cross, and having changed the nature of his cause, he bought Paradise. He deserved indeed to have his cause altered, for he despised not in Christ the likeness of guilt. The Jews had looked down upon the wonder worker; the thief [248] believed in the Crucified One. He recognized the Lord in the man who was suffering with him on the cross, and by his faith did violence to the kingdom of heaven. The thief believed in Christ at a time when the faith of the Apostles was shaken by fear. He deserved indeed to hear the words, *This day shall you be with Me in Paradise.* He had been far from promising himself so much; he commended himself to divine mercy, but with what he deserved before his mind, *Lord,* he says, *remember me when You come into Your kingdom.* Until Our Lord should come into His kingdom, he contemplated being himself in torture, and only asked for mercy at His coming. And being as he was a thief, remembering his sins, he was hesitant. But Our Lord offered the thief what he dared not ask; for, as if meaning, "You ask Me to remember you when I shall come into My kingdom, *Amen, amen, I say unto you, this day shall you be*

with Me in Paradise. See Who it is you trust. You believe that I shall go into My kingdom, and before I go there I am everywhere. Therefore, although I am first to descend into hell, I shall have you today with Me in Paradise. You have asked Me and no other. For My humility - that is, My human nature - descends to mortal men, even to dead men, but My divinity is never absent from Paradise."
Thus the three crosses represented three causes. One of the thieves reproached Christ, the other confessed his crimes and commended himself to the mercy of Christ. The cross of Christ in the middle was a tribunal, not a penalty, and it was from this tribunal that He condemned the reviler and saved the believer. Be in fear, you who revile; rejoice, you who believe. This He will do in His glory which He then did in His humility. . . .

[249] The justice of the martyrs is without a flaw, for they were made perfect in their martyrdom. Therefore it is that the Church offers no prayers for them. She prays for other faithful departed, but not for the martyrs. They were so perfect at their going forth that they pray for us, not we for them. Nor is this in virtue of themselves, but in Him to whose Headship they adhered as perfect members. He is indeed the one Advocate who intercedes for us, sitting at the right hand of the Father - our one Advocate, as He is our one Shepherd. For, He says, *I must bring together other sheep who are not of this fold.* Is not Peter a shepherd similar to Christ? Certainly he is, and others too who are shepherds in the same way; for if he be

not a shepherd, how does Our Lord say to Him, *Feed My sheep*? He is a true shepherd who feeds his sheep; and the words to Peter were not, Feed your sheep, but Mine. Therefore Peter is a shepherd not of himself, but in the body of the shepherd; for if he were to feed his own sheep, they would cease to be sheep; they would become goats. . . .

Let us, then, who are within, honor the martyrs in the tent of the shepherd, in the members of the shepherd, in grace without boldness, in piety without presumption, in constancy without obstinacy, in strength without division. Hence, if you would imitate true martyrs, choose that cause which will enable you to say to God, *Judge me, God, and distinguish my cause from the nation that is not holy*. Distinguish not my torment, for this the unholy nation has, but my cause, which only the holy nation has. Choose, therefore, your cause; hold to the good and just one, and, with the help of God, fear no suffering.

44. JOY OF THE MARTYRS
(*Sermon* 273, 286.1)

OUR Lord not only instructed His martyrs by precept; He also strengthened them by His own example. He suffered first for them in order to give those who were to suffer an opportunity of following in His footsteps: He showed the way and made the path. Death may be according to the body or according to the soul, which both can and cannot die. It cannot die in the sense that its consciousness does not perish, but it can die if it lose God. Just, then, as the soul itself is the life of the body, so God is the life of the soul. In the same way as the body dies when the soul that is its life leaves it, so does the soul die when God leaves it. In order that God should not leave the soul, let it endure in faith, so that it may not fear death for God, and so it will not die forsaken by God. Still, that death which men fear may be a physical fear. But here also Our Lord has strengthened the confidence of His martyrs. How should they doubt about the integrity of their bodily members who are assured that the hairs of their head were numbered? *The hairs of your head,* He says, *are all numbered.* And in another place He speaks more emphatically: *I tell you that the hair of your head shall not perish.* When the Truth speaks in this way, why should human frailty tremble?

[251]
Blessed are those saints whose memory we honor by the celebration of their day of martyrdom. For their temporal life they have received an eternal crown and everlasting life, and they have left us a lesson on these feasts of theirs. When we hear of the sufferings of the martyrs, we rejoice and glorify God in them, nor do we grieve over their death. For if they had not died for Christ, would they be living today? Why should not their confession of Christ do what illness would have done? When the martyrdom of the saints

was being read, you heard the questions of the persecutors and the answers of the confessors. Amongst others, what was the reply of the blessed Bishop Fructuosus? When someone asked this Bishop to bear him in mind and pray for him, Fructuosus answered, I have to pray for the Catholic Church, which is spread from east to west. Who prays for each one by name? But he who prays for all leaves no man out. He whose prayer is offered up for the whole body omits no one of its members. What, then, should you say he meant to signify to the man who asked his prayers? What do you think? No doubt you understand; we call your attention to it. That man begged for his prayers. "And I," he said, "pray for the Catholic Church, which is spread from east to west. If you wish me to pray for you, do not leave that body for whom I pray."

The word martyr is a Greek one, but it is used in the Latin sense by which martyrs signify witnesses. For there are true martyrs and false martyrs, true witnesses and false witnesses. But the Scripture says, *A false witness shall not be unpunished.* If a false witness is not to be without punishment, neither is a true witness to be without a crown. It was easy, [252] indeed, for a man to bear witness to Our Lord Jesus Christ, the Truth, because He is God, but to bear witness unto death was no easy thing. There were certain men whom the Gospel speaks of, princes of the Jews, who believed in Our Lord, but dared not publicly confess Him, it says, on account of the Jews.

An explanation is at once added, for the Gospel goes on to say, *They loved the glory of men rather than the glory of God*. There were some, then, who were ashamed to confess Christ before men, and others somewhat better who were not ashamed of confessing Christ before men, but could not confess Him unto death. These are gifts of God, and sometimes they grow by degrees in the soul. First consider these three kinds of witnesses, and compare them to each other. One believes in Christ, and scarcely ventures to whisper His name; the second believes in Christ, and publicly confesses Him; the third believes in Him, and is prepared to die in his confession for Christ. The first is so weak that he is conquered by shame, not fear; the second is not lacking in confidence, but cannot yet confess unto blood; the third has no more that he can do, for he fulfills the Scripture word, *Fight for the truth unto death*.

The earth has been filled with martyrs as if with a bloody seed, and from that seed the corn of the Church has come forth. The dead have sown Christ more actively than the living. At this present time they are sowing and preaching Christ: the voice of the mouth is silent, the voice of deeds ever remains. They were held and bound and imprisoned, and brought forth before the people; they were tormented and burnt, and stoned and struck, and thrown to the beasts. In all their deaths they were laughed to scorn as if con- [253] temptible men, but *precious in the sight of the Lord is the death of His saints*. Then it was precious

only in God's sight, now it is precious in ours also. At the time when it was a reproach to be a Christian, the death of the saints was contemptible in the eyes of men; they were held in hatred and detestation, and men said to them in a tone of bitter upbraiding, "Do you die thus? Are you thus crucified or burnt?"
And now which of the faithful does not desire these things which were held in derision?

[254]
45. OUR LORD PASSING BY
(*Sermon* 344.5)

THE blind man cried out as Christ was passing by, for he feared that Christ would pass without curing him. And how did he cry? He cried so that he would not be silenced by the crowd. He triumphed over its opposition and won his Savior. In spite of the crowd who strove to silence the blind man, Jesus stood still, and called to him, and said, *What will you that I do? Lord,* he said, *that I may see.* And Our Lord answered, *Receive your sight: your faith has made you whole.* Have a love for Christ; desire the light, which is Christ. If that blind man desired the light of the body, how much more should you desire the light in your heart. Let us cry out to Him, not with our voices, but with our works. Let us live holy lives and despise the world; let all transitory things be as nothing to us. Worldly men, when they see us living in this fashion, will give us, as they deem it, a friendly warning. They love the world and the things of dust without a thought of heaven, and take freely what enjoyment they can find. They will surely censure us if they see us despising these things of earth. They will say, "What mad thing are you doing?" They form the censuring crowd who want to prevent the blind man from crying out. There are some Christians who are against a Christian mode of life, for that [255] crowd itself was walking with Christ, and impeding a blind man who was crying out with all his might for Christ and wishing for the light from the consolation of Christ. There are some Christians of this kind, but let us conquer them by our holy lives, and let our life itself cry out to Christ. He will stand for us, because He stands for ever (*stabit, quia stat*).

For there is a great mystery in this. He was passing by when the blind man cried out, but when He healed He stood still. Let this passing by of Christ make us eager to cry to Him. What is the passing by of Christ? Whatever He bore for us in time constitutes His passing. He was born: in this He has passed, for is He still being born? He grew: in this He has passed, for does He still grow? He was at His mother's breast, and does He still nurse? When He was weary He slept; does He still sleep? Last of all, He was taken and loaded with chains, scourged, crowned with thorns, struck, and spit upon, hung upon a tree, put to death, pierced by a lance, and He rose again from the sepulcher; He is still passing. He ascended into heaven, and sits at the right hand of the Father; that is His permanent place. Cry to Him as much as you can; He will now enlighten you; for inasmuch as *the Word was with God*, He did not pass by, for He was the unchangeable God. And *the Word was God, and the Word was made flesh*. In His human passing the flesh did and suffered many things; the Word was immutable. The heart is enlightened in that Word itself, because in that Word itself the flesh which he took upon Himself is honored. Take away the Word, and what is the flesh? Nothing more than the flesh of any ordinary man. But *the Word was made flesh and dwelt amongst us*, that the flesh of Christ might be honored. Let us therefore cry out to Him and live holy lives. . . .

46. ST. PETER AND ST. JOHN, TYPES OF TWO LIVES
(*On the Gospel of John*, 124)

IT is not a little significant that at His third apparition to His disciples the Lord should have said to the Apostle Peter, *Follow Me*, but of the Apostle John He said, *If I will have him to remain till I come, what is it to you?* When Our Lord had foretold to Peter by what mode of death he should glorify God, He said to him, *Follow Me. Peter turning about, saw that disciple whom Jesus loved following, who also leaned on His breast at supper, and said, Lord, who is he that shall betray You? When therefore Peter had seen him, he said to Jesus, Lord, and what shall this man do? Jesus said to him, So I will have him to remain till I come, what is it to you? follow you Me. This saying therefore went abroad among the brethren, that that disciple should not die. And Jesus did not say to him. He should not die; but, So I will have him to remain till I come, what is it to you?* See up to what point in this Gospel a question is raised, which by its depth exercises not a little the reflecting mind. For why is it said to Peter, and to Peter alone of all who were there, *Follow Me?* The disciples were all following Him as their true Master. But if these words are to be applied to his martyrdom, was Peter the only disciple to die for the Christian truth? Was not the other son of [257] Zebedee, the brother of John, who was openly put to death by Herod after Our Lord's ascension, amongst the seven then gathered together? Someone will say with truth that because James was not crucified the words *Follow Me* were significantly addressed to Peter, who not only suffered death, but the death of the cross as Christ did. Be this so, if no other better meaning can be found. Why, then, is it said of John, *If I will have him to remain till I come, what is it to you?* and why are the words repeated, *Follow Me,* as if John should not follow because He wished him to remain till He come? Who is there who will readily put any other construction on these words than the disciples then put, that because that disciple was not to die, therefore he was to remain on earth till Jesus came? But John himself removed this opinion, declaring that Our Lord had stated positively that this was not to be the case. For why should he add, *Jesus did not say to him he should riot die*, if not to prevent that which was false from remaining in men's minds. . . .

Another thing about these two Apostles, Peter and John, which will not fail to elicit inquiry, is why Our Lord loved John more, whereas Peter loved Our Lord Himself the better of the two? For wherever St. John alludes to himself, in order to do this without mentioning his name, he says, *whom Jesus loved*, as if Jesus had loved only him, and he were to be known by this love, whereas Jesus most truly loved them all. What did he mean to signify by this if not that he was more loved? . . . What greater sign of His greater love could Jesus have given him than in allowing John, who was associated with the rest of the disciples in the work of so mighty a redemption, alone of men to rest his head on the breast of that Savior Himself? Still many proofs may be produced that the Apostle St. Peter [258] loved Christ more than the rest; but not to go at length into other details . . . this is abundantly proved at the time of the third manifestation of the Lord, where, asking him, He said, *Do you love Me more than these?* This He knew perfectly well, and still He put him the question, that we too who read the Gospel should be convinced of Peter's love by Our Lord's interrogation and Peter's answer. But inasmuch as Peter answered, *I love You*, without adding more than these, he answered according to his personal knowledge. For he could not know how much Our Lord might be loved by any other man, because he could not penetrate into hearts. Still, by his former words, *Yes, Lord,*

You know, he, too, stated plainly that Our Lord was asking a thing which He knew. The Lord therefore knew not only that Peter loved Him, but also that he loved Him more than the rest. For all that, if we propose the question whether he who loves Christ more or he who loves Him less is the more blessed, who will hesitate to answer he who loves Him most. Again, if we ask whether the man whom Christ loves more, or the man whom He loves less is the more blessed, we shall answer without hesitation, the man whom Christ loves more. In my first comparison Peter is put before John, but in the second John is put before Peter. Let us ask ourselves a third question, thus: Who of the two disciples is the more blessed, he who loves Christ less than his fellow-disciples and is more beloved by Him, or he whom Christ loves less than the other disciples, whereas he loves Christ more than the one beloved? This is truly a wider question, and the answer requires thought. As far as my own judgment goes, I would answer at once that the man who loves Christ best is the more blessed, and the man whom Christ most loves the happier, if I sought how [259] to defend the justice of Our Redeemer for loving Peter less who loved Him more, and for loving John more who loved Him less.

I will appeal, then, to His manifest mercy, Whose justice is hidden, to solve this most deep question.... Let this be the beginning of our explanation, to remember that in this corruptible body which presses down the soul we are leading a miserable existence. But we who are already redeemed through our Mediator, and have received the token of the Holy Spirit, have hope of a blessed life, although as yet we do not possess it in reality. . . . Even after his sins are remitted, man is forced to bear this life of which it is written: "Is not human life upon earth a temptation?" In it we cry daily to God, *Deliver us from evil*; but it was sin which first caused man to experience that misery. For the penalty is a longer matter than the sin, lest the sin should be thought a small one if the penalty were to end with its commission. . . . This is the condition, sorrowful indeed, but not reprobate, of the evil days which we pass in this mortal life, although we rejoice to see good days during its course. It is a consequence of the just anger of God, of which the Scripture speaks: *Man, born of a woman, living for a short time, is full of wrath,* for the anger of God is not like the anger of man - that is, a perturbation of mind - but a quiet ordaining of a just punishment. In this His wrath, God, not restraining His mercies, as it is written, besides the various consolations of our miseries which He ceases not to show the human race, sent His only Son in the fullness of time, which moment He Himself foresaw. Through His Son He had created all things, that, remaining God, He might become man, and that the Man Jesus Christ might be the Mediator of God and men.

[260]. . . And because they who also walk in Him are not without sins, because sin belongs to the infirmity of this life, He gave them the salutary remedy of

alms, by which their prayer should be helped, when He taught them to say, *Forgive us our trespasses as we forgive them who have trespassed against us.* This is what the Church, blessed by hope, is doing during the days of this calamitous life, which Church the Apostle Peter, in virtue of the Primacy of his Apostolate, represented, being the type of its universality. For as regards what belongs to him individually, he was one man by nature, one Christian by grace, and by a more abundant grace he was at once one and the first of the Apostles. But when the words were said to him, *To you will I give the keys of the kingdom of heaven, and whatever you shall bind on earth shall be bound in heaven, and whatever you shall loose on earth shall be loosed in heaven*, he signified the universal Church, which is shaken in this world by storms, waves, and tempests in the form of various temptations; and it does not fall, because it is founded upon the rock, from which rock Peter took his name. For Peter is called after the rock, not the rock after Peter (*non enim a Petro petra, sed Petrus a petra*), just as Christ is not called after the Christian, but the Christian after Christ. Hence, then, the Lord says, *Upon this rock I will build My Church*, because Peter had said to Him, *You are Christ, the Son of the living God*. Christ was the rock upon which foundation Peter himself was built up. . . . The Church, therefore, which is founded on Christ, received from Him the keys of the kingdom of heaven in Peter's person - that is, the power to bind and to unbind sins. That which the Church is properly in Christ, that

Peter is typically in the rock; in this way Christ is [261] understood to be the rock and Peter the Church. This Church, then, which Peter typified, as long as it abides amidst evils, is delivered from those evils by loving and following Christ. She follows Christ more in those who fight for the truth unto death. But the words *Follow Me* are addressed to all, as Christ suffered for all, of whom the same Peter says, *Christ suffered for us, leaving us an example, that we may follow in His footsteps.* Here, then, is the reason why *Follow Me* was said to him. But there is an immortal life which dwells not in evils, when we shall see face to face what we now see through a glass darkly, as the fruit of great diligence in perceiving the truth. The Church, therefore, recognizes two lives as divinely foretold and commended to her. One is in faith, the other in fruition; one in the days of exile, the other in the abiding dwelling place of eternity; one in labor, the other in rest; one which is in the toil of the journey, the other in the security of home; one in action, the other in the reward of contemplation; one which declines from evil and works good, the other without evil to decline from and with great good to enjoy; one is in combat with its enemy, the other is reigning, having no enemy; one is strong in adversity, the other has no adversity; one holds its carnal appetites in restraint, the other gives itself up to spiritual sweetness; one is filled with solicitude to conquer, the other is triumphant with the peace of victory; one is helped in temptations, the other free from all temptation rejoices in that sovereign help itself; one consoles the needy, the other is passed in a place where the needy are no more; in the one life men forgive the sins of others as their own are forgiven, in the other there is no injury to forgive nor reason for asking forgiveness; in the one life crosses are sent lest men [262] should be puffed up with their good things, while the other is free from all evil in so great a fullness of grace, that the sovereign good is enjoyed without the faintest danger of pride; one discerns between good and evil, the other sees only good things; therefore, one life though virtuous is still poor, while the other is better and blessed. Peter typifies the one and John the other. The one is the life of the earth up to the day of judgment, when it will end: the perfection of the other is reserved till after this world has run its course, but in that to come it will have no end. Therefore to Peter is said, *Follow Me*; but of John it is said, *If I have him remain till I come, what is that to you? Follow Me*. For what is the meaning of these words? As far as I know and can understand, what is it if not, "You follow Me by imitating Me in bearing temporal evils; let him remain until I come to return eternal goods?" It may be better expressed thus, "Perfect works founded on the example of My passion follow Me; but contemplation which begins here must wait till I come to attain its perfection." For the calm possession of patience which endures till death is a following of Christ; and so it remains till Christ comes, when the fullness of knowledge will be made manifest. The calamities of this world are endured here in the land of the dead; there the good things of God will be seen in the land of the living. For we are not to understand, *if I will have him remain till I come* in the sense of waiting, but in that of expectation; because that which is typified in him is not to be fulfilled now, but at the coming of Christ. With regard to that which is signified by him to whom the words *Follow Me* are said, if it be not accomplished here below, we shall not arrive at the object of our expectation. In this life of action the more we love [263] Christ the more we are delivered from evils. But His love for us in our present condition is less, and hence He rescues us from it lest we should be always as we now are. There He will indeed love us with a greater love, because there will be nothing in us to displease Him, or for Him to take away from us; nor does He love us here for any other purpose than to be able to heal us and remove us from those things which are displeasing to Him. Here, then, where He would not have us remain, He loves us less; there, where He would have us go, and in that life which He would not have us lose, He loves us more. In Peter's love of Him, therefore, let us be delivered from this mortality, and in His love for John let us enjoy that immortality.

But this gives us the reason why Christ loved John more than Peter, not why Peter loved Christ better than John. For if Christ is to love us more in the next world, where we shall live with Him for ever, than in this, from which we are delivered in order to live there eternally, it does not follow that we shall love Him less when we ourselves are to be in a higher condition, as it is utterly impossible for us to reach a higher life except by loving Him more. Why, therefore, did John love Him better than Peter, if John typified that life in which He is to be far more loved, unless the words, *I will have him to remain* - that is, to expect - till I come, were said because that love itself, which will then be greatly increased, is not yet ours, but we expect it, that when He comes we may possess it? For as the same Apostle says in his Epistle, *It has not yet appeared what we shall be. We know that when He shall appear we shall be like to Him, because we shall see Him as He is.* Then our love will be greater than our sight. God Himself, who knows what that future life will be in us, loves us more with the love of predestination that He may lead us to it by loving us. And because all the ways of the Lord are mercy and truth, we know our present misery through our own experience, and therefore we love rather the Lord's mercy by which we can help ourselves out of our misery, asking and obtaining it every day for the remission of our sins. This is signified by Peter loving more but being less beloved, for Christ's love for us will be greater in our happiness than in our misery. Because we are not now in the possession of the truth as it will then be revealed to our eyes, we love it less. This contemplation is signified by John who loves less, and waits in expectation both for that revelation and for the fulfillment of His love in us, such as it ought to be, till the Lord comes; but he is more loved because that which is typified in him makes our blessedness.

Still let no man separate these great Apostles. For they were both included in what Peter signified, and were both to become what John signified. The one was a type by following, the other by remaining; but by faith both one and the other endured the evils of this mortal misery, and both looked for the goods of that happiness which was to come. Nor are they alone, for the whole body of holy Church, the Spouse of Christ, which is to be delivered from earthly temptations, and to possess eternal happiness, is with them. Those two lives which Peter and John portrayed are carried on by men who adopt one or the other: for truly in this transitory life they both walked by faith, and in eternity they will both enjoy the one vision. Peter, therefore, the first of the Apostles, received the keys of the kingdom of heaven, unto the binding and loosening of sins for the government of this stormy life, on account of all those holy ones who form an integral part of the body of Christ; for these and for the unbroken repose of that most mysterious life hereafter, John the Evangelist leaned on the Bosom of Christ. And as it is not only Peter who binds and loosens sin, but the universal Church, so it was not John alone who drank from the fountainhead of the Lord's Bosom the mystery that *in the beginning God the Word was with God*, the other things relating to Christ's divinity, together with the ineffable unity of the whole divine Trinity, which *we shall contemplate face to face in that kingdom, and which now, until the Lord comes, are seen in a glass darkly*. John was to glorify these mysteries by his preaching, but it was the Lord Himself Who diffused through the whole world that very Gospel to be imbibed by all His own, each according to their own capacity. Some, and these no insignificant commentators of the Holy Word, have thought that the Apostle John was more beloved by Christ because he was unmarried, and from his boyhood had led a most pure life. There is no certain evidence of this in the canonical books of Scripture; but what much strengthens the supposition is, that the life typified by John will have neither marriage nor giving in marriage.

47. THE WEARINESS OF JESUS
(*Tractates on the Gospel of John*, 15.6)

JESUS therefore being wearied with His journey, sat down at the well. It was about the sixth hour. This is the beginning of mystery. For it is not in vain that Jesus is wearied; it is not in vain that the strength of God is wearied, nor that He, who is the refreshment of our weariness, is tired; it is not for nothing that He is weary, Whose absence makes us weary, Whose presence gives us strength. Still, Jesus is weary, He is weary with His journey; He sits down on the edge of the well, and it is the sixth hour when He thus sits in His weariness. All these details have a meaning and point to something; they appeal to our attention so that we may seek to penetrate their meaning. Let Him then open to us and to you, who deigned to say the words, *Knock, and it shall be opened to you.* It is for you that Jesus is weary with the journey. We find that Jesus is strength, and we find that Jesus is weak: Jesus is both strong and weak: strong, because *in the beginning was the Word, and the Word was with God, and the Word was God: this was in the beginning with God.* Would you know what the strength of this Son of God is? *All things were made by Him, and without Him was made nothing that was made*: and [267] they were made without labor. What, therefore, is stronger than He, by Whom all things were made without labor? Would you know how He is weak? *The Word was made flesh, and He dwelt amongst us.* The strength of Christ made you, and the weakness of Christ re-made you. It was the strength of Christ which called nothingness into being: it was the weakness of Christ which caused that which was made not to perish. He created us by His strength, and He sought us out by His weakness.

He therefore being weak feeds the weak, as the hen does her chickens, for this was the comparison He used of Himself. *How often*, He says to Jerusalem, *I would have gathered together your children, as the hen gathers her chickens under her wings, and you refused*? But you see, brethren, how the hen is sick with her chickens. In no other case of the birds does the mother recognize her offspring. We see many sparrows building nests before our eyes, and nightingales and storks; we see doves making their nests every day of our lives, but we do not recognize the parent birds except in their nests. But the hen so becomes sick with her chickens, that even if they are not following her, and you do not see the offspring, you can recognize the mother. Thus the hen goes croaking about with drooping wings and ruffled feathers, and looking altogether so abject and miserable, that, as I say, if you do not see the chickens, you can tell that she is their mother. Thus it was that Jesus was weak, and wearied with His journey. The way, which spent Him, was the flesh which He had taken for us. How does He, Who is everywhere and in all places, go on a journey? He goes on a journey in this way - unless He had assumed our visible flesh, He would not have come to us. Because, therefore, He [268] deigned to come to us in this manner by putting on the form of a servant in taking flesh, that very taking of flesh is His journey. Hence, what else is His weariness with the journey if not His weariness in the flesh? Jesus was weak in the flesh; but be not weak in your flesh; be strong in His weakness, *for the foolishness of God is stronger than men. . . . There comes a woman.* She was a figure of the Church which was not then justified, but which was to be justified, for this is the result of the conversation. The woman comes in her ignorance, she finds Our Lord, and He touches her soul. Let us see what He does and why He does it: *There comes a woman of Samaria to draw water.* The Samaritans did not belong to the Jewish people, for they were aliens, although they inhabited neighboring countries. It is a long matter to recount the origin of the Samaritans, if we would not become involved in a multitude of superfluous details: it answers our purpose sufficiently to look upon them as aliens. And lest you should think I assert this rashly rather than truthfully, listen to what Our Lord Jesus Himself said of that Samaritan, one of the ten lepers He had healed, who alone returned to give thanks: *Were not ten made clean, and where are the nine? There is no one found to return and give glory to God but this stranger.* It belongs to the type of the reality that this woman, who was the figure of the Church, came from a strange country, for the Church was to come from the Gentiles, and to be foreign to the Jewish race. Let us therefore hear ourselves speaking by her mouth, and recognize ourselves in her, and through her give thanks to God for ourselves. For she was a figure, not the truth, and she herself showed forth the figure, and was made the truth. She believed in Him, Who [269] willed that she should serve as a figure to us. She came, then, to draw water. She had come merely to draw water just as ordinary men and women might do. *Jesus said to her: Give me to drink.* For His disciples had gone into the city to buy food. Then that Samaritan woman said to Him: *How do you, being a Jew, ask of me to drink, who am a Samaritan woman? For the Jews do not communicate with the Samaritans.* You see they were aliens; the Jews even refrained from using the same utensils as they. And because the woman brought a pitcher with her in order to draw water, she was astonished that a Jew asked her to give him to drink, which was contrary to Jewish custom. But He Who asked to be allowed to drink was thirsting for the faith of that woman.

Consider in short Who it is that asks to drink. Jesus answered and said to her: *If you did know the gift of God, and Who is He that said to you, Give me to drink; you perhaps would have asked of Him, and He would have given you living water*. He says, "Give me to drink and I will give you to drink." He is seemingly needy enough to accept your gift, and He is rich as one who is overflowing with good things to bestow. *If you did know the gift of God*, He says. The gift of God is the Holy Spirit. But He is still speaking guardedly to the woman, and getting by degrees into her heart. Possibly He is already teaching, for what is milder or sweeter than this advice: *If you did know the gift of God, and Who He is that said to you, Give me to drink; you perhaps would have asked of Him, and He would have given you living water*. Having gone so far, He stops. The ordinary meaning of living water is that which flows from a source, for rain water collected in tanks and [270] cisterns is not called living water. . . . What then did He who petitioned for water promise in return?

Still the woman was in suspense. *Sir*, she said, *You have nothing to draw with, and the well is deep*. You see what she understood by living water, i.e., the water of that well. "You would give me living water to drink, and I bring a pitcher wherein to draw, and you bring nothing. The living water is here, how can you give it to me?" She understands something different, and as she is thinking of the natural meaning of His words, she knocks, as it were, that the Master may reveal that which is hidden. In her case it was real ignorance, not affected ignorance, which made her knock; she was still an object of pity, the hour for her instruction had not come.

Our Lord speaks a little more plainly about the living water. The woman had said to Him, *Are you greater than our father Jacob, who gave us the well, and drank from it himself, and his children, and his cattle?* "You cannot give me of this living water, because You have nothing to draw it with; perhaps You mean some other well? Can you be better than our father Jacob, who built this well, and used it for himself and his household?" Let Our Lord tell us what sort of living water He had meant. Jesus answered and said to her, *Whoever drinks of this water shall thirst again; but he that shall drink of the water that I will give him shall not thirst for ever: but the water that I will give him shall become in him a fountain of water springing up into life everlasting*. Here Our Lord speaks more plainly. It *shall become in him a fountain of water springing up into life eternal. He that shall drink of this water shall not thirst for ever.* [271] What is more evident than that it was invisible, not visible water which He promised? What can be plainer than that His words had a spiritual not a material signification. . . . Do not let us pass over the fact that the Lord was promising something spiritual. What is, *Whoever drinks of this water shall thirst again*? It is true as far as that water is concerned, and it is true respecting what that water signified. . . . He was promising a certain refreshment and fullness of the Holy Spirit, which she was not then able to understand, and not understanding, what did she answer? The woman said to Him, Sir, *give me of this water, that I may not be thirsty, nor have need to come here to draw water.* Her need forced her to work, and her weakness shrunk from the labor. If only she could have heard the words, *Come to Me all you who labor and are burdened and I will refresh you.* Jesus said this to her that she might toil no more; but she did not yet understand His meaning. . . . Jesus, therefore, seeing that the woman did not understand, and willing her to understand, said, "*Call your husband.* You do not understand what I say because your intellect is deficient; I am speaking according to the spirit, you nearest Me according to the flesh. That which I say belongs neither to the lust of the ears, nor of the eyes, nor of the nostrils, nor of the taste, nor of the touch, only the mind can reach it, only the intellect can draw out its meaning; you are lacking in that intellect, how can you grasp what I say? "*Call your husband*, that is, apply your intellect, for what is there in your having animal life? Not much, for the beasts have it. In what way are you better? Through your intellect, which the beasts have not. What then does *call your husband* mean? You do not understand Me; I am speaking

[272] of the gift of God, but your thoughts are thoughts of flesh and blood; you want to be without bodily thirst, and it is the spirit which I have in view; your intellect is wanting, *Call your husband.*

Still, not having called him, she does not understand. . . . *I have no husband*, she says. And the Lord goes on to speak hidden things. You are to understand truly indeed that this woman had not then a husband, but that she was living in sin with I know not whom, an adulterer rather than a husband. And Jesus said to her, *You have said well that you have no husband. . . . For you have had five husbands, and he whom you now have is not your husband. . . .* The woman said to Him, *Sir, I perceive that You are a prophet.* Her intellect was beginning to dawn, but it had not quite come. She took the Lord to be a prophet, and He was indeed a prophet, for He says of Himself, *No prophet is accepted in his own country.* Again it is said to Moses concerning Him, *I will raise up for them a prophet like unto you from their brethren.* Hence that woman was not far wrong. *I perceive*, she says, *that you are a prophet.* She is beginning to call her husband, and to put forth the adulterer. *I perceive that you are a prophet.* And she begins to ask things which are of constant interest to her. There was a dispute amongst the Samaritans and the Jews, because the Jews adored God in Solomon's temple, and the Samaritans, who were a good way from it, did not adore Him there. The Jews boasted of being better, because they adored God in the temple. The Jews did not communicate with the

Samaritans, because the Samaritans would say to them, "How do you boast of being better than we are, because you have a temple which we do not possess? Did our fathers, who were pleasing to God, adore at [273] that temple? Did they not adore on the mountain where we now are? Thus," they say, "we worship God better on this mountain, where our fathers worshipped Him." Both disputed in ignorance, not having understanding; they were angry with each other and contended, the Jews for the temple and the Samaritans for the mountain. . . . *Woman, believe me,* Our Lord says; for, unless you believe, you will not be able to understand. Thus, *Woman, believe me, that the hour comes, when you shall neither on this mountain, nor in Jerusalem adore the Father. You adore that which you know not: we adore that which we know; for salvation is of the Jews. But the hour comes.* When? *and now is.* What hour is this? *when the true adorers shall adore the Father in spirit and in truth.* Not on this mountain nor in the temple, *but in spirit and in truth. For the Father also seeks such to adore Him.* Why does the Father seek men who will adore Him not on the mountain nor in the temple, but in spirit and in truth? *God is a spirit.* If God were a body it would be necessary to adore Him on a mountain, because a mountain is a corporeal thing; or in the temple, because a temple is a material structure. *God is a spirit, and they that adore Him must adore Him in spirit and in truth.*

We have heard it and it is manifest; we had gone

without and we are sent within. . . . Were you seeking a mountain where you might pray? Humble yourself in order to reach it. But would you mount upwards? Do so without seeking a mountain. In his heart he has disposed to ascend by steps (so speaks the Psalmist) in the vale of tears. *Vale* implies humility. Be all within. And if by chance you seek some high and holy place, let your heart be God's temple. For the temple of God is holy, which you are. Do you wish to pray in the temple? Pray in your own heart. But begin by being God's temple, for He will listen to those who invoke Him in His temple. *The hour then comes, and now is, when true adorers shall adore the Father in spirit and in truth. We adore that which we know, you adore that which you do not know; for salvation is of the Jews.*

48. PASSING FROM DEATH TO LIFE
(*Tractates on the Gospel of John*, 22.6)

LEST you should imagine that you are not to die according to the flesh, and, taking Our Lord's words in a literal sense, should say to yourself: "My Lord has said to me, He who hears My words, and believes Him that sent Me, has passed from death to life: well, I have believed, so I shall not die. I know that you will die the death which you owe to Adam's guilt. He heard the words, *You shall die the death*, and in his person they were addressed to us all, nor can we escape this divine sentence. But when you die the death of the natural man you will be admitted unto the eternal life of the new man, and you will pass from death to life. Now in the interval make this transition unto life. What is this life of yours? It is faith. The just man lives by faith. What are infidels? They are dead. Of such was that dead man, according to the body, of whom Our Lord said, *Let the dead bury their own dead.* Therefore, in this life there are both living men and dead men, and nearly all are living. Who are the dead ones? They who have not believed. Who are the living? They who have believed. What does the Apostle say to the dead? *Arise you who sleep.* You will answer, "He speaks of sleep, not death." Listen to what follows: *Rise you that sleep and arise* [276] *from the dead.* And as if answering the question, "Where shall I go?" he continues, *And Christ shall enlighten you.* When the light of Christ falls upon you as a believer you pass from death to life; remain in Him by Whom you have passed, and you shall not come to judgment.

He explains this Himself by what follows: *Amen, amen I say to you.* For fear we should understand His words, *He is passed from death to life*, as referring to the future resurrection, and wishing to show us how the man who believes passes, and that passing from death to life is in reality passing from infidelity to faith, from injustice to justice, from pride to humility, from hatred to charity, He goes on now to say, *Amen,*

amen, I say to you the hour comes and now is. What is plainer? He now explains His former words, because it is even now that Christ admonishes us. *The hour comes.* What hour? *And now it is when the dead shall hear the voice of the Son of God, and they who hear shall live.* We have already spoken of the dead whom He here mentions. What do you think, my brethren, amongst you who are listening to me, are there no dead? Those who believe and are acting according to the true faith live, and are not dead; but those who either do not believe, or believe like the demons, leading bad lives in fear and trembling, confessing the Son of God without charity, are rather to be regarded as dead. And still this hour is going on, for the hour of which Our Lord speaks is not one of the twelve hours of our usual day. From the time He uttered those words, even until now, and so on till the end of time, this same hour is running its course, and St. John speaks of it in his Epistle when he says, *Little children, it is the last hour.* Therefore it is this very hour in which we are now speaking. May the [277] living live, and may the man who was dead live; let him who was lying dead hear the voice of the Son of God, and arise and live. The Lord cried out at the grave of Lazarus, and he who had been dead four days arose. He who was stinking came forth into the air; he was buried, and a stone had been placed over his remains; and the voice of Our Lord broke the marble of the stone. Your heart is so hard that it has not yet melted at that divine voice. Arise in your heart and come forth out of your tomb. For when thus dead, according to the spirit, you were lying as if in the grave, and were oppressed by the stone of vicious habits. *Arise and walk.* What is the meaning of these words, *Arise and walk*? Believe and confess. For he who believes has risen; he who confesses has come forth. Why do we speak of the man who openly professes his faith as coming forth? Because as long as he was silent he was hidden, but when he confesses his faith he proceeds from darkness to light. And after he has made a confession of faith, what are the ministers of religion told to do? That same thing which was urged upon them at the grave of Lazarus, that is, *Loosen him and let him go.* How is this to be done? Our Lord said to His ministers, the Apostles, *Whatever you shall loose on earth shall be loosened in heaven.*

The hour comes, and now is, when the dead shall hear the voice of the Son of God, and they who hear shall live. How will they live? They will live on Life. And who is this Life? Christ. *I am the way, the truth, and the life,* He says. Will you walk? *I am the way.* Will you be saved from all deception? *I am the truth.* Would you escape death? *I am the life.* These are Our Lord's words to us. We cannot walk except to Him, and we cannot go by any other way but Himself. Now, therefore, it is the hour, it is indeed the hour which will not yet be spent. Men who were dead arise, pass to life, and live at the voice of the Son of God; persevering in His faith He constitutes their life. The Son, therefore, has life, and can give life to those men who believe. And how has He life? As the Father has it. Listen to the Son's own words: *As the Father has life in Himself, so He has given to the Son also to have life in Himself.* Brethren, I will speak according to my ability, for these are words which are disquieting to a small mind. Why did He add *in Himself*? It would have been sufficient for Him to say, *As the Father has life in Himself, so He has given to the Son also to have life*. He added *in Himself*, for the Father has life in Himself, and so has the Son. By the words *in Himself* He wished us to understand something which is hidden in this word. Let us knock that it may be opened to us. O Lord, what have You said? Why did you add *in Himself*? Had St. Paul, Your Apostle, whom You did cause to live, no life? Yes, Our Lord says. How will it be, then, with those men who were dead, and had new life by passing over in faith to Your word; when they have passed shall they have no life in You? *"Yes,"* Our Lord answers; *"for a little before I had said, He who hears My words, and believes in Him Who sent Me, has eternal life."* Therefore, Lord, those who believe in You have life, and You did not say "in themselves." In speaking of the Father Your words were, *As the Father has life in Himself*; and again, in speaking of Yourself, *so He has given to the Son also to have life in Himself.* As He has it so He has given it. Where has He this life? In Himself. In whom does He give us to have life? In Himself. Where was St. Paul's life? Not in himself but in Christ. [279] Where is the life of the faithful? Not in them-

selves, but in Christ. Let us see if this be what the
Apostle tells us: *I live now not I, but Christ lives
in me*. That life which is ours, that is, the life of our
own free will, is only evil, sinning and full of iniquity; our real life, true life, is from God, not from
ourselves. God gives it to us, and we do not give it
to ourselves. But Christ has life in Himself as the
Father has life, because He is the Word of God. His
life is not sometimes good and sometimes evil; this is
man's life. He who was leading a bad life was living
according to his human life; he who was leading a
good one has passed to the life of Christ. As you have
been made a participator in life, you are now what you
were not before, for you were to receive life; but the
Son of God was not first, as it were, without life, and
He did not receive life; for if He had thus received it,
He would not have it in Himself. What is the meaning
of *in Himself*? It means that He should be *the* Life.

49. "THEY COULD NOT BELIEVE"
(*Tractates on the Gospel of John*, 53.5)

*THEREFORE they could not believe, because Isaiah said
again: He has blinded their eyes and hardened their
heart, that they should not see with their eyes, nor understand with their heart, and be converted, and I should
heal them.* People say to us, "If they could not believe,
what sin is there in a man not doing what he cannot
do?" But if they sinned in not believing, they were

able to believe, and did not believe. If, then, they were able, how does the Gospel say, *Therefore they could not believe,* because Isaiah said again: *He has blinded their eyes and hardened their heart,* in order, which is a graver matter, to refer to God the cause of their unbelief, seeing that He Himself has blinded their eyes and hardened their heart? This is said not only of the devil, but of God, as the prophetical text of Scripture testifies; for if we suppose that the words, *He blinded their eyes and hardened their heart,* refer to the devil, it will be difficult for us to show how they sinned in not believing, when it is said of them that they could not believe. Hence, what shall we reply to another testimony of the same prophet, which St. Paul the Apostle quoted, saying, *That which Israel sought he has not obtained; but the election has obtained it, and the rest have been blinded.* As it is written: *God* [281] *has given them the spirit of insensibility; eyes that they should not see, and ears that they should not hear,* until this present day?

You have heard, brethren, the question which is now before us, and you see what a deep one it is; but let us answer it as best we can. They could not believe, because this was what the Prophet Isaiah had foretold; and he had foretold it because God foresaw that it would happen. But if I am asked why they could not believe, I answer at once, because they would not. God indeed had foreseen their perverse will, and He to whom future things cannot be hidden predicted it by His prophet. But, it is objected, the prophet speaks of another cause apart from their will. What is this cause? That God gave them the spirit of insensibility, eyes that they should not see, and ears that they should not hear, and He blinded their eyes and hardened their hearts. I answer that it was even their will which brought this state upon them. God thus blinds and hardens men whom He forsakes and does not help: which He may do by a hidden judgment, never by an unrighteous one. The religion of the good should hold this with a firm and immovable faith, like the Apostle when he was treating the same difficult question. What shall we say then, he goes on; is there injustice with God? God forbid! If, then, we must put away the bare notion of injustice in God, we must confess that both when He helps a man, He does mercifully, and when He does not help He is just, because He does all things not by accident but in measure. If indeed the judgments of the saints be just, how much more so are those of the God of sanctity and justice? They are just, therefore, though hidden. Hence, when similar questions come to be discussed, the difference, that is, between the lot of men, why, for instance, one [282] man should be forsaken by God and blinded spiritually and another enlightened by His presence, let us not take it upon ourselves to pass judgment on the judgment of so great a Judge, but in fear and trembling let us exclaim with the Apostle, *the depth of the riches of the wisdom and of the knowledge of God! How incomprehensible are His judgments and how unsearchable His ways.* Thus the Psalmist says, *Your judgments are as a great deep.*

Urge me not then, brethren, by your expectation to scale this height, or to penetrate into this abyss, or to scrutinize that which baffles scrutiny. I can measure my own strength, and, I think, yours also. This question is above my capacity and my powers of understanding, and so, I imagine, is it of yours. Let us listen, then, together to the counsel of Scripture: *Seek not the things which are too high for you, and search not into things above your ability.* It is not that we may not know these questions, for our divine Master says there is no hidden thing which shall not be manifested; but if we walk according to that knowledge which we have, as the Apostle says, God will reveal to us what we wish otherwise to know over and above our present knowledge and non-knowledge. We have come to the road of faith, and let us hold fast to it; it will lead us to the repose of the King, in whom are hidden all treasures of wisdom and science. For Our Lord Jesus Christ had no sort of envy of those great and specially chosen disciples of His when He said, *I have many things to tell you, but you cannot bear them now.* We must walk, and progress, and grow, that our hearts may be fit for those things which we cannot at present understand. If the last day find us in a state of progress, we shall learn then what we could not learn here.

If, however, any man feel confident that he could [283] throw a stronger and clearer light on this question, God forbid that I should not be readier to learn than to teach. Only, let whoever treats it guard against so defending our free will as to seek to take from us the prayer in which we say, *Lead us not into temptation*; or, on the other hand, of denying our free will and of daring to excuse sin. Let us hear Our Lord, counselling and admonishing, telling us what we should do, and helping us to do it. Too great confidence in their own will puffed certain men up with pride, and too great diffidence in it made others fall into negligent ways. The confident people say, "Why should we ask God not to be overcome by temptation when it is in our own power?" The diffident say, "Why should we try to lead good lives when our doing so is in God's power?" O Lord, O Father, Who are in heaven, lead us not into either of these temptations, but deliver us from evil! Let us listen to Our Lord, saying to Peter, *I have prayed for you, Peter, that your faith may not fail you*; that we may not consider our faith to be so far under the control of our free will as to have no need of the divine assistance. And let us hear the Gospel too, *He gave them power to become the sons of God,* lest we should deem faith to be quite beyond our control, but that we should acknowledge His benefits in both particulars. For we have to return thanks for the power which is given to us, and we have to pray that our weakness may not lead us astray. . . .

It is not therefore surprising that they could not believe when their will was so proud, that, ignoring the justice of God, they sought to act by their own, as the Apostle says of them, they were not subject to the justice of God. Because they prided themselves not on their faith, but, as it were, on their works, they were blinded by their very pride, and struck their feet [284] against a stone. It is in this sense that *they could not* is used where *could not* is to be understood, just as it is said of our Lord God, *If we believe not, He continues faithful; He cannot deny Himself.* St. Paul here uses the word *cannot* of the Almighty. As, therefore, the fact that God cannot deny Himself is praise of the divine will, so when those men could not believe, the fault lies in the human will.

50. THE TWO GENERATIONS OF OUR LORD
(*Tractates on the Gospel of John*, 2.15 and 8.8)

... GOD was first born of men that men might be born of God. For Christ is God, and Christ was born of men. He sought, indeed, only a mother on earth, because He already had His Father in heaven born of God to make us, and born of woman to re-make us. Wonder not, O man, that you are made a son of God by grace, because you are born of God according to His Word. The Word chose first to be born of man that you might be born of God, and reflect within yourself, "God chose to be born of man, and not without cause, because He must have thought me of some worth to do two things for me at once, to deliver me from subjection to death, and to be born for me subject to death Himself." Therefore after the words, *Who are born not of blood, nor of the will of the flesh, nor of the will of man, but of God,* lest we should wonder and be stupefied at so excellent a grace, and look upon the fact of men being born of God as incredible, St. John adds, as if to reassure us, *And the Word was made flesh, and dwelt amongst us.* Why, then, do you wonder that men are born of God? Consider that this very God is born of man, *And the Word was made flesh, and dwelt amongst us.*

He alone is born of a father without a mother, and [286] of a mother without a father: without a mother He is God, without a father He is man; without a mother before all time, without a father at the end of time. His answer, *Woman, what is it to Me and to you?* He spoke to His mother at the marriage-feast, *for the mother of Jesus was there*, and His mother spoke to Him. This is all contained in the Gospel. We know that the mother of Jesus was there, as we know that He said to her, *Woman, what is it to Me and to you? My hour has not yet come.* Let us believe the whole, and seek for the meaning of that which we do not understand. And, first, beware lest fatalists should find in these words, *My hour has not yet come*, a confirmation of their own error, as the Manicheans have done in those other words, *Woman, what is it to Me and to you?* If Our Lord spoke these words to favor the calculations of fatalists, we have committed a sacrilege in burning their manuscripts. But if we acted rightly, imitating apostolic example, the Lord did not speak these words in their sense, *My hour has not yet come.* For vain men, seducers who have been themselves seduced, say, "You see that Christ was bound by fate, for He said, *My hour has not yet come.*" Whom shall we first answer, heretics or fatalists? Both come indeed from the same serpent; both wish to corrupt the virginity of the heart of the Church, which virginity is hers by integrity of the faith. . . .

Why, then, does the Son say to His mother, *Woman, what is it to Me and to you? My hour has not yet come*? Our Lord Jesus Christ was both God and man; as God He had no mother, as man he had a mother. His mother, then, was the mother of His flesh, of His humanity, of the infirmity which He had taken upon Himself for us. He was about to work a miracle, not according to His infirmity, but according [287] to His divinity as God, not as born of weak man. *The foolishness of God is wiser than men.* His mother, then, demanded the miracle; but as if He did not recognize the human womb when about to accomplish a divine act, He seemed to say, "That which does a miracle in Me does not come of you, you have not brought forth My divinity; but because you have brought forth My infirmity, therefore I will acknowledge you when that same infirmity is hanging on the cross." This is the meaning of *My hour has not yet come*. He knew her then Who had indeed always known her. And before He was born of her He knew His mother by predestination, and before God Himself created her of whom He was to be created man. He knew His mother, but at a certain hour in a mystery He does not recognize her: and at a certain hour, which had not yet come, He does recognize her, also in a mystery. For He recognized her when that which she had brought forth was dying. For not that by which Mary was made was dying, but what had been made out of Mary was dying. It was not the Eternity of the Godhead which was dying, but the infirmity of the flesh. His answer, therefore, was to this effect: He distinguished in the faith of believers who He was and how He came. For the God and Lord of heaven and earth comes to us by a human mother. As Lord of the world, of the heavens, and of the earth, He is Lord of Mary also; as Creator of heaven and earth He is the Creator of Mary; but according to what is written, *Made of woman, made under the Law*, He is the Son of Mary. The very Lord of Mary is the true Son of Mary; the very Creator of Mary is also created out of Mary. Wonder not that He is Son and Lord; for as He is the Son of Mary, so is He called Son of David, and therefore is He Son of David because He [288] is Son of Mary. Listen to the Apostle's clear words: *Who was made to him of the seed of David according to the flesh.* Consider Him too as the Lord of David, and let David say it in his own words: *The Lord said to my Lord, Sit at my right hand.* Jesus Himself proposed this to the Jews, and thereby refuted them. How, then, is He both Lord and Son of David? He is Son of David according to the flesh, and Lord of David according to the Divinity: so He is Son of Mary according to the flesh, and Lord of Mary according to His Majesty. Because, therefore, she was not the mother of the Divinity, and He was to accomplish the miracle which she asked for by His divinity, He answered her, *Woman, what is it to Me and to you?*

but lest you should think that I deny you to be My mother, *My hour has not yet come.*" When that infirmity of which you are the mother begins to hang on the cross, then I will recognize you. Let us see if this be true. At the time of Our Lord's passion the same Evangelist who had known Our Lord's mother, and had introduced her to us even at that marriage-feast as the Lord's mother, tells us that *there stood near the cross the mother of Jesus, and Jesus said to His mother, Woman, behold your Son; and to the disciple, Behold your mother.* He commends His mother to the disciple; He Who was to die before His mother, and to rise before His mother's death, commends her; the Man commends man to man. This is what Mary had borne. The hour had come of which He had spoken at the marriage-feast, when He said, *My hour has not yet come.*

(289)
51. THE MARRIAGE FEAST OF CANA
(*Tractates on the Gospel of John*, 8.1 and 9.2)

As we wonder at the things which were done by the Man Jesus, so let us wonder at those which were done by Jesus Our God. It was Jesus our God Who made the heavens and the earth, the sea, and all the beauty of the firmament, the richness of the earth, the fruitful depths of the sea, all those things which are before our eyes were made by Him. And we see them, and if His Spirit be in us, our wonder at them takes the form of praising their Maker. It does not induce us to consider the works apart from their Maker, nor to turn our face, so to speak, to the works, and our back to Him Who brought them forth.

These things, indeed, we see, and they are before our eyes. What of those things which we do not see, as for instance, the Angels, and Virtues, and Powers, and Dominations, and every single inhabitant of that place above the skies who are not visible to our bodily eyes? The angels, nevertheless, have often shown themselves to men when it was necessary that they should. Did not God make all these things also through His Word, that is, His only Son Our Lord Jesus Christ? Who, if not God, made that human soul itself, invisible as it is, which by the works it shows forth in the flesh is a subject of exceeding wonder to [290] wisely thinking minds? And through whom was this soul made except through the Son of God? I speak not yet of the soul of man. Soul, as it is manifested in any brute beast you please, governs in a way its own physical mass. It directs the several senses; the eyes to see, the ears to hear, the nostrils to smell, the palate to distinguish tastes, the members, in short, to discharge their proper functions. Does the body, and not the soul, its inhabitant, do these things? Still, the soul is invisible, and from that which it does, it moves men to wonder. Now bring your thought to bear upon man's soul, to which God has granted the power of knowing his Creator, and of distinguishing between good and evil, that is, between what is just and what is unjust: what great things it does through the body. Consider the whole sphere of the earth encompassed in the human commonwealth, and by how many different administrations, and degrees of administration, in what conditions of citizens, laws, customs, and arts. All this is done by the soul, and its power is invisible. When it is withdrawn from the body you have a mere corpse; but when it is present it acts as a sort of preservative against bodily humors. For all flesh is corruptible, and falls into corruption, unless it be prevented by the soul as a kind of salt. But this is common to the soul of man and of beast; those things pertaining to mind and understanding are more wonderful, as I have said. In them man is renewed after the likeness of his Creator in which he was made. What will this power of soul be when this body shall put on incorruption, and this mortality immortality? If the soul can do so much through corruptible flesh, what will it be able to do through the spiritual body after the resurrection of the dead? Still, this soul of wondrous nature [291] and substance, as I have said, is an invisible thing and an intelligible thing; and this soul was made by Jesus our God, because He is the Word of God. All things were made by Him, and without Him nothing was made. While therefore we see so many great things made by Jesus our God, how can we wonder at the water turned into wine by the Man Jesus? For neither was He so made man as to cease to be God. In Him man was assumed; God was not lost. The same Person therefore wrought this who wrought all things. Let us then not wonder that God wrought all this, but love that He wrought among us, and wrought for our restoration. In those very things which He wrought He signified something to us. I imagine that He did not go without cause to the marriage feast. Apart from the miracle, there is some hidden and mysterious meaning in the thing itself. Let us knock that He may open to us, and inebriate us with invisible wine, for we were water, and He made us wine, and made us wise; we who were formerly without taste, relish His faith. And perhaps it belongs to this very wisdom to understand in God's honor, in praise of His majesty, and in the charity of His most powerful mercy, that which was done in this mystery. Our Lord came as an invited guest to the nuptial feast. What wonder that He went to the marriage at that house, Who came into this world for a marriage? For if He did not come to a nuptial, He has no bride in this world; and what is then the meaning of the Apostle's words: *I have espoused you to one husband, that I may present you as a chaste virgin to Christ.* Why should he fear lest the virginity of the spouse of Christ should be defiled by the devil? *I fear*, he says, *lest as the serpent seduced Eve by his subtlety, so your minds should be corrupted, and fall from the simplicity that is in Christ.* [292] He has therefore here a spouse whom He has redeemed by His own blood, and to whom He has given the Holy Spirit as a pledge. He has delivered her from the slavery of the devil. He has died for her sins and risen again for her justification. What man will offer gifts so great to his bride? Men may offer all sorts of

worldly ornaments, silver, and gold, and precious
stones, horses and slaves, and lands and spoils; but
will any one offer his own blood? If, indeed, a bridegroom be expected to give his blood for his bride, no
man will be found to marry a wife. But Our Lord
dying in all confidence gave His blood for her whom
He was to have in rising again, whom He had already
espoused in the Virgin's womb. For the Word is
the Bridegroom, and human nature is the bride, and
the one Son of God is both of these, and the same is
the Son of man; from that womb of the Virgin Mary,
wherein He was made the Head of the Church, *He
came forth like a bridegroom out of His bride-chamber*,
as the Scripture foretold, *having rejoiced as a giant to
run His way*: He came out of His bride-chamber like
a bridegroom, and went as a guest to the nuptials. . . .
It is God Who works miracles every day throughout
the whole of creation; men have grown to make small
account of them, not because they are slight, but by
reason of their frequency. The rare wonders, however,
which were worked by this same Lord, that is, by the
Word made flesh for us, created greater admiration in
the hearts of men, not because they were more wonderful than those which He works daily in His creatures,
but because the latter are brought about, as it were,
in the ordinary course of things, whereas the former
are seen to be shown forth to the eyes of men as by
the efficacy of a living and present power. We said, as
you remember, that men were filled with wonder at one
[293] man rising from the dead; no one wonders at those
who are daily born into the world out of nothing. Thus,

who is not astonished at the water turned into wine, when this is what God does every year in the vine? . . .

In coming as an invited guest to the marriage-feast, apart from even the mystical meaning, Our Lord wished to bless marriage which He Himself had made. Men were to rise up to condemn marriage, of whom the Apostle spoke; saying, that it was an evil, and that the devil had instituted it; whereas Our Lord Himself when asked in the Gospel whether it was lawful for a man to give up his wife for any cause whatever, answered that it was not lawful except for fornication. In which answer, if you remember, He says, *What God has put together, let man not separate.* And they who are well instructed in the Catholic faith, know that God is the author of marriage, and that as it is from Him, so divorce is from the devil. But in the case of fornication, it is allowable to put a wife away, because, by not keeping the conjugal faith to her husband, it was she herself who first refused to be a wife. Nor are those who consecrate their virginity to God, although they hold a higher rank as to honor and sanctity in the Church, without nuptials; for they too belong to the nuptials of the whole Church, in which marriage-feast Christ is the bridegroom. And for this reason, therefore, Our Lord went as an invited guest to the marriage-feast, that He might establish the chastity of the married state, and show forth the sacrament of matrimony; for the bridegroom of that marriage feast, to whom the words, *You have kept the good wine till now,* were said, was a figure of Our Lord. Christ has kept until now the good wine, that is, His Gospel.

[294]
52. "FROM THAT HOUR THE DISCIPLE TOOK HER TO HIS OWN"
(*On the Gospel of John*, 119)

AFTER the crucifixion of Our Lord had been accomplished, and when the division of His garments, even those for which they had cast lots, was made, let us see what St. John the Evangelist goes on to narrate. *And the soldiers indeed did these things. Now there stood by the cross of Jesus, His Mother, and His Mother's sister, Mary of Cleophas, and Mary Magdalene. When Jesus therefore had seen His Mother and the disciple standing, whom He loved, He said to His Mother: Woman, behold your Son. After that, He said to the disciple: Behold your mother. And from that hour the disciple took her to his own.* This truly is that hour of which Jesus had spoken to His Mother when He was about to turn the water into wine: *Woman, what is this to Me and to thee? My hour has not yet come.* He foretold, therefore, this hour which had not then arrived, in which hour He Who was about to die should recognize her of whom He had been born according to the flesh. At the marriage-feast He Who was to do divine things rebuked the mother, not of His Godhead but of His infirmity, as if He did not know her; whereas, now that He is suffering human pain, He commends her, from whom He was made man, with human affection to His disciple. At the [295] marriage-feast, He Who had created Mary was showing Himself in His strength; but on Calvary that which Mary had brought forth was hanging on the Cross. A lesson, therefore, is here conveyed to us. Our Master in His goodness does Himself what He admonishes us to do, and He instructed His own by His own example, to show us that children, who are filial, should have a care for their parents; as if that tree of the Cross, to which the limbs of Our dying Lord were attached, was also a pulpit from which that Lord preached to us. The Apostle St. Paul had learned some of this sound doctrine, and he taught it when he said, *If any man have not care of his own, and especially of those of his house, he has denied the faith, and is worse than an infidel.* But what relationship can be closer to any man than that of parents to their children, and children to their parents? The Pattern and Teacher of the saints Himself, therefore, exemplified in His own person this most holy precept when He provided her in a certain sense with another son in His own place, and this He did not as God for the creature whom He had created and was ruling, but as Man for the Mother of whom He had been born, and whom He was leaving behind Him. For that which follows explains why He did this. The Evangelist says, speaking of himself, *And from that hour the disciple took her to his own.* Thus he is accustomed to speak of himself as the disciple whom Jesus loved. Jesus indeed loved all, but John better and more intimately than the rest, so that at the Last Supper He allowed him to lean upon His breast; I believe that He meant by this to commend more especially the divine excellence of that Gospel, which He was going to preach through John.

But how did John take the Mother of the Lord [296] as his own? He had been with the other disciples when they said to Our Lord, *Behold we have left all things, and have followed You.* He had also heard the words which were then uttered, *Whoever shall give up these things for Me, shall receive a hundredfold even in this life.* This disciple, therefore, had a hundredfold more than he had given up, into which he was to receive the mother of Him Who was the giver of the hundredfold. Blessed John, however, had received a hundredfold in a society wherein no member called anything his own, but all things were in common among them, as it is written in the Acts of the Apostles. Thus it was that they were Apostles, as if having nothing, and possessing all things. How then did the disciple and servant take the mother of his Lord and Master as his own, when none of them had anything for himself? Is it explained by the passage which occurs a little further on in the same book, *For as many as were owners of lands or houses sold them, and brought the price of the things they sold, and laid it down before the feet of the Apostles. And distribution was made to every one according as he had need.* Are we to understand that the necessary distribution was so meted to this disciple, that blessed

Mary was made into a great deal, being accounted as his mother? Or are we rather to interpret the words, *From that hour the disciple took her to his own*, as meaning that the care of providing her with whatever she required was to belong to John? He took her then, to his own, not as a bit of property, because he had none, but he took the care of her upon him as a duty for which he was personally answerable.

[297]
53. THE WEDDING GARMENT
(*Sermon* 90)

THE nuptials of the King's Son and His Feast are known to all the faithful, and the Table of the Lord is spread for all who have the will to approach it. But it is a matter of importance how a man approaches it, since he is not forbidden access to it. Holy Scripture teaches us that there are two divine feasts; one to which both good and evil people come, the other to which the bad do not come. Therefore the marriage-feast, described by St. Matthew in his twenty-second chapter, has both good and bad guests. They who excused themselves from coming at all are the bad, but not all who entered in are good. I address myself, therefore, to those of you who are sitting amongst the good at that feast, who are mindful of the words, *He who eats and drinks unworthily, eats and drinks judgment to himself.* . . .

But someone objects, "What wonder is it, that one man in the crowd should have escaped the eyes of the master's servants, not having on a wedding-garment? What is one man? It could not have been on his account that they invited both good and bad?" ...
That one man was a class of men, for they were many. Perhaps a careful listener will here answer, "I have no wish to hear your conjectures: I want to have proof that they were many."

[298]
God will help me by His own words, although my ministry will enlighten your minds. Well, then, The father of the family went in that he might see those who were sitting at table. Notice, my brethren, that the business of the servants was merely to invite and to bring the good and the bad. Observe that it is not said, "The servants went in to see the guests, and they saw there a man who had not on a wedding-garment, and they spoke to him." This is not written. It was the king who went in, and the king who found the man, and the king who discerned him and separated him from the rest. This is by no means to be overlooked. But I also undertook to show you that the man without the wedding-garment was one of many. *The king went in to see the guests, and he saw there a man who had not on a wedding-garment, and he said to him, Friend, how did you come in here, not having a wedding-garment? But he was silent;* for he who thus questioned was one whom that man could deceive in nothing. The garment of his heart, not of

his body, was passed in review. . . . The king discovered the man who was hidden to his servants. When questioned he was silent. He is bound, cast out, and is condemned, one out of many. The king had certainly questioned only one, and to one his words had been addressed, *Friend, how did you enter here?* The one was silent, and of him alone it was said, *Bind his hands and his feet, and cast him into the exterior darkness; there shall be weeping and gnashing of teeth.* Why so? *For many are called, but few are chosen.* Who may contradict so manifest a revelation of the truth? . . . Let the few go, cast out the many. He was alone. Truly this one man not only constituted the many, but the many outweighed the number of the good. Many indeed are [299] good, but in comparison with the wicked they are few. Much corn is grown; compare it to the chaff, and you will find few perfect ears of wheat. The same people who are many in themselves are few compared to the wicked. How do we prove that they are many in reality? *Many shall come from the East and from the West.* And where? To that marriage feast, at which both the good and the wicked are present. Our Lord spoke of another feast when He added, *And they shall sit down with Abraham, Isaac, and Jacob in the kingdom of heaven.* That is the feast of which the wicked will not partake. Let us partake worthily of the feast which now is, that we may come to the one hereafter. The same then who are many are few; many in number, few in comparison with the wicked. What, therefore, does Our Lord say? He finds one man and says, Let the many be cast out, let the few remain. For the words, *Many are called, but few are chosen*, mean nothing more nor less than to show plainly how in this feast men are proved worthy of reaching that other banquet of which no sinner will partake.

What then? I would have all of you who now approach the table of the Lord remain with the few; I would not have you be cast out with the many. How will you be able to do this? Put on the wedding garment. Tell us, you say, what this wedding garment is. Beyond a doubt it is that garment which is proper only to the good, who are allowed to remain at table, and destined through the Lord's grace to sit down at that other banquet of which no unjust man is to partake. It is they who have the nuptial garment. Let us see, then, my brethren, what it is which some of the faithful have which the wicked have not. This something will be the wedding garment. If I name the [300] sacraments, you see that they are common to both good and evil. Is it baptism? Without baptism indeed no man reaches God, but not every man who has baptism reaches God. I cannot, therefore, look upon baptism, that is, the sacrament itself, as the wedding garment, which garment I see on the good and on the wicked. Possibly it is the altar, or what we receive from the altar. We see that many eat, and eat and drink judgment to themselves. What, then, is it? Fasting? The wicked also fast. Is it going to church? This the wicked do. Is it, in short, miracle-working? Not only do both good and bad men work wonders, but sometimes the good do not work them. In the days of the people of old, Pharaoh's magi worked miracles, and the Israelites did not work any. Moses and Aaron alone of their number worked miracles; the rest worked none, but they witnessed them, and feared, and believed. Were the wonder-working magi of Pharaoh better than the people of Israel, who could not work miracles, and who were still God's people? In the Church itself, listen to the Apostle: *Are all prophets? Have all the grace of healing? Do all speak with tongues?*

What, then, is that wedding garment? It is this: *The end of the commandment is charity from a pure heart, and a good conscience, and an unfeigned faith,* the Apostle says. This is the nuptial garment. Not any sort of charity; for many men, who are even associated in crime seem to care very much about one another. Those who rob together, who have a similar taste for sorcery, or for actors, for charioteers, or for hounds, care very much about each other; but they have not charity which is *from a pure heart, and a good conscience, and an unfeigned faith*. Love of this sort constitutes the nuptial garment: *If I [301] speak with the tongues of men, and of angels, and have not charity, I am become as sounding brass, or a tinkling cymbal.* Men have come in to the feast having only the gift of tongues, and to them it is said, *Why did you come in here, having not on the wedding-garment? If I should have prophecy,* the

Apostle says, *and should know all mysteries, and all knowledge, and if I should have faith, so that I could remove mountains, and have not charity, I am nothing.* These are chiefly the miracles of men who have not the wedding garment. *If I have all these things*, the Apostle says, *and have not* Christ, *I am nothing.* I am nothing. What then, is prophecy nothing, or is a knowledge of mysteries nothing? It is not these things which are nothing; it is I, who, having them, and having not charity, am nothing. How many good things are of no avail without the one thing. If I have not charity, and give alms to the poor, and confess the name of Christ even unto blood, or give myself up to be burnt, I may do these things from a love of glory, and they are empty. For St. Paul speaks of such things as being done not in the tender charity of devotion, but even from vainglory, as in this passage:]f I should distribute all my goods to the poor, and if I should deliver my body to be burnt, and have not charity, it profits me nothing. This is the nuptial garment. Ask yourselves if you have it, for if so you may sit confidently at the King's banquet. Two things exist in the one man - charity and cupidity. Let charity be born in you, if it be not born already; and if it is born, let it grow, and be fostered, and nourished. But as to cupidity, if it cannot be altogether extinguished in this life - because if we say that we are without sin, we deceive ourselves, and the truth is not in us - in so far as it is in us, in so far are we not without sin. Let [302] charity grow and cupidity decrease, that the former may be perfected - that is, charity; let cupidity

be consumed. Put on the nuptial garment. I speak
to you who have it not already. You are within the
fold and partake of the banquet, and you have not yet
the robe of the Bridegroom; you still seek your own
profits, not the things of Jesus Christ. For the nuptial
garment is put on in honor of the marriage, that is,
of the bride and bridegroom. You know the Bridegroom, Who is Christ; you know the Bride, who is
the Church. Honor the Bride and Bridegroom. If
you have shown them honor, you will be the children
of the marriage. Therefore, my brethren, have
charity. I have shown you the nuptial garment. It
is true that faith is praised, but the Apostle has distinguished what kind of faith. For the Apostle St.
James upbraids certain men who boasted of their faith
and were not leading good lives. *You believe that
there is one God,* he says. *You do well: the devils
also believe and tremble.* Call to mind with me why
Peter was praised and blessed. Was it because he
said, *You are Christ, the Son of the living God*? He
Who pronounced him blessed did not listen to the
words, but looked at the love in his heart. You should
know that the happiness of Peter was not in the words
themselves. The devils, too, had said as much: *We
know who You are, the Holy One of God.* Peter confessed Him to be the Son of God; so did the devils.
. . . Peter spoke in love, the devils out of fear.

Do not, therefore, boast of your faith alone, you who
have come to the feast. Have a care that it is the
right sort of faith, and then you are proved to have on

the nuptial robe. Let the Apostle make the distinction for our instruction; neither circumcision nor uncircumcision avails anything, but faith. Tell us [303] what faith, for do not the devils believe and tremble? "I *do* tell you," he says, "I am even now making the distinction: *but faith that works by charity*.... Have faith with charity, for you cannot have charity without faith." I beg, and admonish, and teach you in the Lord's name, to have faith with charity, because you were able to have faith without charity. I do not exhort you to have faith, but charity. For you were not able to have charity without faith. I mean charity towards God and towards our neighbor: how can this exist without faith? How does the man love God who does not believe in God? How does the fool love God who says in his heart, "There is no God"? You may possibly believe that Christ has come, and still not love Him. But it is impossible that loving Christ you should not believe that Christ has come.

[304]
54. ADORATION OF THE HOLY EUCHARIST
(*On the Psalms* 98.9)

ADORE the footstool of the Lord our God, for it is holy. What have we here to adore? His footstool.... But consider, brethren, what it is He commands us to adore. In another place the Scripture says, *The heavens are My seat, but the earth is My footstool.* Then, does He command us to adore the earth, as He says in this passage that it is His footstool? And how shall we adore the earth when the Scripture plainly tells us, *The Lord your God shall you adore.* Here it says, *Adore His footstool*, but explaining what that is, it says, *The earth is My footstool.* Here I am put into a difficulty: I fear to adore the earth lest He Who made heaven and earth should condemn me; and again, I fear not to adore the footstool of my Lord, because of the words of the Psalm, *Adore His footstool.* I want to know what His footstool is, and the Scripture tells me the earth is My footstool. In my uncertainty I turn to Christ, for it is He Whom I am here seeking, and I find how the earth may be adored without impiety, how His footstool may be properly worshiped. He took earth of the earth, for flesh is of earth, and He received flesh from the flesh of Mary. And because He walked here in that Flesh and gave us that very Flesh to eat unto salvation - but no one eats that Flesh [305] without first adoring it - we find how it is that this footstool of the Lord may be adored. Not only do we not sin in adoring, but we should sin did we not adore. But does the flesh give life? In speaking of the glorification of this same earth the Lord Himself said, *It is the spirit that gives life: the flesh profits nothing.* When, therefore, you turn your face to the earth, wherever it may be, and prostrate yourself, look upon it not as earth, but that Holy One Whose footstool you are adoring, for your adoration is on His account; hence the Psalmist's words, *Adore His footstool, because He is holy.* Who is this Holy One? He Whose footstool you are adoring. And when you adore Him, lest your mind be occupied with the carnal meaning and you should not be quickened by the spirit, He says, *It is the spirit that gives life: the flesh proflts nothing.* Our Lord laid this down after speaking about His flesh. His words were, *Unless a man eat My Flesh, he shall not have eternal life in him.* A certain number of His disciples - about seventy - were scandalized, and said, *This saying is hard, who can bear it? And they went away, and walked with Him no more.* His words seemed hard to them, *Unless a man eat My Flesh, he shall not have eternal life.* They took them stupidly in a literal carnal sense, and imagined that Our Lord was going to cut off parts of His body and so give them to eat, and they said, *This saying is hard.* It was they, not the saying, who were hard. For if they had not been so, if they had been meek, they would have said to themselves: "He would not speak in this way unless His words bore some secret meaning." If they had not been hard but gentle, they would have remained with Him, and would have learned from Him that which they who remained after their departure did learn. For after their going away, His twelve disciples who [306] had remained with Him said to Him, as if grieving over their death, that they were scandalized at His words and had withdrawn from Him. But He instructed them, saying: "It is the spirit that quickens: the flesh profits nothing. The words that I have spoken to you are spirit and life. Put a spiritual meaning upon what I have said. You are not to eat this body which you see nor to drink the blood which

the men who crucify Me are to spill. It is a mystery
which I have laid before you, and in its spiritual sense
it will give you life. Even if it is necessary to give
that mystery a visible celebration, it must be spiritually
understood. Exalt the Lord our God, and adore
His footstool, for it is holy."

[307]
55. MANNER OF RECEIVING THE HOLY EUCHARIST
(Sermon 71.17)

How are we to understand those words of Our Lord, *He who eats My Flesh and drinks My Blood remains in Me and I in him*? Are we to take them as applying also to those of whom the Apostle says, that *they eat and drink judgment to themselves*, eating His Flesh and drinking His Blood? Did Judas remain in Christ, or Christ in Him, he who sold his Master and impiously betrayed Him? although, as the evangelist St. Luke plainly says, he had eaten and drunk of that first sacrament of His Body and Blood, prepared by His hands, with the other disciples. And do so many who either eat that Flesh and drink that Blood with an insincere heart, or apostasize after its reception, remain in Christ, or Christ in them? But there is most surely a certain manner of eating that Flesh and of drinking that Blood by which he who eats and drinks remains in Christ and Christ in him. It is not, therefore, that any one who eats the Flesh of Christ and who drinks His Blood in any kind of a way remains in Christ and Christ in him, but there is a certain manner of receiving which was known to Our Lord when He said these words. Thus again when He says, *He who shall blaspheme against the Holy Spirit* [308] *shall not be forgiven for ever,* He does not mean that every blasphemer is guilty of a sin which cannot be remitted, but that there is a certain kind of unpardonable blasphemy, which He Who uttered this true and terrible sentence wished us to inquire into and to be clear about.

[309]
56. "JESUS DID NOT TRUST HIMSELF UNTO THEM" (JOHN 2.24)
(*On the Gospel of John,* 11.2, 3, etc.)

You have heard that when Our Lord Jesus Christ was at Jerusalem at the pasch upon the festival day many believed in His name, seeing His signs which He did. *Many believed in His name*; and what follows? *But Jesus did not trust Himself unto them.* What is the meaning of this, *They believed in His name, but Jesus did not trust Himself unto them.* Possibly they did not believe in Him, and were pretending, and for this reason Jesus did not trust Himself to them? But the Evangelist would not say, *Many believed in His name* unless his testimony were true. Here, then, we have a great and wonderful mystery: men believe in

Christ and Christ does not trust Himself to men. Because He is the Son of God, He offered Himself of His own will to suffer; and if He had not been willing He would never have suffered, nor even have been born. If He had so willed it He might have been born and not died, and whatsoever else He had willed He might have done, because He is the Almighty Son of the Almighty Father. Let us prove this from the evidence of facts. The Gospel says, when they would have held Him He departed from them, and that when they would have hurled Him down from the top [310] of the mountain He went His way unharmed. And when they came to seize Him, He being already sold by the traitor Judas, who thought he held his Lord and Master in his power, He showed them here too that He suffered by His free will, not because He was obliged. For when the Jews would have seized Him He said to them, *Whom do you seek?* And they replied, *Jesus of Nazareth*. And He said, *I am He.* At this answer they turned back and fell on their faces. By causing them to fall prostrate at His reply He manifested His power in order to show them that He became their prisoner by an act of His will. Therefore He suffered out of mercy. For He was delivered up for our sins, and rose again for our justification. Listen to His words: *I have power to lay down My life and I have power to take it up again. No man takes it away from Me, but I lay it down of Myself that I may take it up again.* Whereas then He had power so great which He preached by His words and manifested by His deeds, what is the meaning of Jesus not trusting

Himself to them, as if they had been going to injure
Him, or to do something to Him against His will,
which is the more curious, inasmuch as they already
believed in His name. For the Gospel speaks of the
same people when it says, *They believed in His name,
but Jesus did not trust Himself to them.* Why? *Because He knew all men, and because He needed not
that any should give testimony of man, for He knew
what was in man.* He who had produced the work
knew it better than it knew itself. The Creator of
man knew what was in man, which man himself, a
creature, knew not. Is not this exemplified in Peter,
for he knew not what was in him when he said, *I will
go with you unto death.* Listen and see that Our Lord
knew what was in man: *Will you go with Me unto
[311] death? Amen, amen I say unto you, the cock shall
not crow this day till you three times deny Me.* Man knew
not what was in him, but man's Creator knew. Many,
however, believed in His name, and Jesus did not trust
Himself to them. How are we to understand this,
brethren? Perhaps that which follows will throw
some light on the mystery here contained. It is true
and manifest that men believed in Him, no one doubts
the Gospel's words and testimony. And again, it is
equally clear that Jesus did not trust Himself to them,
no Christian disputes it, for the same Gospel speaks
and testifies to the fact. . . . Let us see what follows.
*And there was a man of the Pharisees, named Nicodemus, a ruler of the Jews. This man came to Jesus
by night, and said to Him, Rabbi . . . we know that
You are a teacher from God, for no man can do these*

signs which You do unless God be with him. This Nicodemus therefore was one of the number who believed in His name, seeing the signs and wonders which He did. For a little before the Gospel had said that, *When he was at Jerusalem, at the Pasch upon the festival day, many believed in His name.* Why did they believe? It goes on to say, *Seeing the signs which He did.* And what does it say of Nicodemus? *There was a ruler of the Jews, named Nicodemus. This man came to Jesus by night, and said to Him, Rabbi, we know that You are come a teacher from God.* Nicodemus had also believed in His name, and what had his motive been? *No man can do these signs which You do unless God be with him.* If, then, Nicodemus was one of the many who believed in His name, let us see, in his case, why it was that Jesus did not trust Himself to them. Jesus answered, and said to him, *Amen, amen, I say to you, unless a man be born again he cannot see the kingdom of God.* Jesus trusts Himself to those who are born again. They believed in Him, and He trusted not Himself unto them. All catechumens are of this number; they already believe in the name of Christ, but Jesus does not trust Himself to them. ... If we ask a catechumen, "Do you believe in Christ?" he will answer, "Yes," and he crosses himself; he bears the cross of Christ on his forehead, and is not ashamed of the cross of his Lord. Behold he has believed in His name. Let us ask him, "Do you eat the Flesh of the Son of man, and do you drink of His Blood?" He does not understand what we mean, because Jesus has not trusted Himself to him.

As, therefore, Nicodemus was one of this number, he came to the Lord, but he came by night, and perhaps this is significant. He came to the Lord, and he came at night; he came to the Light, and he came in darkness. What does the Apostle say to those who are born again of water and of the Spirit? *You were once darkness, now that you are light in the Lord walk like sons of the light*; and again, *Let us, who are of the day, be sober.* They, then, who are born again, belonged to the night, and are now of the day; they were darkness, and they are light. Jesus already trusts Himself to them, and they do not come to Jesus by night, like Nicodemus; they do not seek the day in the darkness. As such they are even proven to be. Jesus approached them and worked their salvation, for to them He said, *Unless a man eat My Flesh and drink My Blood he shall not have life in him.* By the sign of the cross which they bear on their foreheads catechumens already belong to the great house, but from servants let them become sons. For they are not nothing who already belong to the great house. But when did the people of Israel eat the manna? After the passage of the Red Sea. Listen to the Apostle's interpretation of [313] the Red Sea: *I will not have you ignorant, brethren, concerning our fathers who were all under a cloud, and who all crossed through the sea.* He goes on to say why they crossed the sea, as if anticipating your question, *And they were all baptized by Moses in the cloud and in the sea.* If, then, the sea, which was a figure, was of so great worth, what will be the rite of baptism?

If that which was done as a figure led the people who had crossed the sea to the manna, what will Christ do for His people, whose passage He has Himself guided, in His own true baptism? Through His baptism He has led believers across the sea, after destroying all sins, as if overtaking the enemy in that sea in which all the Egyptians perished. Where did He lead us, my brethren? Where did Jesus lead us by baptism, whose figure Moses then was, as he led the people over the Red Sea? . . . To the manna. What is the manna? *I am the living Bread,* He says, *Who have come down from heaven.* The faithful partake of the manna after the passage of the Red Sea. . . . That Red Sea signified the baptism of Christ. Is the baptism of Christ red if not because it is consecrated by His Blood? Where, then, does He lead believers and baptized Christians? To the manna. The manna, I say. We know what the Jews received, that people of Israel; we know what God rained down to them from heaven; and the catechumens know not that which Christians receive. Let them blush for their ignorance; let them pass through the Red Sea and eat the manna, that as they have believed in the name of Jesus, so Jesus may trust Himself to them.

Observe then, my brethren, what this man answers who comes by night to Jesus. Although he did come to Jesus, still, because he comes by night, he speaks with the infirmity of the flesh. He does not understand [314] what he hears from the Lord, from *the Light which enlightens every man who comes into this world.*

Already Our Lord had said to him, *Unless a man be born again, he shall not see the kingdom of God.* And Nicodemus replies, *How can a man be born again when he is old?* The spirit speaks to him, and he thinks of the animal meaning. He relishes the things of his own flesh, because he has not yet relished the Flesh of Christ. For when Our Lord Jesus had said, *Unless a man eat My Flesh and drink My Blood he shall not have life in him,* some of His followers were scandalised, and said among themselves, *This saying is hard, who can bear it?* They thought that Jesus meant to say that they should eat Him as they did a lamb when it was cooked, and in their horror at His words they left Him, and walked with Him no more. ... When, therefore, He had asked His disciples, *Will you too go away?* Peter, the rock, replied in the name of all, *Lord, to whom shall we go? You have the words of eternal life.* The Flesh of the Lord had been of sweet flavor in his mouth. But Our Lord went on to explain His words, *Unless a man eat My Flesh and drink My Blood he shall not have life in him,* by saying, *It is the spirit that gives life.* Lest they should attach carnal meaning to His words, He said, *It is the spirit that gives life; the flesh profits nothing: the words that I have spoken to yon are spirit and life.*

Nicodemus, who had come by night to Jesus, was not quickened either by this spirit or by this life. Jesus says to him, *Unless a man be born again, he shall not see the kingdom of God.* And he being carnal-minded, for his mouth had not yet tasted the sweetness of the

Flesh of Christ, replies, *How can a man be born again when he is old? Can he enter a second time into his mother's womb, and be born again?*

[315] Nicodernus knew of only one birth, that which comes from Adam and Eve. He knew not yet of the birth which is from God and the Church; he knew only those parents who generate unto death, not yet those who generate unto life; he knew only those parents who give birth to succeeding generations, not yet those who in perpetual life generate men who are to endure forever. Whereas, then, there are two generations, his mind grasped only the one. One is earthly, the other is heavenly; one belongs to the flesh, the other to the spirit; one is mortal, the other is eternal; one is brought about by earthly marriage, the other is born of God and the Church. But both are things which happen only once; neither can be repeated. Nicodemus rightly understood birth according to the flesh; but you in like manner should understand birth according to the spirit. What was it that he understood? *Can a man enter a second time into his mother's womb, and be born again?* Thus if any man propose to you to be spiritually born again, answer him in the words of Nicodemus, "Can a man enter a second time into his mother's womb, and be born again? I am already born of Adam into the world; Adam cannot give me a second birth. I am already born of Christ, and Christ cannot give me a second birth; for as the physical birth cannot be repeated, so neither can baptism."

57. "JESUS FLED"
(Tractates on the Gospel of John, 25.4)

WHY is it said that Jesus fled? Truly indeed He would not have been kept or taken against His will any more than He would have been recognized if it had not been His pleasure. You will now see by what follows that this was done in mystery, not from necessity, but for a significant reason, because He showed Himself to the same crowd who were seeking Him, and discoursing with them He told them many things, and spoke much concerning the bread from heaven. Was He not talking of the bread with them from whom He fled, lest He should be held? Was it not then in His power not to let Himself be taken by them as it was afterwards during His conversation with them? By fleeing, therefore, He signified something. What is *He fled*? His greatness could not be understood. When you are unable to grasp a thing, you say, "It escapes me." *He*, therefore, *fled again into the mountain, Himself alone.* The first-born from the dead ascends into highest heaven, and intercedes for us.

He being alone above, the great High Priest, who entered into the interior of the veil, the people remaining outside (for the high priest of the Old Law, who did this once in the year, was a type of Our Lord). He [317] then being thus above, what had the disciples in the ship to endure? For He having gone to the heights, that ship figured forth the Church. If we do not apply the dangers of that ship as referring before all things to the Church, these things were not types but merely transitory. If, however, we find in the Church the fulfillment of what they signified, their meaning is plain, because the deeds of Christ are a sort of language. *And when evening was come,* the Evangelist says, *His disciples went down to the sea. And when they had gone up into a ship, they went over the sea to Capharnaum.* He speaks of a thing which was afterwards accomplished, as quickly finished. They went over the sea to Capharnaum. He returns to his narration in order to explain how they reached Capharnaum, that is, by sailing over the lake. And while they were bound for the place, which he has already spoken of their reaching, he recapitulates what has happened. *It was now dark, and Jesus was not come unto them.* It was indeed dark, for the Light had not come. *It was now dark, and Jesus was not come unto them.* As the end of the world approaches, there is an increase of error and a greater fear; iniquity is strengthened, and infidelity is more and more frequent: light, in short, which is clearly shown in St. John's Gospel to be one and the same thing as charity, so that he says, *He who hates his brother is in darkness,* is more often extinguished: day by day the darkness caused by the hatred of brothers becomes stronger, and still Jesus does not come. How may we know that it is stronger? Because *iniquity shall abound, and the charity of many shall grow cold.* The darkness grows thicker, and Jesus does not yet come. Increasing darkness, decreasing charity, abounding iniquity, these are the waves which threaten the ship. The winds and tempests are the clamors of the [318] wicked. Hence it is that charity grows cold, and the waves grow boisterous, and the ship is tossed.

And still tribulations are so great that even those who have believed in Jesus, and are striving to persevere unto the end, are fearful of their strength giving way; the Christian is full of alarm when he sees Christ walking on the waves, despising the ambition and the lofty things of this world. Were not these things foretold to him? They were indeed; for when Jesus walked upon the waters they were afraid. Just as Christians, although they put their hope in the next world, when they see the pride of this one brought low, are often disturbed at the breaking up of human things. They open the Gospel and the Scriptures and find all this is foretold, because Our Lord is the first to do it. He humbles the might of this world that He may be glorified by the lowly ones. It is written of this human greatness, *You shall destroy the best established cities*; and again, *The swords of the enemy have failed unto the end: and their cities you have destroyed.* Why, then, do you fear, O Christians? Christ it is Who says, *It is I, fear not.* Why are you afraid at these things? What do you fear? I have foretold them, I bring them about, and it is necessary that they should come to pass. *It is I, fear not.* They were willing therefore to take Him into the ship, recognizing Him, and rejoicing in their new security. *And presently the ship was at the land to which they were going.* They landed at last; they came from water to solid land, from disturbance to security, from the journey to its end.

From the words, *And when the multitude had found Him,* you see that He offers Himself to those people [319] by whom He had feared to be taken when He fled into the mountain. He confirms in every way the fact that all those things were spoken in mystery, and that they were done for some great meaning in order to signify something. Here we see Him who fled the crowd by going to the mountain. Does He not now converse with that very crowd? Let them hold Him now and make Him a King. *And when they had found Him on the other .side of the sea, they said to Him, Rabbi, when did you come here?*

After the mystery of the miracle He instructs them that, if possible, they who have been fed may find other food, and that His words may feed the minds of those whose hunger He has stilled, but only if they are able to understand. And if they do not understand, let that which they do not understand be consumed lest the fragments perish. Let us listen as He speaks to us: Jesus answered and said, *"Amen, amen. I say to you, You seek Me, not because you have seen wonders, but because you have eaten of My bread. You seek Me for the flesh, not for the spirit."* How many there are who look for Jesus merely that He may give them some temporal advantage. One has business, so he seeks the support of priests; another is oppressed by a great man, and he flies to the Church; another wants an intercessor with the man who has a small opinion of him; one wants one thing and one another, and every day the Church is filled with petitioners of this kind. Jesus is scarcely ever sought for on His own account. *You seek Me not because you have seen miracles, but because you have eaten of My bread. Labor not for the meat which perishes, but for that which endures unto life everlasting.* You seek Me for something else; seek Me for Myself. For He implies that He is Himself this food, which becomes clearer in [320] what follows. *Which* (food) *the Son of man will give you.* I believe you were expecting once more to feed on loaves, to sit down and have your hunger stilled. But He spoke of food which does not perish, but which endures unto life everlasting, in the same way as He had said to that Samaritan woman, *If you did know who it is that said to you, Give Me to drink; you perhaps would have asked of Him, and He would have given you living water.* And when she said, *Sir, You have nothing wherein to draw, and the well is deep,* He answered, *If you did know Who it is that said to you, Give Me to drink, you would have asked of Him, and He would have given you water of which he that drinks shall not thirst for ever: for whosoever drinks of this water shall thirst again.* She rejoiced and wanted to have some, thinking she would no longer suffer from bodily thirst, as the labor of drawing water wearied her; and this manner of conversation led her on to spiritual drink, and so precisely the same method is followed here.

58. "LITTLE CHILDREN, IT IS THE LAST HOUR"
(*On the Letters of John*, 3.1, etc.)

LITTLE children, it is the last hour. In these words St. John addresses himself to children, bidding them make haste to grow because it is the last hour. Our bodily age does not lie in our will. Thus no man grows according to the body for willing it, just as no man is born when he pleases; but in St. John's point of view our birth and our growth depend upon our own will. No man is born again of water and the Holy Spirit except by his will, therefore if he choose to grow he can grow, and if he choose to be stunted he can be stunted. What is the meaning of growth? It means progress. What is the meaning of being stunted? Falling away. Whoever knows that he is born, let him listen to those who tell him that he is a child, an infant, let him cleave to his mother's breast and his growth is speedy. The Church is his mother, and the two Testaments of Holy Scripture are her breasts. Here the milk of all mysteries accomplished in time for our eternal salvation is imbibed, so that nourished and strengthened by it a man may be able to eat the food. *In the beginning was the Word, and the Word was with God, and the Word was God.* Christ in His humility is our milk, and the same Christ who is equal to the Father is our food. He nourishes us on milk, that He may feed us on bread, [322] for to touch Jesus spiritually in our hearts is to recognize him as equal to the Father.

Hence He forbade Mary to touch Him, saying to her, *Touch Me not, for I have not yet ascended to the Father.* How is this? He offered Himself to the disciples to be handled, and yet avoided Mary's touch? Was it not He who said to the doubting disciple, *Put in your hands and feel the wounds*? Had He already ascended to the Father? Why then does He repel Mary, saying, *Touch Me not, for I have not yet ascended to the Father*? Are we to conclude that He did not fear the touch of men, only the touch of women? His touch has power to cleanse all flesh. Did He fear to be handled by those to whom He first appeared after His resurrection? Was not His resurrection announced to men through women, in order that the serpent might be vanquished by a counter device? For inasmuch as the serpent had carried tidings of death through woman to the first man, so those of life were broken by women to man. Why then would He not allow Himself to be touched if not to signify that it was a spiritual touch? A spiritual touch proceeds from a pure heart. He attains Christ from a pure heart who acknowledges Him as equal to the Father, but he who does not yet understand the Godhead of Christ reaches His flesh, not His divinity. What great thing is it to reach only as far as the persecutors who crucified Him? It is really a great thing to understand that God the Word was in the beginning; with God, by Whom all things were made, in the manner in which He wished Himself to be known when He said to Philip, *So long a time have I been with you, and have you not known Me yet? Philip, he that sees Me sees the Father.*

But lest any one should be slothful to make progress, [323] let him hear the words, *Little children, it is the last hour.* Make haste to increase and grow, for it is the last hour, a long one indeed, but still the last. He used the word hour for the latter time, because the coming of Our Lord Jesus Christ was in the latter times. But some will say, "How is it the latter time? or the last hour? Antichrist will surely come first, and then the day of judgment." St. John foresaw these objections, and to guard against the over-confidence of men and their thinking in consequence that this was not the last hour, because Antichrist has to come, he said to them, *And as you have heard that Antichrist is coming, even now there are many Antichrists.* Could any hour but the last have many Antichrists?

Whom did he call Antichrists? He goes on to explain. How do we know that this is the last hour? How? Because *even now there are many Antichrists. They went out from us*: here you have the Antichrists. *They went out from us*, therefore let us mourn their loss. That which follows is our consolation, *But they were not of us.* All heretics and schismatics went out from us, that is, they leave the Church; but they would not go out if they were of us. Therefore before they went out they were not of us. If this be so, many who are within and have not gone out are still Antichrists. We go so far as to say this, and why?

in order that there should be no Antichrists amongst those who are within. . . . Antichrist in Latin signifies hostile to Christ. He is not so called, as some think, because he is to come before Christ, that is, that after him Christ is to come; this is neither said nor written, but Antichrist signifies hostile to Christ. You can judge by his own words, whom this applies to, and you will understand that it is impossible for [324] any others than Antichrists to go out; those who are not Christ's enemies simply cannot go out. These remain in His body, and are accounted His members, and members are never at variance with each other. The integrity of the body rests on all its members. And what does the Apostle say about this harmony of members? *If one member suffers, all suffer with it, and if one member rejoices, all the members rejoice with it.* If, therefore, in the glorification of one member all the rest rejoice with it, and in the suffering of one all suffer, harmony amongst the members admits of no Antichrist. And there are some men within who in the body of Our Lord Jesus Christ are to it what bad humors are to the human body, seeing that Christ's body is still under treatment on earth, and that perfect health will only be attained at the last resurrection from the dead. When these humors are removed the body is eased, and so when evil men go out of the Church she is relieved. And in putting forth bad humors the words of St. John may be put in the body's mouth, *These humors have gone out from me, but they were not of me.* What is, *They were not of me*? They were not cut off from my flesh as a part, but they oppressed me like a superfluous weight.

They went out from us; but, be not sad, they were not of us. How is this proved? *Because if they had been of us they would have remained with us.* Hence, brethren, you may see that many who are not of us receive the Sacraments with us, are baptized as we are, and accept with us that which is known to the faithful, Benediction, the Eucharist, and whatever else is in the Holy Sacraments; they accept even the Communion of the Altar with us, and are not of us. Trial proves that they are not of us. When temptation comes upon them, like a sudden gust of wind they [325] fly away, because they were not seed. When at the Day of Judgment the Lord's field begins to be cleared, then, and we must insist upon this, all will fly indeed. *They went out from us, but they were not of us, because if they had been of us they would have remained with us.* Would you know, dear brethren, with what certainty this is said, that those who possibly have gone out and have returned may be proved not to be antichrists nor hostile to Christ? Those who are not antichrists can by no possibility remain outside. But it depends upon the will of every man whether he be antichrist or united to Christ. Either we are members or bad humors. He who makes progress is a member in the body, but he who remains in his sins is a bad humor, and when he goes out those whom he oppressed will be eased. *They went out from us, but they were not of us; for if they had been of us, they would no doubt have remained with us; but that they might be manifested that they are not all of us.* He added *that they might be manifested,* because being within they are not of us, though not manifested, but in going out they are manifested. And you have the anointing from the Holy One, that you may be manifested to yourselves. The Holy Spirit is Himself spiritual anointing, whose sacrament is in visible anointing. He says that all who have this anointing of Christ discern good and evil men, nor is it needful that they should be taught, because this anointing itself teaches them.

59. TWO CITIES: BABYLON AND SION
(*On the Psalms*, 136.2)

UPON the rivers of Babylon, there we sat and wept when we remembered Sion. What are the rivers of Babylon, and how do we sit and weep in remembrance of Sion? If we are its citizens we do not proclaim it by our songs only, but also in our lives. If we are citizens of Jerusalem - that is, of Sion - we are not dwelling as citizens in this life, in the confusion of this world, in this Babylon as citizens, but we are held as captives. It behooves us not only to talk about these things, but also to do them with a devout heart and a holy desire after the eternal city. This city, which is called Babylon, has its lovers who strive for temporal peace, and have no hope beyond it, who place their whole delight in this world, and in this world alone, and we see these men toiling hard for the earthly commonwealth. Still, whoever in this human society lead upright lives, if they desire not the pride of life, perishable exaltation, and pernicious vainglory, but show forth the true faith as far as they can, as long as they can, to all whom they can, in all the things which they see and so far as they understand the character of the earthly state, these God does not suffer to perish in Babylon, for He has predestined them to be citizens of Jerusalem. God knows their state of captivity, and He puts another [327] city before their eyes. This is the city for which they should truly sigh, unto which they should direct all their efforts, and to gain which they should exhort their fellow-citizens, who are fellow-pilgrims, to the best of their power. Therefore, our Lord Jesus Christ says, *He that is faithful in that which is least, is faithful also in that which is greater.* And again, *If you have not been faithful in that which is another's, who will give you that which is your own?*

Still, dear brethren, consider the rivers of Babylon. The rivers of Babylon are all those things which are loved here and which pass away. Supposing, for instance, that a man has chosen agriculture as a pursuit, has grown rich upon it, has his mind fixed upon it, and that it gives him delight, let him look to the end and see that what he loved was not built upon the foundation of Jerusalem, but that it was a river of Babylon. Another man says, "It is a glorious thing to be a soldier; men of agriculture are in awe of the military, and bow down to them and pay them court. If I become a farmer I shall fear the military, but if I become a soldier I shall be feared by the farmer." Foolish man, you have thrown yourself headlong into another river of Babylon which has worse currents than the first. . . .

Another man says, "It is a grand thing to have a lawyer's clever tongue, and to have among all classes of men clients hanging on the lips of their able defender, looking for loss or gain from his mouth, for life or death, for disaster or prosperity." You know not the place into which you have put yourself, for this is another river of Babylon, and its roaring is produced by the waters beating against rocks. . . .
Another man says, "It is a fine thing to travel over the seas, and to do a business in merchandise, to visit [328] many countries, and to draw profits from all. It is a fine thing to have no powerful enemy in the city, to be always going about, and to amuse one's mind by variety of traffic and different nations, and to grow rich by accumulated gains!" This also is a river of Babylon. When will your gains be secure? When will you arrive at peace of mind with them? The richer you are the more you will have to fear. One shipwreck will strip you of everything, and you will weep over yourself in the water of Babylon, because you would not sit and weep by the banks of Babylon.

Other citizens of the blessed city of Jerusalem, knowing that they are captives, consider human desires and the various lusts of men, which impel them in all directions, and drag them into the sea. They witness these things, and they keep clear of the waters of Babylon; they sit by the banks and weep, either for those who are carried away, or for themselves who have deserved to be in Babylon. Their posture of sitting denotes their attitude of humility. Upon the rivers of Babylon, therefore, there we sat and wept, when we remembered Sion. O blessed Sion, where all things are secure, and nothing fluctuates.

Many shed tears which are of Babylon, because they are also glad with the gladness of Babylon. Those who rejoice at their gains and weep at their losses are both of Babylon. You should weep, but at the remembrance of Sion. If you weep over Sion, you should weep when you are prospering according to the standard of Babylon. Therefore it is that the psalm says, *I have found tribulation and sorrow, and I have called upon the name of the Lord.* What is *I have found*? There seemed to be I know not what hidden tribulation which was to be sought after, and this he found as if he had sought for it. And when he had found it what was his gain? He called upon the name of the Lord. There is a wide difference between your finding tribulation and tribulation finding you. The Psalmist says in another place, *The sorrows of hell have found me.* What is the meaning of *I have found tribulation and sorrow*? When a sudden sadness falls upon you by a misfortune happening to you in those worldly affairs which you made your delight; when this sudden sadness finds you out, and it happens in a matter which you thought could not make you sad, *The sorrow of hell has found you.* You imagined you were above, whereas you were below. . . . You found that you were grievously affected by a particular sorrow, by sadness at a certain misfortune, when you perhaps imagined they would not touch you: *The sorrow of hell has found you.* But when you are prospering, all temporal matters are smiling; there has been no death in your family, neither drought perhaps, nor frost, nor blight in your vine, nor acidity in your wine; your cattle have not lost their young, you keep all your worldly rank and dignity, everywhere you have friends ready to serve you, and clients are not lacking to you; your children are submissive, your servants stand in awe of you, your wife is of a quiet disposition, it is what is called a happy home. And in this happy home seek for tribulation, if you are able, that having found it you may invoke the name of the Lord. The divine counsel to weep in joy and to rejoice in sorrow seems somewhat perverse in its teaching. Listen to him who rejoiced in sorrow: *I glory,* he says, *in tribulations.* But see if the man who weeps with joy has found tribulation. Take any man you like, and let him consider that prosperity of his which has made him exult, and puffed him up in a certain sense with joy. He has held his head high and said, "I am a prosperous man!" Let him consider if [330] that happiness is not to pass away, if he can feel certain that it is to last for ever. But if he is not certain, and sees the object of his delight going from him, it is a river of Babylon; let him sit above it and weep. He will sit and weep if he remembers Sion. O what will that peace be which we shall see with God! O blessed equality of the angels! O what a vision and what an ineffable contemplation! Babylon's delights are engrossing; may they not engross and not deceive us. The solace of captives is one thing, and the joy of men released is another. *Upon the waters of Babylon there we sat and wept, when we remembered Sion. On the willows in the midst thereof we hung up our instruments.* The citizens of Jerusalem have their own instruments, the Scriptures of God, the precepts of God, the promises of God, the thought of the next world. But while they work in the midst of Babylon, they hang up their instruments on its willows. The willow is an unfruitful tree, and in this place the tree is meant to signify that no good is to be expected from the willow; in other passages the tree may have a different meaning. Here you must understand sterile trees growing on the waters of Babylon. These are watered by the rivers of Babylon, and bear no fruit. Just as men are lustful, avaricious, and barren in good works, so the citizens of Babylon, to compare them to the trees of that region, feed on the pleasures of transitory things, and like the willows are washed by the rivers of Babylon. You seek for fruit, and nowhere find any. In suffering such men we are mingling with those who are in the heart of Babylon. For there is a great difference between the middle and the outward confines of Babylon.

Some men are not in the thick of Babylon, those, that is, who are not so given up to the pride of life and [331] its pleasures. But as to those who, to put it into plain and brief words, are very wicked, they are in the thick of Babylon, and they are barren trees like its willows. When we meet with them, and find them so sterile that it seems a difficulty to see anything about them by which they may be led to a right faith or to good works, or to a hope of a future world, or to a desire to be delivered from this mortal captivity; we may be able to quote familiar Scripture to them, but because we find in them no fruit by which we may make a beginning, we turn away from them, saying to ourselves: "They cannot yet understand; whatever we may say to them will be taken by them in an evil and hostile way." Delaying, therefore, to bring our Scriptures to bear upon them, we hang up our instruments in the willow trees, for we find no men who are worthy to carry them. . . .

How did the devil enter into the heart of Judas, and urge him to betray the Lord, for he would not have entered in unless Judas had given him the opportunity? In the same way many evil men in the midst of Babylon make room in their hearts by carnal and unlawful desires for the devil and his angels to operate in them and by them, and sometimes they question us and say, *Show us the reason.* Pagans frequently make observations such as, "Tell us the reason why Christ came, and what good He did to the human race? Have not human things declined since His coming, and did they not prosper more then than now? Can Christians tell us what good Christ brought to us? In what way do they think the world has improved because of His coming?" . . . You begin to tell this man of how much good Christ has done, and he does not understand you. You put before him the example of those who carry out the Gospel which you have just heard, [332] who sell all their possessions, and distribute them to the poor, that they may have a treasure in heaven and follow the Lord. You say to that man, "See here Christ's work." How many do this that they may distribute their possessions to the needy, and may become poor, not by necessity but by choice, following God, and looking for the kingdom of heaven. Men laugh them to scorn. "Were these the good things which Christ brought us," they say, "that a man should lose his property, and when he gives it to the needy should be himself needy?" What then will you do? You have no understanding of Christ's good things, for you are full of one who is Christ's enemy, and to him you have opened the door of your heart. You look back upon former times which seem to you to have been more prosperous. Those days were like olives hanging on the trees, which were caressed by the gentle breezes of the wind, and basking in their mellowness. The time came for the olive to be put in the press, for as the end of the year approached, it could not always hang on the tree. It is not without a pregnant reason that certain psalms bear the title, *For the wine-presses.* The tree signifies liberty, the press suffering. When human things are broken up and suffer pressure, you are conscious that there is a growing tendency to avarice, but consider that continency also makes progress. Why are you so blind that whereas you see plenty of the scum of oil in the streets, you cannot see the oil itself in the vessel? This is significant. Men who are leading bad lives are notorious, while those who turn to God, and are cleansed from the stains of their evil desires, are hidden, because in the press itself, or by its operation, the scum trickles out so that it can be seen by all, but the process of straining the oil does not outwardly [333] appear. You rejoice at these things, because you have already been able to sit and weep by the waters of Babylon. But when the authors of our captivity enter into the hearts of men, they question us by the mouths of those whom they possess, and say to us, "Sing us the words of your songs; tell us why Christ came, and what the next world is. I want to believe, tell me your reason for insisting that I should believe." You may answer, "How can you wonder that I insist on your believing? You are full of evil desires; if I speak of the good things of Jerusalem, you cannot understand them: that which you have in abundance must be taken away that you may be filled with that of which you are empty."

Therefore, do not be in a hurry to answer this man; he is a barren tree like the willow. Do not play him your instrument, rather hang it up. He will say, "Tell me about it; tell me the words of your songs; explain me the reason. Do you not desire my instruction?" This man does not listen with an upright heart, and his inquiry does not deserve an answer.... He is not simple, and his questions are insidious. He is not seeking to learn, but to find fault. Therefore, say to yourself: "I shall not answer him, but shall hang up my instrument."

Such was that rich man who asked Our Lord the question, Good Master, what shall I do to gain eternal life? Was he not seeking eternal life after the fashion of those men who petitioned for a song of Sion? The Lord says to him, *Keep the commandments.* Who when he had heard, answered in weariness, *I have kept all these things from my youth.* Our Lord had told him something of the songs of Sion, and He knew that he would not understand, but He gave us an example of how many seem to ask advice about eternal [334] life, and are pleased with us as long as we answer their questions. He gave us a lesson, as if at some future time we should meet the inquiry of such men by the words, *How shall we sing the song of the Lord in a strange land?* See how He answers, *Will you be perfect? Go, sell all you have, and give to the poor, and you shall have treasure in heaven, and come and follow Me.* In order that he may learn many songs of Sion, he should first put away all obstacles and walk free of burden, and thus he will learn something about them. But he went away sorrowful. Let us say in his regard, *How shall we sing the song of the Lord in a strange land?* He went away indeed, notwithstanding which Our Lord gave some hope to the rich. For the disciples who were grieved said, *Who then can be saved?* And He answered them. *That which is impossible to men is easy to God.* The rich have also their particular mode of sanctification, and they have received a song of Sion, that song of which the Apostle speaks, *Charge the rich of this world not to be high-minded, nor to trust in the uncertainty of riches, but in the living God, Who gives us abundantly all things to enjoy.* Adding what they are to do, He strikes a chord of the instrument and does not hang it up: Let them be rich in good works, give easily, communicate to others, lay up in store for themselves a good foundation against the time to come, that they may lay hold of the true life. This was one of the songs of Sion which the rich received, that, in the first place, they should not be high-minded. For riches produce pride, and the proud rich are washed away by the tide of Babylon. What, then, is the counsel given to them? Before all things not to be high-minded. Let them avoid the snare which is produced by riches, that is, pride. . . . Gold, which God made, is not an evil, but the avaricious man is wicked, [335] who, leaving his Creator, turns himself to the creature. Let him, then, avoid the pride of riches, and dwell above the waters of Babylon. He is told not to be high-minded, therefore let him sit; and not to trust in the uncertainty of riches, therefore let him sit above the waters of Babylon. If he has put his trust in the uncertainty of riches, he is dragged into the current of Babylon. But if he humble himself, and be not high-minded, and trust not in the uncertainty of riches, his dwelling is above the waters of Babylon; remembering Sion, he sighs after the eternal Jerusalem, and he gives alms of his substance in order that he may reach Sion. You see what the song of Sion is which is given to the rich. Let them put their hand to labor and not be idle, and let their instrument sound forth when they find a man saying to them, "What are you doing? You are throwing your money away by giving so much in alms; you should lay by for your children." When they see that he is without understanding and recognize in him a willow tree, let them not be eager to explain their conduct or motives to him; let them hang up their instruments in the willows of Babylon.

But they should look beyond the willow trees and sing the songs of Sion without intermission, and do its works. For they do not lose what they give away. Men sometimes leave their property in the hands of servants and it is secure; when they put it into the hands of Christ, is it lost? ....

When you live with those who do not understand the song of Sion, hang up your instruments, as I have said, on the willows in the midst of Babylon; put off that which you have to say. If the willows begin to be fruitful and to be renovated, they will put forth good fruit. Then we shall be able to sing our songs to willing ears. But when your lot is cast with these headstrong men, who ask impertinent questions and oppose the truth, make a point of not seeking to please them, lest you become oblivious of Jerusalem; and let your one soul, which is made one out of many by the peace of Christ, speak; let that captive Jerusalem herself, who is laboring here on earth, say, *If I forget you, Jerusalem, let my right hand be forgotten.* ....

Our right hand is eternal life, our left hand is this mortal life. Whatever you do for eternal life is the work of the right hand. If in your actions you mix with the charity of eternal life the lust of this mortal life, or of human praise, or of any other temporal gratification, your left hand has been aware of what your right hand was doing. And you know that Gospel precept, *Let not your left hand know what your right hand is doing. If, then, I forget you Jerusalem, let my right hand be forgotten.* And this is what really happens; he was not expressing a wish but a prophecy. This, as he said, is what happens to those who forget Jerusalem, their right hand forgets them. For eternal life abides in itself: they cleave to worldly enjoyment, and make their left hand into their right.

Listen to what I am now saying, brethren, that the lesson which I would draw from the right hand may profit you all by God's help. You may perhaps remember that I have already spoken of certain men who make their left into their right hand; that is, who have an abundance of temporal goods, and place their happiness in them, ignorant of what true happiness is, and of what truly constitutes the right hand. Scripture calls such men strange children, as if citizens not of Jerusalem but of Babylon; for one of the psalms says, *Lord, deliver me from the hand of strange children, whose mouth has spoken vanity, and their right hand is* [337] *the right hand of iniquity.* And he goes on, *Whose sons are as new plants in their youth: their daughters decked out, adorned round about after the likeness of a temple; their storehouses full, flowing out of this into that. Their sheep fruitful in young, abounding in their goings forth: their oxen fat. There is no breach of wall, nor passage, nor crying out in their streets.* Is it, then, a sin to be thus prosperous? No; but what is a sin is making it into a right hand, whereas it is the left. Consequently, what does he go on to say, They have called the people happy that have these things. This is why their mouth has spoken vanity, because they called the people happy that have these things. . . . *Blessed,* he says, *is that people whose God is the Lord.* Examine into your hearts, brethren, and ask yourselves if you desire the good things of God, the heavenly Jerusalem, if you long for eternal life. Let all this earthly happiness be to you as a left hand, let that which you will possess for all eternity be your right. And if you should happen to possess the goods of the left hand, do not put your trust in the left. Would you not correct the man who tried to eat with his left hand? If you consider your table dishonored by a guest who uses his left hand, is not the table of God slighted if you make your right hand into the left, and the left into the right? . . . *If I forget you, Jerusalem, let my right hand be forgotten.* . . .

Brethren, let your instruments be heard unceasingly by good works, and sing one to another the songs of Sion. As you have listened willingly, so put in practice the more willingly that which you have heard, if you would not be willows of Babylon, watered by its rivers, and bearing no fruit. But do sigh after the Jerusalem of eternity; let your life follow your Hope Who has gone before you; then we shall be [338] with Christ. . . . Build yourselves up in the rock if you would not be carried away either by the current or by the wind and rain. If you would be armed against the temptations of the world, let the desire of the heavenly Jerusalem grow and be increased in your hearts. Captivity will pass away, happiness will reign. The enemy of the last hour will be vanquished, and we shall triumph with the King in never-ending life.

PART III: THE KINGDOM OF OUR LORD ON EARTH

[341]
1. THE KINGDOM OF CHRIST FORETOLD FROM THE BEGINNING
(*On the City of God*, Bk. 7, ch. 32, and *Letter* 137 to Volusian)

FROM the very beginning of the human race this mystery of eternal life has been announced through the ministry of angels to those whom it was fitting to know it, by certain signs and figures which were adapted to the times. Then the Hebrew people was gathered together into the unity of a sort of commonwealth for the perpetuation of this mystery. In it by the mouth of some having knowledge, and some having it not, that which has taken place from the coming of Christ until now, and which is to take place hereafter, was to be foretold. Afterwards, moreover, for the sake of the testimony of the Scriptures, this people was dispersed amongst the nations to whom eternal salvation in Christ is foretold. For not only all prophecies which are made by word of mouth, nor those precepts of life alone which establish conformity between morals and piety, and are contained in the Scriptures, but also sacred rites and priesthoods, the tabernacle or the temple, all altars, sacrifices, ceremonies, holy days, and everything else pertaining to the service due to God, which has its proper expression in the Greek word *Latria*, were typical signs and figures which, for the sake of that eternal life of the faithful in Christ, we [342] believe to have been fulfilled, which we see being fulfilled, and which we believe will be fulfilled. . . .

Faith opens the door to intelligence, while unbelief closes it. Where is the man who would not be moved to belief, simply by so vast an order of events proceeding from the beginning; by the mere connection of various ages, which accredits the present by the past, while it confirms antiquity by what is recent? Out of the Chaldean nation a single man is chosen, remarkable for a most constant piety. Divine promises are disclosed to this man, which are to find their completion after a vast series of ages in the last times, and it is predicted that all nations are to receive a benediction in his seed. This man being a worshiper of the one true God, the Creator of the universe, begets in his old age a son, of a wife whom barrenness and age had long deprived of all hope of offspring. From him is propagated a most numerous people, which multiplies in Egypt, where a divine disposition of things, redoubling its promises and effects, had carried that family from eastern parts. From their servitude in Egypt a strong people is led forth by terrible signs and miracles; impious nations are driven out; it is brought into the promised land, settled therein, and exalted into a kingdom. Then it falls more and more into sin; it perpetually offends the true God, Who had conferred upon it so many favors, by violating His worship; it is scourged with various misfortunes; it is visited with consolations, and so carried on to the incarnation and manifestation of Christ. All the promises made to this nation, all its prophecies, its priesthoods, its sacrifices, its temple, in a word, all its sacred rites, had for their special object this Christ, the Word of God, the Son of God - God that was to come in the flesh, that was to die, to rise again, to ascend to [343] heaven, Who by the exceeding power of His name was to obtain in all nations a population dedicated to Himself, and in Him remission of sins and eternal salvation unto those who believed.

Christ came. In His birth, His life, His words, His deeds, His sufferings, His death, His resurrection, His ascension, all the predictions of the prophets are fulfilled. He sends forth the Holy Spirit; He fills the faithful who are assembled in one house, and who by their prayer and desires are expecting this very promise. They are filled with the Holy Spirit; they speak suddenly with the tongues of all nations; they confidently refute errors; they proclaim a most salutary truth; they exhort to penitence for the faults of past life; they promise pardon from the divine grace. Their proclamation of piety and true religion is followed by suitable signs and miracles. A savage unbelief is stirred up against them. They endure what had been foretold, hope in what had been promised, teach what had been commanded them. Few in number, they are scattered through the world. They convert populations with marvelous facility. In the midst of enemies they grow. They are multiplied by persecutions. In the straits of affliction they are spread abroad over vast regions. At first they are uninstructed, of very low condition, very few in number. Their ignorance passes into the brightest intelligence; their low ranks produce the most cultivated eloquence; their fewness becomes a multitude; they subjugate to Christ minds the most acute, learned, and accomplished, and convert them into preachers of piety and salvation. In the alternating intervals of adversity and prosperity they exercise a watchful patience and temperance. As the world verges in a perpetual decline, and by exhaustion expresses the coming of its last age, since this also is [344] what prophecy led them to expect, they with greater confidence await the eternal happiness of the heavenly city. And amid all this the unbelief of impious nations rages against the Church of Christ, which works out victory by patience, and by preserving unshaken faith against the cruelty of opponents. When the sacrifice unveiled by the truth, which had so long been covered under mystical promises, had at length succeeded, those sacrifices which prefigured this one were removed by the destruction of the Temple itself. This very Jewish people, rejected for its unbelief, was cast out of its own seat, and scattered everywhere throughout the world, to carry with it the sacred writings; so that the testimony of prophecy, by which Christ and the Church were foretold, may not be thought a fiction of ours for the occasion, but be produced by our very adversaries, a testimony in which it is also foretold that they should not believe. The temples and images of demons, and the sacrilegious rites of that worship, are gradually overthrown, as prophecy foretold. Heresies against the name of Christ, which yet veil themselves under that name, swarm, as was foretold, in order to call out the force of teaching in our holy religion. In all these things, as we read their prediction, so we discern their fulfillment; and from so vast a portion which is fulfilled, we rest assured of what is still to come. Is there a single mind which yearns after eternity and feels the shortness of the present life, that can resist the light and the force of this divine authority?

[345]
2. THE STONE CUT FROM THE MOUNTAIN WITHOUT HANDS
(*On the Psalms*, 98.14)

EXALT the Lord our God, and adore at His holy mountain, for the Lord our God is holy. In the same way as the Psalmist said in another part of this psalm, *Exalt the Lord our God, and adore His footstool, for it is holy* (and we understand what is meant by adoring His footstool), so now, after the glorification of the Lord our God, he commends the Lord's mountain for fear any man should sing His praises elsewhere. What is signified by *His mountain*? We read of it in another place, for the stone was cut out of a mountain without hands, and it broke up all the kingdoms of the earth, and itself grew. This is the vision of Daniel. That stone which was cut from the mountain without hands grew and increased, and it became, he says, a great mountain, so that it filled the whole earth. If we wish to be heard let us adore on that self-same great mountain. This heretics do not do, because that mountain has filled the face of the whole earth; they have clung to a single portion and have lost the whole inheritance. If they recognize the Catholic Church they will adore with us on this mountain. We see before our eyes how that stone which was cut from the moun-
[346] tain without hands has spread, how many regions of the earth it has occupied, and to what nations it has reached. What is the mountain from which the stone was cut without hands? It was the kingdom of the

Jews because, in the first place, they worshiped one God. From them the stone was cut, Our Lord Jesus Christ. He is called *the stone which the builders rejected,* and *He is become the head of the corner.* This stone which was cut from the mountain without hands overcame all the kingdoms of the earth; we see them broken up by it. What were the kingdoms of the earth? The kingdoms of idols and of demons were dispersed. Saturn reigned in the hearts of numerous men; where is his kingdom? And Mercury reigned over many; where is his kingdom? It has been broken up; those kingdoms in which he had been reigning were united under the scepter of Christ. What was the reign of Venus at Carthage, and where is it now? That stone which was cut from the mountain without hands broke up all the kingdoms of the earth. What is the meaning of cut from the mountain without hands? That He was born of the Jewish people without the cooperation of man. For all who are born into the world are born by the cooperation of man. He was born of a virgin, born without hands, for the word *hands* stands for human operation. The hand of man had no part in His birth, in which there was no concupiscence of the flesh, true birth though it was. That stone, therefore, was born from the mountain without hands; it grew, and in growing struck all the kingdoms of the earth. It became a great mountain, and filled the whole earth. This is the Catholic Church, with whom you rejoice to be in communion. But they who are not in communion with her, because they adore and praise God elsewhere than on that mountain, are

[347] not heard unto eternal life, though they may be heard with regard to certain temporal things. Let them not glorify themselves because God listens to them in some things, for He does as much for the Pagans. Do not Pagans cry to God for rain, and He sends it? Why? Because *He makes His sun to shine upon the good and upon the wicked, and His rain to fall upon the just and the unjust.* Boast not, Pagan man, because God sends His rain at your petition, for He rains upon the just and the unjust. He hears you in temporal things; He does not hear you unto eternal life unless you adore on His holy mountain. *Adore the Lord at His holy mountain, for the Lord our God is holy.*

[348]
3. "HE IT IS THAT BAPTIZES"
(*Tractates on the Gospel of John*, 6.8)

IF baptism be holy according to diversity of merit, as merits vary so will baptism vary, and the holier its administrator seems to be, the fuller is thus the grace of him who is administered. Understand, brethren, that the saints themselves, the good who belong to the Dove, to the portion of the earthly Jerusalem, just men in the Church, of whom the Apostle says, *The Lord knows who are His* have different graces, and not equal merits. Some are holier and better than others. Why is it, then, that supposing, for instance, a man be baptized by one of those just and holy men, and another by a man of inferior merit before God, or of inferior rank, or chastity, or life, they have received one and the same thing absolutely, unless it be the power of the words, *He it is that baptizes*? When, therefore, baptism is administered by two men, one being good, and the other better, it does not follow that the baptized person receives in either case the benefit of the minister's goodness or superiority; but be he worthy or worthier, the baptism is one and the same in both, not better in one, nor inferior in the other; and so, when a bad man baptizes, either because the Church is ignorant concerning him, or tolerates him (for evil men are either not known, or [349] they are borne with as the chaff is suffered to grow up with the wheat till the plow is passed over the field), that which is given is the same, nor is it lessened on account of unworthy ministers. It is one and the same through the words, *He it is that baptizes.*

[350]
4. THE VALIANT WOMAN
(*Sermon* 37.2)

WHO shall find a valiant woman? It is difficult to find her, or rather it is difficult to ignore her. Is she not the city built on the mountain, which cannot be hidden? Why then does the Scripture say, *Who shall find her*, when it would have been truer to say, Who shall not find her? . . . And now when you hear the words, *Who shall find a valiant woman*, think not that they are said of a hidden Church, but of that Church which was discovered by one so that it might be hidden from no man. Let us then hear her described, commended, and praised, for she is to be loved by us all as our mother, as the spouse of one man. *Who shall find a valiant woman?* Who does not see this most valiant woman? She is already discovered, eminent, conspicuous, glorious, adorned, and bright, already, in short, she is spread throughout the whole earth. She is more precious than precious stones. What wonder is it that this woman is of greater worth than precious stones? If we think of human treasures and take precious stones in their literal sense, what wonder is it that the Church is found to be of more worth than any precious stones whatever? The [351] comparison is not possible; but still precious stones are contained in her, and they are so precious that they are called living stones. Precious stones, then, adorn her; but she herself is the more precious. . . . There are now, and always have been precious stones in the Church, learned men, full of science, eloquence, and the right understanding of the Law. These are indeed precious stones, but out of their number some have ceased to be jewels in this woman's attire. With regard to doctrine and the eloquence, which makes him renowned, Cyprian was a precious stone, and he remained in this woman's jeweled robe. Donatus was a precious stone, but he broke from the rich folds of her dress. He who remained wished to be loved in her; he who broke away from her sought to make a name for himself without her. Cyprian, in staying with her, gathered fruit for her. Donatus, in receding from her, desired not to gather it but to scatter it. O wicked sons, why do you go after a precious stone which is cut off from the jeweled robe of this woman? You will answer me, "What then? Are you as intellectual as such a man" or, "Can you talk like another?" or, "Are you as learned as a third?" . . . I reply, "Let a man be, if you like, learned, instructed in liberal arts and the mysteries of the Law, a precious stone: give him up for the sake of her who is more precious than precious stones." A precious stone, which does not adorn her, is lying in darkness, wherever it may be; it should have remained on the robe of this woman and adorned her attire. . . . Learn, you merchants of the kingdom of heaven, to estimate the worth of stones; be not contented with any one which does not adorn this woman. . . .

The heart of her husband trusts in her. Most truly did He trust in her, and He taught us, too, to trust [352] in her. For He commended the Church unto the ends of the earth, through all nations, from sea to sea. . . . *The heart of her husband trusts in her*; He, who knows all future things, and cannot be deceived, trusted in her. It is not said that the heart of her children trusted in her, for her infant children were liable to error, whereas no falsehood can deceive the heart of her husband. . . . *Seeking wool and flax, she has done something useful with her hands.* The inspired Word speaks of this woman's matronly wool and flax; we may seek for their meaning. I think the wool signifies something animal, and the flax something spiritual, and this I gather from the manner of our garments, for we wear linen underneath and wool outside. The action of the animal man is visible, that of the spiritual is hidden. Animal activity without the spiritual is hidden. Animal activity without the spiritual, although it seems good, is useless. Spiritual activity without the bodily is laziness. You see a man putting forth his hand to give an alms to the poor; he does it without thinking of God, being desirous of pleasing men; the wool garment is apparent, but it has no linen underneath. You hear another man saying, "It is sufficient for me to worship God in my conscience. What is the use of my going to church, or of my being mixed up outwardly with Christians?" This man wants to have the linen vest without the wool garment. The valiant woman knows not these ways, nor does she commend them. Spiritual things are indeed to be said and to be taught without animal ones; but those who receive them are both to hold spiritual things and to work material deeds in no material spirit. *This woman [353] sought wool and wax, and did something useful with her hands.* This wool and this flax are in Holy Scripture. Many find them but will not do anything useful with their hands. She both found and worked. In hearing you find; in leading good lives you work. . . .

She has put out her hand to useful things. How far has she put out these hands of hers? From sea to sea, and unto the ends of the earth, where she has penetrated. . . .

In this world, therefore, she is laborious, vigilant, solicitous. She keeps her household in severe discipline, and rises by night lest her lamp should go out. She is valiant in tribulation, in tremulous expectation of the promises to come. Her arms are strengthened by the spindle, nor does she eat the bread of idleness; but after the toils of what we may call neediness and poverty, according to this world, what will her portion be in the future, since we read that she rejoiced in her latter days? Would you know? Hear then what that hope is which should keep our lamp burning all through the night. *Her children rose up and became rich.* Now we are living in poverty, and are watching in poverty, and when we die we fall asleep in poverty; but we shall rise up and become rich. On their rising up her children will be enriched.

Many daughters have worked power; you have surpassed and outdone them all.... Who, then, are these other daughters who have worked power, whom the valiant woman has overcome and surpassed? Or what was the power which they worked, and how has she surpassed them? There are unrighteous daughters represented by heresies. Why daughters? Because [354] they too were born of the valiant woman, daughters in the likeness of the sacraments, not in works. They, too, have our sacraments, and our Scriptures, they have our Amen and Alleluia, and many have our creed, hence they are daughters. But would you know what is said to this woman in another place, that is, in the Canticle of Canticles? *As the lily among thorns, so is my beloved amongst the daughters.* It is a wonderful saying to call them at once thorns and daughters. And do those thorns work power? They do indeed. Do you not see the very heretics praying, fasting, giving alms, and praising Christ? I may say that there are amongst their number false prophets, of whom it is said, *They work many signs and wonders, to deceive, if possible, even the elect. Behold I have foretold you.* The thorns, too, work power, of which power it is written, *Have we not eaten and drunk in Your name?* He would not have used the words eaten and drunk of any ordinary food and drink; you know what food and what drink He meant to speak about. And we have done many signs. Many daughters work power, we do not deny it; and thorns bear a flower but no fruit. How has this woman to whom it is said, *You have surpassed and outdone them all,* surpassed them unless it be that she has not only the flower but the fruit?

What is this fruit? *I show unto you a yet more excellent way,* the Apostle says. *If I speak with the tongues of men and of angels, and have not charity, I am become as sounding brass or a tinkling cymbal.* Speaking with tongues is a power which the flowers may have. *And if I should know all mysteries, and all knowledge, and if I should have all faith, so that I could remove mountains* (what power!), *and have not charity, it profits me nothing.* Listen again to further [355] power which may belong to the flower without the fruit. *If I should distribute all my goods to the poor, and if I should deliver my body to be burned, and have not charity, it profits me nothing.* This woman has the more excellent way, from which it was said to her, *Many daughters have worked power.* Many have spoken diverse tongues, have known all mysteries, have done many wonders, have cast forth demons, have distributed their substance to the poor, and have delivered up their bodies to be burned. They are inferior to you, O valiant woman, because they had not charity. *But you have surpassed and excelled them all,* not only by the flower but by a rich and abundant fruit. Consider the beginning of the bunch of grapes itself.... From what comes its beauty? From its hanging on the stem of charity. *Many daughters have worked power, but you have surpassed and outdone them all.*

[356]
5. THE HEAD IN HEAVEN, THE BODY ON EARTH
(*Tractates on the Epistles of John*, 10.3)

IN this we know that we love the children of God. What does this mean, brethren? A little higher up he was speaking of the Son of God, not of the children of God: one Christ was put before us for our contemplation, and we were told, *Whoever believes that Jesus is the Christ is born of God. And every one that loves Him Who begot,* that is, the Father, *loves Him also Who is born of Him,* that is, the Son, Our Lord Jesus Christ. He goes on, *In this we know that we love the children of God*, as if he were going to say, "In this we know that we love the Son of God." Just before he said the Son of God, now he says the children of God, because the children of God make up the Body of the only Son of God, and whereas He is the Head and we the members, the Son of God is one. Therefore he who loves the children of God loves the Son of God, and he who loves the Son of God loves the Father; nor can any man love the Father unless he love the Son; and he who loves the Son also loves the children of God. Who are these children of God? They are the members of the Son of God. And by loving he, too, becomes a member, and through loving he is admitted into the structure of the Body of Christ; [357] and thus there is one Christ, loving Himself. For when members love each other the body is loving itself. And if one member is suffering all the members suffer with it, and if one member exult all the members rejoice with it. And what does he go on to say? *For you are the body and members of Christ.* He was talking a little before of brotherly love, and said, *He that loves not his brother, whom he sees, how can he love God whom he sees not?* But if you love your brother can you love him and not love Christ? How can this be if you love the members of Christ? When, therefore, you love the members of Christ you love Christ; in loving Christ you love the Son of God; in loving the Son of God you love the Father. Love, then, cannot be divided. . . . For if you love the Head you love the members too, but if you do not love the members neither do you love the Head. Are you not afraid at the voice of the Head crying from heaven for His members, *Saul, Saul, why do you persecute Me?* He called the persecutor of His members His own persecutor, and the lover of His members His own lover. You know what His members are, brethren? The Church of God. *In this we know that we love the children of God, because we love God.* And how? Are the children of God and God divided? He who loves God loves His commandments. . . .

Let us run, then, my brethren, let us run, and let us love Christ.

What Christ? Jesus Christ. Who is Jesus Christ? The Word of God. And how does He come to heal those who are sick? *The Word was made flesh and dwelt amongst us.* That which the Scripture foretold, then, was fulfilled. *It behooved Christ to suffer and to rise from the dead on the third day.* Where does His body lie? Where are His members toiling? Where [358] should you be that you may be a member of His body? Penance and remission of sins were to be preached in His name unto all nations, beginning at Jerusalem. Let your charity be spread abroad at the same place. Christ and the Psalmist, that is, the Spirit of God, say, *Your commandment is exceedingly broad*: I know not who placed the limits of charity in Africa. (1) Carry your charity through the whole earth if you wish to love Christ, because the members of Christ are spread abroad on the face of the earth. If you care for a party you are divided, and if you are divided you do not belong to the Body; if you belong not to the Body neither are you under the one Head. What does it profit you to believe and blaspheme? You adore Him in His Head and blaspheme Him in His Body. He loves His Body. If you have cut yourself off from His Body the Head remains united to its Body. That Head cries to you from above, *In vain you honor Me, in vain you honor Me.* It is as if somebody were to kiss you on your cheek and to stamp upon your feet, and perhaps to make you feel his heavy boot while he was holding you in his embrace. Would you not cry out at his words of flattery, and say, "What are you doing, man? you are treading on me." You would not say, "You are treading on my head," for he was embracing your cheek. The head would cry out for its wounded members more than for itself, because it was being honored while they were being ill treated. . . .

Our Lord Jesus Christ, therefore, on ascending into heaven on the fortieth day, specified the place where His Body would have to remain, because He saw that many men would honor Him on account of His ascension into heaven, and He saw that their honor is vain

---

1 Allusion to the Donatists.

[359] if they despise His members on earth. And lest any man should err, and while adoring the Head in heaven should trample on the members on earth, He declared where His members were to be found. For being about

to ascend into heaven, He spoke His last words, and after them He spoke no more on earth. The Head, Who was ascending into heaven, commended the members whom He left on earth, and departed. You no longer hear Christ speaking on earth; you hear Him speaking, but from heaven. And why does He speak from heaven? Because His members were being ill-treated on earth. For to Saul, the persecutor, He spoke these words from on high, *Saul, Saul, why do you persecute Me?* I have ascended into heaven, but am still on earth. Here, I am sitting on the right hand of the Father, while on earth I am still hungry, and thirsty, and a stranger." How, then, being about to ascend into heaven, did He commend His Body on earth? When the disciples questioned Him, saying, *Lord, will You at this time restore again the kingdom to Israel?* He who was leaving them answered, *It is not for you to know the times or moments which the Father has put in His own power; but you shall receive the power of the Holy Spirit coming upon you, and you shall be witnesses unto Me.* See how He understands the spreading of His Body, and in what way He would not be trampled upon: "You shall be witnesses unto Me in Jerusalem, and in all Judea, and Samaria, and even to the uttermost parts of the earth. This is where I am Who am now ascending. I am ascending, indeed, because I am the Head; but my Body is still on earth." And where? It is spread throughout the whole earth. Beware of striking it, or of violating it, or of trampling it under foot. These are the last words of Christ as He was ascending into heaven. Picture to yourselves a

[360] man stretched on a bed of sickness in his own home. He is wasted with illness, and being near death is gasping with his soul, as it were, on his lips. Well, perhaps this man is anxious about some cherished plan very near his heart, and it occurs to his mind, and now he calls his heirs and says to them, "I beseech you to do such a thing." He does violence to himself to speak the words, lest he should die before they are spoken. And when he has said them he gives up his spirit, and the body is carried to the tomb. How will not his heirs bear in mind the last recommendation of the dying man? What will they answer if somebody is found to say, "Do not do it"?" Shall I not do what my father asked me to do with his divine breath, the very last thing I heard him say as he was departing from this world? However I may look upon his other recommendations, these last words of his bind me more than all. I have never seen or heard him again."

Brethren, consider now, with the feelings of Christians, if the last words of a dying man be so sweet and plaintive, and of so great weight to his heirs, what are the last words of Him Who goes, not down into the grave, but Who ascends into heaven? . . . What hope have those men who keep not the last words of Him Who sits in heaven and sees from His place on high whether or not they are treated with contempt? The words of Him Who said, *Saul, Saul, why do you persecute me?* Who reserves a judgment for whatever suffering He sees inflicted on His members?

6. THE SHIP AND THE PILOT
   (*Sermon* 75 and 76)

BUT the boat in the midst of the sea was tossed with the waves. These words of the Gospel admonish the humility of us all to see and realize where we now stand, as well as the goal which we should heartily aim at reaching. For that ship, which is bearing the disciples and laboring in the waves under a contrary wind, is significant. Nor was it for nothing that Our Lord left the crowd and went up into the mountain that He might pray in solitude. Then, coming to His disciples, He found them in danger, and walking upon the sea, He soothed them by getting into the boat, and He calmed the waves. What wonder, indeed, is it, if He Who created all things, is able to calm all things? Still it was after He had got into the boat that they that were in the boat came and adored Him, saying, *Indeed, You are the Son of God*; for before this proof of it they were afraid, seeing Him walking upon the sea, and they had said, It is an apparition. But He getting into the boat took away the fear from their hearts, for their minds were in greater danger because of their doubt than their bodies from the waves. . . .

The ship, then, which carries the disciples, that is, the Church, is tossed and shaken by the storms of temptation. The adverse wind, that is, the devil, is never quiet. He is always armed against it, and seeks to prevent it from getting into calm waters. But greater is He Who intercedes for us. For in this, our stormy passage, He encourages us by coming to us and strengthening us, lest starting up in terror we should cast ourselves into the sea. Should the waves beat against the ship it is still a ship. It alone carries the disciples and receives Christ on board. It is in danger indeed on the waters, but without it we should at once sink. Keep then in the ship and call to God. For in default of all tactics, when the helm does not act, and the sails, if they are hoisted, serve only to increase, instead of diminishing the danger, when human means and helps are at a total standstill, the sailors have yet no other resource than prayer and supplication to God. Will he Who allows the ship to enter port forsake His Church and not lead it into rest?

Still, brethren, the one great disturbance in this ship is caused by the Lord's absence. Can a man who is within the pale of the Church be without the Lord, and under what circumstances can this be? When he is conquered by a sinful lust. As there is a mysterious meaning attached to the words, *Let not the sun go down upon your wrath, nor give you place to the devil*, and they are understood to refer not to that sun which dominates the heavenly bodies, and is visible to us and to the beasts alike, but to that light which only the pure hearts of the faithful see, as it is written, *He was the true light which enlightens every man who comes into this world*. For this visible light of the sun shines upon the smallest and most insignificant of the animal creation. There is, therefore, the true light of justice and wisdom which the mind, disturbed by anger, and covered by it as with a cloud, ceases to see; then it is that the sun seems to go down upon the wrath of man. Thus it is in this ship when Christ is absent; each man [363] s shaken by his temptations and his sins and his lusts. For instance, the Law says to you, "Do not bear false witness against your neighbor." If you understand the witness of truth you will have the light in your mind; but if you yield to the lust of a sinful gain, and determine in your mind to bear false witness, from that moment the tempest begins to frighten you in the absence of Our Lord; you are tossed by the waves of covetousness, and endangered by the storm of your concupiscences, and as if Christ were absent you are nearly sinking.

What, then, is the meaning of Peter's daring to walk to Him on the waters; for Peter commonly personifies the Church? How else are we to interpret his words, *Lord, if it be You, let me come to You upon the waters*, than in this way, "Lord, if You are true, and if You can lie in nothing, let Your Church too be glorified in this world, because the prophecy foretold this concerning You. Let her, therefore, walk upon the waters and thus come to You, for to her it was said, *The rich among the people shall long for Your countenance*."

This Gospel . . . concerning Our Lord Who walked on the sea, and the Apostle Peter, who walking began to totter through fear, to sink through want of courage, and who emerged from the waves by confession, puts before us the sea as an image of this world, and Peter the Apostle as the type of the one Church. For this Peter, who is first in Apostolic rank, the most zealous in the love of Christ, frequently acts as spokesman for all. Upon the interrogation of Our Lord Jesus as to whom men thought He was, and when the disciples had answered Him by quoting the various opinions of [364] men, He turned again to St. Peter, saying, *But whom do you say that I am?* And Peter replied, *You are Christ the Son of the living God.* The one answered for all, unity in many. Then the Lord said, *Blessed are you, Simon Bar Jona, because flesh and blood has not revealed it to you, but My Father Who is in heaven.* Then He added: *And I say to you,* as if meaning, Because you have said to Me, You are Christ, Son of the living God, so I say to you, *You are Peter.* He had previously been called Simon. But the name of Peter was given to him by the Lord, and it was given in this form that it might signify the Church, because Christ is the rock, and Peter is the Christian people. For the rock is the royal name, and therefore, Peter was called after the rock, not the rock after Peter; just as Christ is not called after a Christian, but the Christian after Christ. *You are Peter* therefore, Our Lord says; *and upon this rock,* which you have acknowledged and confessed, saying, "*You are Christ, Son of the living God,*" *I will build My Church,* that is, upon Myself, Son of the living God. I will build you upon Myself, not Myself upon you . . .

This same Peter named blessed after the rock, bearing the figure of the Church, holding the first place amongst the Apostles, having heard in a short space that he was blessed, that he was Peter, and again that he was to be built upon the rock, was grieved when he was told of the Lord's future Passion, for Our Lord foretold it to His disciples as soon to come to pass. Peter feared that he would lose by death Him Whom he had confessed as the source of life. He was disturbed, saying, "Lord, far be it from You, this shall not be. Spare Yourself, Lord, I will not have You die." Peter said to Christ, "I will not have You die;" but better were Christ's words, "I will die for you." Then [365] He reproved him whom He had praised shortly before, and called him Satan whom He had declared blessed. *Go behind Me, Satan,* He says; *you are a scandal unto Me; because you savor not the things that are of God, but the things that are of men.* Being what we are, what would He have us make ourselves, when He so reproaches us for being human? Would you know? Listen to the psalm: *I have said, you are all gods, and sons of the Most High.* But in savor human things, you are all as men to die the death. The self same Peter, who was so lately blessed, is now Satan in one moment of time, at an interval of only a few words. You wonder at the change of names, but look to the cause.... Consider why he is blessed. "Because flesh and blood has not revealed it to you, but My Father Who is in heaven; therefore blessed, because flesh and blood has not revealed it to you. If flesh and blood had revealed it to you, it would have come from yourself; but... because it was My Father in heaven, it comes from Me, not from you. Why from Me? Because all things which the Father has are Mine." Now you have heard the reason why he is blessed and why he is Peter. Why is he that which we look upon with horror, and which I will not name again? Why if not that he was speaking as a man? *For you savor not the things that are of God, but the things that are of men.*

Let us, members of the Church, who consider this, discern what is from God and what is from ourselves. For then we shall not stumble; we shall be founded on the rock, and shall be proof against wind and storm and wave, that is, the temptations of this present life. But look at Peter who then personified us. At first he has confidence, then he hesitates; now he confesses Our Lord to be immortal, now he is afraid lest He [366] should die. Therefore if the Church of Christ has strong men, she has also weak ones; she is bound to have both one and the other, hence St. Paul's words, *We who are strong should carry the burdens of the weak.* When St. Peter said, *You are Christ, Son of the living God,* he signifies the strong; but inasmuch as he hesitated and was afraid, and wished Christ not to die, fearing death, not recognizing life, he is the figure of the weak ones of the Church. In this one Apostle, that is, in Peter, the first and chief of the Apostolic band, in whom the Church was shadowed forth, each kind was typified, the weak and the strong, because the Church exists not without one and the other.

So it is with regard to the Gospel scene now before us. "*Lord, if it be You*" Peter says, "*bid me come to You upon the waters.* For I cannot do this thing of myself, but through You." He recognized what he had of himself, and what from Him by Whose will he believed he could do that of which no human infirmity is capable. "Therefore, If it be You, command; because when You command it shall be done." . . . And the Lord said, *Come.* And Peter stepped upon the waters without the slightest hesitation at the word of command from Him Whose presence sustained and bore him up, and began to walk. He could do what the Lord can do, not in himself, but in the Lord. *You were darkness, and are now light, but in the Lord.* That which no man can do either in Paul, in Peter, or any other of the Apostles, he can do in the Lord.

Peter, therefore, walked upon the waters at the Lord's bidding, knowing that he could not do it of himself. He could do by faith that which human infirmity left to itself could not have accomplished. These are the strong ones of the Church. Hear with all [367] your ears, and understand and act. For we have not to do with the naturally firm ones that they may become weak, but with the infirm, that they may become strong. Presumption prevents many from becoming strong. No man is made strong in God unless he feels his own weakness in himself. God sets aside a free rein for His inheritance. . . . This I say and I repeat, this take to heart and act upon: no man becomes strong in God who does not first feel himself weak ... So Peter says, *Bid me come to You upon the waters.* As a man I dare, but I call upon one Who is more than man. Let the God Man command man to do that which as man he cannot do. *Come,* He says. And Peter descended and began to walk upon the waters. This he did at the bidding of the Rock. Behold what Peter could do in the Lord; what could he do of himself? Seeing the strong wind, he was afraid; and when he began to sink he cried out, *Lord, save me!* He had confided in the Lord, and been strong in Him; as a man he tottered, and turned again to the Lord. . . . Immediately stretching out the help of His right Hand, He raised the drowning man, and reproached him for his want of confidence. *O you of little faith, why did you doubt?* You were trusting in Me: did you doubt Me?"

[368]
7. HERESIES AND HERETICS
(*On the Psalms* 7.14, 21.31, 54.2)

AND in His bow, the Psalmist says, *God has prepared the instruments of death: He has made ready His arrows for them that burn.* I should be inclined to take this bow to mean the Scriptures, in which the strength of the New Testament, like a nervous force, as it were, has softened and overcome the hardness of the Old Testament. From this bow the Apostles, like arrows, are sent forth, and divine praises are sung. . . .

But because, besides the arrows, the Psalmist speaks of God as having also prepared instruments of death, it may be asked, "What are these instruments of death?" Possibly heretics? For proceeding from the same bow, that is, the Holy Scriptures, they too penetrate souls, not for the sake of inflaming them with charity, but in order to infuse into them a deadly poison, which does not happen except where it is desired. Hence this very disposition of things is to be attributed to Divine Providence; not that Providence makes sinners, but Providence disposes of men who sin. For they who read with a sinful motive are forced to put a wrong construction upon the text so that their sin may be punished. Still by their destruction the children of the Catholic Church, pressed, as it were, by goads, are roused from sleep, and come to the true understanding of Holy Scripture. It is necessary that heresies should [369] arise in order that the elect, as St. Paul says, may be made manifest, that is, manifest to men, for they are manifest to God. . . . But you, who wish to have your own property and not the great unity of Christ (for your ambition is to be powerful on earth, not to reign with Him in heaven), have your own houses. And sometimes we go to you and say, "Let us seek the truth, let us find the truth." And you answer us, "You keep to what you have; you have sheep of your own; we have ours; leave our sheep alone as we leave yours alone." Thank God our sheep are His sheep too. What did Christ purchase by His blood? O may they indeed be neither ours nor yours, but may they be His Who redeemed them and signed them.

Neither he that plants is anything, nor he that waters; but God gives the increase. ... I labor for the name of Christ, you for Donatus. For if you consider Christ, He is everywhere. You say, "Behold He is on this spot." I say, He is everywhere. O you children, praise the Lord, praise the name of the Lord. From where comes their praise, and how long does it last? *From the rising of the sun until the going down thereof, praise the name of the Lord.* Behold the Church which I preach. Behold the price which He paid, His redemption, this Church for which He shed His blood. But what do you say to this? You say, "I, too, am gathering for Him;" He says, *He who gathers not with me, scatters.* You are dividing unity and seeking your own possessions. And why do these possessions bear the name of Christ? Because for the sake of keeping them you have inscribed them with the titles of Christ. Is not this a not infrequent case in private life? A man uses a great name, which he usurps, to protect his house against a strong man's invasion. He wishes to remain in possession, and to [370] strengthen the frontal of his house with a title which does not belong to him, that when it is read the greatness of the name may ward off an invasion into it. This is what the Donatists did when they condemned the Maximinianists. They busied themselves with the judges and went through the form of a council, as if producing the title deeds that they might seem to be bishops. When the judge asked, "What other bishop is there here belonging to Donatus party?" the Court answered, "We know of none save the Catholic bishop Aurelius." Fearing the laws, they spoke of only one bishop, but in order to get a hearing of the judge, they usurped the name of Christ; they affixed His titles to their own property. . . . And consider, brethren, wherever a great man finds his own titles, does he not claim the property as his right, and say, "My name would not be here if I were not proprietor? My titles have been used, the inheritance is mine, for where I find my name, I claim the thing as mine."

Does a man change the titles? The title remains what it was; the owner may be changed, not the title. Thus, in the case of those who have the baptism of Christ, if they return to unity, we do not change or destroy their titles, but acknowledge the title deeds of our Lord and King. . . .

Again the 54th psalm says, *Cast down, Lord, and divide their tongues.* ... It is good for those to be cast down who have exalted themselves unduly; it is fitting that the tongues of those should be divided, who have been guilty of conspiracy; let them conspire unto good, and let their tongues be at one. . . . *Cast down, Lord, and divide their tongues.* Cast down, why cast down? Because they have exalted themselves. *Divide,* why *divide*? Because they have conspired together for evil. Call to mind that tower [371] which proud men built after the Deluge: what did they say? "Lest we perish in the Deluge let us build a high tower." In their pride they fancied they were safe, and they built a lofty tower, and the Lord divided their tongues. They began not to understand each other, and from this source diversity of languages arose. For previously there had been only one, but one tongue was for peaceful and humble men. When those men were guilty of the conspiracy of pride, God spared them in causing the division of tongues, lest understanding each other they might have constituted a pernicious unity. Through proud men tongues were divided; through the humble Apostles they were gathered into unity; the spirit of pride scattered tongues, the Holy Spirit brought them together. For when the Holy Spirit came down upon the disciples, they spoke all languages, and were understood by all; diverse tongues were brought together. If, therefore, they be still unbending Gentiles, it is fitting that they should have division of tongues. If they wish for one language, let them come to the Church, because as the language of the flesh is in diversity, so the voice of faith in the heart is one. *Cast down, Lord, and divide their tongues. . . . He shall redeem my soul in peace from them that draw near to me.* For with regard to those who are not near me the thing is easy. I am not so liable to be deceived by a man who says to me, "Come and worship before the idol;" he is very far removed from me. . . . But in the case of a Christian he strikes you on your own ground. *He shall redeem my soul in peace from them that draw near to me; for in many things they were with me.* Why did I say, *They draw near to me.* Because, *in many things they were with me.* There are two thoughts in this verse.

[372] *In many things they were with me*: we both had baptism, in that they were with me: we both had the Gospel, in that we were together: we honored the feasts of the martyrs, in that they were with me: we kept the Paschal solemnity, in that they were with me. But they went not wholly with me: in heresy they were not with me, in schism they were not with me. They were with me in many things; in a few things they were not with me. But in these few in which they are not with me, the many in which they are with me profit them not. For consider, my brethren, how many things St. Paul enumerates, and he says if one be lacking, the rest are of no avail. *If I speak with the tongues of men and of angels, and if I should have prophecy, and all faith, and all knowledge, and should know all mysteries, so that I could remove mountains, and if I should distribute my goods to the poor, and deliver my body to be burnt*; how many things he mentions, yet let charity be lacking, they are more as to number, but it is greater as to excellence. Therefore, they were with me in all the sacraments; in the unity of charity they were not with me. In many things they were with me. Again, in another sense, For they were with me in many things; they who separated themselves from me were with me in many, not in a few things. For throughout the world the seed is scarce and the chaff plentiful. What then does he mean to say? They were with me as chaff, not as wheat. And chaff has a likeness to wheat; it proceeds from the same seed, grows in one field, is nourished by the same rain, has the same reaper, goes

through the same process of threshing, has the same harvest, but it does not replenish the same garner. *For they were with me in many things. . . . And his heart has drawn near.* Whose heart are we here to [373] understand if not the heart of Him by Whose anger they are divided amongst themselves? How has His heart drawn near? It has drawn near that we may understand His will. Truly indeed the Catholic faith has been made clear through heretics, and through those whose opinions are evil; men whose opinions are good have been proved. For many things were hidden in Scripture, and when heretics were cut off they stirred up the Church of God with questions; the hidden things were revealed, and the will of God was manifested. Hence, it is written in another psalm: *The congregation of bulls with the cows of the people; that they who are tried with silver may be put without Let them be put without,* he says, that is, let them appear and be made manifest. Hence, in the art of money coining, men are called *exclusores* who extract the piece from the confusion of the block. Therefore, many who would be well able to study and relish the Scriptures were hidden in the people of God, nor, in the total absence of calumniators, did they propound the solution of difficult questions. Before, indeed, the attacks of the Arians, was the Trinity ever perfectly defined, or had penance been properly discussed before the obstinacy of the Novatians? So again, baptism was not perfectly defined till the attack of the Rebaptisers from without. Nor were the sayings relating to the very Unity of Christ itself made clear until separation began to agitate weak brethren, when those who knew how to treat and answer these objections brought to the light the obscure points of the Law by their words and controversy, lest feeble men torn by the aunts of the impious should perish. . . .

[374]
8. THE CATHOLIC FAITH STRENGTHENED BY HERETICS
(*On the City of God*, Bk. 18, ch. 51)

THE devil seeing the temples of the demons deserted, and the human race hastening to follow the lead of the saving Mediator, stirred up heretics, who, bearing the name of Christians, should resist the teaching of Christianity. As if they could be tolerated without a word of reprehension in the city of God, just as the city of confusion suffered in its ranks philosophers who held different and conflicting opinions. If, therefore, they who have erratic and depraved opinions in the Church of God, being admonished to have just and true ones, offer a contumacious resistance, will not give up their pestilential and deadly tenets, but persist in holding to them, then they become heretics, and going out they are looked upon as fighting in the enemy's camp. Even thus their very sin is an advantage to the true Catholic members of Christ, for God makes a good use of the wicked, and *to them that love God all things work together unto good.* For with regard to all the enemies of the Church, whatever error may blind their eyes, or wickedness deprave them, if they receive power to afflict her body, they exercise her patience; or if it be by an non-docile spirit alone that they oppose her, they exercise her wisdom. But that even enemies may be-loved, they exercise her kindness, or it may be her [375] generosity, whether her arms in treating with them are gentle words of teaching, or the severe warn-ings of discipline. On this account the devil, who is the prince of the city of confusion, is not allowed to harm the city of God during its days of exile by stirring up his own weapons against it. Beyond a doubt, Divine Providence brings about its prosperity in temporal things that it may not be broken by adversity, and its trial in adverse things that it may not be spoiled by prosperity. The one and the other are so regulated that we see here an application of the Psalmist's words: *According to the multitude of the sorrows in my heart, Your consolations have rejoiced my soul.* Hence again St. Paul says, *Rejoicing in hope, patient in tribulation.*

For it must not be supposed that those other words of his, *All who wish to live completely in Christ shall suffer persecution*, can fail to apply to any epoch of time. When, in the absence of persecution from those with-out, there seems to be peace, and there is peace in truth, which brings with it much consolation, principally to the weak, still men are not lacking within indeed, they are numerous who torture the feelings of holy people by their evil lives, because they draw down blas-phemies on the name of Christian and Catholic. The dearer this name is to those who wish to live completely in Christ, the more they deplore that in consequence of the wicked within, it is less loved than their piety could desire. The heretics themselves, who are supposed to have the Christian name and sacraments, and scriptures and profession, cause deep sorrow to the faithful ones, because, on account of their dissensions, they force many men wishing to become Christians to hesitate. And many reprobate men find even in heretics a reason for blaspheming the Christian name, since heretics do bear the Christian name after a fashion. By [376] these and similar human errors and human depravities do they who wish to live completely in Christ suffer persecution, even should no active enemy vex their body. They bear this persecution, not in their bodies, but in their hearts. Hence the words, *According to the multitude of my sorrows in my heart* - he does not say, "in my body." But again, when it is borne in mind that the divine promises are immutable, and that St. Paul says, *The Lord knows those who are His, and whom He foreknew He also predestined to be made conformable to the image of His Son*; not one of them can perish. Consequently, the same psalm goes on to say, *Your comforts have given joy to my soul.* But the very sorrow felt by the good who are persecuted by the lives either of bad or false Christians, is a profitable sorrow, because it springs from that charity in virtue of which they would not see sinners perish, nor have them prevent the salvation of others. In short, even their repentance is a source of great rejoicing. It fills holy souls with a joy as sweet as their previous anguish was keen. So it is in this world, in these evil days, not only from the time of the bodily presence of Christ and His Apostles, but from that of Abel himself, the first just man whom his wicked brother killed, so will it be hereafter until the end of time, that the Church progresses in her exile through the persecutions of the world and the consolations of God.

9. THE GIFT OF THE DOVE WITHOUT THE DOVE
(*On the Gospel of John*, 6.9)

WHERE were the disciples sent that they might be the ministers of baptism in the name of the Father, and of the Son, and of the Holy Spirit? Where were they sent? *Go*, our Lord said, *and baptize all nations.* You have heard, brethren, from where that inheritance comes, *Ask of Me and I will give you the nations as an inheritance, and the ends of the earth as your possession.* You have heard how the law was promulgated out of Sion, and the word of the Lord from Jerusalem, for it was there that the disciples heard the words, *Go, and baptize the nations in the name of the Father, and of the Son, and of the Holy Spirit.* . . .
In the name of the Father, and of the Son, and of the Holy Spirit. He is one God, as it is not in the *names* but in the name of the Father, Son, and Holy Spirit. One name signifies one God, just as the seed of Abraham signified one seed, as St. Paul explains the words, *In your seed all nations shall be blessed.* He said not, *And to his seeds*, as of many, but as of one, *And to your*

seed, which is Christ. As then the Apostle wished to show you that the unity of seed pointed to the unity of Christ, so here in the name, not in the names, as [378] there in your seed, shows that God the Father and the Son and the Holy Spirit are one God.

But the disciples say to Our Lord, "Behold we have heard in Whose name we are to baptize; You have made us ministers, and have said to us, *Go and baptize in the name of the Father, Son, and Holy Spirit*: where shall we go?" "Have you not heard where? To My inheritance. You ask, Where are we to go? To those whom I have bought with My blood. To whom then? To the nations," He says. . . . The Apostles were sent to the nations, and if to the nations, therefore to peoples of all tongues. This is what the Holy Spirit signified by the division of tongues on the Day of Pentecost, and by the unity of the Dove. By this unity tongues are divided and the Dove is one. Has there been concord in the tongues of the nations and discord in the one tongue of Africa? What is more evident, my brethren? There is unity in the Dove and concord in the tongues of the nations. Pride indeed once caused the division of tongues, and many sprung out of one. If pride produced diverse tongues, the humility of Christ brought them together. That which the Tower had parted the Church unites in harmony.

Many tongues sprung out of one, and, be not surprised, it was the work of pride. (1) One tongue springs out of many; wonder not, for this is the work of charity, because although there is diversity of sound in various tongues, we invoke one and the same God, and we keep one and the same peace From where, then, came the manifestation of the Holy Spirit as that of unity if not in the Dove, that the words *My Dove is one* might be addressed to the Church dwelling in

1 This is an argument against the Donatists.

[379] peace. How could His humility better be shown forth than in a dove, which is gentle and mournful, as opposed to the raven, which is a type of pride and self-sufficiency. . . .

. . . And why was the Dove the indication of some bidden thing, that after Our Lord's baptism the Dove, that is, the Holy Spirit in the form of a dove, should have descended upon Him, and remained upon Him, inasmuch as John recognized in the coming of the Dove a certain special power to baptize in the Lord? Because, as I have said, the peace of the Church was strengthened by this special power. It may happen that a man have baptism without the Dove, but that it profits him without the Dove is impossible. Be attentive to my words, my brethren, for heretics beguile our brethren who are cold and lukewarm by this fallacious argument. Let us be simpler and more fervent. "Well then," they say, "have I or have I not received baptism?" I answer, "You have." "Then if I have, you have nothing to give me, and I am safe

on your own showing? I say that I have received
it, and you say so too; the mouth of both of us agrees
as to my certainty, what then can you promise me
more? Why do you want to make me a Catholic
when you have nothing further to give, and admit
that I have already received that which you say you
have? When I say, *Come to us*, I mean to imply
that you have not got something which you acknowledge that I have. Why do you say, Come to us?

The Dove teaches us why. It shall answer in the
person of Our Lord, and the answer is, "You have
baptism, but not the charity in which I cry." Have
I the Sacraments and not charity? Do not complain: show me how the man who divides unity can
have charity? The heretic says, "I have baptism,"
[380] and I answer, So you have, but your baptism
with out charity profits you nothing, for without charity you are nothing. For baptism, even in him who
is nothing, is not a small thing, indeed it is a great
thing through Him of whom it was said, He it is that
baptizes. But lest you should imagine that, great as
it is, it can profit you anything if you are not in unity,
the Dove descends on the baptized man, as if to say,
"If you have baptism, belong to the Dove, lest that
which you have should avail you nothing." Therefore we say, "Come to the Dove," not that you may
begin to have something new, but that what you
already have may become profitable to you. Your
outside baptism was unto damnation; if you have it
within, it will begin to work your salvation.

Not only did your baptism not avail you anything, it was also bad for you.

Even holy things may do us harm; in the good they work in a salutary way, in the bad they are instruments of judgment. Surely, brethren, we know what we have received, and that it is most holy, and no man says that it is not holy, for what are the Apostle's words? *He who eats and drinks unworthily, eats and drinks judgment to himself.* He does not say that the thing itself is evil, but that a bad man by receiving unworthily receives a good thing unto judgment. Was that supper which Our Lord gave Judas an evil? Assuredly not. The physician would not give poison: He gave salvation, but Judas, who was not at peace, by receiving unworthily, received unto perdition. So also is it with him who is baptized. A heretic says to me, "We have baptism." I acknowledge that you have it, and take care, for this very possession will be your condemnation. Why? Because you have the gift of the Dove without the Dove. If you have the gift [381] of the Dove with the Dove then your possession is safe. . . . Come, then, to us, and do not say, "I have already got what you have, and this is enough for me." Come, the Dove is calling you with sweet, plaintive cries. . . . Come to the Dove, to whom it is said, *My Dove is one, the only one of her mother.* You see the one Dove over the head of Christ, do you not see the tongues of fire on the whole face of the earth? It is the same Spirit in the Dove, and the same Spirit in the Tongues; and if both Dove and Tongues represent the same Spirit, then the Holy Spirit is given to the whole earth, and you have cut yourselves off from this Holy Spirit to croak with the raven, not to moan with the Dove....

Again, do not say, "I do not come to you because I was baptized outside." Make a beginning in charity and in fruitfulness, and let its fruit be found in you, or the Dove will send you into the ark. This is what you find in Scripture. The ark was built of imperishable wood: men who are faithful to Christ, holy men, are as imperishable wood. Just as the righteous are called living stones of which the temple is built, so are they who persevere in faith likened to imperishable wood. In that ark, then, the wood was imperishable, for the Church is the ark, and it is here that the Dove baptizes. That ark was borne on the waters, the imperishable wood was watered from within. Certain wood we find which was watered from without, that is, all the trees which were in the world. Still there was no difference in the quality of the water; it was all water, and had come from the sky or the depths of sources. The imperishable wood of the ark and the wood without the ark were washed by one and the same water. The dove was sent out, and at first it found no resting-place for its feet, it returned to the [382] ark, for all things were full of water, and it chose rather to go back than to be again exposed to the waters. But the raven was sent out before the waters were dried up, and it would not return after being again washed by them, but died in them....

Still you say, "We have baptism." This is true; a sacrament is a divine thing, and I will admit that you have baptism. What are the same Apostle's words? *If I should have prophecy, and should know all mysteries and all knowledge, and if I should have all faith, so that I could remove mountains*, lest you should say, "I have believed, and that is sufficient."

But what does St. James say? *The demons themselves believe and tremble.* Faith is a great thing, but it profits nothing without charity. The devils confessed Christ. Believing, but not having charity, they said, *What have we to do with You?* They had faith without charity, therefore they were devils. Glory not in merely believing, for in this you may be likened to the devils. Say not to Christ, *What have we to do with You?* for the unity of Christ is speaking to you. Come to the home of peace, return to the embrace of the Dove. You have received your baptism without; if you will have its fruit return to the ark.

10. JACOB AND ESAU IN THE CHURCH
   (*Sermon* 4.2, 5.4)

WHOM did Isaac represent when he wished to bless his first-born son? He was already old; years imply age; by years I understand age, and by age the Old Testament. Because therefore they, who were under a cloud, did not understand the Old Testament, it is said of Isaac that his eyes had grown dim. The dimness of his physical eyes signifies the dimness of Jewish minds; the years of Isaac typify the ancient character of the Old Testament. ... It is not strange that he wished to bless his first-born son; but the youngest, disguised as the eldest, receives the blessing. The mother is a figure of the Church. For, brethren, you must see the Church not only in those saints whose sanctity began after the coming and birth of Our Lord; all the saints of all time belong to this same Church. Nor is it true that father Abraham does not belong to us because he lived before Christ was born of a virgin, and we so long afterwards, that is, we are made Christians after the Passion of Christ, as the Apostle says, We are the children of Abraham by imitating the faith of Abraham. We, then, belong to the Church by imitating him, and shall we shut him out from the Church? This Church is typified in Rebecca, Isaac's wife; this Church was shown forth even in the holy prophets, who had understanding concerning the Old Testament, because those temporal promises signified something spiritual. . . . What, then, is the meaning of the youngest under the figure of the eldest receiving the blessing, unless it be that under figure of the promises of the Old Testament made to the Jewish people, a spiritual blessing has descended to the Christian people? Understand my meaning, brethren: they are told of a promised land, so are we: the Scripture seems to speak to the Jews as Jews of the promised land, and to us is given the meaning of the promised land, who say to God, You are my hope, my portion in the land of the living. But it was our mother who taught us so to speak, that is, the Church teaches us in the holy prophets how to understand those temporal promises in a spiritual sense.

But the blessing could not be ours unless, cleansed from our sins by the birth of regeneration, we learn how to bear with the sins of others. For the same mother brought forth these two sons. Listen, brethren, she bore one hairy son and one smooth son. The hairs signify sin, but the smoothness gentleness, that is, immunity from sin. The two sons are blessed, because the Church blesses the two kinds. Just as Rebecca brought forth two so does the Church, one being hairy, the other smooth. For there are men who, even after baptism, will not give up their sins, and wish still to do what they did before. For instance, if they practiced frauds, they want to continue practicing them; if they perjured themselves, they want to go on committing perjury; if they were immoral or drunken, they do the same things now none the less. Well, this is Esau who was born a hairy man. What does Jacob do? His mother says to him, Let your father bless you, and he answers, "I fear to approach [385] him." For there are men in the Church who fear the contact of sinners, lest by their intercourse they should, as it were, lose in unity, and perish through heresies and schisms. . . .

Esau, then, comes back late, bringing with him what

his father had asked for, and he finds his brother blessed in his place, and the blessing is not repeated for him. This is because those two men signified two peoples one blessing typifies the unity of the Church. But two peoples are signified in Jacob himself, though they are shadowed forth in a different way. In truth Our Lord Jesus Christ, Who had come to the Jews and Gentiles, was not received by the Jews who belonged to the eldest son. He chose out, however, some be longing to the youngest son, who had begun to desire and understand the promises of the Lord in a spiritual sense, These did not look upon that promised land which they desired, in an earthly sense, but they wished for that spiritual city in which no man is born according to the flesh, because no man dies there either in body or in spirit. . . .

There are bad men in the Church belonging to Esau, for they too are children of Rebecca, children of our mother the Church and born, of the same womb. Consequently, they enjoy the dew from heaven and the fruitfulness of the earth; from the heavenly dew they have the whole body of the Scriptures and divine teaching, whereas the fruitfulness of the earth gives them all visible sacraments, for a visible sacrament belongs to the earth. Both good and evil men have all these things in common in the Church. For they too have the sacraments and partake of them; they know the mystery of wheat and wine which the faithful know. . . .

These things are common to both, but the inheritance of the nations belongs only to spiritual men, because they belong to the Church which has filled the whole earth. Listen, brethren, and understand as much as you can, or according to what God gives you to understand. Every spiritual man sees that the Church which is spread through the whole earth is one, true, and Catholic, ascribing nothing to herself, bearing with the sins of men whom she may not purge from the Lord's field until the supreme Reaper shall come. He, Who cannot be deceived, will make clean His field, and will put the wheat into the garner, but will deliver the chaff to be burned, because it is for Him to cut off the chaff and separate it from the wheat, and prepare the garner for the full ear and the fire for the refuse. He bears with sinners, therefore, because He knows that He is to cut them off in the end. There are sinners in all peoples, and carnal men in the mass of the spiritual whom they serve, for the spiritual do not serve, but they profit by the failure of the carnal. . . . This Jacob, then, signifies the Christian people, for he is the youngest son, and the Jewish people is represented by Esau. The Jewish people, indeed, sprung from Jacob, but, in a figurative sense, they are typified more strictly by Esau. . . . Consider this mysterious meaning. The Jew is the servant of the Christian, which is manifest, because Jacob has filled the whole earth, as you see. And that you may know that these things were spoken of the future, read what history says, and you must conclude that the words, *The elder shall serve the younger*, were not fulfilled in these two. We read that Esau acquired many riches, and began to reign in all abundance, but that Jacob sought to feed his neighbor's sheep. And when he had set out on his return he feared his brother, and sent him I know not how many sheep as a gift, together [387] with a servant who was to say, *Behold the gifts of your brother.* He would not see him before he had propitiated him with presents. And when Jacob came in to Esau, he fell down before him from afar. How is it then true that the elder shall serve the younger when the younger seems to worship the elder? But these things were not accomplished in history that they may be understood as prophecies relating to the future. The younger son took the birthright, and the eldest lost it. Jacob has filled the earth, he has conquered peoples and kingdoms. The Roman Emperor, himself a Christian, commanded that the Jews should not come up even to Jerusalem. Scattered over the earth, they have become, as it were, the keepers of our books. Like servants, who, when they go to their Lord's audience, carry their documents, and sit outside, so has it been with the eldest son in regard to the youngest.

The Church, then, who says, *Judge me, God, and discern my cause from that of the unrighteous people,* wishes to be discerned not from Esau, for already she is distinct from him, but from bad Christians. For you have heard how this Jacob, who is a figure of the Christian people, struggled with the Lord. God appeared to him, that is, an angel in the figure of the Lord. Jacob struggled with him, and wished to hold and keep him. . . . And what does God say, the angel, that is, in His person, when Jacob prevailed. He touched him on his thigh, and it withered, and therefore Jacob was lame. God says to him, *Let me go, for it is now morning.* And Jacob answers, *I will not let You go unless you bless me.* And he blessed him. In what way? By changing his name. *You shall not be called Jacob, but Israel; because you have prevailed with God, you shall also prevail against men.* Here is the blessing. You see before you one [388] man; he is touched in one member and withers, and in another way he is blessed. The same man is partially paralyzed and lame, and still he is blessed and vigorous. . . . Jacob's withered thigh is an image of bad Christians, that in the one Jacob both a blessing and a malediction may be portrayed. He is blessed in the righteous, and he is lame in the unrighteous. . . . Now the Church is lame, one foot is strong, the other is disabled. Consider what the Pagans say, brethren. Sometimes they find good Christians, who are serving God, and they wonder at them, and are brought to the faith. Sometimes they happen to be brought into contact with men of evil lives, and they say, "See what Christians are!" These unrighteous men, however, belong to the breadth of Jacob's withered thigh. But the touch of the Lord is the correcting and vivifying hand of the Lord. Jacob, therefore, is blessed in part, and is paralyzed in part. The Lord shows forth these evil men in the Church. Hence it is written in the Gospel that when the blade had sprung up there appeared also the cockle, because when men

begin to make progress they are sensible of the
presence of evil ones. . . . But now we must bear
with the cockle until harvest time, lest pulling it
out, we should also pull out the seed. The time will
come, however, for the Church to be heard in her cry,
Judge me, God, and discern my cause from the unrighteous people. It will be in the day of the Lord's
coming in His glory with His holy angels. All
nations will be gathered together before Him, and He
will separate them, as a shepherd separates sheep from
goats. And the just shall be placed on the right, and
the unjust on His left hand. The just will hear the
words, *Come, you blessed of My Father, receive the
kingdom,* but the unjust, *Go into everlasting fire
which is prepared for the devil and his angels.*

11. OUTWARD CATHOLICS AND BAD CATHOLICS
(*Seventeen Questions on Matthew*, 1)

*WHILE men were asleep, his enemy came and sowed
cockle among the wheat and went his way.* When the
pastors of the Church were less vigilant than usual, or
when the Apostles slept in death, the devil came and
sowed cockle among those whom the Lord interprets to be evil sons. But, it is asked with reason, are
these heretics or bad Catholics? The heretics themselves may be called bad sons, because, built up on the
same Gospel seed and the name of Christ, they turn
away to false teaching through the influence of iniqui-

tous opinions. When He speaks of them as being oversown on the wheat, it seems to signify that they belong to the one communion; still, because the Lord interprets the field itself to be the world, not the Church, they may well be taken to mean heretics, for it is not the communion of one Church or one faith which will hold them together with the good in this world, but only the bond of the common Christian name. Thus, they who are wicked in the one faith come rather under the category of chaff than of tares, because the chaff and the wheat grow together from the same root. The net which contains both good and bad fish is a fair image of bad Catholics; for the sea, which typifies the [390] world, and the net which seems to show forth the communion of the one faith, or of the one Church, are distinct things. There is this difference between heretics and bad Catholics: heretics believe that which is false, but bad Catholics, believing that which is true, do not carry out their faith in their lives.

Men are accustomed also to ask in what schismatics differ from heretics? The answer to this question would be to say that it is not difference in faith which makes schismatics, but a falling away from communion. It may be questioned, however, whether they are to be classed with the tares. They seem to be more like spoiled ears of corn, as it is written, *The bad son will be corrupted by the wind,* or broken ears of corn, or like ears which have been cut or torn off from the root. The higher the ears of corn stand the slighter they are, and so it is with men; the prouder they are, the weaker they are. Nor does it follow that every heretic or schismatic be separated bodily from the Church. For if he believe that which is erroneous concerning God or concerning any dogmatic teaching pertaining to the structure of the faith, so that he is not guided by the moderation of a patient inquirer, but is obstinately credulous, and at variance by opinion and error with what he imperfectly knows, then he is a heretic, and he is in spirit without though he seems to be bodily within. The Church contains many men of this kind, because they do not so defend their own false opinions as to gain the attention of the multitude; when they do this they are banished from the pale. Again, all men who are so envious of the good as to seek opportunities for excluding or defaming them, or who are so ready to defend their own crimes, if they should be alleged against them or brought forward, as to try to stir up even party spirit or disturbances in the Church, [391] all such are already schismatics; they have departed from the spirit of unity, although by not having found a favorable opportunity, or by their secret maneuverings they may be outwardly partakers of the mystery of the Church.

Therefore, those only are to be rightfully looked upon as bad Catholics who, although they believe those truths which belong to the teaching of the faith or are in a disposition of mind to seek what they do not know, and to discuss it in a spirit of piety without prejudice to that truth, who love and honor as much as possible the good, or those whom they take to be good, are still leading bad and immoral lives in opposition to the teaching of their faith.

[392]
12. THE HIDDEN CHILDREN OF THE CHURCH
(*On the City of God*, Bk 1, ch. 34, 35; Bk. 18, ch. 49)

IT is said that Romulus and Remus, in seeking to increase the population of the city which they were founding, set up a place of sanctuary, that whoever took refuge in it should be free from all account. A remarkable anticipation, telling for the honor of Christ. They who conquered the city followed the example of those who founded it. But was it a great thing if the former did for supplying the number of their citizens what the latter did to preserve the multitude of their enemies?

These, and such like arguments, which may perchance be enlarged and dwelt upon, may serve the redeemed family of Christ, Our Lord, the exiled city of Christ, Our King, as an answer to the objections of its enemies. Let it be mindful that amongst those very enemies themselves future citizens are hidden, so that it may not account it a useless labor, even for the sake of those future citizens, to bear with hostile men until confessors become its portion. As, indeed, the city of God, during its days of exile, has out of these two ranks of men some who are united with it by the communion of the sacraments, who still will not be with it in the eternal inheritance of the saints, and they are partly hidden and partly known. They even do not scruple to join the very enemy in murmuring [393] against God, whose sign they bear upon themselves. At one time they are with the enemy at the theater, at another they are filling the churches with ourselves. We are by no means to despair of the conversion even of such men, if future friends be hidden amongst bitterest enemies, who know not their own destinies. . . . Therefore, in this corrupt world, and in these evil days of time, during which the Church, through her present lowliness, purchases for herself the high place to come, and is made wise by sharp fear and bitter pains, by travail and the conflict of temptations, with only hope for her joy; in these evil days when she rejoices over one sound man, many reprobate ones are found amongst the number of the good. Still, as in the Gospel net, both are gathered together, and in this world, as in the sea, both swim after the same fashion when taken in the nets until the shore is reached, and then the wicked will be separated from the good, and in the good, as in His own temple, God will become all things to all. Hence we now see the fulfillment of His prophecy Who spoke in the psalm, and said, *I have declared and spoken, they are multiplied beyond number.* This now takes place from the time that He declared and spoke first by the mouth of His precursor St. John, and then by His own mouth, saying, *Do penance, for the kingdom of heaven is at hand.* He chose disciples, whom He called also apostles, men humbly born, unknown, and illiterate, that however great they might be, or whatever great thing they might do, it would be Himself in them Who was living and doing. Amongst the number there was one bad disciple. Christ made use of him with wise purpose, in order to carry out His Passion, and to show His Church an example of bearing with evil men. After He had sown the Holy Gospel as far as was necessary by His bodily presence, [394] He suffered and died and rose again, showing forth by His Passion what we should bear for the truth, and by His resurrection what we have to hope for in eternity, saving the depth of the mystery by which His blood was shed for sinners. He spoke with His disciples on earth for forty days, ascended into heaven in their sight, and after ten days sent the promised Holy Spirit. The great sign of the highest importance of His coming down on those who had believed was, that each one of them should speak the languages of all peoples, signifying in this way the future unity of the Catholic Church throughout all nations, and her thus speaking the tongues of every people.

[395]
13. PETER AND JUDAS IN THE CHURCH
(*Tractates on the Gospel of John*, 1.10)

THEN one of His disciples, Judas Iscariot, he that was about to betray Him, said: Why was not this ointment sold for three hundred pence and given to the poor? Judas said this, not because he had a care for the poor, but because he was a thief, and having the purse carried the things that were put therein. Here you see that Judas did not become bad when he betrayed Our Lord to the Jews who tempted him. But many who are careless of the Gospel narrative fancy that Judas went wrong from the moment that he accepted money from the Jews to betray Our Lord. It was not then; he was already a thief, and he was following Our Lord as a reprobate, because it was a following of body, not of heart. He was number among the twelve, but he had not the apostolic spirit, and was a twelfth in figure. On his failing, and another succeeding to his place, the apostolic body was completed in truth, and its number remained unbroken. What, then, my brethren, did Our Lord Jesus Christ wish to teach His Church in choosing to have one reprobate among the twelve, if not that we should bear with the wicked and not divide the Body of Christ because of them? Behold there is a Judas among saints, and Judas is a thief; and lest you should make light of this, he is not an ordinary [396] thief, but a sacrilegious one. He is a thief of treasure, even of divine treasure, even of sacred treasure. If a distinction be made in courts of justice in judging the circumstances of any particular theft or peculation, for a theft of public property is called a peculation, and a private robbery is not judged in the same way as a public one, how much more severely is a sacrilegious thief to be punished who has dared to steal, not from any ordinary quarter, but from the Church. He who steals anything from the Church is like the reprobate Judas. Such was this Judas, and still he came in and went out with the holy eleven. With them he assisted at Our Lord's Supper itself; he might converse with them, he could not defile them. Peter and Judas ate of the same bread, and yet what has the righteous man in common with the reprobate? For Peter received bread unto life, and Judas unto death. The food of salvation is like a good odor, and as a good odor so strengthening food gives life to the good and poison to the evil. For he who eats unworthily eats and drinks judgment to himself - judgment to himself, not to his fellow-man. If it is to himself and not to you that he eats judgment, be steadfast yourself in good, and bear with the wicked, that you may come to the reward of the good, and may not fall a prey to the torments of the wicked.

Take example by what Our Lord did when on earth. What need had He of purses to whom angels ministered, unless it was because His Church was one day to have them? Why did He give admittance to a thief except to teach His Church patiently to bear with thieves? But he who had been accustomed to take money out of the purse did not hesitate to sell his Lord Himself for money. Let us see how Our Lord answers him. Consider, brethren, He does not say to him, "You say these things because of your theft." He [397] knew that Judas was a thief, and did not betray him, but rather bore with him, and gave us an example of patience in bearing with evil men in the Church. But what follows? *For the poor you have always with you, but Me you have not always.* We understand well enough that we have the poor always with us; His words are true. When is the Church without the poor? *But Me you have not always*; what is the meaning of this? ... Be not afraid, it is spoken to Judas. Why then did he not use the second person singular, you instead of you? (1) Because there is more than one Judas. The one reprobate signifies the body of the evil, just as Peter typifies the communion of the good, the body indeed of the Church, but as far as it concerns the righteous. For if the mystery of the Church were not exemplified in Peter, Our Lord would not say to him, *To you do I give the keys of the kingdom of heaven; whatever you shall bind on earth shall be bound in heaven, and whatever you shall loose on earth shall be loosed in heaven.* If this be said only for Peter, it is not said for the Church. But if in the Church too those things which are bound on earth are bound in heaven, and those things which are loosed on earth are loosed in heaven, because when the Church excommunicates, the excommunicated man is bound in heaven, and when she reconciles him he is unloosed in heaven; if this be done in the Church, Peter in accepting the keys signified the Church of the good. If in Peter's person the good in the Church are signified, Judas is the type of evil men in it. To them it is said, *Me you have not always.* For what is not always? and what is always? If you are just, and if you belong to the body which Peter signifies, you have Christ both in this life and in the next; in this present life

---

1 *Habebis* [singular], not *habebitis* [plural].

[398] by faith, by the sign of the cross, the sacrament of baptism, by the food and drink of the altar. You have Christ in this present life, but you will have Him always, for when you depart hence you will go to Him Who said to the thief, *Today you shall be with Me in paradise.* But if you are wicked you seem to have Christ in this present life, because you go to church, and sign yourself with the sign of Christ, and are baptized with the baptism of Christ. You mingle yourself with the members of Christ, and go up to the altar of Christ; you have Christ in this present life, but because of your evil life you will not always have Him.

[399]
14. ON SACRIFICE
(*On the City of God*, Bk. 10, ch. 4, 5, 6, 7)

Now, not to speak of other things which pertain to the worship of God, surely no man will dare to say that sacrifice is due to any other than God alone. Many details in divine worship were usurped in order to give honor to men, and they were practiced either by excessive abjectness or by loathsome flattery, but so practiced that the subjects towards whom they were exercised should be held to be men worthy of esteem and veneration. If much be given to them it becomes a question of adoration; but what man ever judged that sacrifice should be offered except to one whom he knew, or imagined, or pretended to be God? The great antiquity of the rite of offering sacrifice to God is clearly proved by the two brothers Cain and Abel. God rejected the sacrifice of the elder of these two while He accepted that of the younger. But who would be so demented as to suppose that the things offered in sacrifice supply a need in the uses of God? Holy Scripture proves this in many places, but for brevity's sake we may quote that single sentence of the psalm, *I said to the Lord, You are my God,* for You require not my good things. We must believe, then, that God has no need not only of cattle nor of any other corruptible thing whatever, but not even of man's justice, and that the whole worship of God, rightly [400] understood, profits man not God. No one will say that he has benefited a fountain by drinking its waters, nor the light by seeing.

A true sacrifice is every work which is done that we may cleave in holy union to God, that is, with a reference to that great end by which we may become truly happy. Hence mercy itself, if it be not done for God, is no sacrifice. For sacrifice, even when made or offered by a man, is a divine thing, and so the ancient Latins termed it. Therefore a man who is consecrated in God's name, and given up to God, inasmuch as he dies to the world in order to live unto God, is a sacrifice, for that also belongs to mercy which a man exercises towards himself. Thus it is written, *Have pity on your soul, pleasing God.* When we chastise our body by temperance, and do it as we ought, for God's sake, in order that we may not yield our members as instruments of iniquity unto sin, but as instruments of justice unto God, we accomplish a sacrifice. The Apostle admonishes us to do this when he says, *I beseech you therefore, brethren, by the mercy of God, that you present your bodies a living sacrifice, holy, pleasing unto God, your reasonable service.* If, therefore, the body, which the soul uses as a sort of servant or instrument, whose good and lawful service is referred to God, is a sacrifice, how much more does the soul become a sacrifice when it has God as its direct object, that, inflamed with divine love, it may put off the form of earthly lust, and in submission to Him as to the Unchangeable Form may be reformed, pleasing Him because it has partaken in His own beauty? This the same Apostle goes on to say, *And be not conformed to this world, but be reformed in the renewal of your mind, that you may prove what is the good, and the acceptable,* [401] *and the perfect will of God.* As, then, true sacrifices are works of mercy which we do either for ourselves or for our neighbors with a reference to God for the sole object of works of mercy is to deliver us from misery and so to make us happy, and this is only accomplished by that good of which it is written, *It is good for me to adhere to my God* - so the whole city of the redeemed itself, that is, the company and society of the saints, may be offered as a universal sacrifice to God by the great High Priest, Who offered Himself up in the Passion for us that we in the form of servants might be the body of so great a Head. He offered up His human nature, and was offered up in it, for according to it He is Mediator, and Priest, and Sacrifice.

When then the Apostle had exhorted us to present our bodies as a living sacrifice, holy, pleasing unto God, our reasonable service, not to be conformed to this world but to be reformed in the newness of our mind, that we may prove what is the will of God, which good and acceptable and perfect sacrifice we ourselves are, he goes on: *For I say, through the grace that is given me, to all that are among you, not to be more wise than it behooves to be wise, but to be wise unto sobriety, and according as God has divided to every one the measure of faith. For as in one body we have many members, but all the members have not the same office, so we being many, are one body in Christ, and every one members one of another. And having different gifts according to the grace that is given us.* This constitutes the sacrifice of Christians, *Being many, we are one body in Christ.* The Church, too, frequents the mystery of the altar which is known to the faithful, and in which she is shown that in that which she offers she may herself be offered up. Those immortal and blessed ones in heaven, who rejoice in the possession of their Creator, [402] are immutable in His eternity, unerring in His truth, holy by His gift, because they have a merciful love for us in our mortal vicissitudes, in order that we may become happy for all eternity, would not have us sacrifice to them, but to Him whose sacrifice they know themselves to be in common with ourselves. For with them we are one city of God, whom the Psalmist addresses in the words, *Glorious things are said of you, O city of God*, part of which city we ourselves are here in exile, and part of which is in the heavenly ones for our consolation. Those words of Holy Scripture, *He that sacrifices to gods shall be put to death, save only to the Lord*, speak to us from that City on high, where the intelligible and unchangeable will of God constitutes the law from that heavenly court, so to speak (for we are thought of in that place), which is ministered to us by angels. So many miracles testify to these Scripture words, and the law and precepts, that it is clear to whom the immortal and blessed ones would have us sacrifice, who wish us that which they have them selves.

15. SACRIFICES OF THE OLD LAW, TYPES
(*Questions on the Gospel of Luke*, 1.2)

WHEN the Lord said to the leper who was cleansed, *Go, show yourself to the priest, and offer for your cleansing according as Moses commanded, for a testimony to them*, He seems to give His sanction to the sacrifice which was commanded through Moses, since the Church has not received it. This He may be understood to have commanded, because the most holy of holy sacrifices had not then begun to be offered, the sacrifice of His Body. For at that time He had not offered Himself as a holocaust in His Passion. When this His sacrifice was confirmed in the faith of peoples, that temple in which the sacrifices of the Old Law had been accustomed to be offered, was destroyed. This was done according to Daniel's prophecy. The typical sacrifices were not to be taken away until that which they signified was confirmed by the combat of the apostolical preaching, and the faith of believing peoples.

[404]
16. OUR LORD THE DAILY SACRIFICE OF THE CHURCH
(*On the City of God*, Bk. 10, ch. 20; Bk. 17, ch. 20; *On the Psalms*, 33)

OUR true Mediator, then, inasmuch as Christ Jesus taking upon Himself the form of a servant is made the Mediator of God and man, while as God He receives sacrifice together with the Father, being God as He is, chose, as man, rather to be the sacrifice than to receive it, lest anyone should draw the conclusion even here that sacrifice was to be offered to a creature. Thus He is at once the priest, Who offers Himself, and He is the offering. He willed that this mystery should be the daily sacrifice of the Church; as the Body of which He is the Head, the Church, learns through Him to offer herself up to God. The old sacrifices of the saints were so many signs and types of this true Sacrifice which was shadowed forth through many signs, just as one thing might be set forth by a multiplicity of words, so that it should be much emphasized without causing weariness to the mind. All false sacrifices ceased in presence of this supreme and true sacrifice.

... The sacrifice of the Jews, according to the order of Aaron, used to consist, as you know, in offerings of cattle, and this was typical; the Sacrifice of the Body and Blood of the Lord, which the faithful and readers of the Gospel know, did not then exist, which [405] Sacrifice is now spread over the whole earth. Put, therefore, these two sacrifices before you, the one according to the order of Aaron, the other according to the order of Melchizedek. For it is written, *The Lord has sworn, and He will not repent: You are a priest forever according to the order of Melchisedech.* Who is the priest for ever according to the order of Melchizedek? Our Lord Jesus Christ. Who was Melchizedek? He was the King of Salem, and Salem was the city which learned men have identified with the later Jerusalem. Thus, before the Jews reigned at Jerusalem, Melchizedek, who is described in the Book of Genesis as a priest of the most high God, was there. It was Melchizedek who met Abraham after he had delivered Lot from the hands of his persecutors, and had vanquished those by whom he was held so as to release his [nephew]. Great indeed was Melchizedek, since Abraham was blessed by him. He offered up bread and wine, and blessed Abraham, who gave him a tenth [of what he had]. Consider what he offered and whom he blessed. And afterwards it was written, *You are a priest forever according to the order of Melchizedek.* These were the words of David inspired by the Holy Spirit, spoken long after Abraham's day, but Melchizedek belonged to Abraham's times. To whom does David point when he says, *You are a priest forever according to the order of Melchizedek*, if not to Him Whose Sacrifice is known to you? . . .

Again with regard to that passage in the Book of Proverbs which we touched upon in treating of the barren woman who bore seven children, it was always at once understood to mean only Christ and the Church by those who knew Christ to be the wisdom of God. *Wisdom has built herself a house, she has* [406] *hewn out seven pillars. She has slain her victims, mingled her wine, and set forth her table. She has sent her maids to invite to the tower, and to the walls of the city: Whoever is a little one, let him come to me. And to the unwise she said: Come, eat my bread, and drink the wine which I have mingled for you.* Here, indeed, we acknowledge that the Wisdom of God, that is, the Word co-eternal with the Father, built for Himself a house of the human body in the virginal womb, and that He joined to this body, as members to the head, the Church, that He offered up the martyrs, as victims, prepared a table of wine and bread, in which the priesthood according to the order of Melchisedech is also apparent. We acknowledge that He called to Himself the foolish and the unwise, because, as the Apostle says, *He chose the weak things of this world that He might confound the strong....* To become a partaker of that table is to begin to live. For what is a more credible meaning of the words of Ecclesiastes, *There is no good for a man but to eat and drink*, than to apply them to that table of His Body and Blood which the Priest Himself, the Mediator of the New Testament according to the order of Melchisedech, shows forth? For, this Sacrifice has succeeded to all the sacrifices of the Old Testament which were offered up as types of the future, and on this account we recognize the voice of the same Mediator, speaking in prophecy in the 39th Psalm: *Sacrifice and oblation You did not desire, but You have perfected a body for me.* His Body is offered in place of all former sacrifices and oblations, and is administered to those who assist. . . .

[407]
17. HOW CHRISTIANS HONOR THE MARTYRS
(*On the City of God*, Bk. 8, ch. 27)

WE do not build temples, nor institute priesthoods, nor services, nor sacrifices in honor of our martyrs themselves, because it is not they but their God who is our God. We do indeed honor their shrines as those of holy men of God, who fought for the truth even unto the death of their body, in order that the true religion might be manifested and false and untrue religions overcome: and if these feelings were in the heart of any men before, they repressed them out of fear. Who amongst the faithful ever heard of a priest standing at the altar, raised even over the holy body of a martyr unto the honor of God, and saying, "I offer you this sacrifice, O Peter, or Paul, or Cyprian," whereas at their shrines sacrifice is offered to God Who made them both men and martyrs, and associated them to His holy angels in heavenly honor; that in that sacrifice we may both give thanks to the true God for their victories, and may also encourage ourselves by the help of the same God unto the winning of similar crowns and palms from the renewed commemoration of them. Whatever services, then, are held on the spots of martyrdom and do honor to shrines, they are not sacrifices to the dead as if they were gods. Or whoever may take even his food in the same way to the martyr's tomb, which indeed is not done by [408] Christians of the better sort, and in most places no such custom exists, still, whoever follows it, and after offering his food, prays, and takes it away either to eat or to distribute to the needy also, does so in order to sanctify that food for himself by the merits of the martyrs in the name of the Lord of the martyrs. He who knows the one Sacrifice, which is also offered up there, knows that these practices are not sacrifices to the martyrs.

[409]
18. THE EUCHARIST A PERPETUAL MARRIAGE FEAST
(*Tractates on the Letters of John*, 2.2)

WHAT did Our Lord show us as written in the Law of

Moses, in the Prophets, and Psalms concerning Himself? Let Him tell us. St. Luke has stated it in a few words, that, in the great amplitude of the Scripture text, we might know what we are to believe and how we are to understand it. The pages and books, numerous indeed, which have come down to us, all give us Our Lord's few and simple words to His disciples on this subject. What were they? *That it behooved Christ to suffer and to rise again on the third day.* This is told us of the Bridegroom, *That it behooved Christ to suffer and to rise again.* He commended the Bridegroom to us. Let us see what He says of the Bride, that recognising the Bride and Bridegroom you may not come in vain to the nuptials. For every celebration is a marriage feast, the marriage feast of the Church. The Son of the King, Who is Himself a King, is to espouse a bride: and they who assist are the bride. It is not here, as in carnal marriages, where those who attend at the marriage and she who is married are different persons: in the Church, they who assist, if they assist worthily, become the bride. For every Church is the spouse of Christ, and the flesh of Christ is the beginning and first fruits of Christ: therein the Bride is joined in the flesh to the Bridegroom. When, in truth, He wished to commend His own Flesh, He broke bread: and in the breaking of the bread the eyes of His disciples were opened, and they knew Him. . . . For your information He said these words, *That it behooved Christ to suffer and to rise again*; and what does He now add to them, that after commending the Bridegroom, He might commend the Bride? *And to preach penance in His name, and remission of sins to all nations, beginning by Jerusalem.* You have heard the words, brethren. Hold them fast. Let no one have doubts concerning the Church, which is spread through all nations; let no one question its having risen in Jerusalem, and filled all nations. We recognize a field in which a vine has been planted, but when the vine has grown to its perfection we recognize it no longer, because it fills the whole field. From where did it begin? From Jerusalem. Where has it reached? To all nations. Few remained in darkness. All shall come to the light. In the meantime, while the Church includes every people, the farmer deemed it well to uproot some useless weeds; thus heresies and schisms came about. Do not allow yourselves to be uprooted by those who have been weeded out, rather do all you can to move them to be re-sown in the vineyard. It is manifest that Christ suffered, rose again, and ascended into heaven, and the Church also has been made manifest, because in her name penance and remission of sins are preached through all nations. From what place did she begin? From Jerusalem. A vain and foolish man hears this, and what more can I call him than blind who sees not this mighty mountain, and who shuts his eyes to the light which is shining on the candlestick? . . . Where did the Church begin if not there where the [411] Holy Spirit descended from heaven, and filled the place in which the one hundred and twenty were assembled? The twelve had been ten times multiplied. One hundred and twenty men were sitting there, and the Holy Spirit came down and filled the whole place, and there was a sound as of a mighty wind, and parted tongues as it were of fire. . . . They began to speak with diverse tongues, according as the Holy Spirit gave them to speak. And all the Jews who were there out of every nation heard each man his own tongue, and they were astonished that those simple and unlearned men should have suddenly mastered not one or two languages but every language. This union of every idiom showed that every language was to be represented in the faith. But these men who love Christ much, and will not, therefore, hold communion with the city which put Him to death, honor Christ so that they restrict him to two languages, the Latin and the Punic, that is, the African tongue. Does Christ hold communion with only two tongues? For Donatus has no more than two. Let us bestir ourselves, brethren, and see rather what the gift of the Holy Spirit was, and believe what was foretold concerning it. Let us consider the fulfillment of the Psalmist's words, *There are no speeches nor languages where their voices are not heard*. And lest it should be understood that those languages were heard in one place only, and not rather that the gift of God belongs to all languages, listen to what follows: *Their speach has gone forth into all the earth, and their words unto the end of the world*. How is this? Because He has set His tabernacle in the sun, that is, in a place visible to all. His tabernacle is His flesh; His tabernacle is His Church; and she is set in the sun, not in the night, but in the day. . . .

19. THE FOOD OF THE CHURCH
(On the Psalms, 33.6, On the Gospel of John, 26.2 and 27.2)

... THE sacrifice of Aaron ceased, and the sacrifice according to the order of Melchizedek began. Someone, then, I know not who, has changed his countenance.(1) Who is this mysterious person? yet not mysterious, for Our Lord Jesus Christ is known to all. In His Body and Blood He willed to be our salvation. What made Him put before us His Body and Blood? It was His humility, for unless He had been humble He would not be made food and drink. Think of His almightiness: *In the beginning was the Word, and the Word was with God, and the Word was God.* Behold the eternal food; but the angels eat, the heavenly powers and spirits eat, and eating they are nourished, and that which feeds and rejoices them remains whole and entire. What man may venture upon that Food? What heart is fit to partake of it? It was necessary then that that banquet should be converted into milk, so as to be made accessible to the little ones. How does food become milk except by the process of eating? For this is what the mother does, and the infant partakes of her food; but as the child is incapable of eat-

---

1 A commentary on the title of the 33d Psalm: *For David when he changed his countenance before Achimelech, who dismissed him, and he went his way.*

ing bread, the mother eats it first, and at the

lowly breast the infant sucks the milk, which is the bread itself. How, then, has the wisdom of God fed us with this self-same bread? Because *the Word was made flesh and dwelt amongst us.* You see His humility: for it is written that *He gave them bread from heaven,* man ate the bread of angels; that is, man has eaten that eternal Word of God, equal to His Father, Whom the angels feed upon, Who being in the form of God, thought it not robbery to be equal with God.

The angels are nourished by Him; but He humbled Himself that man might eat of the angels bread, *taking upon Himself the form of a servant, in habit found as a man, He humbled Himself, becoming obedient unto death, even the death of the cross,* that from the cross He might show forth to us the new sacrifice, the Body and Blood of the Lord. Because *He changed His countenance before Achimelech,* that is, before the kingdom of His Father, for the kingdom of His Father was the kingdom of the Jews. How the kingdom of His Father? Because the kingdom of David was the kingdom of Abraham. For the kingdom of God the Father is rather the Church than the people of the Jews; but according to the flesh the people of Israel was the kingdom of the Father. . . .

He changed then His countenance before Achimelech, . . . and He dismissed him and went his way. Whom did he dismiss? The people of the Jews themselves, and went his way. You seek for Christ amongst the Jews and no longer find Him. Why did he dismiss him, and go his way? Because He changed His countenance. They, cleaving to the sacrifice of Aaron, did not receive the sacrifice according to the order of Melchizedek, and they lost Christ; the Gentiles to whom He had not sent prophets, began to possess Him. [414] For He had sent His forerunners to the Jews, David himself, and Abraham, Isaac and Jacob, and Isaiah and Jeremiah, and all the other prophets. A few grew to know Him in this way, for although they were in reality many, they are few in comparison to those who perish. We read that the few were thousands; still it is written, *a remnant shall be saved.* You seek circumcised Christians and do not find them. In the early times of the faith, many thousand Christians were of the circumcision. If you look for them now, you do not find them. *He changed his countenance before Achimelech, and dismissed him, and went his way. . . .* The names are changed to excite in us a desire to understand the mystery, lest we should think that the Psalms only commemorate or narrate that which took place in the Book of Kings, and instead of seeking for the figures of future things, we should be content to accept them as facts accomplished and ended. What does the change of names signify to you? There is something hidden here, strive to penetrate its meaning, do not be contented with the letter, because the letter kills; but desire the spirit which vivifies. The spiritual understanding is the salvation of the believer.

Consider how David dismissed King Achish. I have said that the name of Achish is interpreted to mean *how is it.* Call to mind those words of Our Lord Jesus Christ when He spoke of His Body: *Unless a man shall eat My Flesh and drink My Blood, he shall have no life in him; for My Flesh is food indeed, and My Blood is drink indeed.* And His disciples who were following Him were frightened, and scandalized at His words, and not understanding Him, they thought Our Lord meant I know not what difficult thing; that they were to eat that very body which they saw, and [415] to drink His blood, and they could not bear it. They might have been saying, how is it? For in the person of Achish, error and ignorance and foolishness are personified. When a man says *how is it?* he means that he does not understand, and a want of understanding constitutes the darkness of ignorance. Therefore ignorance reigned in their hearts like a sort of King Achish; that is, they were ruled by the might of error. But he said, *Unless a man eat My Flesh and drink My Blood.* Because He had changed His countenance, it seemed like madness to give His flesh to men to eat, and His blood to drink. Thus David was accounted as a madman when Achish himself said, *Why have you brought this madman to me?* Does it not seem a madness to say, *Eat My Flesh and drink My Blood?* and are not the words, *Whoever shall not eat My Flesh and drink My Blood, shall not have life in him*, those of a madman? So they appear to Achish, that is, to foolish and ignorant people. Therefore he left them and went away; their intellect forsook them, so that they could not understand him. And what did they say to him? They seemed to say, *how is this?* which is the interpretation of Achish. For their commentary was, *How can this man give us His flesh to eat?* They deemed Our Lord a madman, and thought He was demented, and that He did not know the meaning of His own words. . . . And he (David) was carried in his own hands.(1) Who can understand, my brethren, how a man is able to accomplish this? For who is carried in his own hands? A man may be carried by others, but no one is carried by himself. We do not find it accomplished literally in David, but

1 This reference to 1 Sam. 21.13, is translated in the Vulgate by *and slipped down between their hands.*

[416] we do find it in Our Lord. For Christ was carried in His own hands when speaking of His own Body. He said, *This is My Body.* He carried that Body in His own hands. . . .

What is the meaning of the words, *And his spittle ran down upon his beard!* For this it did when he changed his countenance before Achimelech or Achish, and he dismissed him and went his way. He sent away those who did not understand. To whom did he go? To the Gentiles. Let us then understand that which was incomprehensible to them. The spittle ran down upon David's beard. . . . The spittle may signify infantile words. . . . And were not those infantile words, *Eat My Flesh and drink My Blood*? But these infantile words concealed His power. The beard is understood to signify strength. What then is the spittle running down upon His beard if not infantile words which covered His almightiness? . . .

I am the Bread of Life, He says. From where came their pride? *Your fathers,* He says, *ate manna in the wilderness, and are dead.* Why, having eaten, did they die? Because they believed what they saw, and did not understand what they did not see. They are your fathers because you are like them. For, my brethren, as far as this physical strength is concerned, do we not also die although we eat of the bread which comes down from heaven? They are dead just as we too shall die, by the death of the body, as I have said. But as regards that death of which Our Lord warns them, and by which their fathers had died; Moses and Aaron and Phineas, and many men pleasing to God, had eaten of the manna, and they did not die. Why? Because they understood the visible food with a spiritual mind, they hungered after it, and partook of it in a spiritual way that they might be spiritually replen- [417] ished. Now at this present time we accept a visible food: but the sacrament and the power of the sacrament are different things. How many men approach the altar and die, and die by this very participation. Hence the Apostle says, *He eats and drinks judgment to himself.* For it was not the Lord's chalice which was poison to Judas, and yet he drank of it, *and when he had drunk, the devil entered into his heart.* The evil was not in the thing, but in a wicked man misusing a good thing. See, then, my brethren, that you eat the heavenly Bread with a spiritual mind, and bring innocence to the altar. If your sins be of daily occurrence, yet let them not be deadly. Before coming to the altar, ponder the words which you say, *Forgive us our trespasses as we forgive them that trespass against us.* Forgive and it will be forgiven you. Come with confidence, it is bread and not poison. . . .

In no way are the people of Israel said to have displeased God more than by murmuring against Him. Hence Our Lord, wishing to show them that they are true sons of these men, says, *Why do you murmur one with another?* discontented children of discontented fathers. *Your fathers did eat manna and are dead*, not because the manna was evil, but because, they ate of it unworthily. . . .

The whole sum and substance of that which Our Lord spoke concerning His Body and Blood, i.e., the promise of eternal life through partaking of it, His wish that eaters and drinkers of His Body and Blood should remain in Him and He in them, the want of understanding in non-believers, the carnal comprehension of spiritual things which had scandalized them, the consolation Our Lord offered to His disciples who remained after the others had left Him to their loss, [418] the question which He put to them to try them that their answer about staying with Him might be of use to us, *Will you, too, go?* let all this help us to eat the Body and Blood of Christ, not only in the sacrament, which many evil men do, but also unto a spiritual participation, that we may remain members of the Lord's body, and feed on His Spirit, and not be scandalized if many who now partake of the sacraments with us in this life, are one day to suffer eternal torments. For now the body of Christ is mixed like the corn of a harvest field, but the Lord knows those who are His. If the farmer knows what he is doing in thrashing out the corn because of the hidden ear, and if the thrashing out does not finish the work which the winnowing is to do, so we are certain, brethren, that all we who are in the Lord's body, and remain with Him that He, too, may remain in us, must of necessity live amongst the wicked as long as the world is to last. By the wicked I do not mean men who blaspheme Christ; few men blaspheme Him with their tongues, but many by their lives, and with such as these it behooves us to live unto the end.

20. SACRIFICE OF THE ALTAR APPLIED TO THE DEPARTED
(*Handbook to Laurentius*, ch. 29)

IT cannot be denied that the souls of the departed are benefited by the piety of their relations on earth when the Holy Sacrifice of the Mediator is offered for them, or alms are distributed in the Church. But these things profit those who, while on earth, so lived as to deserve their future suffrages. For there is a certain manner of life which is not sufficiently good not to require this consolation after death, and yet not bad enough to make it useless. There is, of course, a state of goodness which may dispense with these helps, and one of wickedness which renders them unavailing when once this life is over. Hence it is here on earth that a man gains the merit or demerit which will either profit him hereafter or turn to his damnation. Let no one hope to gain merit there with God for what he has neglected to do here. These practices, then, which the Church encourages for the departed are not contrary to the Apostle's words, *For we shall all stand before the judgment seat of Christ, that every one may receive the proper things of the body, according as he has done, whether it be good or evil.* Each man while in the body acquired this merit for himself by so living as to render these suffrages availing. They do not benefit [420] all the departed, and why, if not on account of the different life which each led in this world? When, therefore, sacrifices, either of the altar or of any alms whatever, be offered up for all the baptized dead, they serve as thanksgiving in the case of perfect souls, as a propitiation for those who are guilty, yet not grievously so; while in the case of the wicked, though they do not help the dead, they serve as a certain consolation to the living. They profit those whom they profit either as a perfect remission or as softening the rigor of their condemnation.

After the resurrection indeed, and when the last judgment shall have taken place, those two cities, that is, the city of Christ and the city of the devil, will reach their respective ends, one being the city of the good, the other the city of the wicked, but both being composed of men and angels. By no possibility will the good have the will to sin nor the wicked the means of sinning, neither will they be able to incur death. The good will live possessing perfect truth and happiness in eternal life, the wicked will live miserably in eternal death, without the power of dying, because, both good and bad will endure for ever. But as in that eternal happiness one will have a higher place than another, so in that abode of misery some will be less tormented than others.

[421]
21. SAVED YET SO AS BY FIRE
(*On the Psalms,* 37.3)

IT will come to pass that certain souls will be reproved by the wrath of God and chastised in His anger. Perhaps not all who are corrected will be cleansed, but it is certain that some will be saved in this way. This is certain because it is stated in so many words, *Yet so as by fire.* But some will be reproved and will not be cleansed. For He will indeed reprove those to whom He shall say, *I was hungry and you gave Me not to eat, I was thirsty and you gave Me not to drink*; and continuing with the other works of mercy He will reproach the wicked on His left hand with their sterility and want of kindness; to them it will be said, *Depart into everlasting fire, which is prepared for the devil and his angels.* These were the more terrible evils which the Psalmist feared quite apart from those of this life, in which he cries out and groans, saying, "*Rebuke me not, Lord, in Your indignation.* Let me not be amongst the number of those to whom You will say, *Depart unto everlasting fire, which is prepared for the devil and for his angels.* Neither chastise me in Your wrath. May You cleanse me in this life, and make me so that there may be no need of the cleansing fire which awaits those who are to be saved yet so as by fire." Why is this, unless it is that on earth [422] they build up wood, hay, and combustible matter on the foundation stone. If they were to build up gold, silver, and precious stones they would be secure from both fires, not only from that eternal fire which is to torment the wicked, but also from that other fire which is to cleanse those who are to be saved by fire. For it is written, *He himself shall be saved yet so as by fire,* and because St. Paul says, *He shall be saved,* that fire is made light of. Though some shall indeed be saved by fire, that fire will be more grievous than anything which a man can suffer in this life. And you know how much the wicked have suffered, and may suffer here below, still these great sufferings of theirs might have fallen equally upon the good. What have the laws imposed upon malefactors, thieves, adulterers, criminals, and desecrators, which the martyr has not endured for his bearing witness to Christ? These temporal evils, therefore, are far less grievous, and still you see that men will do anything you please in order to avoid them. How much more wisely do they act who obey the law of God, lest they should suffer those more cruel torments?

[423]
22. ALMS, PRAYER, AND SUPPLICATION FOR THE DEAD
(Sermon 172)

THE blessed Apostle admonishes us not to be sorrowful concerning them that are asleep, that is, our dear dead, as others who have no hope, which hope is that of the resurrection and of eternal life. For the Scripture is accustomed to adopt this most correct term in their regard, that when we hear them spoken of as those who sleep, we may have the greater confidence in their awakening. Hence, too, the Psalm says, *Shall he that sleeps rise no more?* A certain sadness over the dead whom we love is in a manner natural, for it is not our judgment but our nature which shuns death. Nor would death have befallen man had it not followed his sin as a penalty. Thus, if animals who are created for a certain period of time, try to escape death and love their life, how much more does man, who was so created that, if he had chosen to live without sin, he would have lived for ever? Hence of necessity we must be sad when our dear ones leave us by death; for although we know that they do not leave us on earth forever, but are only preceding us who are shortly to follow, still death itself, which our nature shrinks from when it strikes someone we love, grieves the affection which is in us. Therefore the Apostle did not exhort us not to be sorrowful, but only not to be like others [424] who have no hope. We grieve, then, over the necessity of losing our friends in death, but with the hope of again seeing them. This necessity causes us anguish, but the hope consoles us; our infirmity is tried by the one, and our faith is strengthened by the other: on the one hand our human condition sorrows, on the other the divine promise is our salvation.

In like manner, funeral pomp and show, a costly tomb, and the erection of rich monuments, solace the living if you will; they profit not the dead. But there is no sort of doubt that the dead are helped by the prayers of Holy Church and the Sacrifice of salvation, and by alms, that God may deal more mercifully with them than their sins have deserved. For the universal Church carries on the tradition which has been handed down by our fathers, that of praying for those who have departed hence in the communion of the body and blood of Christ by commemorating them at a particular place in the sacrifice itself, and by remembering to offer it also for them. Who indeed may doubt that works of mercy, which are offered up in their memory, relieve them for whose sakes prayer is not vainly made to God? Most surely these things profit the departed, but such among them who have lived so as to deserve this consolation after death. Thus it is vain for the relations of those who have departed this life without that faith which works through charity and without its sacraments, to offer up for

them these acts of piety. While here on earth they
had not the pledges of that faith, or they did not
receive the grace of God, or received it in vain, and
laid up to themselves treasures of anger, not of mercy.
It is not, then, that new merits are bought for the
dead, by their friends doing some good work for them,
but these acts follow them in consequence of their own
[425] previous actions. It was in the flesh that they merited any consolation which might be applied to them
after they had ceased to live in this world. And, therefore, at the termination of his mortal life, a man can only
receive that which he has merited for himself during
its course.

Kind hearts, then, may be allowed to sorrow in
moderation over their dear departed ones, and to shed
peaceful tears by reason of their mortal condition. The
joy which comes from faith should quickly dry them
up, for by this joy the faithful believe that when they
die they leave us for a short time and pass to better
things. Let them take consolation even from the
sympathy of others, as exhibited either at funerals or
by mourners, lest the complaint of those who say, *I
waited for one who would sorrow with me, and there
was nobody, and for consolers and I found none*, should
be true. A proper care should be shown for the tomb
and for burial, for such care is reckoned in Holy Scripture amongst good works; nor is the praise bestowed
upon it confined to those who buried the bodies of
patriarchs and other holy people, or corpses in general,
but it is extended to those who performed the same

office for the Body of Our Lord Himself. Then let men carry out these last offices for their dead and solace their human grief in so doing. But let them who have a spiritual as well as a natural affection for their friends who are dead according to the flesh, though not according to the spirit, show a far greater solicitude and care and zeal in offering up for them those things which help the spirits of the departed - alms, and prayers, and supplication.

[426]
23. THE HOLY SPIRIT THE SOUL OF THE CHURCH
(*Sermon* 267.3, 268.2)

Is the Holy Spirit no longer given, brethren? Whosoever thinks this is not worthy to receive Him. He is still given. Why, then, does no one speak the tongues of all nations, as they spoke who were filled with the Holy Spirit on the day of Pentecost? Why? Because that which was then signified is now fulfilled. And what is that? When we were celebrating Lent, you remember that we spoke to you of how Our Lord Jesus Christ commended His Church to His disciples and ascended into heaven. The disciples asked when the end of the world should be, and He answered, *It is not for you to know the times or moments which the Father has put in His own power.* He was then promising that which He has now fulfilled. *You shall receive the power of the Holy Spirit coming upon you, and you shall be witnesses unto Me in Jerusalem, and in all Judea, and Samaria, and even to the uttermost part of the earth.* The Church was then confined to one house, and she received the Holy Spirit. She was composed of a few men, but she spoke the tongues of the whole earth. See now the fulfillment of those beginnings. For what was signified in that infant Church which spoke in all tongues if not the majestic [427] Church which we now contemplate, speaking the tongues of all peoples from sunrise to sunset? That which was then promised is now fulfilled. We have heard of old, we see now. *Hear, daughter, and see,* was said to the Queen herself. *Hear, daughter, and see.* You did hear the promise; behold the completion. Your God declined you not; your Bridegroom deceived you not; He Who purchased you with His own Blood deceived you not; He Who from foul made you fair, from impure a virgin, deceived you not. You were promised to yourself; but promised in a few, fulfilled in multitudes.

... Let no man, therefore, say, "I have received the Holy Spirit, why can I not speak the tongues of all nations?" If you would have the Holy Spirit, my brethren, listen to what I am going to say: the spirit in us, which constitutes the life of every man, is called the soul, ... and you see what the part of the soul is in the human body. It nourishes all the members, sees in the eyes, hears through the ears, smells through the nostrils, speaks with the tongue, works with the hands, walks with the feet; it operates in all the members that they may have life; it vivifies each one of them, and ascribes to each its proper function. For the eye does not hear, nor the ear see, nor the tongue see, nor do the ear and eye speak, still they are living members, . . . the functions are special, life is common to all. So it is in the Church of God; in some saints it produces miracles, in others it confesses the truth, in others it keeps virginity, in others the chastity of the married state, one thing in some, and another thing in others; each one has his proper function, but the same amount of life is common to all. The Holy Spirit is to the body of Christ, which is the Church, what the soul is to the human body: the Holy Spirit does for [428] the whole Church that which the soul does through all the members of one body. But observe what you must be on your guard against, what you must note, and what you must fear. It happens in the human body, or rather that a member of this body may chance to be cut off, say a hand, a finger, or a foot, does the soul still exist in the amputated member? As long as it was part of the body it was a living member, but when once cut off its life ceases. So it is with a man who is a Catholic Christian, as long as he is joined to the body, when cut off he becomes a heretic, for the soul ceases to exist in an amputated member. . . . If one member be in any suffering all the other members suffer by sympathy. Still as long as it forms part of the body it may suffer indeed, but it cannot die, for what is death except a giving up of one's spirit? If a member be cut off from the body is it still animated by the soul? And yet the member is recognized as being what it is, a finger, or a hand, or an arm, or an ear, as the case may be. It may keep its form when cut off from the body, but it cannot have life. Thus it is with the man who is separated from the Church. You may ask him if he has the sacrament, and baptism, and the creed, and may find all three. This is the outside likeness; unless you are nourished by the indwelling soul it is in vain that you boast of having the external form.

[429]
24. "THEY HAVE PARTED MY GARMENTS AMONG THEM"
(*Tractates on the Gospel of John*, 118)

WE must not pass over briefly that part of the Gospel which relates to the division of Our Lord's garments and the lots cast for them by the soldiers. For although all the evangelists have mentioned the fact, St. John lays the most stress upon it; they speak obscurely about it, and he most openly. Thus St. Matthew says, *After they had crucified Him, they divided His garments, casting lots for them.* And St. Mark has, *And crucifying Him, they divided His garments, casting lots for what each was to have.* St. Luke says, *Dividing His garments they cast lots.* But St. John mentions the number of divisions, which was four, that all might be taken by the soldiers. Hence it follows that there were four soldiers who carried out the orders of their chief in crucifying Him. His words are clear enough. The soldiers, therefore, when they had crucified Him, took His garments, and they made four parts, to every soldier a part, and also His coat, which coat they took is here to be understood that the sense may be, "They took His garments and made four parts, to every soldier a part, and they also took His coat." He spoke thus to show us that no further lots were cast for His other clothes, only for His coat, which they took with His other garments, but did not [430] divide in the same way. He goes on to explain this: *Now the coat was without seam, woven from the top throughout,* and he says why it was they cast lots for it. *They said then one to another, Let us not cut it, but let us cast lots for it whose it shall be.* It is evident that with regard to the other garments they had equal parts, so that it was not necessary to cast lots, but the coat alone could not be equally divided among them without being torn, which would have been a useless cutting up of His clothes. Instead of this they chose rather that one should have it by lot. The Prophet's testimony is in accordance with the Evangelist's narrative, as St. John at once adds, *That,* he says, *the Scripture might be fulfilled, saying: They have parted My garments among them, and upon My vesture they have cast lots.* In the first place, he speaks of them as dividing and not casting lots; and when they do cast lots he does not speak of them as dividing. He is altogether silent about lots with regard to His other garments, and afterwards says, *And upon My vesture they have cast lots,* that is, for the remaining coat. On this matter I will say what He shall give me to speak, having first refuted the calumny of those who think they see a discrepancy amongst the evangelists, by showing that no one of their accounts contradicts St. John's narrative.

For St. Matthew in saying *they divided His garments, casting a lot,* meant to signify that the tunic, for which they cast lots, was included in the great division, because in dividing all the garments of which the coat formed a part, they cast lots for it. So again St. Luke says, *Dividing His garments they cast lots,* and doing this they came to the coat for which they cast lots, in order to make a complete division of His garments amongst them. What is the difference between saying as St. Luke does, *Dividing His garments they cast lots,* or as St. Matthew says, *They divided His garments, casting a lot,* except that St. Luke spoke of lots, putting the plural for the singular, which is a not infrequent manner of speaking in Holy Scripture, although some manuscripts are found to have *lot* in the singular. St. Mark alone seems to have raised a question on the subject, for in the words, *Casting lots upon them,* what every man should take, he would appear to say that lots were cast for all the garments, not for the coat alone. But here again the obscureness is due to his brevity, for casting lots upon them is equivalent to casting lots as they were dividing, which they did. For the division of all His garments would not have been complete unless it had been made clear who was to take the coat, so that an end might be put to the contentions of the dividers, or rather that all strife might be forestalled. His words *what every man should take*, even if signifying lots, do not apply to all the garments which were divided, for lots were cast for the coat. Thus because he had omitted to describe it, and to say how it alone remained over and above the equal division of the rest, and that they cast lots for it lest it should be cut up, he adds, What every man should take, that is, who should take it. The whole may be thus rendered: they divided His garments, casting lots amongst themselves as to who should have the coat which remained over and above the equal division of the rest.

Perhaps someone may ask what the division of His garments, and the casting of lots for His coat signifies. The garment of Our Lord Jesus Christ which was divided into four symbolised the four parts of His Church, which is spread through the whole earth, and the earth consists of four parts. The Church is distributed equally, that is, uniformly in these parts. Hence in another place He speaks of sending His angels to gather His elect from the four winds, and what are the four winds if not the four parts of the world, north, south, east, and west? As to the coat, it signifies the unity, which is formed by the bond of charity, of all the parts. The Apostle was to speak of this charity. *I show you*, he says, *an excellent way*, and in another place, *To know also the charity of Christ which surpasses all knowledge*, and again, *But beyond all these is charity which is the bond of perfection.* If, then, charity be a more excellent way, and if it surpass knowledge, and be enjoined before all things, it is indeed reasonable that the coat by which it is signified should be spoken of as woven from the top. It is without seam for fear it should come unsewn, and it falls to the share of one because it gathers all together in one unity. As amongst the Apostles who were also twelve, which is four divided into three, when they had all been questioned, only Peter answered, *You are Christ, the Son of the living God*, and the answer made to him is, *I will give to you the keys of the kingdom of heaven*, as if he alone had received the power of binding and loosening, whereas Peter spoke those words for all the rest, and received that power as if he represented unity in his person; one, therefore, is a figure of all because unity belongs to all. So here when St. John had described the coat as woven from the top, he adds *throughout*. If we apply this to what the coat really signifies, no man is found outside who belongs to the whole; from which word *whole*, as the Greek language shows, the Church is called Catholic. But what else is signified by the lot except the grace of [433] God? Coming thus to one it came to all, as by the casting of lots all were satisfied, and so it is that the grace of God in unity reaches all men; and when lots are cast it is not the person or personal merits which decide the question, it is the secret ordering of God.

25. THE TWO CAPTURES OF FISH
(*On the Gospel of John*, 122.1)

AFTER this Jesus showed Himself again to the disciples at the sea of Tiberius. And He showed Himself after this manner. There were together Simon Peter, and Thomas who is called Didimus, and Nathaniel who was of Cana of Galilee, and the sons of Zebedee, and two others of His disciples. Simon Peter said to them, I go a fishing. They say to him, We also come with you. With regard to this fishing of the disciples it is accustomed to be asked why Peter and the sons of Zebedee returned to that which they had been previous to the Lord's calling them, for they were fishermen when He said to them, *Come after Me, and I will make you to fishers of men.* Then indeed they followed Him, in order, having left all things, to cleave to His teaching, so much so that when that rich man to whom He had spoken those words, *Go, sell what you have, and give to the poor, and you shall have a treasure in heaven*, had left Him sorrowful, Peter said to Him, *Behold, we have left all things, and have followed You.* How is it, then, that now they seem to have left their apostleship, to become what they formerly were, and to take back what they had given up, as if unmindful of the words which they had heard, *No man putting his hand to the plow and looking back is fit for the kingdom of heaven*? If they had done this after the death of Jesus and before His resurrection from the dead (which indeed they could not do, for on the day of His crucifixion their minds were wholly absorbed in Him until His burial, which took place before the evening; and the next day was the Sabbath, on which day they, following the custom of their fathers, might not work; and on the third day the Lord rose again, and revived their hope in Him which they were already beginning to lose) we should suppose that they had so acted from the despair which had taken hold of their minds. Now, after He had returned to them living from the tomb, after the sure proof of His risen flesh which He had put before their eyes and hands, not only that they might see it, but even that they might touch and feel it; after examining the marks of His wounds, and hearing St. Thomas' confession of faith, who had said beforehand that he would not believe in any other way; after receiving the Holy Spirit by His breathing upon them, and hearing with their own ears His words, *As the Father has sent Me so do I send you. Whose sins you shall remit they are remitted, and whose sins you shall retain they are retained* - they at once become that which they had previously been, fishers, not of men but of fish.

We must answer those who take objection to their so acting in this way. Provided that they were faithful to their apostleship, they were not forbidden to seek the necessaries of life by their calling; for it was a perfectly lawful calling, whenever they had not other means of living. Will indeed anyone dare to think or to say that the Apostle St. Paul did not share in the perfection of those who had left all things to follow

Christ, because, lest he should be a burden to those to whom he preached the Gospel, he gained his bread by [436] his handiwork? In doing this he gave an additional truth to his own words, *He labored more than all*; adding, *Not I, but the grace of God with me*, that his power to labor by soul and body, even more than all the rest, should also be attributed to the grace of God, which power enabled him not to cease from preaching the Gospel, and yet not to live by the Gospel in the way that the other apostles did; for in how many nations, who were in total ignorance of the name of Christ, did he not sow the Gospel seed farther and wider than they? When he speaks of living by the Gospel, that is, of having necessary food, he shows that it is not incumbent on the Apostles, but that they have power so to live. He alludes to it in these words: *If we have sown unto you spiritual gifts, is it a great matter if we reap your carnal things? If others be partakers of this power over you; why not we rather? Nevertheless we have not used this power.* And a little further on: *They who serve the altar partake with the altar: so also the Lord ordained that they who preach the Gospel should live by the Gospel. But I have used none of these things.* It is quite evident, then, that it was in the power of the Apostles to live only on the Gospel, though it was not a command, and to reap carnal things from those to whom they had sown spiritual ones, by preaching the Gospel, that is, that they might receive physical support, and, as soldiers of Christ, the salary which was due to them. . . . A little before, this same soldier had spoken in noble language on the subject: *Who serves as a soldier at any time, at his own charges?* he says. And still this was what he himself did, since he labored more than all the others. If, then, blessed Paul did not use with the rest the faculty which indeed he shared with all other preachers of the Gospel, but served at his own charges, [437] lest he should offend the peoples who were total strangers to the name of Christ, by making His doctrine appear venal, he learned an art which he did not know, since he had not been brought up to work, that while the master labored with his hands, none of his audience should be pressed for money. How much more, then, should blessed Peter, who had been a fisherman, exercise the craft which he knew, if at that time he had not any other means of living?

But someone will object: "And how was it he could find none, when Our Lord had made the promise, *Seek first the kingdom of God and His justice, and all these things shall be added to you*"? Even here, too, the Lord fulfilled His promise. For who else provided fish for the net? He allowed them to be in that want which should compel them to go and fish, for no other reason than to show forth a preordained miracle; in which, at the same time, He would feed the preachers of His Gospel, and would strengthen that Gospel itself by the great mystery signified in the number of the fish. This is what we now have to speak about, following His own guidance.

Simon Peter said to them: I am going fishing. They

who were with him said to him: We will also come with you. And they went forth and entered into the ship: and that night they caught nothing. But when the morning had come, Jesus stood on the shore: yet the disciples knew not that it was Jesus. Jesus therefore said to them. Children, have you any meat? They answered Him: No. He said to them: Cast the net on the right side of the ship; and you shall find. They cast therefore: and now they were not able to draw it for the multitude of fishes. That disciple therefore whom Jesus loved said to Peter: It is the Lord. Simon Peter, when he heard that it was the Lord, girt his coat [438] *about him (for he was naked), and cast himself into the sea. But the other disciples came in the ship (for they were not far from the land, but as it were about one hundred yards), dragging the net full of fish. As soon then as they came to land, they saw hot coals lying, and a fish laid thereon, and bread. Jesus said to them: Bring here some of the fish which you have now caught. Simon Peter went up, and drew the net to land, full of large fish, one hundred and fifty-three. And although there were so many the net was not broken.*

This is the great mystery in St. John's great Gospel, and it was written at the end to give it more weight. There were, therefore, seven disciples present at that taking of fish, Peter, and Thomas, and Nathaniel, and the two sons of Zebedee, and two others whose names are not given, and by their number of seven they signify the end of time. The course of all time runs in a term of seven days; and thus it was that Jesus stood on the shore when the morning had come, because the shore is also the end of the sea, and therefore signifies the end of the world. Peter having drawn his net to land, that is, on shore, also points to that same end of the world. This the Lord Himself explained in another place when He made the comparison of the net cast into the sea, which, He says, they draw out to the shore. He explains what was meant by this shore. So shall it be at the end of the world, He says.

But that parable was a figure of speech which did not set forth a fact; as, however, in this passage which tells us what will come to pass at the end by a real event, so the Lord signified in a second capture of fish what the Church should be in our times. The first He did in the beginning of His preaching, the second after His resurrection, to show that the first capture of fish signified both good and evil men whom the Church [439] now holds within her pale; but that the second signified only the good, whom the Church shall hold for all eternity, after the resurrection of the dead at the end of the world has been accomplished. At the first capture Jesus did not, as in the second, stand on the shore when He commanded them to take the fish; but going up on to Simon's ship, He asked him to put off a little from the land, and, sitting in it, He preached to the crowd. And when He had ceased speaking, He said to Simon, *Launch out into the deep, and let down your nets for a catch.* And there the capture of fish remained in the ships. They did not as here draw their net on to the shore. By these signs, and any others which may be discovered in the first capture, the Church in this world is signified; in the second, the Church, as she will be at the end of time, is set forth. This is why the one takes place before, and the other after, the resurrection of the Lord, because, in the first, Christ showed us to be called; in the second, to be risen again. In the former, the nets are not cast in on the right, lest only the good should be signified; nor on the left for the wicked alone, but in all directions. Let down your nets, He says, for a catch, that we may understand the good and the bad to be mingled together. Here He says, *Cast in your net on the right of the ship,* in order to signify those who stand on the right, who are only the good. In the first capture the net broke, in order to signify the division caused by schisms; of the second, that peace of the saints where schism will be no more, the Evangelist was able to say, *And whereas they were so many,* meaning so big, *the net did not break,* as if he had borne in mind the time when it did break, and commended this good by comparison with that evil. Before the resurrection so great a multitude of fish [440] was taken, that two ships full of it were nearly sinking, that is, they were weighed down in the water, for they did not sink, although they were in danger. Why are there so many things in the Church which cause us to groan? Is it not because a vast multitude of people are entering in who threaten to overthrow discipline with their corrupt morals, which are far removed from the ways of the saints, and the number is so great that it cannot be held in check? In the second capture they cast in the net on the right, and they were not able to draw it out for the multitude of fish. What is the meaning of *they were not able to draw it out*? Does it not signify that those who belong to the resurrection unto life, to the right hand, who depart while within the Christian pale, typified by the nets, will be known only on the shore, that is, at the end of the world after the resurrection? Therefore they were not able so to draw the nets as to place the fish which they had caught within the ship, as they had done on the former occasion when the fish broke the net and weighed down the ships. After this life is over the Church holds these members of the right hand in the sleep of peace, as if in the hollow of the ship, until the net reaches the shore where it was dragged, as it were, two hundred cubits. . . . Lastly, in the first capture the number of fish is not expressed, as if it realized the fulfillment of the prophet's words, *I have declared and I have spoken; they are multiplied above number.* Here, on the contrary, they are not multiplied above number, but it is fixed at one hundred and fifty-three. . . .

It is not, therefore, for nothing that these fish are said to be so many and so big, that is, one hundred and fifty-three large fish. For thus it is written: *Simon Peter drew the net to land full of large fish, one hundred and fifty-three.* After the words, *I have not come to destroy the law but to fulfill it,* Our Lord, Who was to give the Spirit, by Whom the law might be fulfilled, adding, as it were, seven to ten,(1) said a little further on in the same passage, *He, therefore, that shall break one of these least commandments, and shall so teach men, shall be called the least in the kingdom of heaven. But he that shall do and teach, he shall be called great in the kingdom of heaven.* Such a man as this, therefore, may belong to the number of the big fish. But he that is the least, who is unfaithful in his conduct to his own preaching, may be found in that Church which is typified by the first capture of fish, and which contains both good and bad men; for it too is called the kingdom of heaven, and He alludes to it in the words, *The kingdom of heaven is like unto a net cast into the sea, and gathering together of all kinds of fish.* Here He wishes both good and wicked men to be understood, and He speaks of them as drawn out on the shore, that is, awaiting the final separation at the end of time. And in order to show that the least are the reprobate, who teach good doctrine with their mouths and deny it by their bad lives, that they are not to be even the least in eternal life, but not there at all, after the words, *He shall be called the least in the kingdom of heaven,* He added at once, *I say unto you, unless your justice abound more than that of the Scribes and Pharisees, you shall not enter into the kingdom of heaven.* The Scribes and Pharisees are undoubtedly they who sit in the chair of Moses, and He says of them, *All things whatsoever they shall say to you, observe and do; but according to their works do not, for they say and do not*: that which they teach

---

1 Seven gifts of the Holy Spirit to the ten commandments of the Law.

[442] by their words they break by their works. It follows, therefore, that he who is the least in that kingdom of heaven, which is signified by the Church on earth, shall not enter into the kingdom of heaven of the Church in glory; because, by teaching that which he does not practice, he will not be among those who do what they preach, and therefore he will not be one of the large fish; *he who shall do and shall teach shall be called great in the kingdom of heaven.* And because he is great here on earth, he shall therefore be one day in heaven, where the least shall not enter. They shall be so great in heaven that the least there is above the greatest here. But they who are great here, that is, who in that kingdom of heaven, where the net gathers together both good and evil men, do the good which they teach, shall be greater in the eternal kingdom of heaven. Thus do the fish typify those who belong to the right hand and to the resurrection unto life. . . .

[443]
26. THE CHURCH IN ST. AUGUSTINE'S DAY A CHURCH OF MIRACLES
(*On the City of God*, Bk. 22, ch. 8)

MEN say, "Why do not the miracles, which you talk about as having been worked, take place now?" I might indeed reply that they were necessary before the world believed for the very purpose of making it believe. The man who still seeks for wonders in order that he may believe, is himself a great wonder for not believing what the whole world believes. But the motive of those who act thus is to deny faith even to the miracles of the first ages. How, then, is it that Christ's ascension into heaven in the flesh is everywhere celebrated with so much faith? How, in civilized times which reject everything beyond human agency, could the world without any miracles have so miraculously believed incredible things? Or are we to say that they were credible, and that the world accepted them because they were credible? Why, then, do these men not believe? Our argument is therefore brief; either setting out from something unseen and incredible, they grounded their faith on incredible things, which, however visibly took place; or the "something" was beyond a doubt so credible as to need no testimony of miracles to convince any man, and unbelievers are thus convicted of gross infidelity. I would say this to refute the vainest doubters. For we cannot deny that [444] many miracles have taken place to prove that one grand and saving miracle by which Christ in His risen flesh ascended into heaven. All are recorded in the most infallible books of Scripture in which the facts themselves are related together with what those facts were intended to prove. Some were manifested in order to create faith; others through the faith which they evoked stand out in brighter light. They are read to the people that they may be believed, nor would they be read to the people unless they were believed. For even now miracles are worked in His name, or through His sacraments, or through the prayers or commemorations of His saints, but these are not so well known as to be noised abroad with the same great renown as the first miracles. The canon of Holy Scripture, which it was important to define, involves the reading of these miracles in all places, so that they are living in the memory of all the people, but as to the modern ones, wheresoever they are worked, they are hardly known to the very city or inhabitants of the place in which they occur. For it often happens that even in the place itself it is only the few who know about these things, the rest being in complete ignorance, and this is especially the case in a large city. And when they are related elsewhere to other people, they are not sufficiently supported by authority to be credited without difficulty or doubt, although they are related by Christians addressing Christians.

The miracle which was worked at Milan while we were there, when a blind man received his sight, may have been brought before many people for various reasons. Milan is a large city, the Emperor was there at the time, and the wonder took place in the presence of an immense crowd who were assembled together before the bodies of Saints Protasius and Gervasius. As these remains were hidden and no man had the slightest traces of their resting place, it was revealed in a dream to Bishop Ambrose. The relics were found accordingly, and on the very spot the blind man put off the shadow of his former darkness, and saw the light of day.

But at Carthage, who, save a very few, know of the cure which was granted to Innocent, an ex-officer in the imperial prefecture? It took place in our presence, and we saw it with our own eyes. When we returned to Africa, my friend Alypius, that is, and I we were not priests at that time, but already serving God, he who with all his household was most pious, received us into his own house, and we took up our abode with him. He was in the hands of doctors who had already operated upon him for many and grievous fistulas, and they were treating those which remained by various appliances of their art. In the operation he had suffered protracted and violent pains. But one sinus amongst many escaped the eyes of the doctors, and was so hidden away that they did not touch it, whereas they ought to have laid it bare with their instruments. When, therefore, they had cured those fistulas which they had opened, this one remained untouched by their remedies. Innocent suspected the cause of their delay, and dreaded another operation which a doctor friend of his declared would be necessary. The others had not admitted him the first time even to see how they performed it, and Innocent who had ordered him out of the house in anger and would hardly see him, now exclaimed, "Are you going to cut me up again? Are the words of the man, whom you refused to meet, to come true?" They laughed scornfully at the unskillful doctor, and tried [446] to calm the man's fears by hopeful words. Many days went by, and nothing that they did was of any good.

Still they persisted in saying that they meant to heal the sinus with medicine, not by the operating knife. They called in another doctor of most mature age, who had a considerable reputation with the faculty. Animonius, this was his name, for he was still living at the time, examined the place, and promised the same result as they from their care and skill. Thus reassured, Innocent tried to joke about the matter with his family doctor who had predicted another operation, as if he was already restored to health. What happened? After many days had gone by without any result, the doctors, worn out, owned with confusion that he could not possibly be cured without an operation. Innocent grew pale with anguish. When he had collected himself and was able to speak, he bade them depart and not come back to him, and all that the poor man in his sorrow and direful necessity could think of was to call in a certain Alexander, who was then looked upon as a wonderful surgeon, and Alexander should do for him what he in his wrath would not have the others do. But when the latter had visited him, and examined with his professional eye their mode of treating the fistulas, being a man of honor, he persuaded Innocent to allow those who had done so much for him as to cause his own wonder, to have the entire benefit of his cure, adding that he could not by any chance recover without an operation. It was, he said, quite contrary to his feelings of propriety to take from men, the traces of whose medical devices, industry, and labor he could see and admire in the fistulas, the reward of so much toil for the slight thing which there remained to be done. They were restored to favor, and it was arranged that with the [447] assistance of this same Alexander they should open the fistula; otherwise they all pronounced him incurable. The operation was put off till the following day. But when they had gone, the grief of that house, in consequence of the intense anguish of its master, became so great, that we could scarcely keep from bitter tears. It might have been his funeral. Every day he was visited by holy men, the then Bishop of Uzalis, Saturninus of blessed memory, the priest Gelosus, and the deacons of the Church of Carthage; amongst whom, and the sole present survivor, was our bishop, whom we must name with due respect, Aurelius. Dwelling with him upon the wonderful works of God, I have often talked over this incident, and have found that his memory was very keen in the matter. When, according to their custom, they visited Innocent in the evening, he asked them in a burst of tears to be so kind as to be present on the following day, he would not say at his pain but at his death. For he was so overcome by fear at the thought of his former sufferings that he made sure he should die under the doctor's hands. They comforted him, exhorted him to have confidence in God, and to submit courageously to His Will. Thereupon we went in to prayer, where we made use of our customary genuflections and prostrations. He threw himself down on the ground as if someone impelled him to remain prostrate, and then began his prayer. Who can explain in words how he prayed, with what anointing, and floods of tears, and groanings and sighs which shook all his body, and nearly took away his breath. I was not conscious whether the others were praying or whether their attention was diverted by this prayer. I was unable to pray; all that I did was to say in my heart, "Lord, if You hear not this prayer, whose prayers will [448] You hear?" For it seemed to me that he could not pray more and live. We rose from our knees and departed after receiving the Bishop's blessing, he asking them to return on the following morning, and they admonishing him to be calm. The dreaded day came, and those servants of God were present according to their promise; the doctors had arrived, and everything was prepared for the needs of the hour; fearful instruments were brought out in the midst of the astonished suspense of the bystanders. But they who had the greater authority with him were striving to fortify his drooping courage, and were soothing down in the bed the parts which the knife was to touch. The bandages are removed, the place is uncovered, the doctor examines it, and fully prepared with his instrument looks for the fistula. He searches and feels, and feels and searches in all possible ways; he finds the mark of a scar perfectly healed. I cannot describe our joy in words, nor the praise and thanksgiving which we all poured forth to our almighty and merciful God in the midst of happy tears; this must be imagined rather than expressed.

In the same city of Carthage, Innocentia, a most religious woman belonging to one of the first families of the place, had a cancer in the breast, a disease which doctors pronounce to be incurable. Usually the member affected is either cut off from the body, or life may be somewhat prolonged by means of constant treatment, but death, however much delayed, is said to be inevitable, and recovery quite impossible. This was the sentence which Innocentia had heard from the lips of an experienced doctor who was a great friend of her family, and she had turned herself exclusively to God. At the approach of Easter she was warned in a dream that whatever baptized [449] woman she should first meet in that part of the baptistery which was reserved to women, should sign the part affected with the sign of the cross; she did this and was immediately cured. When the doctor, who had told her to use no remedies if she wished to prolong her life a little longer, had examined her, and found that she, whom he knew by previous examination to have had cancer, was perfectly cured, he besought her to tell him what she had done. He wished, it seems, to become acquainted with the remedy which would prevail against the received opinion of the faculty. When he heard from her what had happened, he showed scorn both in voice and face, so that she feared he would ridicule Christ. It is related that he answered in a respectful tone, "I thought you were going to tell me some great thing." And as she was already shocked, he added quickly, "What wonder did Christ work in curing a cancer when He raised a man to life who had been dead four days?" When I heard of this miracle and was much vexed that so great a one happening in that city to a person by no means obscure should be so little known, I thought it was my duty to admonish her, I had almost said to scold her, for her silence. Upon her answering me that she had not kept the matter quiet, I made inquiries of those ladies who might very possibly have been her friends at the time whether they had known of it or not. They told me that they were in total ignorance of the fact. "Well," I said to her, "is this what you understand by not keeping it quiet, since you leave your very intimate friends in ignorance on the subject?" And because I had questioned her briefly, I induced her to relate the whole thing from the beginning in their presence. They listened in great astonishment and glorified God. [450] As Bishop Proejectus was carrying the relics of the glorious martyr St. Stephen, at the baths of Tibilis,(1) an immense multitude of people came together to his shrine. A blind woman in the crowd begged that she might be led to the bishop who was carrying the relics. She gave him the flowers which she had in her hand, and received them back again, and at once her eyes were moved, and she recovered her sight. To the utter amazement of those present she led the way rejoicing, and no longer required to be shown it by another.

At Calamae there was a man, foremost amongst his class, Martialis by name, who was already very old, and who detested the Christian religion. He had a daughter, a Christian, and a son-in-law who was baptized in the same year. As he was ill they besought him with entreaties and tears to become a Christian.

He refused absolutely and put them away from him in violent indignation. The thought suggested itself to his son-in-law to go to the shrine of St. Stephen, and there to pray with all his strength that God would put a good mind into his father-in-law so that he should believe in Christ without delay. This he did with many sighs and tears, and with sincere desire of soul. In going away he took a flower, which he chanced to find, from the altar, and that evening he laid it under his father-in-law's pillow, and so the night passed. Before dawn Martialis cried out, asking them to run for the bishop, who happened to be with me at Hippo. Hearing that the bishop was absent, he asked for priests to come to him. They went, he declared himself a believer, and was baptized, to the astonishment and joy of all. As long as he lived the words, "Christ, receive my spirit," were on his lips

1 In Numidia.

[451] although he did not know that these were blessed Stephen's last words when he was stoned by the Jews. They were also his own last words, for not long afterwards he too departed this life.(1)

1 The above is a selection of four miracles out of twenty recorded by St. Augustine as having taken place within his own knowledge.

PART 4. BEHIND THE VEIL

[455]
1. HAPPINESS OF THE SAINTS
(*On the City of God*, Bk. 22, ch. 30)

WHAT will that happiness be where there will be no evil, where no good thing will be lacking, where we shall be engaged in the praises of God, Who will be all things to all? For I know not what other occupation will be ours in that place where weariness will be no more, nor any laborious necessity. The psalm also gives me a lesson on the subject in the words, *Blessed are they, Lord, who dwell in Your house, they shall praise You for ever and ever.* The incorruptible body in its outward figure and inward structure, which body we now see divided into various members according to our needs, will then make progress in the praises of God, because those needs will be no more, but happiness, full, certain, secure, and everlasting will be ours. Every detail now hidden, connected with physical harmony as it exists inwardly and outwardly throughout the bodily structure, of which details I have already spoken, will not then be hidden, but together with the other great and wonderful things there will enkindle in rational minds the praise of so mighty a Creator at the sight of the intellectual beauty thus displayed. I dare not venture an opinion as to how those bodies are to move about, because I am not able to form one. Their movements and their rest will be in keeping with their appearance itself, for in that place no lack

[456] of harmony will exist. The body will be at hand to carry out the wishes of the spirit, nor will the spirit take delight in anything which is not becoming to both spirit and body. It will be the reign of true glory, where no man will be subject to be falsely praised or flattered, and of true honor, which will be denied to no one deserving of it, nor offered to any undeserving of it, nor will any undeserving man covet it there, where only the perfect find a place. It will be the reign of true peace, because no man will suffer contradiction either from himself or from others. The reward of virtue will be the very Giver of virtue Himself, for He, than Whom nothing better or greater can exist, promised Himself as its reward. What else do the words signify which He spoke through His prophet, *I will be their God, and they shall be My people,* unless it be, "I will satisfy their cravings, I will be all those things which men may honestly desire, life and health and food and plenty, glory, honor, peace, and all good things?" This also is the true interpretation of what the Apostle says, that God may be all things to all men. He will be the fulfillment of our desires, Who will be seen without end, loved without weariness, praised without fatigue. This reward, and this love, and this act of praise will be as that eternal life itself, common to all.

For the rest, who is capable of thinking, how much more of saying, what degrees of honor and glory will be given as a reward for merits? There is no doubt that they are to be given. And that blessed city will also possess this great good, that no inferior will be envious of any superior whatever, just as now the angels do not envy the archangels. Each will be as unwilling to possess that to which he was not called, although bound by the most peaceable bond of union [457] to him who has been so called, as in the body it is not for a finger to be as an eye, while at the same time its compactness as a bodily structure embraces both these members. Therefore one will have some gift inferior to that of another, and will so have it as to possess the further gift of wishing for nothing more.

Nor will they be lacking in free will because of their incapability of taking delight in sin. Indeed it will be much freer, delivered as it will be from delight in sin, even unto an unswerving delight in not sinning. For the first free will which was given to man in his original state of righteousness was able to resist sin, but was also liable to commit it; the latter free will, however will be the more powerful in that it will be unable to sin. This truly is due to God's gift; it is not in the nature of the thing:, for it is one thing to be God and another thing to participate in God. By His nature God cannot sin; the participator in God receives from Him the gift of not sinning. But the degrees of the divine gift were to be kept in this way, that a first free will should be given to man by which he was enabled not to sin, and a last free will by which he should be unable to sin: the first was to be a means of meriting, the second was to belong to the reward. And because this nature used its liberty of sinning to sin, it is liberated by a more abundant grace, that it may be led to that liberty in which it cannot sin. As the possibility of not dying constituted the first immortality which Adam lost by his sin, and the impossibility of dying will constitute the last immortality, so the possibility of not sinning constituted the first free will, and the impossibility of sinning will constitute the latter free will. The will which loves piety and justice will be as undying as our happiness. By sin indeed we have retained neither piety nor happiness, but with our lost [458] happiness we have not lost the wish for happiness. Because it is most true that God cannot sin do we therefore deny His free will? Free will, then, in that eternal city will be one in all, and personal in each; it will be delivered from all evil, and filled with all good, it will enjoy without ceasing the delights of eternal joys, in oblivion of sin and punishment, yet not so forgetful of its own delivery as not to be mindful of gratitude to its deliverer.

As far, therefore, as reasoning science is concerned, knowledge will then retain the memory of past evils, but, as far as the sense of experience goes, it will be absolutely oblivious. For the most skillful doctor is acquainted with nearly all diseases of the body as they are known to medical science; but as they are experienced by the body, he is unacquainted with many from which he has not himself suffered. As, therefore, there is a double knowledge of evils, one by which they are apprehended by the intellect, the other by which they are a matter of personal experience (it is truly one thing to have an acquaintance with all vices by the study of wisdom, and another to acquire this knowledge through a bad life); so there is a double oblivion of evils. An educated and learned man forgets the same things in one way, and a man who has learned them by personal experience in another; the former forgets by ceasing to study, and the latter by ceasing to experience them. According to this last oblivion, the saints will not remember past evils; for they will be so far removed from evils that the memory of them will be almost obliterated from their senses. Still by that same intellectual knowledge which will be great in them, they will not only remember past things, but will not be ignorant concerning the eternal misery of the damned. Otherwise if they are not to know of their [459] former misery, how will they *sing the mercies of the Lord for ever*, as the psalm says? Truly there will be nothing more joyful in that eternal city than this canticle in praise of the grace of Christ, by Whose blood we are redeemed. There the Psalmist's words, *Be still and see that I am the Lord*, will have their fulfillment. It will be in reality that great sabbath without night, which the Lord extolled in the first beginnings of the world, about which it is written, *And God rested on the seventh day from all His work which He had done. And He blessed the seventh day, and sanctified it, because in it He had rested from all His work which God created and made.* When we are fed and supported with the fullness of His blessing and sanctification, we ourselves shall be the seventh day. In our heavenly rest we shall see that He is God; that when we fell from Him we wished to belong to ourselves, hearing the seducer's word, *You shall be like gods*; and forsaking the true God, by Whose action we should become gods, not by forsaking Him, but by participating in Him. For what have we done without Him if it be not that our strength has failed in His anger? Refreshed by Him, and made perfect by a greater abundance of grace, we shall rest for ever, seeing that He is indeed God, of Whom we shall be full when He is Himself all things to all His creatures. For our good works, when they are understood to be rather His than ours, will then be ascribed to us as a means of gaining this long sabbath. For if we attribute them to ourselves, they are servile works, and it is written of the sabbath, *You shall do no work therein.* Thus it is said by the mouth of the Prophet Ezechiel, *Moreover, I gave them also my sabbaths, to be a sign between Me and them: and that they might know that I am the Lord that sanctify them.* We shall know this perfectly [460] when we attain that perfect rest, and we shall see perfectly that He is God.

If the number of the age, like that of days, be computed according to that manner of reckoning which seems to be expressed in the Scriptures, this eternal sabbath will be more apparent because it is found to be the seventh. Thus the first age, after the fashion of a first day, counts from Adam till the Deluge, not by the lapse of time, but by the number of generations, for it contains ten. From the Deluge, according to the Evangelist St. Matthew, three ages follow up to the coming of Christ, each of which are unfolded by fourteen generations; the first from Abraham to David, the second from David until the transmigration to Babylon, the third from the captivity of Babylon up to the birth of Christ in the flesh. In all, therefore, this makes five. We are now in the sixth, which is not to be measured by generations, because it is written, *It is not for you to know the times which the Father has put in His power.* After this age God will rest as if on the seventh day, for He will make this same seventh day rest in Himself, and we shall constitute it. It would indeed take a long time to go minutely now into each one of these ages. The seventh, however, will be our sabbath, which will have no evening. The Lord's Day is like an eternal eighth day, consecrated by the resurrection of Christ, and typifying the eternal rest not only of the spirit, but also of the body. In that sabbath we shall rest and we shall see; we shall see and we shall love; we shall love and we shall praise. This is what will come to pass at the end of time, and what will last for ever and ever. For what other end have we than to reach the kingdom which has no end.

[461]
2. THE VISION OF THE BLESSED IN ETERNAL LIFE
(*On the City of God*, Bk. 22, ch. 29)

LET us now consider, with God's gracious assistance,

what the occupation of the saints is to be in their immortal and spiritual bodies, living in the flesh not according to the flesh, but according to the spirit. If I would truly describe what their action is to be, or rather what their rest and leisure are to be, words fail me. For I have never seen this with my bodily senses. But if I assert that I have seen it with my mind, that is, with my intellect, what is our intellect compared to the excellence of heaven? In that place there is *the peace of God*, which, as the Apostle says, *surpasses all understanding*. Whose understanding is this if not ours, or perhaps that of the holy angels, for it is not the understanding of God. If therefore the saints of God are to be in peace, it is to be that peace which surpasses all understanding. There is no doubt that it surpasses ours; but if it also surpasses that of the angels, so that he who said all understanding included even them in his restriction, we must gather from the words that neither we nor any of the angels can know the peace of God in which God rests, as He knows it. This peace therefore surpasses all understanding, except His own. But because we, according to our measure, have been made participators of His peace, we shall arrive [462] at the perfection of peace in ourselves, amongst ourselves, and with God, as far as it can be attained by us; in this manner, and according to their measure, the holy angels know it, but men in a far lesser degree, however much they may excel in spirit. We must bear in mind the greatness of the man who said, *For we know in part, and we prophesy in part, until that which is perfect shall come*. And again, *We see now through a glass in a dark manner; but then face to face.* Thus do the holy angels see, who are also called our angels, because they have been delivered from the powers of darkness, and receiving the pledge of the Spirit, have been translated to the kingdom of Christ. We have already begun to belong to these angels with whom we shall share in common the holy and ineffable kingdom of God, of which I have already written so many pages. In the same way, therefore, are the angels of God our angels as the Christ of God is our Christ. They are God's because they have not left God; they are ours because they have begun to reckon us amongst their own citizens. Our Lord indeed says, *See that you despise not one of these little ones: for I say to you that their angels in heaven always see the face of My Father, who is in heaven.* Therefore, as they see, so shall we also see; but we do not yet see as they see. This is why the Apostle uses the words which I have just quoted: *We see now through a glass in a dark manner but then face to face.* This sight, then, is reserved for us as a reward for our faith, of which St. John the Apostle also speaks: *When He shall appear,* he says, *we shall be made like to Him, for we shall see Him as He is.* The face of God must be understood to mean His manifestation, not the particular member which we have in our human bodies, and call by this name. Consequently, when I am asked what the saints will [463] do in their spiritual body, I do not speak of what I see, but of what I believe, according to the Psalmist's words, *I have believed, therefore I have spoken.* I say, then, they are to see God in their body, but whether by the body, as by the body we now see the sun, and moon, and stars, and sea, and earth, and those things which are in them, is no small question. For it is hard to say that the saints will then have bodies so constituted that they will not be able to open and shut their eyes when they please, and harder still, to think that whoever shuts his eyes in heaven will not see God. For if the Prophet Elijah saw his servant Gehazi, whom he had cleansed from leprosy, in another place, taking the gifts which Namaan the Syrian gave to him, and thinking, wicked servant that he was, that no one knew what he had done, how much more, in their spiritual body, will the saints see all things, not only if they shut their eyes, but also that which takes place out of their bodily presence. Then that perfect state of things will come to pass of which the Apostle speaks: *We know in part, and we prophesy in part. But when that which is perfect is come, that which is in part shall be done away.* Then in order to show, as best he could, by some analogy, how far removed that future life is from the life, not of any kind of men, but of those who on earth are held to be particularly holy, he says: *When I was a child I spoke as a child, I understood as a child, I thought as a child. But when I became a man I put away the things of a child. We see now through a glass in a dark manner; but then face to face. Now I know in part; but then I shall know even as I am known.* If, then, in this life, where the prophetical office of remarkable men is to that future life what babes are compared to a youth, and yet still Elijah saw his absent servant receiving gifts, how, when our perfect state comes, and the corruptible body no longer presses down the soul, but an incorruptible body proves no hindrance, will those saints in glory need their bodily eyes for sight, which Elijah did not require in order to see his servant at a distance? For according to the interpreters of the Septuagint these are the Prophet's words to Gehazi: *Did not my heart go with you when the man turned back from his chariot to meet you? and you did receive money?* According to the priest Jerome's interpretation from the Hebrew, it is, *Was not my heart present, when the man turned back from his chariot to receive you?* The Prophet speaks of having seen it with his heart, and in his unshaken confidence he was indeed wonderfully assisted from on high. But how much more fully will all be endowed with this divine help in that day when God is to be all things to all men? Even then, however, the corporeal eyes will carry out their functions, and will be in their proper place, and the spirit will make use of them through its spiritual body. For the fact of the Prophet's not having required them to see a man at a distance did not prevent him from using them in order to see objects within the range of his vision, which he could still have seen by the spirit if he had shut his eyes, as he did see things which were taking place beyond his bodily presence. Therefore far be it from us to say that the saints in glory, if they shut their eyes, are not to see God, Whom their spirits are always to see. But whether when their bodily eyes are open they will see with them is next the question. For if in the spiritual body they are able to use even those spiritual eyes themselves only as far as we can now use our mortal ones, beyond a doubt God will not be visible by them. They will therefore be something of a far higher order if that incorporeal nature which is [465] not contained in place, but is everywhere whole and entire, is to be seen by their medium. It is not because we say that God is in heaven and on earth (for He says by the Prophet, *I fill the heavens and the earth*) that we are to think of Him as partly in heaven and partly on earth. He is whole and entire in heaven, and whole and entire on earth, not alternately in one and alternately in the other, but in both at once, which is beyond the power of any corporeal nature. Therefore a greater intensity of vision will be given to those eyes, not a keener sight after the fashion of what serpents and eagles are said to have (for with all their keen sight these same animals can see nothing but bodies), but the power to see incorporeal things. And perhaps this great power of sight was granted temporarily to the eyes of holy Job even while still in this mortal body, when he said to God, *With the hearing of the ear I have heard You, but now my eye sees You. Therefore I convict myself, and do penance in dust and ashes.* There is no reason why the eye of the heart should not be here signified, of which eyes the Apostle says, *That the eyes of your heart may be enlightened.* But no Christian man, who honestly receives those words of God our Teacher, *Blessed are the pure of heart for they shall see God*, can doubt that God is seen by those inward eyes in the day of sight. Whether He will also be seen then through our bodily eyes is the question which now occupies us.

The words *all flesh shall see the salvation of God* may without the least suggestion of difficulty be looked upon as equivalent to *and every man shall see the Christ of God,* Who was most truly seen in His body, and Who will be seen in His body when He shall judge the living and the dead. There are numerous other passages of Scripture to prove that He is Himself [466] the salvation of God, but the words of that venerable old man, holy Simeon, declare it more emphatically. When he had taken the infant Christ into his arms he said, *Now You do dismiss Your servant, Lord, according to Your word, in peace. Because my eyes have seen Your salvation.* That which the above mentioned Job is found in the translations from the Hebrew to have said, *And in my flesh I shall see God,* foretold without doubt the resurrection of the flesh, but he did not say *through my flesh.* If he had, Christ the Lord might have been understood, Who through the flesh will be seen in the flesh. As they stand they mean, *In my flesh I shall see God,* as if he had said, "I shall be in my flesh when I see God." And when the Apostle speaks of face to face, he does not force us to believe, that through this corporeal face, where we have our bodily eyes, we shall see God Whom we shall see in spirit without ceasing. For unless there was also a face according to the interior man, the same Apostle would not have said, *But we all beholding the glory of the Lord with open face are transformed into the same image from glory to glory, as by the spirit of the Lord.*

Nor do we understand the Psalmist's words in a different sense, *Come to Him and be enlightened: and your faces shall not be confounded.* By faith which is proved to belong to the heart, not to the body, we approach God. But as we do not know what the means of access are which a spiritual body has (for we are indeed treading on unknown ground) when we find certain things not otherwise intelligible, in which we are not assisted and supported by the authority of Holy Scripture, the words of the Book of Wisdom must of necessity be verified in us: *The thoughts of mortal men are fearful, and our counsels uncertain.*

If we could be perfectly certain of the truth of that reasoning of philosophers by which they maintain that [467] things within the domain of the intellect so appear to the mind's eye, and sensible things, i.e., physical things, to the bodily sense, as to render the body unable to grasp intellectual things, and the mind of itself unable to grasp physical things, then it would follow of necessity that no bodily eyes, even if they belonged to a spiritual body, could by any possibility see God. But both true reason and prophetical testimony set this reasoning at nought. For what man will so far dispute the truth as to presume to say that God does not know these physical things? Has He then, a body through whose eyes He may note them? Likewise, from what we were just saying about the Prophet Elijah, is it not sufficiently apparent that corporeal things are also apprehended by the spirit, not by the body? For when Gehazi took the gifts, it was certainly a material act, which however the Prophet saw by his spirit, not by his body. As, therefore, it is evident that bodies are seen by the spirit, what if the power of the spiritual body should be such that the spirit may be seen by the body? For God is a spirit. Consequently a man does not know by any inner consciousness acting through his bodily eyes that very life of his by which he now lives in the body, and which nourishes and vivifies his physical members, but he sees life in others, because it is a visible thing. For how do we discern living bodies from bodies which do not live unless it is that our vision embraces at once the body and life, which we can only perceive through the body. But we cannot see life out of the body by our bodily eyes. Although it may be, and is, extremely probable that we shall see the material bodies of the new heaven and the new earth, in the same way as we shall see God everywhere present and governing even all corporeal things, through the medium of our renovated [468] bodies, which will enable us to see with the greatest clearness in whatever direction we cast our eyes; still it will not be then as it is now, when the invisible things of God are seen through the comprehension of material things in a dark manner and in part. Here on earth the faith in us by which we believe is of greater worth than the sight of corporeal things which we discern by our bodily eyes. But just as we do not believe in the life of men whose life and movement we see around us from the moment we see it, because we see it, while we are not able to see their life out of the body which we still observe by the body without any ambiguity, so whatever may be the spiritual light which we shall bear in our bodies, we shall see God, Who is incorporeal, governing all things, through our bodies. Either, therefore, God will be so seen through those eyes that in so high a state of excellence they will have something akin to the mind by which a man is able to discern incorporeal things, this, however, is difficult if not impossible to prove by any examples or testimony from Holy Scripture; or, which is easier to understand, God will be so familiar and so distinguishable to us that He will be seen by the spirit by each one of us in each one of us, He will be seen by each in each other, He will be seen in Himself, in the new heaven and the new earth, and in every existing creature. He will be seen also through bodies in every body wherever the eyes of the spiritual body direct their glance. Our thoughts also will be apparent to each other. For the Apostle's words will then be fulfilled. After he had said, *Judge not any man before the time*, he added, *until the Lord come, Who will bring to light the hidden things of darkness, and will make manifest the counsels of hearts: and then shall every man have praise from God.*

[469]
3. THOUGHT IS TRANSPARENT IN THE GLORIFIED BODY
(*Sermon* 243.5)

IN that society of the blessed, my brethren, each one

will see the thoughts of every other, which thoughts God alone now sees. There, no one would wish to have a secret thought, because no one will have a wicked thought. Hence the Apostle says, *Judge not before the time*; that is, lest you judge rashly when you do not see with what intention a man is acting. If something be done which may be done with a good intention, be not harsh: take not upon yourself more than human nature has a right to claim. God alone sees the heart, but man may only judge of those things which are manifest. *Judge not*, then, *before the time*. What does *before the time* mean? He goes on to say what. *Until the Lord come, Who will bring to light the hidden things of darkness, . . . and will make manifest the counsels of the heart.* This is bringing to light the hidden things of darkness, making manifest the counsels of the heart. Now, therefore, our thoughts are our own, and each man sees his own in the light, because he knows them; but they are dark to our neighbors who do not see them. In heaven that which you are conscious of having thought will be known to others. What can you fear? Now you
[470] wish to hide and to shield your thoughts, for perhaps you have an evil thought, or a dishonest thought, or a vain thought. There you will have only good, and honorable, and true, and pure, and sincere thoughts. As now you wish to see your face, so there you will delight in seeing your conscience. For, dear brethren, will not knowledge itself belong to us all? Do you imagine that you will recognize me in heaven because you knew me on earth, and that you will not recognize

my father, whom you did not know, or any other bishop you like to mention who may have occupied my place in this church? You will know all. They who are there will not know each other from seeing their faces; it will be a higher kind of knowledge. There, all will see as prophets are accustomed to see here, and in far greater degree. They will see by God's light when they are filled with God. There will be no evil thought, and no thought which will not be known.

4. ETERNAL LIFE: AMEN AND ALLELUIA
   (*Sermon* 362.27)

LET no man, therefore, brethren, ask in a perverse refinement of subtlety what bodies in the resurrection of the dead will look like, how tall they will be, how they will move and walk about. It is sufficient for you to know that your flesh will rise again in the same form in which Our Lord appeared after His resurrection, in the very flesh of man. But do not fear corruption on this account, for if you do not fear corruption you will not fear the words, *Flesh and Blood shall not possess the kingdom of God*; nor will you fall into the mistake of the Sadducees, which you would inevitably do if you supposed that men are to rise again in order to marry wives, to have children, and to do the actions which belong to mortal life. If you ask what that life will be, who amongst us can answer your question? It will be the angels' life. Whoever is able to show you the life of the angels will be able to explain that future state, for men will be equal to the angels. But if the angels' life be hidden, let no one seek to know more, lest he mistake his own imaginings for the real solution. His search is hasty and eager. Keep to the proper path, and if you do not forsake it you will come to the true country. Hold then to Christ, brethren, keep the faith in the true way, and you will [472] be led to that which you cannot now see. The hope of the members rests on that which was manifested in the Head; that foundation showed forth what our faith is to build up, that it may be perfected hereafter by vision, lest when you think you see you should be deceived by an erroneous impression into believing something which has, so to speak, no existence, and having strayed from the proper path you fall away, and do not reach the heavenly country by the straight road, or in other words, do not reach the reality through faith.

You will say, "How do the angels live?" It is sufficient for you to know that corruption enters not into their lives, for it is easier to tell you what will not be there than what will be there. I, my brethren, can briefly enumerate a few things which will not be there, and this I can do because we have had experience of them, and know that they will not be in heaven. What will be there we have not yet conceived. *For we walk by faith and not by sight: while we are in the body, we are absent from the Lord.* What,

then, will not be there? Marrying a wife in order
to found a family, because death enters not in at
those doors; there will be no growth where there is
no advance in years; nor refreshment, where there is
no weariness; nor business, where there is no poverty;
nor the praiseworthy works which good men are
forced to do by reason of the needs and necessities of
this life. I say, not only that the acts of thieves and
usurers will have no place there, but also that those
things too will be absent which good men accomplish
for the removal of human needs. It will be a perpetual Sabbath, which the Jews celebrate in time, but
which we refer to eternity. It will be an ineffable
rest, which cannot be expressed in words, but, as I
[473] said, it is expressed in a certain way, by enumerating those things which will not be found there. We are
looking up to that rest, and are being spiritually regenerated for it. For as we are born in the flesh unto
toil, so we are spiritually born again unto rest, as Our
Lord's words signify, *Come unto Me all you who
labor and are burdened, and I will refresh you.*
He feeds us here, and perfects us hereafter: He promises here, and fulfills hereafter: He speaks to us
here in parables which have their accomplishment
hereafter. When, then, in that blessedness we are
made perfect according to both soul and body, and are
safe forever, these matters of worldly business will be
no more, nor will the good works of Christians, which
call forth admiration on earth, be found there. For
what Christian is not praised for giving bread to the
hungry and drink to the thirsty? for clothing the

naked, showing hospitality to the stranger? for quieting the angry, visiting the sick, burying the dead, and for consoling the mourner? These are great works, full of mercy, and praise and grace, but even they will not be there because they are called forth by a state of need and misery. Whom are you to comfort with food and drink in that place where no man either hungers or thirsts? Or will you clothe the naked there where all are clothed with immortality? You have heard the Apostle describing the garments of the saints, *For this corruptible body must put on incorruption.* The word *put on* signifies a covering. This garment Adam lost that he might clothe himself in one of skins. Or are you to open your house to strangers when all men are in their own home? Will you visit the sick there where all will be strong with one and the same strength of incorruption? Will you bury the dead where life is eternal? Will you appease angry men where all things are peace? Will you console mourners where all are to rejoice for ever? The end of misery, consequently, and of these works of mercy, will be simultaneous.

What, then, shall we do there? Have I not already said that it is easier for me to say what will not be there than what will be? Thus much I know, brethren: we are not to be idle when we fall asleep, for our mortal sleep itself is given to refresh our weariness. Our weak body could not bear perpetual activity in the senses unless, by unconsciousness of those senses, it were renewed so as to be able to encounter a repetition of that ever-recurring working of the mind; and just as our new life is to come through death, so might it be likened to our awakening from sleep. There will be no sleep in that life, for where death has ceased the image of death will also cease. Nor need any man fear weariness when he hears that he will always be awake, and not employing himself. This I can affirm, but how it is to be I am unable to explain, because it is not given me to see; still I may say something without presumption about our occupation there, because it is based on Scripture. Our whole being in heaven may be summed up in two words, *Amen* and *Alleluia*. What do you say, brethren? I see that you hear and are glad. But do not let a material interpretation of these two words sadden you. If, for instance, one of you were to stand up day after day saying *Amen* and *Alleluia*, he would be overcome with weariness, and fall asleep over the words, and only long to be silent. Consequently he would think to himself that this is a miserable life and an undesirable one. Who, you ask, will endure the repetition of *Amen* and *Alleluia* for all eternity? I will explain my meaning, therefore, if I can, and as far as I can. We shall say [475] *Amen* and *Alleluia* not with words which pass but with the love of our souls. For what does *Amen* mean, and what does *Alleluia* mean? *Amen* means it is true, and *Alleluia* means *praise God*. Because then God is the immutable Truth, Who is without decline or progress, without loss or increase, without the shadow of falsehood, Who is ever the same, unchangeable and eternally incorruptible, and because those things which we do as creatures in this life are, as it were, figures of the reality carried out in our mortal bodies, and certain signs in which we walk by faith; when we come to see face to face that which we now see *in a glass darkly*, then we shall say in an ineffably different way, *It is true*, and in saying this we shall indeed say *Amen*, but ever replenished we shall be ever insatiable. For as nothing will be lacking, it will be a complete satiety, and because this will be a never-failing source of delight, it will be a sort of perpetual longing in the fullness of all desires, if we may so speak. In the same measure, therefore, as ever insatiable, you will be nourished with the truth, in that same measure you will say in the ever-enduring reality, *Amen*. Who can explain *what eye has not seen, nor ear heard, nor the heart of man ever conceived*? Because, therefore, we shall see the truth without any weariness, and with enduring delight, and shall contemplate it in the fullness of certainty, the love of that same truth will make our hearts burn, and cleaving to it with sweet and chaste embrace, in which the body will have no part, we shall praise Him in like manner with a spiritual voice, saying, *Alleluia*. For in their joy at their common glory all the inhabitants of that heavenly city, burning with charity towards each other and towards God, will say *Alleluia*, because they will first say *Amen*.

[476] Hence this life of the saints will so fill their bodies themselves, which will be then transformed into heavenly and angelic ones, and so nourish them for all eternity that no mortal requirement will take them

away from that most blessed contemplation and praise of the truth. Thus that very truth will be their food, and that eternal rest like sweet repose. For when the banquet of those who are sitting down is mentioned, as Our Lord says, *Because many shall come from the east and the west, and shall sit down with Abraham, and Isaac, and Jacob in the kingdom of My Father*; the meaning intended to be conveyed is that they shall be fed in a great rest on the food of the truth. This is the food which is the never-failing source of refreshment: it fills and remains entire; you consume it and it is not consumed. That food is not such as we eat here, which is consumed to give nourishment, and disappears in order to maintain life in the man who eats. And that sitting down mentioned by Our Lord is eternal rest; the meat at that banquet will be the incommutable truth, and the banquet itself eternal life, that is, seeing things as they really are. *For this is eternal life,* says St. John, *that they may know You, the one true God, and Him Whom You have sent, Jesus Christ.*

In many passages which we cannot enumerate the Scripture proves that eternal life in the contemplation of the truth will not only endure in a manner which human speech fails to describe, but that it will endure in delight. Thus it is said, *He who loves Me keeps My commandments, and I will love him, and will show Myself to him.* As if then He were asked for the reward and fruit of keeping His commandments, He says, *I will show him Myself,* thus describing perfect

[477] happiness to be the knowledge of Him as He is. So again, *Dearly beloved, we are now the sons of God, and it has not yet appeared what we shall be. We know that when He shall appear we shall be like to Him, because we shall see Him as He is.* Therefore St. Paul's words are, *But then we shall see Him face to face,* because in another passage he has also said, *We are transformed into the same image from glory to glory, as by the Spirit of the Lord.* And it is written in the Psalms, *Be still and see that I am the Lord.*

Perfect sight will follow perfect leisure. But when will perfect rest come if not after the troubled days of earth have passed away, the days of human needs which now involve us, and which will last as long as the earth bears thorns and tribulations to sinning man, that he may eat his bread in the sweat of his brow. When, therefore, the time of the earthly man has passed wholly and entirely away, and the day of the heavenly man is in its full perfection we shall see Him best, because our rest will be perfect. For when at the resurrection of the just corruption and want are over, there will be no further cause for toil. By the words *be still and see,* it was as if He had said, Sit down and eat. We shall rest then, and shall see God as He is, and seeing Him we shall praise Him. And this will be the life of the saints, the occupation of those who are at peace; we shall give praise for all eternity. Not for one day only will our praise last; but as that day will not be a temporal day, so our praise will not have the end of a temporal day, and we shall praise for ever and ever. Listen to the voice of Scripture speaking to God according to this our desire: *Blessed are they who dwell in Your house, they shall praise You for ever and ever.* Turning to God, let us pray [478] to Him for ourselves and all His people who are with us in the courts of His house, may He grant to keep and protect them, through Jesus Christ His Son Our Lord, Who lives and reigns with Him for ever and ever. Amen.

INDEX

ABRAHAM, example of a good rich man, 91.
Ambrose, St., advice to St. Monica, 44.
Apostles, fishermen after the resurrection, 435.
Augustine, St., his struggle, 10.
—prayer for St. Monica, 23.
—life in episcopal house, 26.
—his role as arbitrator, 33.
—advice to a great man, 47.
—language to the Holy Father, 57.
—correction of a bishop, 59.
—address to his people, 64.
—view of the earth, 304.
—of the right hand, 336.
BABYLON, willows of, 320.
Baptism, independent of administration, 348.
—unto condemnation, 380.
Birth according to the Spirit, 315.
Blasphemy towards the body of Christ, 358.
Brethren of our Lord, 172.
CANCER cured, 449.
Capture of fish after the resurrection, 438.
Carried in His own hands, 415.
Love, order of, 216; the nuptial garment, 300.
Christianity a great miracle, 443.
Church, a tent, 128; regal priesthood of, 182; scandals in, 199; two lives in, 261; breasts of, 321; precious stones of, 351; wool and flax of, 352; the weak and strong in, 366; hidden citizens of, 392; daily sacrifice of, 404; mountain and light, 410; every language in, 411; life of, 427; unity of, 431.
Conversion through prayer, 450.
Curiosity, vain, 331, 333.
DAYS of eternity, 106.
Definitions due to attacks, 373.
ESAU in the Church, 385.
Holy Eucharist, daily bread, 207; adoration of, 305; how to receive it, 307; different ways of showing honor to, 46; sum and substance concerning, 417.
Evil a deficiency, 136.
Eyes of the mind through visible things, 223.
FAITH a voluntary act, 143; an altar, 180; before understanding, 342;

and works, 150; without works, 151; without charity, 276.
False Catholics, 390.
Feeding and being fed, 211.
Fire, action of, 134.
Flame and light simultaneous, 237.
God's Face, secret of, 127; Lord of the vineyard, 175; born to us through human mother, 287.
Going by night to the Light, 312.
Good and bad guests at earthly banquet, 297.
HEAVEN, 476.
Heretics as antichrists, 323; as bad humors in the Church, 324;
Human ear and Word of God, 87; passing by of Christ, 255.
Hunger of Our Lord, 241.
IGNORANCE due to impurity, 232.
Image of God in the human heart, 255.
Interior mind, 273.
JACOB's withered thigh, 388.
Jesus, Divine Sonship of, 238.
John, type of the blessed life, 265.
Justice of the martyrs, 249.
KING at the marriage feast, 298.
Kingdom foretold, 341.
Knowledge of the saints, 458.
LANGUAGE of miracles, 228.
Lazarus, name of, chronicled, 119,
Legacy of Our Lord, 359.
Leprosy, interpretation of, 181.
Light, comparison as to, 86.
Lovers of Babylon, 326.
MAMMON of iniquity, 123.
Marriage-feasts of Our Lord, 291.
Mark of just, 191.
Martyrs, true and false, 251.
Miracles, 444. of creation, 225; Fistula cured, 448.
Mary, mother of Jesus at Cana, 286; virginity of, 171.
Mystery of prosperity, 110, 113, 156.
NET cast into sea, 125.
New Testament, promises of, 139, 384.
OCCUPATION of the blessed in heaven, 474.
Old Testament, view of, 81; expectation of, 98; promises of, 159, 161.
PEARL of great price, 187.
Peter's fall, 220; called the rock, 260; his confession,

302; pilot of the ship, 363; typifies the good, 397.
Poverty, quality of, 91, 92.
Purgatory, 421.
Purity of intention, 319.
RIGHTEOUSNESS, 166.
Rivers of Babylon, 327.
Romans, reward of the, 131.
SABBATH of the inner man, 109; of the saints, 472.
Sacrament of Confirmation, 325.
Sacrifice due to God alone, 399; of the altar, 406, 408; for the departed, 419, 424.
Sight of the saints, 462, 465.
Scandal of heretics, 375.
Seamless garment, 429.
Sleep of Our Lord, 129.
Son of Mary on the Cross, 294.
Songs of Sion, 334.
Sound as food of our ears, 86.
Spiritual rising, 239.
Stone from the mountain, 346.
Suffering unto justice, 145.
Sursum corda ("Lift up your hearts"), allusions to, 83, 100.
TEARS of the just and of sinners, 96.
Thirst of Our Lord, 269.
Thorns and daughters, 195, 354.
Thought in the saints, 469.
Traitor in the Church, 395.
UNBELIEF due to man, 280.
Unbinding of grave clothes, 245.
Understanding through purity, 231, 322; through faith, 271.
Unity of the Dove, 378; salt of the multitude, 212.
Usurpation of title-deeds, 370.
VALUE of the cause, 247.
Virginity of Mary, 171.
WALKING to God, 215.
Wine of the marriage-feast, 293.
YOKE of Our Lord, 102, 121; of riches, 104; of the world, 189.
Zacchaeus, a type, 203.

THE END

Made in the USA
Middletown, DE
06 September 2023